WALKING SAFARIS OF AFRICA

WALKING SAFARIS OF AFRICA

GUIDED WALKS FROM THE CAPE TO KENYA

DENIS COSTELLO

PELAGIC PUBLISHING

Dedicated to my parents for inspiring my curiosity

First published in 2025 by
Pelagic Publishing
20–22 Wenlock Road
London N1 7GU

www.pelagicpublishing.com

Walking Safaris of Africa: Guided Walks from the Cape to Kenya

Copyright © 2025 Denis Costello

The moral rights of the author have been asserted by him in accordance with the Copyright, Designs and Patents Act 1988.

All rights reserved. Apart from short excerpts for use in research or for reviews, no part of this document may be printed or reproduced, stored in a retrieval system, or transmitted in any form or by any means, electronic, mechanical, photocopying, recording, now known or hereafter invented or otherwise without prior permission from the publisher.

https://doi.org/10.53061/ERAW7063

A CIP record for this book is available from the British Library.

ISBN 978-1-78427-505-1 Pbk
ISBN 978-1-78427-506-8 ePub
ISBN 978-1-78427-507-5 PDF

Cover photograph: Sundown in Mashatu Game Reserve, Botswana (Roger and Pat de la Harpe Photography)

Back cover credits: main image Walk Botswana; inset Denis Costello

Designed and typeset in Minion and Gill Sans by BBR Design, UK

Printed in India by Replika Press Pvt. Ltd.

Contents

List of maps	viii
Foreword	x
Preface	xii
Acknowledgements	xiii

1. Introduction — 1
    Walking safari styles — 4
    Cape to Kenya — 11

2. Planning a walking safari — 28
    Booking — 28
    Getting there and around — 30
    Money matters — 31
    Responsible safari travel — 34
    What to wear — 36
    What to carry — 37
    Trail tech — 41
    Health and hazards — 41

3. The walking safari experience — 44
    Walking guides — 44
    On the trail — 52
    Walking and wildlife — 54
    Staying safe on trails — 55
    Taking a rest — 63

4. South Africa — 65
    Walking safaris in South Africa — 66
    The Cape — 77
    Zululand — 82
    Kruger National Park and Greater Kruger — 94
    Greater Mapungubwe Transfrontier Conservation Area — 118
    The Waterberg, Pilanesberg and Madikwe — 124
    Kalahari borderland reserves — 128

5. Namibia — 132
    Walking safaris in Namibia — 132
    Sossusvlei — 133

Kunene Region 136
Etosha 140
Kwando River 141

6. Botswana 142

Walking safaris in Botswana 142
Okavango River Delta 143
Northern Botswana 153

7. Zimbabwe 157

Walking safaris in Zimbabwe 157
Victoria Falls area 163
Hwange National Park 165
Matobo National Park 170
Gonarezhou National Park 171
Chizarira National Park 175
Matusadona National Park 175
Mana Pools National Park 178

8. Zambia 187

Walking safaris in Zambia 187
Liuwa Plain National Park 188
Kafue National Park 189
Lower Zambezi National Park 193
South Luangwa National Park 200
Luambe National Park 214
North Luangwa National Park 216

9. Malawi 224

Walking safaris in Malawi 224
Liwonde National Park 224
Majete Wildlife Reserve 229
Nkhotakota Wildlife Reserve 231

10. Mozambique 233

Walking safaris in Mozambique 233
Gorongosa National Park 233
Niassa Special Reserve 234

11. Tanzania 237

Walking safaris in Tanzania 237
Ruaha National Park 243
Nyerere National Park 249
Mikumi National Park 252
Ugalla River National Park 253

Katavi National Park	253
Mahale Mountains National Park	254
Gombe National Park	254
Saadani National Park	255
Mkomazi National Park	255
Burigi-Chato National Park	256
Tarangire National Park	257
Lake Manyara National Park and the Eyasi basin	260
Ngorongoro Conservation Area	264
Serengeti National Park	268

12. Kenya — 282

Walking safaris in Kenya	282
Greater Mara conservancies	286
Amboseli National Park	298
Chyulu Hills	299
Tsavo National Park	300
Laikipia Plateau	302
Samburu and the Mathews Range	320

Afterword	327
Safari operator contacts	328
Useful websites	335
Bibliography	336

Maps

1. Key map — ix
2. South African Cape — 12
3. South African Lowveld, Zimbabwe and Southern Mozambique — 13
4. Namibia — 14
5. Botswana, Western Zambia and Western Zimbabwe — 15
6. Eastern Zambia, Malawi and Southern Tanzania — 16
7. Kenya and Northern Tanzania — 17
8. Zululand and Kingdom of Eswatini — 83
9. Great Limpopo Transfrontier Park — 95
10. Northern Kenya — 303

LIST OF MAPS

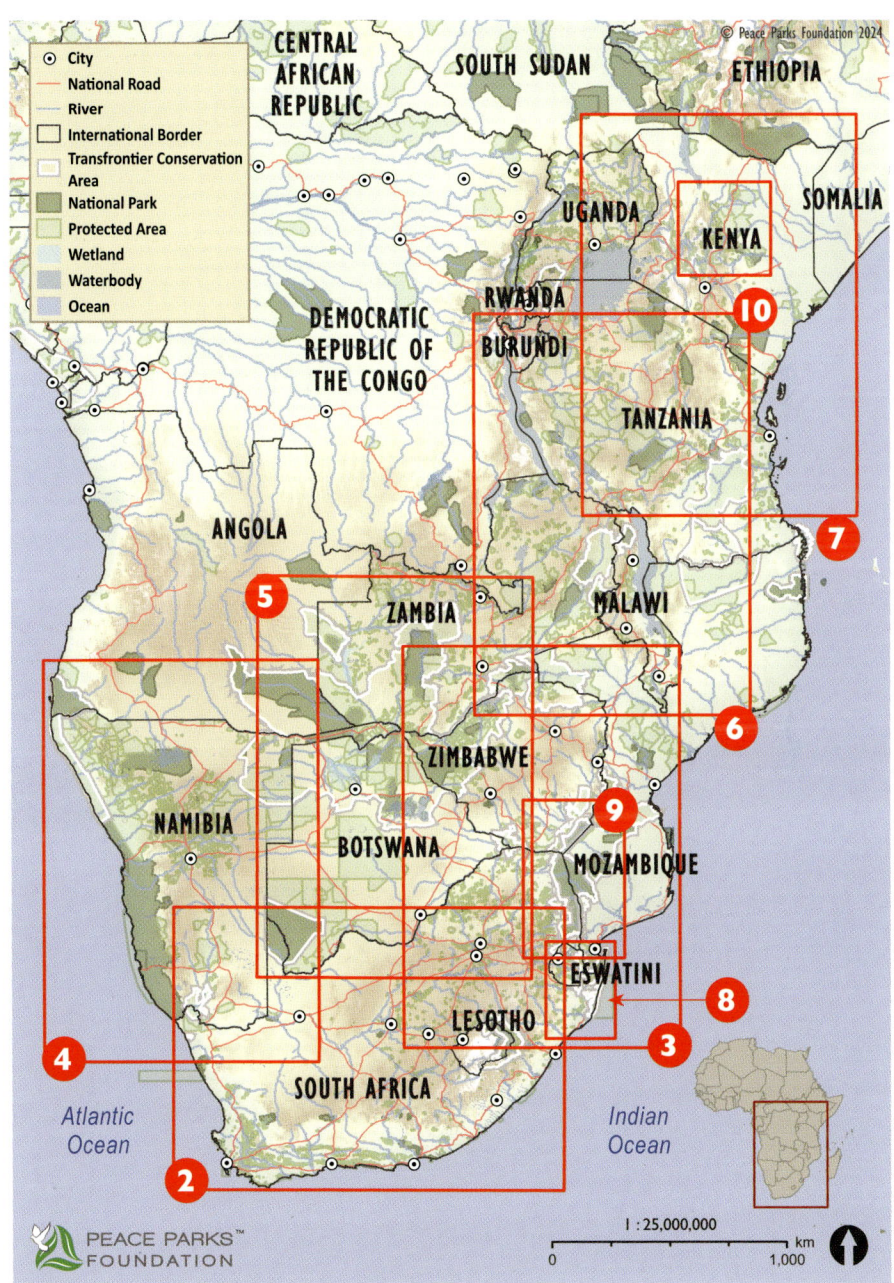

Map 1: Key map

Foreword

A couple of decades ago, one of my earliest assignments for Peace Parks Foundation was to Mana Pools in Zimbabwe. I cherish the memory of resting in the shade of an ancient ana tree after a walk, watching a family of elephant effortlessly ford the Zambezi from Zambia. I sat still and unnoticed as they joyfully splashed in the waters mere metres away, the embodiment of the freedom of wildlife that has space to roam with no regard for our human borders.

It was a moment when I felt humbled and vulnerable in the enormity of nature, and a confirmation that I was blessed to have taken a path in life that would allow me to wander often in African wilderness. On foot, we experience these parts of the world at their most wild and raw, which awakens our primordial senses. We are uplifted by an extraordinary emotional and spiritual connection that takes us back in time and traverses great distances.

For hundreds of thousands of years, humans and animals have walked trails in Africa, well-trodden paths across the grassy plains and through dense forests, curated and maintained by the largest of the herbivores. Walking through the bush is one of the most natural and unintrusive activities we can undertake in these wild spaces. We enjoy the bounty of nature up close and leave nothing but footprints.

Following in the footsteps of a local guide on a wilderness trail, learning first hand from their deep knowledge of the bush, pausing to listen when they stop, scanning the horizon as they do in the hope of seeing through their sharp eyes, is an experience like no other. Traditional skills and indigenous knowledge embody a deep-rooted understanding of nature and enhance the safari experience. Through formal employment, these stewardship roles support those for whom cultural preservation and access to nature's resources are a human right. Walking safaris become a platform for cultural exchange and mutual learning by fostering engagement with indigenous peoples and local communities and respecting their traditions.

For 28 years, Peace Parks Foundation's vision and mission has been to encourage peaceful coexistence between people and nature, across vast transboundary landscapes, known as peace parks. Their scale and connectivity transcend political borders, and their greater ecosystems encompass the many wilderness areas it's possible to experience, on foot, that are showcased in this book. The use of walking trails speaks to the very core of what Peace Parks is – an organisation that prioritises the health and harmony of landscapes, works to conserve them at scale, and is proud to share them with the world in order to better protect them.

The value of experiencing these unique landscapes first hand cannot be overstated. These ecosystems are natural wonders and crucial players in the planet's health. By becoming immersed in these environments, we cultivate a deeper understanding of the delicate balance between human activity and nature's resilience, and the vital importance of living in harmony with the landscape. Adventures on foot are a journey back to our roots, and the route to protecting and preserving where humankind came from. Our connection to each other and nature is universal, and is something we must be conscious of wherever we travel.

FOREWORD

Space for nature to thrive: the Lanner Gorge is at the heart of the Great Limpopo Transfrontier Conservation Park.

There is a greater consciousness now than ever before. We have powerful knowledge about the impacts of humans on nature, and the connection between peace and prosperity. The span of experiences featured in this excellent guidebook is heartening testimony to the yearning for visitors to engage with nature deeply, and their desire to understand the intertwining of climate change, biodiversity and ourselves. Expanding this understanding helps make what Peace Parks Foundation does possible, and I am hopeful for a future in which people and nature not just survive, but thrive.

I'm pleased to see that most Peace Park Foundation operational areas are featured, including Lower Zambezi-Mana Pools. No doubt the young transborder elephants I once met there are now adults, and, somewhere amid the floodplain woodlands, a group of walkers is sharing quiet moments in their company.

Werner Myburgh
Chief Executive Officer,
Peace Parks Foundation

Preface

Travelling Africa, seeking out its best walking safaris, has been the pleasure of a lifetime. Everywhere, I met fascinating people working to protect wilderness areas, sharing their wisdom and stories. It makes me optimistic for the conservation of these precious habitats.

During those travels I was sometimes asked 'what's the best place in Africa for a walking safari?' This I answer honestly. Everywhere in this book has the potential to hit number one when the stars align – a safe and knowledgeable guide (and good guests); the right weather; and the undefinable serendipity of whatever is found along the trails.

'OK, then, so what's your favourite place to walk?' Now I must think, as this changes from time to time. This answer is subjective, and I need to consider what I really enjoy. I think of standout trees, especially baobabs. And shady woodlands, perhaps fever trees or winter thorn. It should be buzzing with life – bees, birdsong, a healthy ecosystem. There must be interesting wildlife around, with at least some fresh tracks and the potential of a pulse-racing encounter – elephant, rhino, lion. Water is a key ingredient, a place to sit awhile and to wait and watch. Even better if there's a chance to mix walking with a water-based safari.

This leads me to a tributary of the Zambezi, and it's not the Luangwa but the Shire River. Malawi's Liwonde National Park is small by African scale but has it all from a walking safari perspective: not too many visitors, a profusion of animals, incredible birdlife. Baobabs and fever trees aplenty. Good guiding and lodges. Overnight walks to a fly-camp available. So, I won't dodge the question, and say that Liwonde is my favourite place for walking safari. For now, at least.

As a country, Malawi is highly vulnerable to climate change, and is already suffering from disrupted rainfall patterns and the increased impact of tropical cyclones. This raises another question that can't be avoided: is it moral to for us to indulge in wildlife tourism and its associated carbon production? The answer is an unqualified 'Yes'. Liwonde, and all of Africa's protected areas, cannot survive without visitors. The parks and their people need us come, to enjoy, to learn, to appreciate the conservation work – and to leave light footprints behind.

Acknowledgements

This book would have been impossible to write without the help of people with far greater experience in African wilderness walking than mine. The narratives by guides Mark Thornton and Andrew Booth are valued contributions that bring the text to life. Many other guides helped with their local knowledge, and I'd like to thank Noelle van Muiden in South Africa, Grant Reed in Botswana, Adam Jones in Zimbabwe, Robin Pope, John Coppinger and Brent Harris in Zambia, Richard Beatty and Ethan Kinsey in Tanzania, and Andreas Fox and Calum Macfarlane in Kenya.

I'd especially like to thank Peace Parks Foundation for a wonderful Foreword and for contributing the maps. Alex van den Heever's piece on tracking is an essential feature, and Sivuyile Manxoyi shared a fascinating expert overview of African starlore. Thanks to the many lodges and walking safari operators for their help in gathering information and images, and to African Parks and other organisations that smoothed the way. My special appreciation goes to Kim Paffen for the contribution of her exquisite photographs, and thank you Katherine Kelly for the assistance with proofing.

Lastly, I'd like to applaud the multitude of working walking guides. Their knowledge, good humour and tireless commitment to sharing their Africa are integral to every walking safari in the book.

There are few better memories than sharing a moment on foot with an elephant in its natural habitat.

KIM PAFFEN

1 Introduction

Walking in wilderness is the most natural thing in the world. As humans, we have been sharing dusty trails with elephants in Africa for at least 300,000 years, and our other hominid cousins have done so for a couple of million years. Thanks to the dedicated preservation of ancient skills, we too can tread in the footsteps of our long-gone ancestors by going on a walking safari.

The Swahili word for journey has been on a journey itself. Its origins are in Arabic, where 'safara' means to unveil or discover. In East Africa, this became 'safari', a journey of discovery, historically undertaken on foot with pack animals. In the nineteenth century and well into the twentieth, 'safari' was the term in East Africa for expeditions to the interior in search of hunting riches – ivory, hides and meat. In post-war Africa, the depletion of wildlife coincided with a growth in interest in the appreciation of nature conservation, and the age of the photographic safari arrived. The term 'safari' now means exploring the African wilderness with the expectation to encounter wildlife in its natural habitat.

In this book, a walking safari refers to an expertly guided walk in a conservation area where at least some of Africa's big game might be met – elephant, buffalo, lion, leopard, rhino. Yes, that definition is a bit arbitrary, but it helps to decide what to include, where to draw a line. Needless to say, there are countless other ways to enjoy African nature on foot, guided and unguided, but that's another book.

Exploring the wilderness on trails made by wild animals themselves feels right. Meeting these animals is a thrilling part of a walking safari, but there's much more than that: it's a genuinely immersive experience, a chance to gain a deeper appreciation for the entire ecosystem. On a safari vehicle, we are looking at wilderness; on a walking safari we are really in the wilderness. Walkers encounter fascinating smaller creatures, seedpods and flowers, fungi and feathers, bones and burrows, middens and nests. They learn the art of tracking, discover fossils, rock art and prehistoric tools. Bush skills, geology, folklore, bushveld cooking, astronomy, stories of lives lived in the wilds – all of these elements can be part of an enriching walking safari.

Above all, taking part in a walking safari is an opportunity to disconnect from the modern world for a while and simply enjoy the serenity of African wilderness and all its sights, scents and sounds. It's a 'slow safari', a therapeutic engagement with nature rather than a superficial chase for star animals. The American ecologist Edward O. Wilson popularised the word 'biophilia' with his 1984 book of the same name. Coming from Greek and meaning a 'love of life', biophilia is our 'innate tendency to focus on life and life-like processes'. A yearning for nature is genetically hardwired into us, Wilson argued. 'From infancy, we concentrate happily on ourselves and other organisms,' he wrote. 'We learn to distinguish life from the inanimate and move towards it like moths to a porch light.'

The personal benefits are evident, but by choosing to walk, we can benefit conservation of habitat and its wildlife. Walking safaris are literally low impact. Our footprints blend and blur with those of the wildlife, and in a few days all trace of us has disappeared. While it

Zambia's South Luangwa National Park is renowned for its walking safaris.

would be wrong to overplay the benefits of walking for wilderness areas, they are real. In modern conservation, there's a continuous struggle to balance the income needs of reserves, and the desire to protect them from development. Lodges and camps require roads, water extraction, waste pits, sewage treatment, supply traffic. Park management plans are designed to minimise the negative impact of tourism, while maintaining the financial benefits. Large parks have zonal designations, with areas reserved as 'low use' wilderness, barring vehicles and lodges and allowing the bare minimum in terms of access. By utilising these areas for walks, there are tangible benefits in their protection: the walking guides can keep an eye out for anything untoward, reporting poaching evidence or injured animals. But the main benefit is simply the fact that the wilderness zone is being used at all – it helps defend it from more intrusive usage.

Because of their immersive nature, walking safaris create life-long champions for conservation. This was very much the overt goal of walking pioneers such as South African Game Ranger Ian Player. He patrolled on foot or horseback and simply could not countenance ploughing roads through pristine bushveld. By bringing people – especially young folk and future influencers – into wilderness areas on foot, he knew he had the perfect environment to teach the value of habitat conservation, to kindle a love affair with nature and to

Five reasons to go on a walking safari

1. Experience the joy of genuine immersion in wilderness.
2. Get up close and learn about nature's smaller treasures.
3. Share an experience with our earliest ancestors.
4. Spend time with the most experienced guides.
5. Help to preserve traditional skills and knowledge.

INTRODUCTION

A walking safari is an opportunity to enjoy some of nature's smaller wonders.

instil a desire to do whatever it takes to defend the remaining wilderness for the benefit of all.

In the same era, another conservationist was taking a different tack. In Zambia's Luangwa River valley, Norman Carr recognised that money from adventurous wildlife tourists was a way to shift the focus from hunting conservation to real conservation, and introduced the idea of wilderness trails. While these pioneers can be thanked for creating the modern availability of walking safaris, we should be even more grateful to the legions of walking guides and trackers who make it a safe and fascinating activity. Skills that are as old as humankind – tracking, trailing, navigation, ethnobotany, survival, knowledge of animal behaviour – are preserved by African guides. The availability of such guides, combined with a modern desire for 'active travel', for real engagement with the world, is behind the growth in walking safari opportunities. The adage that it's better to die with memories than regrets applies; and there are few better memories than sharing a moment on foot with an elephant or lion in its natural habitat.

Walking safari styles

Walking safaris range from gentle one-hour strolls to intensive backpacking expeditions, and this variety of walking safari styles makes them widely accessible. You don't need to be particularly outdoorsy to enjoy most of them, just have a keen curiosity and a readiness to be active. Participants on walking safaris soon learn that it's all about the stops and not the walking. It's not unusual to pause every 100 m to examine a plant, to decipher some tracks, to train binoculars on a bird, to touch a rubbing post or claw marks on tree bark. Every walk includes a healthy

Walking by the Mara river in Kenya.

Who can take part in a walking safari?

Out on a trail, the maximum number of walkers is six to eight: this is regarded as the most that can be safely managed in big game areas. For lodge-based walks, there's usually no minimum number, but some multi-day walks have a minimum booking requirement, typically four. The starting age for doing walking safaris varies but is never lower than 12 if it's in an area with potentially dangerous game. The primary concern for younger children is keeping control of the group in the event of an unexpected close animal encounter, and the fact that small children might be seen as prey by some animals is a consideration. For multi-day walks and backpacking, the usual minimum age is 16, but for Ezemvelo KZN Wildlife in South Africa it's 14, and some privately run trails cater for families with a minimum age of 12. The policy for older walkers differs from place to place and depends on the nature of the walk. The aim is to reduce the risk of a medical emergency in the bush, especially in hot conditions. Some walk operators request a recent medical certificate of fitness for those of a certain age – check with the operator in advance if concerned.

At some point before setting out on a trail, participants are asked to sign an indemnity. At lodges, this is normally done directly on arrival along with a refreshing drink. The indemnity form asks for the names and ages of participants, and for information about any medical conditions or infirmities they have and informs walkers of the risks involved. In signing the form each participant confirms that they indemnify the walk operator against any harm they may experience. It often includes a section where walkers can mention special interests such as botany, ornithology, tracking or invertebrates.

It's important to recognise that although a walking safari is not an adventure sport, it's not risk-free, and while this guidebook endeavours to only include walking operators with a reputation for high standards, it cannot vouch for the safety of individual guides or venues. If in doubt, be sure to ask the walk operator for confirmation that the guides have the appropriate training to guide on foot.

It's best to provide advance notification to the trail operator of any disabilities or health conditions that might impact on the feasibility of a walk. A growing number of safari companies have wheelchair friendly accommodation and vehicles, but owing to terrain, guided walks are not feasible for those with reduced mobility. That said, the right guides can ensure such guests share in the richness of walking safari discoveries by not just focusing on the big game while on a drive, but interpreting tracks, flora, geology and everything that makes walking fascinating. Let them know you are interested in these, and not just chasing the photogenic wildlife.

Other disabilities do not preclude enjoyment of bush walks, especially in private reserves and concessions, which can tune the experience to match individual needs. In an area where close encounters with big game are likely, hearing impairment can increase the element of risk and should be discussed with the guide in advance. For those with limited or no vision, bespoke walks are feasible, especially in reserves where the risk is lower because of open terrain and lower wildlife densities, and the sounds, scents and tactile wonders of African nature offer a rewarding experience.

period of sitting in silence in the shade of a tree or on a rocky lookout, soaking in the balm of nature.

Regardless of the style of walk, guides always adjust the pace and distance to the walkers. They are designed to be enjoyable immersions in nature, and not part of your fitness regime. Walks steer clear of steep slopes, thorny thickets and deep water crossings. In brief, walking safaris are for everyone, and it's just a matter of picking the most suitable ones. A typical dawn walk from a lodge or camp will cover 4–8 km over three hours. Walks from dedicated walking camps tend to be longer in duration and distance than those from lodges and are more enjoyable if you are an active walker. Backpacking trails are a further step up and demand fitness.

Apart from on backpacking or animal-ported trails, it's normal to have a game viewing vehicle available. It's used to reach walking areas, which are often zones with restricted access, meaning there can be excellent close animal encounters with no other visitors around. Where allowed, the vehicle is used for a night drive back to camp, a time when there's the chance to spot crepuscular wildlife. There's no need to feel you will miss out on good photo opportunities from a vehicle by choosing a walking safari.

Wilderness trails camps

Wilderness trails camps are the mainstay of the walking safari world and are recommended for those who want to make walks the central activity of their safari. A variety of terms can be used for this style of camp: wilderness trails camp, bush camp, explorer camp, expedition camp and so on. What makes a wilderness trails camp? These are always smaller camps, to suit the size of a walking group, with a maximum of eight beds. Trails camps are more basic than safari lodges, and don't have fancy extras such as swimming pools, spas and photo hides. Typically

Remote Africa Safaris Chikoko Tree camp in South Luangwa National Park can only be accessed on foot.

off grid and unfenced, they provide a rich immersion in nature. In most cases, trails camps are seasonal, with all traces removed before the rains arrive. There are exceptions – the SANParks Wilderness Trails camps in Kruger National Park are fixed structures with plumbing and are open almost all year.

One thing such camps have in common is a decent walk of three to four hours every morning, returning to the camp for breakfast or brunch. In the afternoon, there's usually a short walk/drive/sundowner drink combination and a night drive back to camp (where permitted). 'Wilderness trails' is a term that can be misunderstood. Coined by Norman Carr, it refers to exploration of wilderness on foot rather than by vehicle. It rarely refers to a particular route walked, in contrast to named and marked trails such as the Otter Trail or Appalachian Trail. Guides and their guests wander wherever they wish on trails created by animals – hence the plural 'trails' rather than 'trail'.

Wilderness trails examples
SANParks Wilderness Trails (page 98)
Hwange Bush Camp (page 166)
The Bushcamp Company (page 201)

Canvas tents are the norm, although a speciality of Zambia is the seasonal walking camp constructed using bush materials – dried grasses and reeds, split bamboo and woven mats. The Meru-style tent is commonly used and is named for Mount Meru in Tanzania, rather than Meru in Kenya. These are A-frame tents made of steel tubing, with walls of canvas and mesh, PVC floors and a separate awning to help keep them cool. They are spacious – typically 3.5 m wide and 3.5–5 m long, with an option for a bathroom extension and often set on a platform long term or for a season. Bathroom facilities may be shared or en suite, and in camps without plumbing, shower water is heated before being transferred to a suspended bucket or a tank to feed a shower. While some wilderness trails camps utilise composting toilets, it's increasingly common to find flush toilets. Folks who consider themselves 'non-campers' are usually very pleasantly surprised by their experience of African tented safari camps.

Mobile walking safaris
On a mobile walking safari, guests walk to overnight in a new camp location each day, giving the sense of a journey. This can mean walking between fixed camps or making use of a fly-camp that's relocated ahead of the walkers by vehicle, boat or pack animal. The ability to walk with just a daypack while the camp and kit is transferred can be called 'slack packing'. This style of walking safari is generally pretty comfortable, with full camp facilities including a composting toilet and warm showers. Camp-to-camp mobile walking safaris are popular in the Luangwa River valley, while pack animal supported safaris are a Kenyan speciality. There are good examples of vehicle-supported mobile safaris in the Serengeti and Okavango, with Robin Pope Safaris in South Luangwa, Tropical Ice in Tsavo and Africa on Foot in the Kruger.

Mobile walking safari examples
Africa on Foot (page 107)
Dorobo Safaris (page 239)
Karisia Walking Safaris (page 307)

The 'fly' in fly-camp is nothing to do with the insect but relates to the 'fly' of a flag, or a sheet used to create a simple overnight shelter – a 'flysheet' can go overhead or on the ground. A fly-camp is a tented camp designed to be simple to set and transport. Note that in this book the term 'fly-camp' is used in its most popular

Fly-camps typically feature a suspended bucket shower and short-drop toilet.

sense – a temporary camp that's set up just for one or two nights for a particular group. Some operators use the term for a camp that's set for months, but in this text that's referred to as a seasonal camp.

Tents are typically dome tents: a tent made for two, about 2 or 3 m square and big enough for a couple of camp cots and for an average human to stand. Beds range from a thick 'bedroll'-style mattress to a camp cot or stretcher or even a real bed. Typically fly-camp toilets are composting style, referred to as 'long drop' or 'short drop'. This means a seat over a hole in the ground, with ash or sand to be added to the pit after use. When used properly, they are odourless. Suspended bucket showers are the norm.

Backpacking safaris

Backpacking is the most demanding style of walking safari and always mobile in nature. It's the purest form of wilderness exploration, and what North Americans refer to as backcountry hiking: exploring wilderness where there's no human, nor signs of humans. You carry everything needed and leave nothing behind. Drinking water is sourced from springs or by digging in sandy riverbeds, as elephants do; the toilet is a hole scooped in the ground and washing is done sparingly with whatever water is to hand. Hikers need to be capable of covering up to 15 km on a hot day with a pack weighing 15 kg or more. On some trails it's possible to camp in one spot for two nights and explore for a day unencumbered. The ultimate in backpacking safari style is the primitive trail, where walkers sleep out under the stars with, at most, a mosquito net. Backpacking trails in big game areas are rare to find outside South Africa and Zimbabwe.

Backpacking safari examples
Ezemvelo KZN Wildlife Primitive Trail (page 88)
Kalahari Primitive Trail (page 128)
Luangwa Wilderness Walking Trail (page 215)

INTRODUCTION

At night on a primitive trail sleep-out, guests must take turns to keep watch.

Lodge to fly-camp walks

A variation on the mobile safari is a lodge to fly-camp walk. Typically, the fly-camp is set up on request at an attractive location within walking distance of the lodge. Your belongings stay at the lodge and overnight bags are sent ahead by vehicle or pack animal, along with the camp and its crew. Then, guides and guests set off in the warm light of the late afternoon to walk for a couple of hours, to arrive before sunset. The fly-camps are very comfortable, and there's a trend to increased use of mesh to give that 'under the stars' experience; some camps used cube-shaped tents akin to large mosquito nets with a synthetic floor. With dinner cooked on the campfire, a night or two of fly-camping is a highly romantic adventure.

Lodge to fly-camp walking examples
Mashatu (page 119)
African Environments (page 239)
Asilia Naboisho (page 286)

A bed in the bush: dome tents at a fly-camp in Liwonde National Park.

Lodge walks

The simplest form of walking safari is when you stay at a lodge and swap out a morning game drive for a walk instead. This is how many safari travellers get their first taste of the excitement of going on foot. In this book the style is referred to as a 'lodge walk', and hundreds of lodges include walks as an activity – too many to mention all by name. In some parks it's the only way to have a walk, so such lodges are included.

There are a couple of pitfalls to watch out for when planning to include a lodge-based walk in your safari. First, many lodges are open all year, but only offer walks in the dry season. Secondly, check they actually have trained walking guides on staff and enough guides to guarantee a walk. At some lodges, the walk may be an 'all guests or none' option owing to guide or vehicle availability on a particular day. Finally, lodges that run walks after the morning drive is over should be avoided – you want to be out on foot at dawn when it's cool and game viewing is at its best, then use the middle part of the day for rest.

Lodge-based walking examples
Tuli Wilderness (page 121)
Chiawa Safaris (page 197)
Lewa House (page 316)

There's an almost infinite variety of safari lodges, each attempting to set its own personality. They range from the intimate to the semi-urban in scale and have a longer season than wilderness trails camps. Safaris can be a once-in-a-lifetime experience and lodges go to extraordinary lengths to create memories. Some sport enormous tents or rooms, multiple baths and showers, and private plunge pools. Beds on sleep-out decks, in treehouses, in hides – there's always something innovative. For walking safari travellers, it's hard to recommend the places that go over the top – gyms, spas, wine cellars, air-conditioned rooms – as they tend to create a distance between the visitor and the natural world.

The best lodges for walks are small in scale and open to nature.

A season for trails

The time of year is the most important consideration when planning a walking trip. Walking safaris are a dry season activity: the grass is short and the bush is thin, making it easier to avoid any unplanned animal encounters. Rivers are low and fordable, and wildlife is concentrated at remaining water sources and easy to find. In the past, the dry season followed a reasonably predictable pattern, but in recent years climate change appears to be having a real impact, so it's risky to book walking trips at the beginning or end of the season.

The heat is the second climatic factor to consider, but less important than rainfall. In equatorial East Africa there's no great annual variation in temperature, but in Southern Africa the hot and humid summer months are best avoided. The problem is not so much the walking temperature – walks take place in the early morning or late afternoon, times that afford pleasant conditions all year. The issue is staying cool at night or during the midday downtime, as walking camps tend to be off grid and sans swimming pools – and this is why most of them close in the hottest months of the year.

Apart from the time of year, the time of the month can be considered. Most of us live in areas with nocturnal light pollution, and the crystal clear night skies of Africa are a wondrous revelation. If we travel when there's a new moon, we can see a million more galaxies besides our own. On the other hand, full moon is a magical time to be camped out in the wilds.

Cape to Kenya

From genteel walks in the Cape to camel-ported expeditions in the mountains of northern Kenya, an alluring choice awaits. Based on this book's definition of a walking safari, the content spans the countries where people 'go on safari'. With apologies to Madagascar, Ethiopia, Gabon and other fascinating African wildlife travel destinations, it covers guided walks in the countries of Southern and East Africa. The text is organised from south to north from the Cape to Northern Kenya. Why? Because that's how, broadly speaking, the season moves. One can walk in the Cape in the southern summer months, and in the main walking areas of South Africa the season starts in April. By May, it's usually possible to find good walking in Botswana and Zimbabwe, and in June the waters have receded in the parks of Zambia and Malawi. Southern Tanzania dries out at around the same time, and it's the peak walking season in northern Tanzania and Kenya. By October, walks are winding down all over Africa, except where they are starting again ... in the Cape.

In the following pages you will find location maps, an at-a-glance overview of Africa's prime walking safari zones, what makes each special, seasonality information and some tips on factors that can help to steer a destination decision.

Subsequent chapters are organised by country reluctantly; modern borders are an impediment to our ancestral urge to roam freely, and fences are but one manifestation of our war on nature.

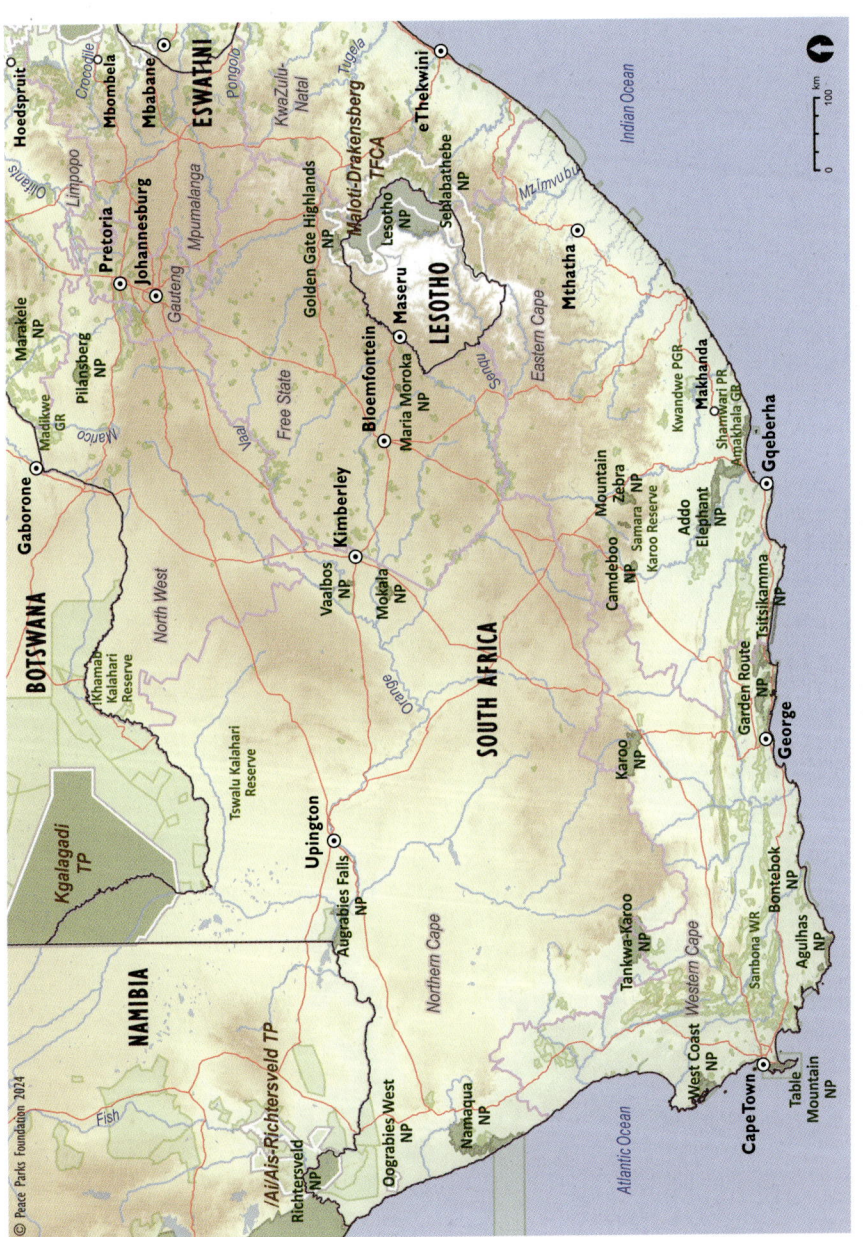

Map 2: South African Cape

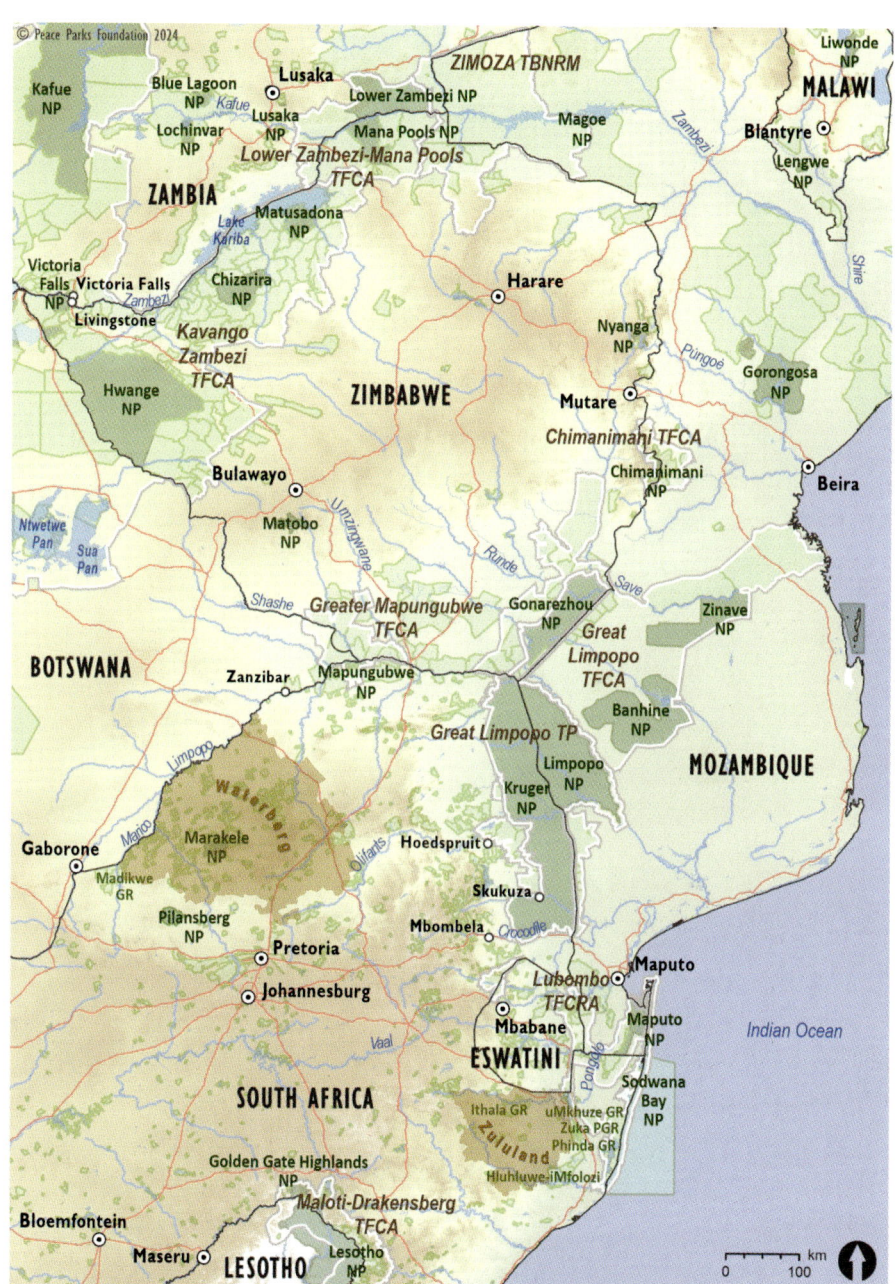

Map 3: South African Lowveld, Zimbabwe and Southern Mozambique

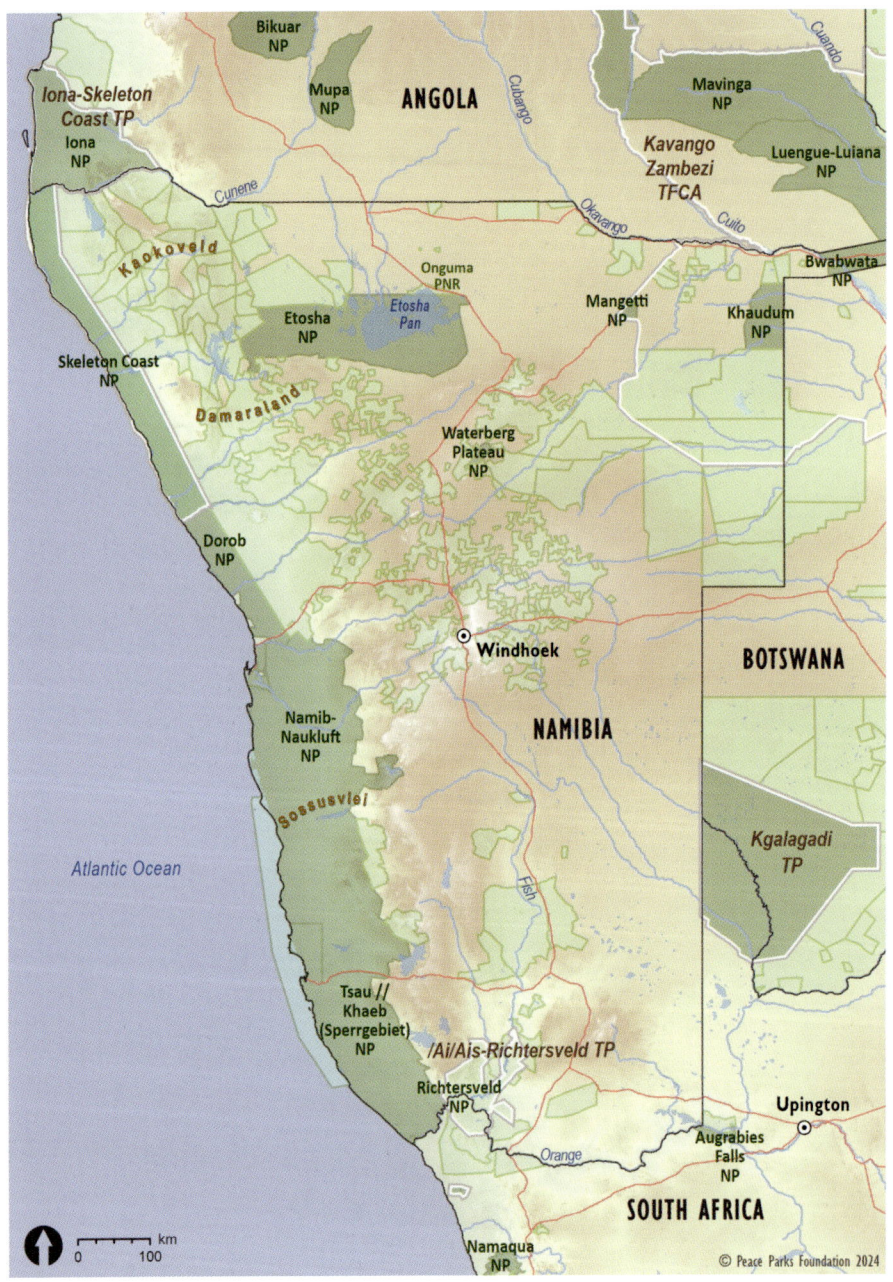

Map 4: Namibia

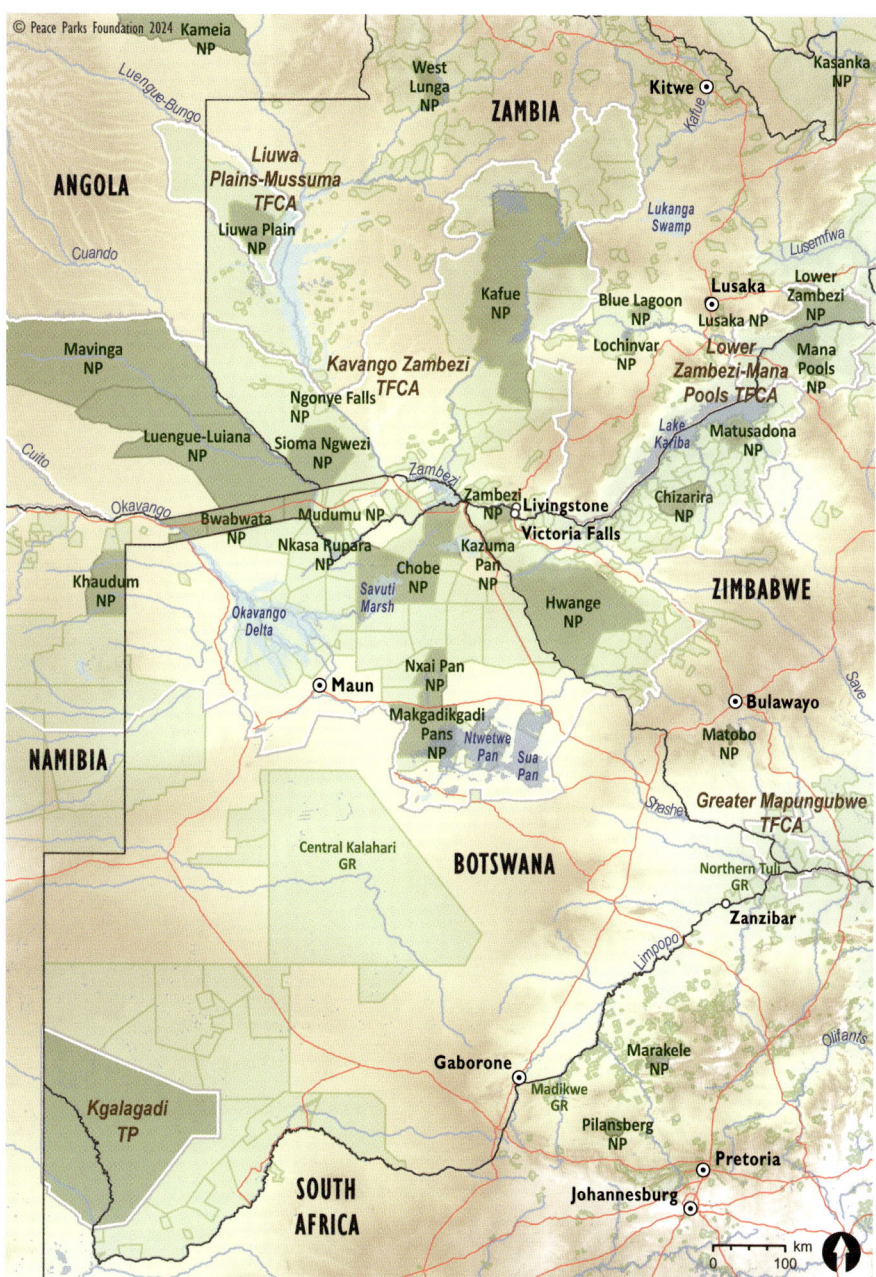

Map 5: Botswana, Western Zambia and Western Zimbabwe

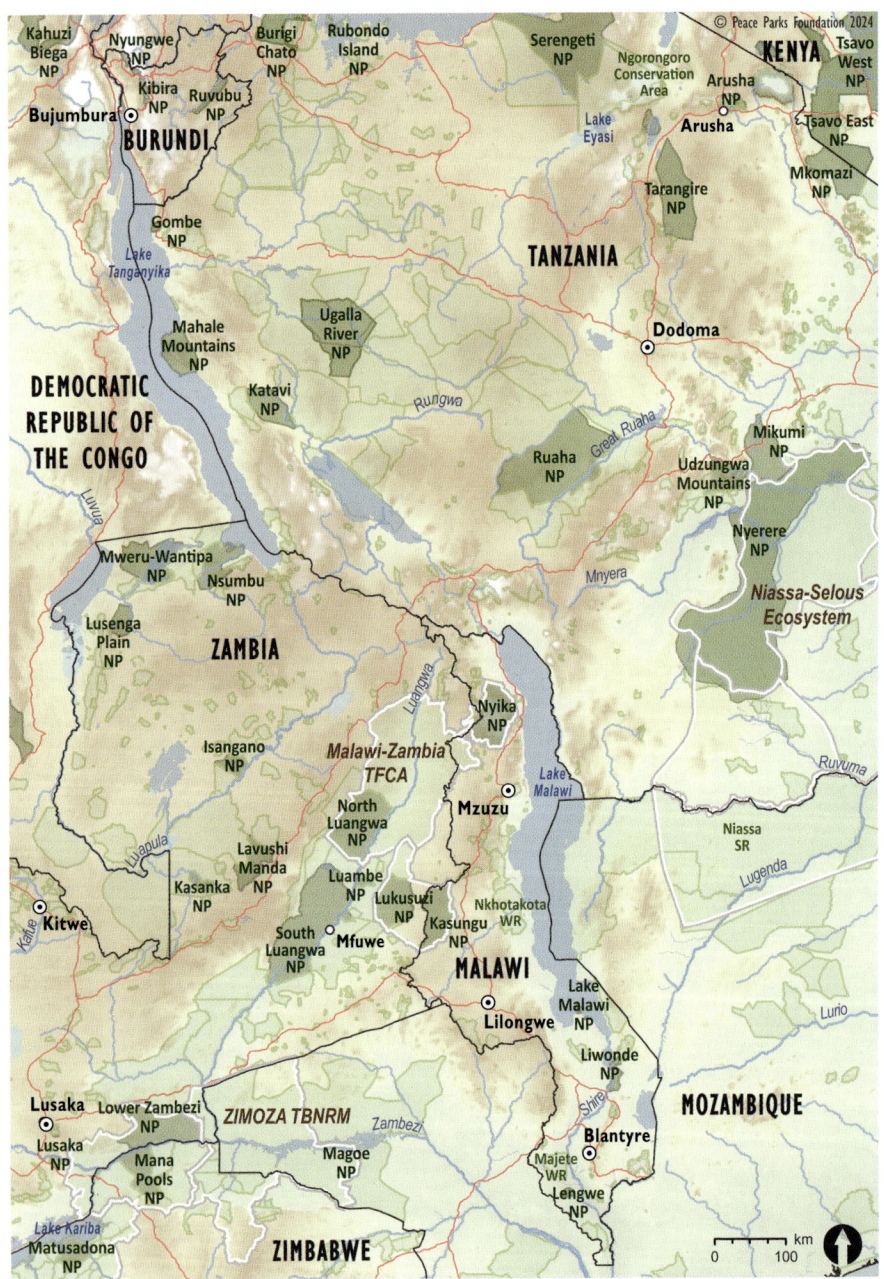

Map 6: Eastern Zambia, Malawi and Southern Tanzania

Map 7: Kenya and Northern Tanzania

The Cape

WHERE The reserves of Western and Eastern Cape Provinces, South Africa.

WHY Discover beautiful fynbos and Karoo landscapes, and a climate that's amenable to walks at a time of year not practicable in other parts of Africa. Western Cape province has a couple of private reserves with lodge-based walks that are perfect to combine with the Garden Route, while the Eastern Cape reserves are wilder with a fascinating mix of habitats and walking terrain.

WHEN Walking can be enjoyed at any time of year and is at its best during the southern hemisphere summer from October to April.

J	F	M	A	M	J	J	A	S	O	N	D

The Great Karoo is a distinctive landscape of the Cape interior.

South African savannah

WHERE The savannah biome of South Africa that spans Zululand, the Lowveld, the Waterberg and the Kalahari borderlands.

WHY Walk with all of Africa's typical megafauna, including white and black rhino, and choose from the widest range of walking styles from primitive trails to the height of luxury. This area encompasses one of the world's greatest wilderness areas, the Kruger National Park and adjacent Greater Kruger reserves. South Africa is suitable for self-drive, and its state-owned parks offer the continent's most affordable walking safaris.

WHEN Throughout this zone, it's a winter walking destination: April to September are the best months.

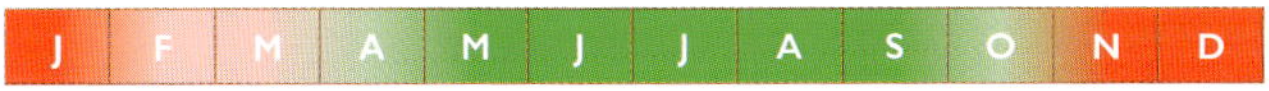

The Kruger National Park is typical savannah with all of Africa's most loved animals.

The 'Arid Eden'

WHERE The Kgalagadi Transfrontier Park and Namibia.

WHY Enjoy short walks in a stark and stunningly beautiful landscape, spot desert-adapted wildlife and spend time with Khoisan guides, guardians of a long history of survival skills in a harsh environment. Walks take in interesting ethnobotany and rock art, and while animal numbers are low compared to other destinations, it's marvellous to spot gemsbok or (in northern Namibia) elephant on the move against a backdrop of rocky mountains or sand dunes.

WHEN April, May, September and October are the ideal months to avoid intense heat by day or cold by night.

J	F	M	A	M	J	J	A	S	O	N	D
			A	M				S	O		

Iron-rich red sands are typical of the coastal desert landscape of the Namib Sand Sea.

The Okavango

WHERE The Okavango Delta and north-east Botswana.

WHY A geographic anomaly, the inland delta of the Okavango River is one of the most desirable wildlife destinations on earth. The geography is perfect for shunning the vehicle in favour of exploration on foot and by boat. The flat terrain makes for easy walking and, in addition to the many lodges with walks, there are specialist operators with mobile tented camps who can offer lower-cost itineraries.

WHEN The drier months from June to October are best for walks, with walk/mekoro combinations more likely early in the season.

| J | F | M | A | M | J | J | A | S | O | N | D |

The Okavango Delta is made for exploring on foot and on water.

Zambezi River basin

WHERE Northern Zimbabwe, Zambia and Malawi.

WHY The Zambezi and its tributaries water vast areas of wilderness and some of the most important walking safari destinations in Africa, adorned with woodlands of baobab, mahogany and winter thorn. Matusadona, Mana Pools and Lower Zambezi national parks are all directly on the Zambezi, while its basin encompasses the parks of Hwange in Zimbabwe and Kafue in Zambia. To the east, large tributaries such as the Luangwa and Shire Rivers are havens for wildlife and walkers.

WHEN The Zambezi basin is the most seasonal destination, and the dry season from May to October is the time to travel for walks.

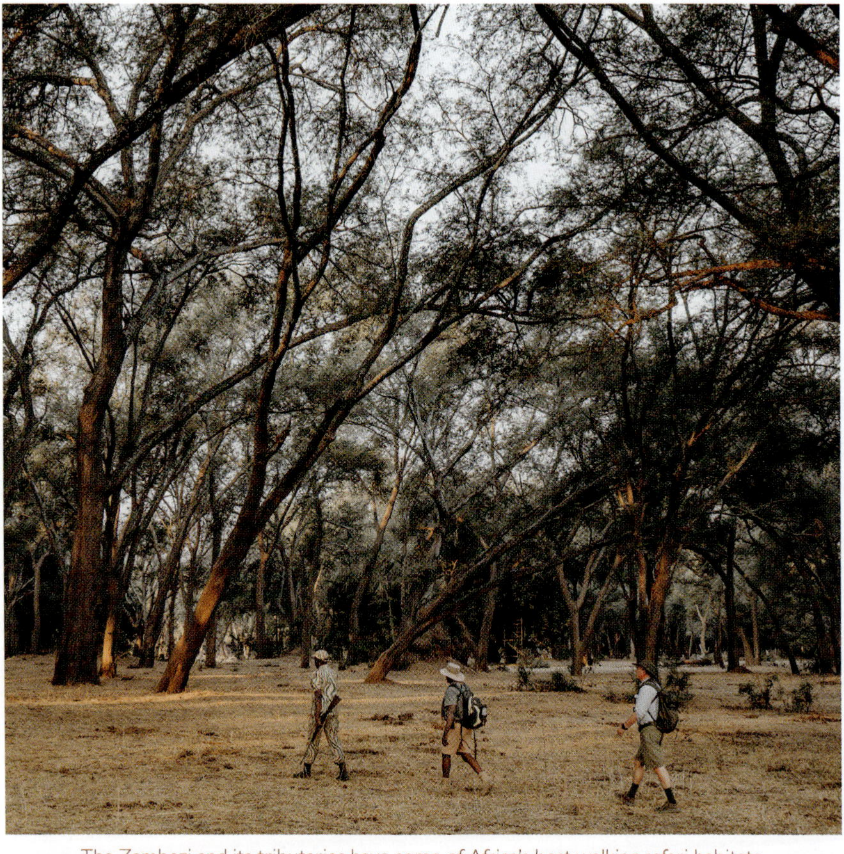

The Zambezi and its tributaries have some of Africa's best walking safari habitats.

The Southern Rift Valley

WHERE Tanzania's 'southern circuit' behemoths, Ruaha and Nyerere.

WHY These big parks with low volumes of visitors grant endless room to explore on foot and so are ideal for those who wish to escape other humans. Ruaha in particular has a dramatic terrain with opportunities for longer walking expeditions. Additionally, the national parks of Ugalla River and Katavi offer solitude, while on the shore of Lake Tanganyika, the Mahale Mountains can only be experienced on foot.

WHEN The climatic pattern is similar to the Zambezi basin, with walking ideal in the dry season from June to October.

J	F	M	A	M	J	J	A	S	O	N	D

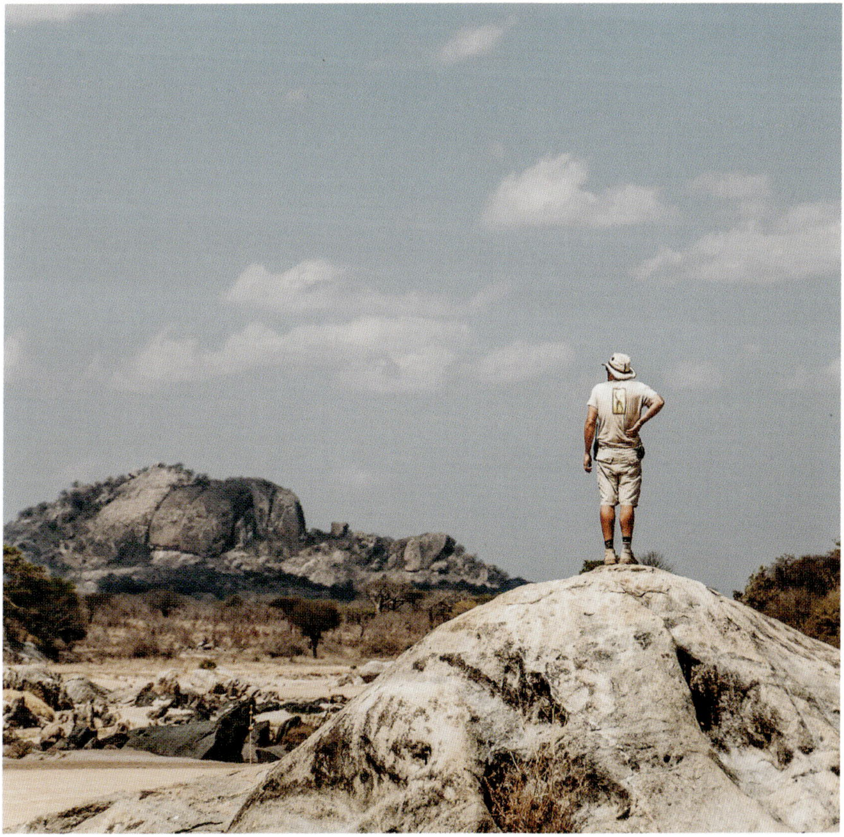

KICHAKA EXPEDITIONS

Southern Tanzania has space to escape the crowds on foot.

The Serengeti–Mara system

WHERE Northern Tanzania and Southern Kenya.

WHY The Great Rift valley is the quintessential safari destination, a land of lions atop rocky outcrops gazing over endless grasslands studded with acacias and sprinkled with plains game. It's the domain of semi-nomadic pastoralists, the Maasai, Samburu and other herders, who have shared the land with wildlife for countless generations and make for interesting guides. The Serengeti is a walking safari hotspot, with some of the longest mobile walking safaris in Africa.

WHEN For walks, the ideal time in the Serengeti and other 'northern circuit' parks is during the May to October dry season. The same season applies to walks in Kenya's Mara conservancies.

J	F	M	A	M	J	J	A	S	O	N	D

The Serengeti has small camps, designed for walking.

The Northern Rift Valley

WHERE Laikipia plateau and northern Kenya.

WHY The well-watered, rolling landscape of Central Kenya's Laikipia Plateau is one of the great walking safaris zones of Africa and offers a rich selection of charming family-owned lodges. It's one of the best places to approach rhino on foot. Beyond, northern Kenya is increasingly wild, a mix of volcanic forested mountains and open arid plains, a land for multi-day expeditions supported by camel or donkey in the company of Samburu and Laikipiak Maasai guides.

WHEN Walking is good at any time, although April and May are the most likely months for rainfall.

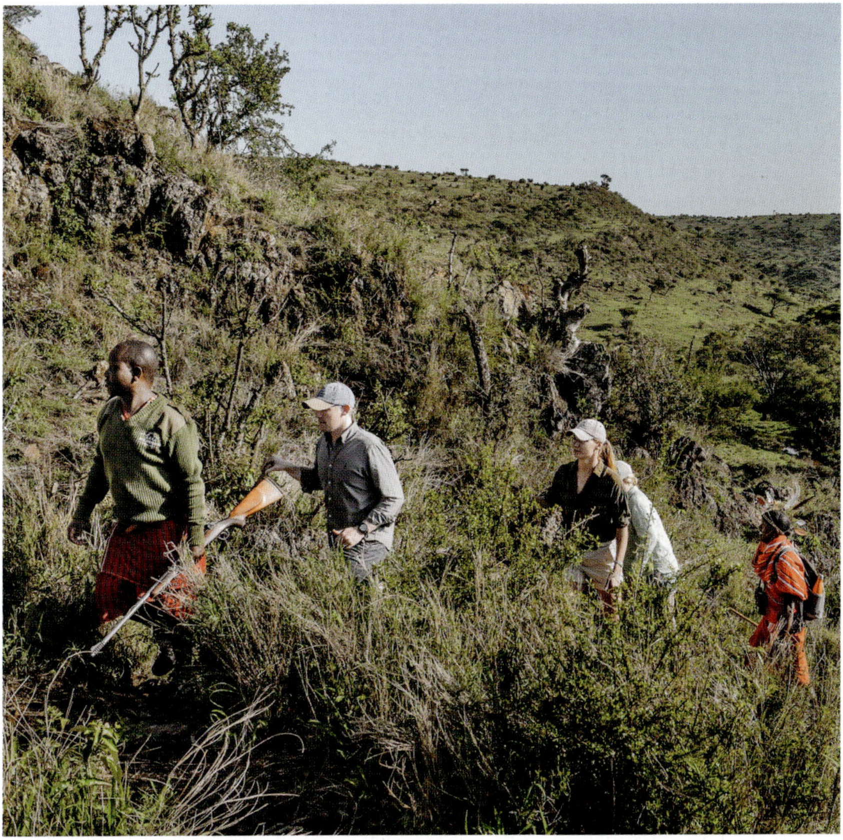

The well-watered Laikipia Plateau is a hotspot for walking safaris.

Decision considerations

There are a few aspects to consider to help zero in on the destination that suits your style. The list here leaves out perhaps the biggest decision factor of all, the cost – and that's a topic for Chapter 2.

Flight factors

Unless you are lucky enough to live locally, a big chunk of a safari trip time can be chewed up with flights. For most outside Africa, the closest country with decent flight connections is Kenya: Nairobi has direct flights from the USA, Europe, Middle East and Asia. It has a well-oiled internal flight network, meaning it's possible to arrive in Nairobi on an overnight flight, take a connection and be on safari the same day.

Next best in terms of travel time is northern Tanzania, as there's an international airport near Arusha that has direct flights from Amsterdam and the Arabian Gulf. From there it's a short hop by air, or a longer one by road, to some of the best walking safaris destinations in East Africa. South Africa is longer in travel time, but tends to be cheaper in flight costs, owing to more competition on routes.

Combinations

It's tempting to supplement safaris with other activities, especially for those who are not dedicated parks addicts. South Africa's Cape and Garden Route are among Africa's most beautiful destinations, with vineyards and maritime wildlife among the attractions, and some fine walking. Zululand reserves can be blended with cultural and historical sights, and a stunning coastline. Itineraries in Zimbabwe and Zambia can easily take in Victoria Falls and its myriad adventure activities. Walks in Liwonde National Park and the Luangwa River valley are often paired with sedate stays on Lake Malawi. In a similar way, safari visitors to Tanzania and Kenya can split the trip with coastal relaxation in Zanzibar, Lamu and other Indian Ocean idylls.

Other activities

One of the attractions of the walking safari is spending less time bouncing on rutted tracks in a 4x4, but it's not the only way. Water-based safaris are never less than outstanding and can often be combined with walking. The best places to do this are the Okavango Delta, Mana Pools, Lower Zambezi, Liwonde and Nyerere. A mix of walking and horseback safaris can be found in Botswana, Hwange, Serengeti and in Kenya. Safaris by balloon are big in the Serengeti, and fishing is famous on the Zambezi and in the rivers of Laikipia.

African culture

Walks everywhere have an element of ethnobotany, the science of traditional plant uses, but it's especially strong in Zululand, Namibia, Tanzania and Kenya. Rock paintings and petroglyphs, some of them very old, are a fascinating aspect of walks throughout Southern Africa. Walks in the Greater Mapungubwe Transfrontier Conservation Area provide the chance to appreciate the history of a bygone African kingdom.

Romantic Africa

Umbrella acacias, guides wrapped against the morning chill in colourful traditional attire: this is East Africa – Kenya and Tanzania.

INTRODUCTION

East Africa's Maasai bring their interesting cultural dimension to walks.

Off the beaten track

Each country has some out-of-the-way walking safari destinations, but for sheer vastness and low visitor numbers it's hard to beat Ruaha and Nyerere in Tanzania and Kafue in Zambia.

Expeditioner style

For those who like a challenge, some longer walks each day, the sense of a journey on foot, then the places to head for are Northern Kenya, Tsavo, the Serengeti and the Luangwa River valley. To take part in totally self-sufficient backpacking trails, there are limited options: South Africa, Zimbabwe and Zambia.

Special animals

It's memorable to meet a rhino on foot in the wild, and the best chance of this is in South Africa or Laikipia. If tallying birds is a goal, then East Africa is the place – there are over 1,000 species recorded in Kenya and Tanzania.

2 Planning a walking safari

Booking

It's hard to return from a safari in Africa and not to start dreaming of the next visit. People who take walking safaris tend to be repeat visitors, seduced by the sensual and tactile natural experience. An impromptu decision to take a walk during a stay at a lodge or camp is feasible – management is keen to give guests what they want, and if there's a qualified guide available, they will take you out. But generally, it's better to plan walks in advance of arrival, especially if there are logistics required, such as when fly-camping. When it comes to booking dates and venues, there's a choice of methods.

Specialist tour operator

Travel agencies are an endangered species, but they are very much alive in the safari sector and it's a good idea to use one. A safari can be an expensive and special trip, marking a life milestone or special family gathering, and a specialist safari agency or tour operator can handle tricky African travel logistics, seasonality, visas, health factors, dietary needs, security questions and special interests. The majority of safaris are booked via an agency in the traveller's home country.

Some agencies are more knowledgeable about walking safari options than others, as it's regarded as a niche activity. A badly informed agent could sell a trip where you arrive at the lodge to find it's the wrong season for walks; or that walks needed prior booking; or that the walk is scheduled after morning drives; or requires a long drive to another reserve. This book is designed to make it easy to avoid these pitfalls, so you can request particular venues for walks. Booking through an agency in your home country works well when you want to include walks in the mix of activities, taking part in what are referred to as lodge-based walks in this book. Your travel agreement is with the agency, which makes the arrangements with a chain of service providers behind the scenes.

Direct booking

Booking directly with a walk operator is a fine option, especially for the specialist walking companies that are covered in this book. In this case, it's perfectly feasible to arrange your own flights and liaise directly with the in-country safari operator for your transfers and accommodation. You will find contact details on the websites which are listed on pages 328–334. Quite a few companies have multiple camps within a park or country and will stitch together the trip. And, although in competition, camps that run walks are often happy to act as safari agencies themselves – to be a single point of booking and payment, and arrange for the accommodation and internal transfers to other venues.

In this case, your agreement is with the company operating the walk. They will usually quote the price in US dollars, apart from in South Africa, where it's more usual to pay in South African rand. This route will not be cheaper than using an agent, as camp owners won't undercut their main source of business. Smaller

PLANNING A WALKING SAFARI

camps might not have the resources (or communications links) to do travel planning with individual travellers, in which case they will refer you to an agency they work with, either in your home country or an Africa-based safari company.

Policies vary, and some operators of trails camps and mobile walking safaris will only take group bookings. Others are 'open' and accommodate individuals – Foreign Individual Travellers or FITs in the industry parlance. For solo travellers, the dreaded 'single supplement' is standard practice. In fact, it's so prevalent that it's worth mentioning by name walk operators who do not surcharge single travellers: the camps of Robin Pope Safaris in Zimbabwe, Zambia and Malawi, Remote Africa Safaris Mwaleshi Camp in Zambia, fly-camping safaris with Maasai Trails, Karisia Walking Safaris and Kitich Forest Trails in Kenya and Serian in Tanzania. During off-peak periods, some companies such as Wilderness and Kwando Safaris waive single supplements. For backpacking trails, where hikers provide their own tents, solo hikers are not at a disadvantage.

Private walking guides

Private guiding and walking safaris have a good fit. The premier advantage of travelling with a qualified private guide is to benefit from walking with some of the best and most experienced guides, folks who build their reputation on their knowledge and communication skills, and simply being interesting travel companions. Many have specialist qualifications that can sync with visitor interests, such as ornithology, tracking, flora and photography. Apart from the actual guiding experience, guides have personal knowledge of the overnight lodgings and walking locations. Travelling with one opens the door to exploring areas on foot that would otherwise not be accessible, either because the lodges don't have walks-qualified guides, or because there are no lodges at all. The daily pattern is determined by the guests and their guide, rather than being subject to the needs of a lodge or other guests. On a multi-destination itinerary, the private guide and guests develop a rapport and maximise the variety of experiences, rather than repeating similar activities and interpretations. There's consistency and a continued narrative, and the guide knows how to tie in each destination. Although it adds somewhat to a safari cost, this is not excessive, especially if shared with a small group of friends or family.

Andreas Fox is a private walking guide based in Nairobi.

Local walking safari specialist

Apart from using a home country agency or booking directly, there's a third option that's especially valuable in the world of walking safaris: using an Africa-based safari company that knows walking safaris. Experienced walking guides often work independently as guide trainers, private guides and as safari agents. Throughout this book, you will find reputable companies included. Although listed in their home country chapters, most are happy to organise trips in all of the countries covered in this book. This option is especially good for repeat visitors, who can build up a relationship with the company and its guides that offers peace of mind for subsequent trips. As these are small companies with a lot of local expertise, you should play nice: don't pick their brains and then book direct. Be careful when booking through in-country agencies that are not specialised in walks, and if in doubt, contact the walk operator directly, and ask for their advice.

Getting there and around

The best airline options for safari travellers are Ethiopian, Qatar Airways, Emirates and Kenyan Airlines. Kenyan flies direct to Nairobi from New York and a number of cities in Europe, the Middle East and Asia. Ethiopian has an even bigger network and modern aircraft, and has good connections with most safari destinations, including a recently added route to Maun in Botswana. South African Airways, Kenya Airways and Emirates fly to Lusaka, Zambia. South African Airways, Kenya Airways and Ethiopian Airways fly to Lilongwe, Malawi. For direct flights from the USA, at the time of writing, Delta flies to Johannesburg and United Airlines to Cape Town.

There are efficient internal air networks in the main safari destinations. For individual travellers, the costs are managed by sticking to scheduled services or charter flights at 'seat rates'. Propeller plane flights stay low and are often a highlight of a trip – the romance of seeing wildlife as you come in low to land at a dusty airstrip is magical.

South Africa can be a good destination for self-drive tourism, but in other countries rental is more expensive and trips take a higher degree of planning. High ground clearance vehicles are needed to access the reserves, usually a Land Cruiser or similar. Renting vehicles fully customised for wild camping is a popular way to travel in Namibia, Botswana and Zimbabwe, and to a lesser degree in the countries further north. There are excellent resources to help plan routes and where to stay, especially Tracks4Africa. With this style of travel, it's trickier to organise walking safaris. When staying at a campsite in some parks it's possible to book a ranger escort, but they are there to protect and are not really nature guides; and there's the question of where to fit them in the vehicle on the drive to the walking zone. To take walks when travelling with a vehicle, the easiest thing is to stay a night or two at a lodge or camp that welcomes self-drive visitors and avail yourself of their hospitality and guiding. Some specifically target this market, with facilities for self-catering guests, and these include Tuli Wilderness in Tuli Block, McBrides Camp in Kafue, the camps near Mfuwe gate in South Luangwa, and Mvuu Camp in Liwonde.

Money matters

Once decided on dates and a destination, buy travel insurance. It's pretty much mandatory and a tour agency or lodge will want to see evidence of it. It's important to start the policy before booking and paying for the trip, so that cancellation may be covered. An accident on a trail may require helicopter rescue and flight evacuation, and insurance ensures the best level of care if hospitalisation is needed.

Safaris require advance payment by credit card or by bank transfer. Cancellation fees vary, so check conditions and dates carefully when you make a booking. At many lodges, especially at the higher end, walks are included as an activity but this should be verified when booking so there are no surprises.

Conservation fees, which go towards park protection, road maintenance and so on, are usually charged separately and can be a substantial additional cost; some parks charge in excess of $100 per person per day. Community levies are a common and important additional fee. Check in advance in case any activity or local fee requires payment in dollar cash: no issue for US visitors, but a headache for other nationalities.

In general, tipping is common in the safari sector in Africa and can be a substantial part of the income of guides and other staff. In South Africa it's a good idea to pick up some rand from an ATM, and in other countries dollars and euro (and no doubt other currencies) are welcome. It's normal for lodges to facilitate a pooled gratuity for camp staff, and separate tips for guides and trackers. How much? Some lodges suggest $10–15 per guest per day, but of course it's up to the guest. Walking guides have undergone additional training compared with other guides, often at their own expense, so being generous with tips will have a positive influence in encouraging more guides to get qualified and thus expand the number of venues where walks are available.

For obvious reasons, the world of walking safaris is not one to cut corners: it's essential to have a competent expert guide. Most walking safaris fall into the more expensive end of safari travel. That's not to say high-quality walking safaris are impossible at a lower cost, and that will be covered. But first, let's look at what influences walking safari prices. Safari travel in general is not cheap and it was always thus. In the 1950s and 1960s, only the seriously rich and footloose could afford to indulge in a safari in Africa, and today the experience is far more affordable, but still a comparatively expensive form of travel. In part, this is simply because of the costs of provision: high concession fees and taxes and the logistics of building in remote locations. While wage rates are low, a large number of staff is required to run a lodge or camp, and it adds up to a hefty fixed wage bill. Imported solar systems, vehicles and fuel are at rich economy cost levels and more. By definition, the wilderness areas with the best walking are remote, which adds to the cost of building and supply; often flying by small aircraft is the only practical access route for both guests and camp supplies. In many places, lodge owners take on the costs of road maintenance, fencing and even anti-poaching teams. Supply and demand is another cost driver: there's a finite amount of conserved lands where safaris can take place and a growing number of people who want to enjoy a safari. This leads to a ratcheting up of concession fees (paid by a lodge) and conservation fees (paid by the guest).

Provision of walking safaris costs more than vehicle-only safaris. Walking guides have special skills and extra training; the more expensive lodges are the ones likely to invest in their guides and make walks available on the activity list. When lodges offer fly-camping, they need additional staff to set camp, cook and assist, and an extra vehicle for logistics, so a supplemental fee is sometimes charged. In most cases, when on a sleep-out, guests pay for their room back at the lodge: it's there in case of a change of mind or bad weather. As for the smaller specialist trails camps and bush camps, these come with their own costs. Typically, they only operate for half the year, have a small number of beds, and have to be completely constructed and deconstructed each season. Mobile walking safaris can be the most expensive of all. You might wonder how sleeping in a dome tent with a long-drop toilet nearby can cost more than a fancy lodge – until you take part in such a safari and witness the logistics involved.

What does this all add up to in numbers? As a rough guide, $400–$700 per person per night would pay for the majority of walking safari experiences. There are a few more expensive and plenty that are less expensive, and some ways to reduce costs. Firstly, there are travel money-saving tips that apply to safari travel in general: plan ahead and try to find the sweet spot to book when flight prices are at the minimum. Sign up to newsletters and look for special deals. Ask an agency for a discount.

Then there are some that don't apply: walking is not a low-season activity, and in fact the best walking destinations are the most likely to be closed completely during

The Pafuri Triangle is one of South Africa's hidden secrets and a superb walking destination.

the 'green' season, owing to inundation. Even shoulder seasons are problematic for walking, with thick vegetation and high temperatures reducing their feasibility. Walking is a dry season activity.

Some ideas follow on how to experience high-quality walking safaris without it costing the earth.

Stay longer

Walking safaris are by definition a form of slow travel. If you enjoy the steady beat of exploration on foot, you're probably a person who does not want to race around with two nights here and a night there. So pick a place, get immersed, get to know the staff, maybe even start to recognise individual animals. You will save money by sticking with the same operator for a week or two through discounted rates and minimising air and road travel. The ultimate slow safari is to take a nature training course (see page 48). These field-based courses can involve a significant amount of time on foot, and the longer the course, the cheaper it is on a per night basis.

Go to less visited destinations

The high-profile high-volume parks can charge more and still stay busy. So head for lesser known destinations such as Liwonde in Malawi, the Tuli Block in Botswana and the Pafuri area of Kruger, all of which present excellent good-value walking. They really appreciate visitors.

Stay outside the park

But not too far outside. The sort of low-budget safaris that require visitors to drive for hours and then negotiate the gate procedures before starting their game viewing are a bad fit for walking. It's ideal to stay in the park, but it's sometimes feasible to stay at cheaper lodgings and enter the park at dawn for a walk. Examples are the Kruger National Park gate walks, lodges near the main gate for South Luangwa National Park and near the gates of Tarangire and Lake Manyara National Parks in Tanzania. Many parks have buffer zones known as Game Management Areas or Wildlife Management Areas that are unfenced from the parks and contain pretty similar habitat and wildlife. Walks in these areas can be rewarding and less costly, but always ensure they are led by qualified staff if big game can be encountered.

Go to South Africa

It's a bit misleading to generalise, as there are individual exceptions, but of the countries covered in this book, the least expensive for a walking safari is South Africa. This is thanks to its having a large domestic market, and a big chunk of its safari industry is geared to that market. As well as the many walks in state-owned parks, private reserves have lodges that afford high-quality experiences at costs much less than those of similar level properties further north. In the publicly owned parks, non-residents do pay higher conservation fees than locals, but they are still a fraction of those charged in East Africa.

The other aspect that makes South Africa affordable is the ability to travel like a local. With the appropriate precautions, rent a vehicle, stock up on food and self-drive to the state-owned parks and get stuck in. Every lodging has an individual *braai* (barbecue) stand, and either individual or shared kitchen. There are restaurants in the bigger camps. Game drives and walks can be booked at camps in the Kruger, Hluhluwe-iMfolozi and a few other parks. Activities in SANParks and Ezemvelo KZN Wildlife parks are priced separately from accommodation and run at very reasonable rates; it's possible to have a professionally guided walk for the price of a cinema ticket in New York or an art exhibition in London.

Take advantage of local rates

Residents of the countries covered in this book can ask for the local rate. Regional discounts, such as for the Southern African Development Community (SADC) countries, are available too.

Go backpacking

If you are fit and have the kit – a lightweight tent, sleeping bag, camping stove – then backpacking safaris are the way to go. Essentially you are just paying for the services of the professional guide and the conservation fees, which are low in the main place for this style, South Africa.

Take a guided nature walk

Finally, change the definition of 'walking safari'. To keep the content manageable, this book is restricted to expertly guided walks in areas with at least some of Africa's megafauna. There are countless places that have guided walks in areas without dangerous game present; these are usually referred to as 'nature walks' and are less expensive, as there's no requirement for the higher level of training or armed escort associated with walking safaris. And they can be shared with younger children. Even without an expert guide, there's plenty of wonderful wilderness walking in Africa. From South Africa's coastal trails, with their whales and otters, to the Simien mountains with their gelada baboons and Ethiopian wolves, it's a continent begging to be explored on foot.

Responsible safari travel

Around our planet, there's no wilderness area that's not subject to pressure from human activity. It's easy to become demoralised by the cascade of bad news and especially the interwoven slow motion catastrophes of climate change and destructive land use. In Africa, this is especially acute. Its people have played little role in creating the climate emergency, but are suffering the effects, a problem compounded by rapid population increase. The continent has the world's fastest growing population, and while UN projections see the global population peaking at around 10 billion by the 2080s, Africa's will still be growing: from 140 million in 1900, to 1.4 billion in the mid-2020s, 2.5 billion by 2050 and 4.1 billion by the end of this century. In economies that remain dominated by agriculture, the threat to wildlife habitat in this scenario is obvious. Yet there are reasons to be optimistic. Throughout Africa, there has been a transformation in how wilderness reserves are viewed, thanks to better management practices that distribute the economic benefits more equitably. Flagship parks are not just vehicles for national pride but vital revenue generators. And that's why wildlife tourism is important.

Africa's wilderness needs visitors. It's an attractive concept to set aside huge self-sustaining areas for nature and lock humans out, but it can't work. If reserves are not generating money through tourism, other more destructive forces take over – logging, charcoal production, mining, hunting, livestock farming, slash and burn agriculture. Unfortunately, we have seen many examples of this process play out in places where tourism collapsed owing to wars and unrest. The depletion of wilderness areas, which act as carbon

North Luangwa National Park is part of the Malawi–Zambia Transfrontier Conservation Area.

sinks, would far outweigh any gains by reduced tourism air travel. Thankfully, we have illustrations of places that have recovered remarkably well through good management. If there's a name to warm the heart of conservationists, it's African Parks. Working with national government agencies, this formidable non-governmental organisation has been remarkably successful in its mission to rehabilitate degraded conservation areas over the last 30 years. It has focused on less well-known parks, often difficult to access and with few tourism facilities. By investment in park infrastructure – roads, fences, staff facilities – and then carefully managed wildlife introductions and development of tourism facilities, it has demonstrated a replicable model that gives hope for habitat protection wedded to economic benefit for local communities.

Another development that's cause for optimism is the proliferation of enormous Transfrontier Parks. The driving force behind them is the Peace Parks Foundation, established in 1997 by HRH Prince Bernhard of the Netherlands, President Nelson Mandela and Dr Anton Rupert. There are now ten of these designated, each defining lands in state, community and private ownership that can be considered one ecosystem. Progress has been steady and there are tangible results to these projects, which recognise that successful ecosystems require scale and international cooperation.

As individuals, we are playing a beneficial role in spending money on safari travel. It's important that we endeavour to minimise our impact on these sensitive habitats, and we can do that through our travel choices. One tactic is to embrace slow safari – go to one place, stay there and don't bounce around on unnecessary journeys. When visiting a lodge or camp there are obvious things we can do to help them – minimise water usage, don't ask for imported products, buy local crafts. Waste management is a huge problem in Africa. In developed countries with efficient recycling, less than 10% of plastic made is ever recycled for reuse, so it's not surprising that in Africa, if you leave waste plastic it will (at best) end up in a pit fire – sometimes surprisingly close to the lodge. It's easy for us to bring home everything we carry in, especially hazardous waste such as batteries. There's a single-use plastic bag ban in Kenya and Tanzania, but it's OK to have packing aids such as Ziplock bags, which go home with you. Good lodge operators are proud of their eco-credentials and delighted to be asked for a tour – see how waste disposal works, how water is treated and energy generated, where tree planting is taking place. Safari operators are investing in green technology: bio-waste plants that make cooking gas, biofuels for vehicles, sustainable firewood, solar plants and electric vehicles. A great many support environmental initiatives that combat deforestation, and some reserves have achieved carbon neutrality.

By choosing walking safaris over other forms of safari, we can have a positive impact. Walking camps are small and transitory and have less environmental impact on a site and in their servicing – water usage, goods trucked in, waste out. By exploring on foot, we ensure wilderness zones get used and are not taken over for more destructive uses. The lowest impact walking safaris are the 'leave no trace' style, which range from backpacking to camel-supported expeditions. A few days after humans pass through, their tracks are already blurred by the animals that own the trails.

What to wear

Bush walkers should wear neutral-coloured clothing in bush shades – green, grey or khaki. Dark shades are better than light ones, as bright colours and white are not natural and will alert animals to your presence, but avoid black and navy, which attract tsetse flies. Camouflage patterns are not recommended, as they are used by military and rangers.

A hat is essential, ideally one with a brim that shades your neck and ears from sunburn. A light buff is a handy item that can protect your face from dust during a drive, be worn as a bandana, or be used to shield your neck from sun.

Take a look at the feet of professional walking guides, and you'll find everything from hiking boots to sandals. The lesson here is to wear what is comfortable to you and not something new from the shoebox. Hiking boots provide ankle support and are recommended for backpacking, but for other walks many people happily use trail shoes; avoid mesh style uppers which admit sand and seeds. The best compromise is lightweight but waterproof ankle boots. Beware of low-quality footwear as summer heat can melt the glue on the soles. Despite what some guides might have on their feet, it's best to avoid sandals for walks. Whatever footwear you bring for use around camp should be suited to using for walking in an emergency – if your walking shoes fall apart or get stolen by a hyena – so should not be flip-flops.

Ankle gaiters can be useful to stop grass seeds from infesting your socks. Don't get the high waterproof style, which are too hot for use in Africa. There are canvas and leather short gaiters on sale in outdoor shops in South Africa and online, including the Rogue and Solomon brands. Some folks prefer to wear low-cut

PLANNING A WALKING SAFARI

Shades of green and khaki are less conspicuous to wildlife.

socks instead of long ones, as the seeds are easier to remove from skin than from cloth or wool.

It's fine to wear shorts, leggings or breathable hiking pants. Jeans are adequate for short walks but not for longer trails, as they become heavy in the heat or rain. If you're in doubt about what to wear, check with the guides on the evening before the walk; they'll be able to tell you if there are ticks around, if the trails are thorny or if rain showers are expected, and you can adjust your wardrobe to suit the conditions. You'll need a medium-weight fleece for pre-dawn travel in open vehicles and for evening wear. Bring a light waterproof coat or poncho to protect against showers. It's wise not to set off on a walk with too many layers, as after warming up they'll be a burden for the rest of the trail.

Look for unscented sunscreen and avoid using perfumes or strong-smelling soaps and creams, as the scents are easily detected by animals. It's best to leave any valuable jewellery at home. If your trip involves domestic flights on small aircraft, check the restrictions – soft luggage with a maximum weight of 15 kg is common.

What to carry

It's essential to carry water on bush walks. Bring a reusable bottle from home and fill it at the camp from the filtered source; alternatively, walk operators can usually supply a water bottle. Outdoor equipment stores sell water containers and pouches with a shoulder strap, which allows your hands to remain free, and the insulated versions even keep a drink cool for a while. Don't put ice in metal containers because of the noise this makes while walking.

Packing for backpacking

It's worth giving some extra thought to your gear when heading into the *veld* with a full backpack. While it's not necessary to reach the level of sawing your toothbrush in half, careful planning, especially of meals, can shave a few kilograms off the load and make a multi-day trail more enjoyable. A simple rule for what to include in your backpack kit is 'if in doubt, leave it out': it's much more common to regret having carried something along than having left it behind. Pack the essentials, and only then consider including one or two luxuries.

Keeping your pack weight under control is key to enjoying a backpacking safari.

Essentials

Backpack	60–70 l is a good size for a three- or four-day trip.
Tent or mosquito net	Check the plan with the trail leader to ensure the correct choice is packed; for some primitive trails no shelter is needed.
Sleeping mat	As lightweight and compact as possible. For inflatable mattresses put a tarp underneath for protection from thorns.
Sleeping bag	A one- or two-season bag (5 °C) is fine for most of the year, and a three season bag (0 °C) during winter.
LED head torch	Rechargeable models are fine. When used at a low setting they have a burn time more than adequate for the hours needed on a trail. If bringing a battery model, pack spare batteries.
Camping stove, accessories and fuel	Gas canisters are lighter than liquid fuel. Neither can be carried on flights, so if flying consult in advance with the trail leader to identify the best fuel and source.
Utensils	These should include a bowl, mug, fork and spoon (or spork), and a camp knife or multi-tool.
Water containers	Set off with a minimum of 2 l in bottles or bladders, and at least the same again in storage capacity for use at the camp.
Water purification	Chlorine drops and tablets can be bought at pharmacies or outdoor equipment stores; add fruit powder to flavour the water.
Sun protection	A hat with a brim, sunblock and lip balm, and sunglasses if desired.
Anti-insect lotion	A DEET-based cream or spray, or DEET-free alternatives such as Natrapel 8 Hour and Picaridin.
Wash kit	The soap in the wash kit should be biodegradable.
Camping towel	A lightweight microfibre towel. A smaller towel is useful for drying feet after a river crossing.

Toilet tissue and lighter	Pack these in a Ziplock bag. Guides usually provide a small shovel or auger for bush toilets.
First aid items	Guides carry a first aid kit, but it's handy to have a small personal one to treat sprains, cuts or blisters.
Personal medicines	Include malaria prophylaxis if required in the area where you will be walking. Pack rehydration sachets for replacing electrolytes.
Compressible stuff sacks	A waterproof sack to keep electronic items dry. A sack for dirty clothes and another one to carry out rubbish
Trail wear	Breathable hiking gear in earth shades, a swimsuit if river bathing is an option, and a set of spare underwear and socks for each day. This is where weight can be saved. It's possible to do a four-day trail in one set of clothing, with a spare set for evening wear. The evening set can be worn on the final day.
Evening wear	Long pants or leggings, a fleece top and a beanie in winter.
Trail boots	While trail shoes can be fine for most walks, the added weight carried when backpacking means that boots with ankle support are needed.
Camp shoes	Sandals or lightweight shoes for evenings at camp.
Camp meals	Freeze-dry hiking meals. South African outdoor stores such as Cape Union Mart, Trappers and Outdoor Warehouse carry these, or order from The Trailfood Co.
Snacks	Biltong, energy bars, hard-boiled eggs, crackers, dried fruit and nuts; teabags, coffee and hot chocolate sachets are all good.

Non-essentials

Treats	At the end of the day, it's nice to have a reward such as chilli sauce or sweets.
Rain gear	If rain is forecast, bring a poncho or light waterproof.
Compact binoculars	They can have a harness to stop them swinging.
Gaiters	Ankle-high gaiters are helpful to keep grass seeds, dust and ticks off your socks and out of your shoes.
Trekking poles	Useful at river crossings and on loose slopes; they take some load off legs.
Repair kit	This can include a sewing kit, and duct tape for ad hoc repairs to boots, sleeping mats and other kit.
Power bank	To charge a camera or phone.
Chair with back support	Naturehike is a good brand with models that weigh less than 1 kg.
Pocket shower	A lightweight 10l bag with a shower head and cord for suspension from a tree.
Day pack	Sometimes a backpacking camp stays put for two nights, in which case it's useful to have a light day pack for snacks, water and swimwear.
Small tarpaulin	It's hard to stay clean on a trail. A small tarp or flour sack weighs little; it can be stuffed into a side pocket of your pack and used when sitting or lying on the ground.

Binoculars are a must for most walkers.

It's feasible to do without a day pack and just carry a water bottle on a shoulder strap, but it's better to have a small pack, preferably in neutral colours and with pockets for small items. The type of pack with an integrated hydration bladder is a handy option; alternatively, it's good to have one with secure side pockets for easy access to water bottles. Useful items for the pack include sunblock, lip balm, personal sanitary items, hand sanitiser and a waterproof stuff sack in case of rain. Try to avoid Velcro fasteners and the noisy types of plastic bag; Ziplock bags are good for tissues and snacks. The pack should have space to stow a fleece after the day warms up and to hold a light raincoat or poncho if this could be needed on the walk. It's sensible to take along a small personal first aid kit – a few blister plasters, antiseptic wipes and Band-Aids, rehydration sachets and a pair of tweezers. Energy snacks such as dried fruit, trail mix or muesli bars are good to have, and many walk operators supply snacks, either carried by the guide or distributed to walkers in advance. These typically include packets of fruit juice, biltong (dried meat), fresh or dried fruit and biscuits or crackers.

A pair of binoculars is an essential item for most walkers. A good size for walking is 10x42, although the smaller 10x25 does the job. It's best to keep them to hand, as an animal encounter is no time to be removing backpacks or fiddling with zippers. If your pack has a chest strap, you can tuck compact binoculars behind it while still having quick access to them. Lightweight harnesses are available that keep the equipment from swinging while you walk.

There's a strong argument for leaving your camera in the vehicle or at the lodge. A camera can soon become burdensome on a walk, especially if it has a heavy zoom lens and assorted accessories.

Realistically, the best wildlife shots will be taken from a steady perch on a vehicle or at a hide. Modern smartphones provide a fine alternative and can easily be carried in a belt pouch or pocket for quick access. They are not going to capture great shots of birds or other wildlife on a walk, but are good for macro shots, people and landscapes. It's best practice to not share photos of rhinos without removing the location metadata of the image.

Don't forget to switch your phone to 'airplane mode' – nothing would be more embarrassing than a phone sounding at a critical moment. And look for a belt pouch with a magnetic flap instead of a zip or Velcro fastener. For recharging, almost all venues have some way to charge devices; even those that are off grid have solar charging. Check the local plug socket type before travel and pack a suitable adapter.

Trail tech

Going on a walking safari can be a good opportunity for a tech detox, and on multi-day trails, especially backpacking trails, it's recommended that you leave behind watches, phones and other gadgets, and just enjoy tech-free immersion in nature. That said, a smartphone is still a handy thing to carry. Apart from being a means of taking photos on trail – and an alarm clock for early starts – it can be used to access increasingly sophisticated nature apps. Your walking guide will be a living encyclopaedia of natural history, and usually has reference books to hand, but apps can be fun to supplement the info when back at camp. To be useful, the apps should work offline, through a downloadable database. Here are a few downloads to consider.

- **BIRDS** Merlin – free app from Cornell Lab, with downloadable country bird packs; Roberts Bird Guide 2 – best for Southern Africa, pricey but comprehensive; eGuide to birds of East Africa. Before playing calls from a birding app check with the guide if it's appropriate – in general, we don't want to interfere with natural behaviour.
- **MAMMALS** Stuarts' African Mammals and Stuarts' South African Mammals.
- **REPTILES** Frogs of Southern Africa; ASI Snakes – free app invaluable for identifying snakes, especially venomous ones.
- **PLANTS** Seek – free app from iNaturalist; eTrees of Southern Africa.
- **TRACKS** Stuarts' Tracks and Scats; iTrack Africa.
- **STARS** Stellarium Mobile; Sky Map; StarWalk 2.
- **MAPPING** There are various apps that can record a trail on GPS-enabled devices, such as a watch. If you decide to use one, let the guide know. It's polite to refrain from waymarking features: the guide's personal discoveries – special trees, springs, denning sites – are not for sharing with the world.

Health and hazards

Heatstroke and sunburn are the biggest walking safari health risks. Never set out without a hat, sun protection and plenty of water, and keep a few sachets of rehydration powder in your pack. When walking, the sun quickly evaporates sweat from exposed skin, so it's not evident how quickly you can dehydrate. Watch out for the symptoms, such as a headache or cramping. During hot conditions, keep up water intake at camp. In bush camps a wrap (called a *kikoi* in East Africa) is often provided to provide traditional cooling, and it works well when soaked and worn next to skin.

Secondary health hazards on walks are insect bites and thorn scratches. They should be treated at the first available rest stop with a wipe of an antiseptic swab. The tropical zone destinations in this book have a year-round malaria risk, apart from Laikipia, where the risk is low. Namibia, Botswana and South Africa have seasonal risk in certain areas; take medical advice on prophylaxis before travel. In any case, it makes sense to avoid being bitten by mosquitos: apart from malaria parasites carried by *Anopheles* species, other mosquito species transmit dengue and yellow fever and other viruses. Keep tents zipped up and cover arms and legs – especially the feet and ankles – after sundown. Mosquito nets are standard at the camps and lodges in this book, and visitors are often pleasantly surprised at the lack of mosquitos during the dry season.

In fact, if there are tales of insect woe, they are more often directed at the tsetse fly rather than the mosquito. These insects operate by day and can give a painful bite and transmit disease such as 'sleeping sickness'. They can penetrate clothing and seem to regard deterrent sprays as an invitation. They are not a pest associated with walks in particular – indeed, lumbering game viewing vehicles are magnets for tsetse, and they are less prevalent during the dry walking season. In areas where tourists and tsetse overlap, traps are used and seem quite successful in reducing populations. We should thank the tsetse for being partly responsible for the conservation of Africa's wilderness areas. Without them, more land would have been given over to cattle ranching, and the wild animals eliminated. The fly itself has been largely eradicated in Southern Africa, but is found in other parts of Africa, especially the Zambezi valley and the parks of Zambia, Malawi and Tanzania.

Cooling down in a river after a walk is one of the pleasures of wilderness walking, and guides will advise where it's safe to do so in flowing, shallow water sans crocodiles. Avoid paddling in stagnant water – the main risk is from bilharzia, a parasite transmitted by freshwater snails. If a walk requires wading through still water, it's a good idea to dry your feet thoroughly after the crossing, using a small towel carried for that purpose. Ticks can be found in any areas with long grass, especially in wet season months. Check with the guide prior to the walk, and they can advise if shorts are appropriate. 'Pepper ticks' – the juveniles – are tiny and hard to spot but can be irritating. As ticks can transmit disease, bite areas should be monitored. Mopane bees, also known as 'sweat bees' or 'mopane flies', are not biters but are annoying in other ways, appearing in clouds and targeting moisture in the eyes, nostrils and mouth.

The idea of annoying little biters can be off-putting for people thinking of travelling to Africa, but in many years of walking the author has experience of ticks just twice and mopane bees once, and mosquitos and tsetse have never been a problem when on trail.

When deciding on a walking safari destination, should personal safety be a factor in the selection? In short, no. There's a tendency for news media to give higher prominence to violent incidents, especially if an animal is involved, and overlook the mundane, which can lead us to irrational fears. In reality, the most dangerous activity in Africa is road travel, and there are ways to minimise the risks.

PLANNING A WALKING SAFARI

Flying is safe, and often the only practical means to reach many of the venues in this guide. Even if a road transfer is possible, it eats into time that could be spent in the bush and will probably be stressful and not much cheaper. So, where possible, price the flights in. Where road transfers are necessary, plan the itinerary so that they take place in daylight. After dark, pedestrians, wild and domestic animals, potholes and badly lit vehicles are real dangers. And that's before considering often lamentable driving standards, which is a problem by day and night. Unless you are an Africa 'old hand', let somebody else do the driving. Don't be shy about insisting on safe speeds and mobile phone usage.

Statistically, some countries have higher rates of violent crime, and South Africa stands out in this regard. However, as globally, crime is primarily an urban phenomenon, and frankly, if your interest is to get deep into wilderness as quickly as possible, then there's hardly a city in sub-Saharan Africa worth detaining you. At most, you might have an overnight in transit, but from Nairobi to Lusaka to Johannesburg, these transit cities all have pleasant lodges in leafy suburbs. As safari travellers, we are privileged to see only the best aspects of Africa. It's quite standard to arrive at an international airport and fly to a reserve via propeller plane, and spend the entirety of a visit in the calm surroundings of the natural world.

3 The walking safari experience

Walking guides

Here's something to try while out on a bushwalk. As you move, scan the ground in front and see if you can spot any interesting tracks. Are they fresh? Glance at the grasses: could they show the recent scent markings from a hyena? At the same time, keep an eye on the middle distance for any potential dangers. Is the dark shadow ahead a log or a resting buffalo? That moving branch, is it a baboon or a feeding elephant? Think about where you are headed – are you walking towards thick bushveld or a steep slope? Check that giant sycamore fig: there could be a roosting eagle owl in there.

Simultaneously, listen for the sounds of the bushveld. Is that the call of a rare and interesting bird? Is the other sound an alarm call of an antelope? Maybe there's a lion or leopard ahead. Think about the wind: do you know which direction it's coming from? Oh, and what about the guests behind you? Are they all together or has someone stopped for a photo and fallen behind? Are they looking happy or is it time to find shade for a rest and rehydration? When you stop, have a think: could you find your way back to the vehicle or camp from here?

You get the picture. Guides are not just leading the way; they are using all of their senses to navigate the bushveld safely, while creating an enjoyable experience for their guests. As a walker you can relax and enjoy, but the guide is working hard. It needs a special character to be a good walking guide. After all, it's tougher work than vehicle-based nature guiding. The best walking guides have a genuine love for nature, are constantly learning themselves and can empathise with the excitement of a first-time trail walker. That said, even the finest of guides can tire of repeating information to a silent audience, and walkers gain more by being 'good guests': getting engaged, helping with spotting, showing interest and asking questions. During a walk, keep questions relevant to what's at hand and save others for rest breaks or campfire chats.

Depending on local conditions, number of guests and policies, you might find yourself on a trail with just the guide, carrying a rifle. In Southern Africa, under the Field Guides Association of Southern Africa (FGASA) protocols, it's usual to have two guides, or a guide and a tracker; if there are two armed guides, they are referred to as 'first rifle' and 'second rifle'. Apart from providing a second pair of eyes and maintaining situational awareness, walking with a backup is a way to mentor upcoming walking guides in the field; don't assume the guide at the front is the most experienced. When there are two rifles, it's normal for both to walk at the front, as this is where animal encounters happen, and it lets the guides confer and plan any actions. In some places, the practice is for one guide to walk at the back, where it's easier to keep an eye on the group.

North of the Limpopo River in Zimbabwe and Botswana, it's common to walk with a single armed guide, while north again beyond the Zambezi River the walking party tends to get bigger.

In Zambia and East Africa, it's normal to have a walking guide to focus on interpretation who is aided by an armed scout or ranger employed by the park (see box, 'Is my guide a ranger?', page 48). The ranger's primary duty is to escort, but they are often proficient trackers and happy to share their knowledge of nature alongside the guide. The ranger normally walks at the front, followed by the guide, then the guests, and they confer with the guide in the event of any potentially dangerous animal encounters. In Zambia, it's usual to have an assistant guide, who walks at the back; referred to as a 'tea bearer', they are much more than a porter for the snack break: they are helping to spot animals, and are often guides in training to lead trails, so are listening in and gaining experience.

A specialised form of guide is the tracker. This is a person who has perfected the art of identifying spoor and trailing wildlife, through traditional or formal training. Apart from showing amazing skills, trackers add a lot to the safety of a walk, as they are usually drawn from the local community and are adept at detecting potentially dangerous animals. Naturally, trackers always lead the group, and may be 30 or 40 m ahead. Depending on their skillset, they may either work alongside a guide or act as the guide themselves.

Most of the walking safaris in this book require an armed escort for safety, but it's not always necessary. For example, in Namibia and other arid zones, buffalo are generally not present, and the open terrain makes avoiding elephant easier. If considering doing a bush walk in a big game area and there's no armed escort, it's important to investigate why – especially if the other operators in the area walk with rifles. It may be a lack of qualification or a licensing issue, in which case it'd be wise to not walk.

Guide training

Staff who are qualified to guide on foot are always more experienced than those who are only permitted to drive. Apart from their natural history knowledge and 'soft' guest skills, they have additional special training. Mainly, this is to ensure safety – navigation skills, situational awareness, recognising animal alarm calls, reading animal behaviour, tracking. Trails guides keep alive skills that humans developed over hundreds of thousands of years and are in danger of being lost in the modern era. Walking safaris would not be possible without these guides, and spending time in their company is one of the extra benefits of walking.

To work as a guide in Africa, one needs to be a citizen or have residency, but it's possible to share in the training programmes out of interest (see page 48). The guide training regime and recognition varies from country to country. Some excellent guides may have no formal training but vast experience, but the trend is towards formal certification of guide qualifications. It takes a high level of commitment to qualify as a walking guide, and this ensures high levels of safety and quality in trails guiding in Africa.

The biggest driver for formalised guiding standards is the Field Guides Association of Southern Africa (FGASA). Based in South Africa, this member-based organisation has developed a set of guiding protocols and courseware and FGASA is accredited to oversee guide training by the government training and certification body for the tourism sector. Under the FGASA system, the courses and assessments are complemented by mandatory logging of work in the field, and in the case of trails guides, this is significant. Before being allowed to lead guests on foot, they must first qualify as a field guide, pass first aid training, and do their Advanced Rifle Handling (ARH) training and assessment. This involves learning to use a rifle with a minimum calibre of .375, and more usually .458, ethically at close range, with the emphasis on speed of reaction and accuracy. Then, the guide completes theory and practical training, and is vetted by a qualified mentor before starting to guide under supervision and logging their hours and Potentially Dangerous Animal (PDA) encounters. There's a minimum of 100 mentored hours in the *veld* as first or second rifle and then 50 hours in a workplace setting before the final trails guide assessment. Ultimately, a person with the FGASA Professional Trails Guide certification will have a minimum of 600 hours in the field and will have logged 300 PDA encounters. With additional hours logged, further tracking skills attained, and a demanding assessment passed, a guide can reach the next level of Special Knowledge and Skills (Dangerous Game) Trails Guide. The most vital specialised skill for trails guides is tracking (see page 56), and guides who have attained the highest levels in both tracking and trails guiding are referred to as 'FGASA scouts'; there are fewer than twenty in Africa.

In Botswana, a Full Professional Guide may conduct all tourism activities including walking with guests, with or without a rifle, in areas with PDAs. The qualification requirements are in a state of transition at the time of writing. The Botswana National Credit and Qualifications Framework (NCQF) Levels 4 and 5 guide qualifications make provision for guides to first become Backup Trails Guides with the basic weapons and speed-shooting proficiency and the ability to provide support to a lead trails guide. The requirements for this qualification include 50 hours on foot with a qualified mentor, an assessment of Viewing Potentially Dangerous Animals (VPDA) on foot in a backup role, theory training and encountering the pre-requisite elephant, buffalo and big cats on foot. There are demanding safety requirements to step up to become a lead trails guide, including facing the dreaded 'nagmerrie' (Afrikaans for the nightmare). Similar to one of the FGASA ARH tests, this involves a lion target on a motorised sled that 'charges' the candidate at close to 50 kph.

In Zimbabwe, guides take great pride in their training regime, regarded as the toughest in world. All Zimbabwean professional guides are qualified to guide on foot. It starts with a series of four exams that test the candidate's knowledge of relevant law, habits and habitats, firearm ballistics and a general paper that covers just about any topic a guest might ask about Zimbabwe. The exams are challenging, but with them under their belt the guide can start the journey as an apprentice guide: under the mentorship of a fully qualified guide, they can conduct game drives within the national parks. In the years ahead, the apprentice guide will grab every opportunity to spend time on foot with their mentor, logging dangerous game encounters. Unlike under the FGASA system, there's no formal assessment and certification at this point. Instead, when the mentor considers the apprentice ready, they will be allowed to lead a group, with the mentor a few steps behind. A full debrief after each walk is a must, highlighting the positives and negatives, all the while adding to the log book.

At some point during these years of learning, the guide must pass advanced proficiency in bush first aid and their rifle handling. This is similar to the FGASA rifle test, focusing on speed and accuracy at close quarters; where it differs is that Zimbabwean apprentice guides are given responsibility to dispatch problem animals, a task that normally falls to a park ranger, so they have real experience of rifle usage before facing an emergency situation. The stress of any dangerous animal encounter is surpassed by the oral exam, when the guide is faced with up to ten experienced examiners, all of them professional guides. Armed with a recommendation from their mentor and a full logbook, assessment day starts with questions around a table that's filled with props – animal skulls, seed pods, grasses and leaves, pieces of skin. There's a final stage, the most challenging of all, known as 'the proficiency'. This is a week-long practical exam conducted annually. The candidate links up with three others who have passed the oral exam, and they set a tented camp in the bush, just as they would for their guests. Tents, beds, furniture, showers and toilets, kitchen and all the extras must be put in place over two days. Then the 'guests' arrive – the examiners – who inspect the camp with a critical eye. For the rest of the week, they act like the most curious of guests, going on walks and drives, and peppering the guide with questions that cover geology and astronomy and everything in between.

Across the Zambezi River, Zambia's wildlife safari guides follow a progressive curriculum through a training programme defined by the Technical Education Vocational Authority (TEVETA) with qualifications recognised by the Zambia Qualifications Authority and UNESCO. The entry level is the wildlife safari transfer guide programme, which delivers theoretical and practical training in all aspects of nature. Those working as a transfer guide gain skills in communication and guest etiquette, sharing knowledge while learning from qualified guides. The second stage involves deeper nature training, and after passing this stage they can take guests on game drives as a wildlife safari driving guide. After two further years of training, they can apply for the highest accreditation which is the wildlife safari walking guide. These guides spend many hours assisting on trails before taking their assessment. Rifle training for guides is not a requirement in Zambia, as armed escorts are always conducted by wildlife police officers employed by the national parks.

In Tanzania, the recently formed Field Guide Association of East Africa aims to formalise guide training certification. For now, the onus for standards is on the walk operators and some have in-house trainers, while others bring in expert trainers as needed, and rigorous firearms assessments are part of that. Lead guides will all have had a long apprenticeship with many hours on foot – and many big

Zimbabwean professional guide Spike Williamson at work in Hwange National Park.

Is my guide a ranger?

The answer to this question is 'it depends'. In Africa the term 'ranger' is usually reserved for staff in reserves who do not deal directly with visitors. Their job description can include a wide range of tasks involved in looking after a park or reserve and its wildlife: anti-poaching patrols; dealing with injured animals or animals in places they should not be; enforcing park rules; supporting research activities and community outreach; inspecting infrastructure and reporting. But not interpretive guiding – that's the job of nature guides.

It's the guide's responsibility to run a trail or walk – determine the route, pace and duration and interpret the natural world for the guests. Guides qualified to lead on foot have various names: trails guide or trails officer in South Africa, professional guide in Zimbabwe, wildlife safari walking guide in Zambia. In places, a guide or tracker is referred to as a *fundi*, which in Swahili describes any expert, specialist, or craftsman. In this book, the term 'trails guide' is used when referring to guides qualified under the FGASA system, and otherwise 'walking guide' is used.

If a ranger – sometimes called a scout or wildlife police officer – is walking at the front and carrying a large bore rifle, their main concern is dealing with a dangerous animal. Normally, they will have received special training on the safe escorting of trail walkers. If they are carrying a military style rifle such as an AK47, or trailing the group, then they are present for general security – a deterrence to any nefarious humans. Rangers are often from local communities and have deep knowledge of local culture, nature and are proficient trackers – essential for their anti-poaching work.

---

game encounters – under their belts. The national park authority is strict on who they permit to do the overnight walking safaris in the wilderness zones, such as those in the Serengeti.

The Kenya Professional Safari Guides Association (KPSGA) recognises three levels of safari guiding expertise, Bronze, Silver and Gold, with guides being assessed based on a combination of years of experience and exams set by the KPSGA. There's no defined category for walking guides, but rifle-carrying guides will have undergone additional training and assessment that includes firearm use and trails specific skills. Some follow the FGASA Trails Guide syllabus, a high standard that's recognised as such throughout Africa, while others gain their walking guide training in Tanzania. Many Kenyan guides come from the Samburu and Maasai tribes, with a tradition of semi-nomadic cattle herding. These guides may not have the KPSGA recognition but have a deep knowledge of their natural environment and many years of experience of guiding guests in safety in their areas.

Nature training on foot

One of the joys of walking safaris is the constant opportunity to learn something new, and it's possible to formalise this aspect by taking an ecology field course with a training company. The core business of these companies is to provide mentoring and training to aspiring professional guides, but they also have courses for people interested in developing their knowledge as part of a bushveld walking holiday. Anyone can join a trails guide training course, a fantastic way to experience maximum time on foot in wilderness in the company of some of Africa's most knowledgeable guides and like-minded nature lovers. Note that these courses are training focused, and participants pitch in on all aspects; they aren't the sort of safari where you get pampered with a cold towel and open bar after a day in the bush.

There are options in South Africa and in Botswana, and courses are identical to those undertaken by career students; they follow the syllabuses developed by the Field Guides Association of Southern Africa (see page 45). Successful graduates who are not local citizens or legal residents may be able to take up unpaid work placements, but there are barriers that will likely stymie dreams of becoming a full-time professional guide. Normally, trails guide students complete the field guide course before, but it's not absolutely essential if joining out of interest. Field guide course graduates are issued with a Nature Site Guide certificate, and the terms field guide and nature guide are rather confusingly interchangeable.

If students want to carry a rifle on trails and do the Advanced Rifle Handling (ARH) training and assessment, they must firstly attain the South African Professional Firearm Training Council (PFTC) rifle handling qualifications. This can be done via a number of trainers; it takes a few days and covers safety and basic rifle skills. If passed, the student can then go on to do the ARH as part of the trails guide training. However, people doing these courses for fun can elect to skip the rifle part and won't walk armed or complete the assessments. Trails guide field courses range from four to six weeks, and walks are more intensive than on normal walking safaris. They aim to maximise the number of PDA encounters, as the students need to log a certain number in order to pass the course. They usually include a backpacking and sleep-out experience, and this aspect can be challenging.

African Guide Academy is the only FGASA-accredited training company in Botswana; it operates a fascinating range of nature training courses. Most students come to take courses for the experience of studying nature in the Okavango rather than to pursue a guiding career. Courses are run from Kwapa Training Camp in the southern Delta and a wilderness trails camp in the same area. The unfenced camps are set in a wildlife-rich area amid a landscape of river channels, floodplains, lagoons and a diversity of habitats that includes riparian woodland, savannah, mopane scrub, climax mopane woodland and grasslands. The southern Okavango tends to be dry as it only receives floodwaters in exceptional years, but if water is present there's a chance to gain mekoro safari skills.

Nature Guide and Trails Guide are both 28-day courses, but the modular design means they can be split over two two-week stays. Kindle versions of courseware can be bought online in advance to give participants the chance to get a start before travel. Track & Sign and Wilderness Trails courses are both seven nights; they incorporate a significant amount of time learning skills while on foot, and there's a specialist birding course.

In line with the FGASA syllabus, it's best to do the Nature Guide training before taking on Trails Guide, but not essential when doing the courses out of general interest. If guests do both courses, they can sit the exams and do the rifle and trails guiding assessments and qualify as a certified Apprentice Trails

Guide. In fact, African Guide Academy offers both the FGASA and Botswana Qualifications Authority (BQA) backup guide qualifications, with the latter easier to attain. It's important to note that getting qualified in either certification is just the first step, and many hours of mentored walks and logged big game encounters are required before leading a trail, but with several years of repeat visits it's feasible. One way to get those hours is to take part in the Wilderness Trails course, but this can also be simply booked as a stand-alone course for the experience. For this course, participants leave Kwapa to overnight in a low impact wilderness trails camp. There's maximum time on foot and a mix of nights spent in tents in camp and sleep-outs with a night watch.

Kwapa Camp is a two-hour road transfer from Maun. Lodgings are in large Meru-style tents with en suites.

Participants should have a reasonable level of fitness and have a driving licence. The minimum age is 18 to follow the FGASA syllabus and 16 for the BQA. Doing trails guide training in Botswana costs more than in South Africa but has the advantage of being conducted in one of the world's greatest wildernesses. In South Africa, there's more choice of training providers and more course dates.

Based in Northern KwaZulu-Natal, **Bhejane Nature Training** is a FGASA-approved training company that presents a full suite of guiding courses and attracts a mix of career students and nature enthusiasts from both South Africa and overseas. As well as Field Guide and Trails Guide courses, Marine and Coastal Guiding is offered thanks to their location not far from the Indian Ocean coastline of the iSimangaliso Wetlands Park. Bhejane

Taking a break during an EcoTraining trails guide course in northern Kruger.

runs its courses from the Gobandlovu Base Camp in Kuleni Game Reserve. It's well located in a wildlife-dense area close to Phinda Private Game Reserve and uMkhuze Game Reserve, and field trips range north to the Ndumo Reserve, known for its prolific birdlife, and Tembe Elephant Park. The base camp has shared accommodation in wooden huts or safari tents. Field practicals are run from the Bhejane Outpost camp which is set in various reserves in Zululand. The Outpost is much more rustic than the main camp, the accommodation in dome tents with bucket showers, flush toilets and solar power.

Bushwise Field Guides is a long-standing training company that welcomes non-career students alongside aspiring professionals, all the way up to trails guide. Rather than following the FGASA programmes, the company is accredited by the International Field Guide Association, and the guide qualifications are the same as those attained through other government-accredited South African trainers. Bushwise runs a couple of interesting online courses of 8 or 12 weeks' duration that participants can follow at their own pace from home. The camp-based Field Guide is a 60-day course which may be too long for time-limited overseas participants, but an option is to do the online Field Guide course followed by the condensed 17-day Field Guide practical in South Africa. This is hosted at a camp in Greater Makalali, a wildlife-rich private reserve 60 km from Hoedspruit. The trails guide practical course is operated from the Bushwise camp adjacent to Makalali and likewise lasts 17 days. If spaces are available, non-career participants can join as observers, with no special prior requirements. They are treated in the same way as career students and can expect to spend six to eight hours in the bush daily. Part of the training is a three-day primitive trail, so be prepared to carry a backpack and sleep out in the wilds.

The largest private guide training company in Africa is **EcoTraining**, which has developed a collection of online and field courses that are geared to both the professional and the nature enthusiast. As well as year-long guide training programmes, there are fascinating shorter courses covering specialist topics including birding and wildlife photography. The EcoQuest course, which is run over one or two weeks, can be regarded as an intensive safari, as the learning is done in the field rather than the classroom and it spans the natural world from plants and animals to ecology and astronomy. The online courses are a fascinating way to improve knowledge of nature from home, and as they are run live, provide the chance to interact with some very experienced trainers. Some participants find 'their tribe' with fellow alumni and follow up with real life travels in Africa. The online option makes it possible to do a lot of the Field Guide course remotely, and then finish it with a 35-day field practical, instead of the usual 55-day programme.

Short field courses of particular interest for walkers are the wilderness skills and tracking courses, both of which involve significant time on foot. The six-day Wilderness Trails Skills course covers essentials for surviving on foot in the wild, such as navigation, water-sourcing and campsite selection. The EcoTracker courses run over one or two weeks, and there's a 28-day EcoTracker: Animal Monitoring course targeted at professionals that utilises some of Africa's best trackers as trainers. 28-day Trails Guide training courses are run by EcoTraining in a number of Greater Kruger reserves, and other career or short wildlife courses are available in Mashatu in Botswana and a training camp on the Mara River in Kenya. For trails guide training, the pick of the camps is the one in the Makuleke Contractual Park in northern Kruger. The unfenced camp is located in a grove of nyala trees on the edge of the floodplain of the Limpopo River and can accommodate 16 students in en-suite A-frame huts.

Motsumi Bush Courses is the company of Bennet de Klerk and his team of specialist trainers. Based near Rustenburg, 100 km west of Pretoria, Motsumi covers the full range of FGASA courses, including trails guide. Bennet grew up on a Kalahari game farm and absorbed a love for the bushveld at an early age. After leaving university he worked as an overland safari guide on trips around Southern Africa, before landing up in Pilanesberg National Park and beginning a full-time career in guide training. He is a guide and assessor at the highest trails guide qualification level, Special Knowledge and Skills (Dangerous Game), and has had a military career to the rank of lieutenant-colonel in the South African defence forces.

For non-career students, Motsumi runs a one-week Bush Enthusiast Course. This is an opportunity to gain a deeper appreciation of the natural world in the company of expert trainers and involves plenty of time on foot. The course base is Mooihoek Mountain Retreat, overnighting in cabins or tents, which, while simple, have the essentials – hot water and proper beds. The field activity takes place in the Magaliesberg Mountains and Pilanesberg. Near the retreat, there are unusual rock formations, shallow caves, interesting vegetation and some relatively well-preserved Anglo Boer War sites. On the wetter eastern side of the mountains, Kgaswane Mountain Reserve has beautiful natural waterways, with swimmable pools, small rapids and waterfalls. Of the six nights, three are spent at a rustic camp in Pilanesberg National Park. Over the week, every aspect of the natural world is touched upon, from geology and astronomy to flora and fauna, tracking and animal behaviour. Evenings are devoted to storytelling by the campfire under the stars.

On the trail

Each walk in a big game reserve starts with a safety briefing. The rules defined by the Field Guides Association of Southern Africa may not be part of the pre-trail briefing throughout Africa but are always applicable:

1. Walk in single file.
2. Stay close together behind the rifles.
3. Never run.
4. Keep silent while walking.
5. Obey all commands without question.

As a guest, you don't need to walk with apprehension but observe these rules to ensure the guide can do their job and keep you safe. After the briefing is a good time to ask questions about the rules or let the guide know of any special interests you have.

Guides have a good knowledge of their area and its interesting features but are explorers at heart, so every walk is different. The group walks silently in single file: it's orderly, low impact and it presents a smaller profile to wildlife, and therefore is less likely to alarm them. The group should stay together; there's no need to walk on the heels of the person ahead, just in a compact bunch so that if there's a sighting, everyone has a chance to see it. The guides should never be out of view. Trail walkers are encouraged to swap

THE WALKING SAFARI EXPERIENCE

A typical trails camp day

05:00 You wake in darkness and tune your ears to the nocturnal bush sounds. Is that a frog or an African scops owl? The cough of a hippo is echoed by the eerie call of a hyena.

05:30 Don the walking attire and fleece for chill pre-dawn air. The camp is unfenced, so you get an escort to the common area, where flasks of hot water are ready for the first cup of the day.

05:50 The eastern sky is turning rosy, so there's no time for a big breakfast, just a few bites. You climb into the game viewing vehicle.

06:00 The crepuscular light reveals the last of the night roamers: maybe a bat-eared fox or porcupine; with luck, an aardvark or even an aardwolf (no relation).

06:15 It's bright enough for the guide to scan the sand for new tracks as they drive.

06:30 The engine off, you climb down and get the daypack comfortable. The sounds have changed. Now, there's a baboon squabble in the trees. You pay attention as the guide gives a safety briefing.

07:00 The walk is into its rhythm and sunlight filters horizontally through the trees, casting long shadows. The alarm bark of an impala sounds.

08:30 You reach the perfect shady spot for a snack and rest break. As you sit still, animals appear.

10:00 After more walking, the heat starts to weigh. The vehicle and its ice box are welcome sights. You drive back to camp to brunch and a cooling shower.

11:00 A nap, a book. Sit with the binoculars and spot new birds. Repeat.

16:00 The heat has eased. The trail shoes are back on as the group gathers for a muffin or slice of cake. You drive out of camp again, enjoying a typical slow game drive.

17:00 You park and walk, but not too far. You reach a focal point – a river, a waterhole, a vantage point. It's the bewitching hour, a golden light. Drinks are involved.

18:30 The sun is well down as you start the drive back. A high-powered torch with a red filter is deployed. The nocturnal animals are emerging: sengi and spring hare, maybe a lion on the move.

19:00 At camp there's time for another shower before meeting by the campfire for dinner and conversation.

21:00 You are back in your tent. The night music of the African wilds is again your companion. Is that the deep saw of a leopard?

The middle part of the day is devoted to rest and relaxation at camp.

When there's a natural barrier and the animal feels safe, viewing can be very close.

positions in the line, as those near the front see more. Every 10 or 15 minutes, the lead guest should step to the side, let the others pass and continue at the tail. Walkers who need to stop for any reason should communicate this to the guides with a low whistle or finger or tongue click, not by shouting.

The guides will stop for interesting things such as tracks, dung, burrows, special plants, birds and insects, and, of course, bigger animals. Usually, it's not the goal of trail walking to seek out wildlife such as elephant, rhino, lion and buffalo, but encounters will happen, and when they do, the guide will take a decision on the course of action. Depending on the situation – the type of animal, the number of them, the density of the bush – the guide may decide it's safe to go nearer. The aim is to stay in the animal's 'comfort zone' where either they are not aware of human presence or are aware and carry on with natural behaviour. Sometimes wildlife can be approached up to a surprisingly close distance, especially if there's a natural barrier such as a body of water, steep slope or fallen tree. It's important to stay still and quiet at an animal encounter. Apart from the primates, who can easily spot a human, the eyes of most animals are conditioned to detect movement, not to identify the shape of a human standing still.

Walking and wildlife

Even for the most experienced wilderness explorer, big game area walking is different. It's exciting to anticipate what we may meet along the way, and just about every walk will involve some interesting wildlife encounters. Why are guides always a step ahead and the first to spot an animal? Yes, it's because they are at the front, but they are also using their experience. They develop a feel for which animals are likely to be in which habitat. They know the plants that attract feeders and become familiar with favourite resting spots. Guides learn the pattern of movement, when and where animals seek water in the morning or evening. They know in which type of tree a species of bird likes to roost or feed. Above all, guides use their acquired skills to detect which animals are nearby – primarily by listening for tell-tale sounds and looking at tracks and other evidence of an animal's presence, such as fresh droppings, scent markings, scratch marks, bent, broken or nibbled vegetation, and disturbed ground where an animal has dug for food or minerals. Experienced guides even detect nearby animals by scent. Sound is vital: the alarm call of a bird or monkey can indicate a predator, and the crack of a big branch is an elephant feeding. Hearing oxpeckers can mean that buffalo are close. Guides can detect the low grunts that lions use to communicate with their young.

While listening and scanning the bush, the guides have an eye on the tracks as they walk. This is in itself quite a skill, and one of the most interesting aspects of walking safaris. Walkers can begin to learn not just which tracks belong to which animals, but how fresh they are, how to estimate the size of the animal from the tracks and the number of individuals. Spoor is of interest for safety reasons and allows for animal encounters under controlled conditions. It can be fun to try to follow the fresh track of a leopard, lion, or rhino, an activity known as trailing. The guide will weigh the merits of doing so; if the bush is dense or the animal has young in tow, then the best decision would be to take another direction.

Nature being nature, walks don't always live up to expectations. There's no guarantee of seeing anything, and animal sightings can be especially difficult if it's windy or the bush is thick. It's relatively rare to find big cats while walking, and antelopes and other small mammals tend to be quite skittish around people on foot. The key to enjoying walks is to just feel the peace of nature, soak up the small things and treat anything else as a pleasant surprise.

Staying safe on trails

Walking safaris are very safe when professionally guided and when guests behave in accordance with their guide's instructions. It's not risk free, but arguably safer than game driving, and definitely safer than the drive from the airport.

In the outdoor activity community, the Lemon Theory is cited when teaching safety. Its premise is that adverse incidents are not necessarily caused in a chain reaction, but through a number of unrelated factors synchronising like lemons lining up in a casino fruit machine. An example in the walking safari field might go as follows. A cranky old buffalo is resting out of sight behind a bush ahead of the walking group. A guide zones out for a moment and has not noticed some telling aural and visual clues that there may be buffalo nearby. A guest is lagging behind the group and does not hear the guide's instruction when the animal stands up. Any one of these on its own might not create drama, but the combination can be deadly. As guests, it's up to us to play our part in not making lemons, and that means listening to the guide. Their first job is to protect both their guests and the wildlife from harm. Thanks to high training standards

The art of tracking
Alex van den Heever

Born out of necessity in the wilderness of Africa, animal tracking is an ancient skill honed for reasons of survival. As cities rose and the hunter-gatherer way of life waned, the past six decades saw these abilities dwindle quickly. Yet in the wild spaces of private reserves and national parks, a handful of master trackers persists. Their daily quest to find wildlife benefits the experiences of visitors, aids in conservation efforts and thwarts poaching. Modern tracking may be more intense than its ancestral roots, but it's given rise to some incredibly skilled individuals.

To track is to blend physical vigour with sharp vision, creativity, memory and logical thought. The world's elite trackers add a special spark to this mix – a swift synthesis of their surroundings, entwined with a deep-rooted understanding of the animals they know so well. Many are adept at imitating the behaviours they observe, a testament to their acute observational skills. The craft of tracking is not static; it demands curiosity, continuous learning and years of refining. Tracking an antelope under the sweltering sun demands not just stamina but empathy and insight into the creature's life – its diet, habitat, and behaviours. As Renias Mhlongo – a world-renowned tracker with whom I have spent 30 years – remarks, 'one must put the animal in your heart'.

With time, trackers become attuned to the land and its vegetation, the season and the day's rhythm – all of which guides their intuition. Despite appearances, tracking is not a mystical art but the result of relentless practice and a deep understanding of nature. It is, in essence, a profound ecological literacy. Analysing tracks goes beyond knowledge of the wild; it involves scrutinising the minutiae. Distinguishing between a young white rhino's track and an adult black rhino's involves keen perception of delicate physical nuances.

Effective tracking is a dance between the macro and the micro, an exhausting process that sharpens all senses. Trackers construct mental canvases of the animals' lives, their movements and their interplay within their domain. It's crucial not to fixate on a single creature lest other vital clues go unnoticed. For instance, a tracker focused on a black rhino might overlook the faint distress call of a shrike, signalling a hidden leopard nearby. The seasoned tracker knows the principles but remains ever responsive to the environment's cues. Tracking may seem enigmatic to the untrained eye, but it is a genuine skill that can be mastered through dedication and experience.

Tracks and signs: the language of the wild

Tracks and signs lay the groundwork for tracking, much as learning the alphabet is essential before one can read and interpret the marks left by animals. These signs include all forms of evidence that animals have been present, from footprints (spoor) to signs of feeding, and from dropped feathers to bones, hairs and scents, each one a critical clue for a tracker.

Every track tells its own story, shaped by factors such as the animal's size, age, health and the ground it travels over. No two creatures, even of the same species, leave identical marks. The variety

Renias Mhlongo and Alex van den Heever deciphering tracks.

of movements an animal makes – from a slow walk to a full sprint or a sudden turn – all contribute to the complexity of their tracks. The signs of older animals or those with injuries often stand out owing to their unusual nature, and these are the subtleties that trackers learn to decipher.

The type of ground – whether it's a layer of fine silt or shifting gravel – greatly affects the clarity of a track. More often than not, the tracks are incomplete or distorted, requiring a tracker to piece together the puzzle. By eliminating animals that couldn't have made a particular sign, trackers narrow down the possibilities. Clear tracks are rare; the terrain's nature often complicates the imprint left behind. Different grounds, from soft sand to rocky soil, can result in dramatically different track impressions.

The challenge of trailing

Trailing is the intricate skill of piecing together animal signs to locate the creature itself. It's akin to a detective assembling clues to pinpoint a suspect. A successful tracker blends signs with the environment to deduce an animal's path and destination. This discipline is perhaps the most challenging to master, demanding both logic and creativity. It's about focusing on the minute details and then zooming out to understand them within the environment's larger tapestry. Only those dedicated to practising trailing day in and day out stand to truly master this ancient African art.

Trailing is not steeped in mystique; it's a tangible skill just like any other. In the past, hunter-gatherers depended on trailing to secure food, tracking animals not for trophies but for essential nourishment. However, from around the 1960s, with the push of urbanisation and political shifts, such as those during apartheid in South Africa, traditional hunting practices waned, disconnecting people from the land.

Today, trailing has found new relevance. Professional trackers in the ecotourism industry use it to locate wildlife for visitors. Field rangers rely on it for anti-poaching operations and to gather data for wildlife conservation studies. This skill remains vital, bridging the gap between ancient practices and modern conservation needs. Mastering the trail of animals is an art often perfected by those with years of field experience. Herders and hunters, for instance, have accumulated experience in following these natural pathways. Yet anyone can learn to track with proficiency given the right knowledge and practice.

Trails guides take great pride in their expertise, and each walking experience described in this book presents a chance to acquire and gradually master tracking skills. Developing even a foundational skill set in tracking significantly enhances the experience, providing a valuable toolset that can be applied to wilderness walking anywhere in the world.

The cornerstone of tracking is understanding animal behaviour – knowing their social habits, preferred habitats and diets. Recognise the general tendencies of a species, then zero in on the individual quirks. For example, a leopard at Londolozi was known to target greater cane rats within certain areas of the reserve. Knowing her preferred hunting spots allowed trackers to predict her movements accurately. Animals, especially those with padded feet such as lions and leopards, often opt for the easiest routes. However, trailing an aardvark can be a dizzying endeavour owing to its erratic path in search of ants and termites. Understanding such behaviour is key to predicting the animal's next steps.

Seasons dictate patterns too. Elephants may visit the same water sources during dry spells, while leopards might choose elevated spots during summer afternoons to enjoy a cool breeze. Regular tracking reveals the patterns of animals such as rhinos, from their territorial edges to their preferred wallowing spots.

The nature of the ground plays a critical role in tracking. Begin by noting how undisturbed ground looks; any disruption, whether slight or stark, becomes a potential clue. Sandy terrain can distort track sizes, while mud tends to enlarge them. Harder surfaces might show only partial prints. Trackers must judge the size, shape and texture of tracks, which vary with age. Fresh tracks can be darker or lighter than the soil, fading to blend in over time. Sometimes only the texture, such as the unique pattern of a rhino's footprint, is what identifies a track.

When deciphering animal signs, study the scene thoroughly. Check for additional tracks or signs before making a judgement. A single ambiguous mark might be clarified by another sign nearby. Look for disturbances in the earth and vegetation – anything from upturned stones to broken branches can be telling.

and long experience, guides do this very well.

Reserve owners, walk operators and guides know that safety is paramount to the continued availability and success of walking safaris. Safety considerations come into play long before anyone puts on their boots, with intensive guide training and adherence to strict policies. When planning a walk, guides check the weather conditions and will only go out when these are favourable. They will determine a route that avoids unnecessary risks such as steep slopes, deep river crossings and

Gait analysis reveals much about an animal's actions or intentions. A swiftly moving lion might be intent on joining its pride or sensing a rival. A slow-moving predator could be stalking its prey. Other fauna and bird calls can also inform trackers. Zebras dashing in one direction might signal nearby lions, while peaceful impalas could suggest predators have passed. Different bird calls can indicate various predators; for example, white-crested helmet shrikes make distinct sounds when they spot leopards.

Understanding individual animals and their reactions to human proximity is crucial, not only for tracking but also for safety. Interestingly, expert trackers with years of practical experience record surprisingly few dangerous encounters. Karel Benadie, a Master tracker who co-founded Tracker Academy with Renias and me, has followed dangerous animals such as black rhinos for decades without incident, thanks to his heightened sense of awareness.

It's essential to view the larger scene. Focusing solely on the ground limits vision and can be unsafe. By broadening your view, you can 'read' the landscape and see signs from a distance, such as fresh leopard scat, that can guide you on the trail. Frustration can lead novice trackers to rush, increasing the likelihood of missing vital signs. In such cases it's best to pause, regroup at the last known track and consider the animal's possible path. If the terrain is too tough for clear tracks, look ahead to softer ground or search in arcs. However, too slow a pace might mean never catching up with the animal. The key is to adapt your speed to the terrain and develop a tracking rhythm that suits your style and experience.

Tracking, to me, is like uncovering the secretive story of an animal, and indeed of nature's own script. It's a practice where every discovery is a lesson that reveals the subtle interactions in nature that we mostly don't notice. I remember how, just recently, a seemingly insignificant dew drop on a grass blade unveiled the complex passage of a hunting leopard – a small insight that connects to a much larger understanding of the leopard's story – which enabled us to find her. This passion for tracking deepens my appreciation for the symbiosis between human advancement and the natural world. By preserving the art of tracking, we safeguard not just an ancient skill but embrace a sustainable ethos in land use that benefits both our species and the tapestry of life we share this planet with.

ALEX VAN DEN HEEVER established the Tracker Academy alongside Renias Mhlongo and Gaynor Rupert, and it stands as Africa's pioneering accredited tracker training school. The academy prioritises training unemployed individuals from rural communities adjacent to large wildlife areas, giving them the skills to work in safari lodges and contributing to vital anti-poaching efforts.

thick bush. They know that guests want an enjoyable experience more than a physical challenge, and won't take chances that could result in a guest suffering from exhaustion or heatstroke. There are simple rules for keeping safe on trails, with one overarching principle: listen to the guide. This means paying attention at the pre-walk briefing, and especially to follow instructions when close to animals.

By design, the reserves included in this guide have no managed trails along fixed routes. Walkers follow natural tracks made by animals: these are

The trails group always walks in single file.

mostly a pleasure to walk, but they can be uneven, sandy, rocky, or strewn with thorn branches and piles of dung. The most basic trail hazard is a trip or fall, especially when trying to spot wildlife while on the move. African bush can be spikey – so don't be tempted to reach out to grab something to prevent a fall. Footwear needs to have a reasonably thick sole to protect against spines. If thorny bushes can't be avoided, then carefully use your hand or a trekking pole to move them to the side. Don't follow too close to the person in front, to avoid a branch whip. Another technique to protect yourself is to use a backpack as a shield, by reversing into the thorn branch and then swivelling through to the other side.

Staying silent while moving is not only more enjoyable for all, but it lets the guides listen for signs of what wildlife is around. In most cases, big game encounters happen in controlled conditions. Guides will detect an animal ahead and then indicate the plan to the group. If it's a bachelor buffalo, a bull elephant in musth, predators feeding or animals with young, the likely action will be to change direction to give the animals a wide berth and let them be.

The main risk while walking is an unexpected close encounter. Lone buffalo have a knack for sitting inconspicuously in the shade, and even a family of elephant can be hard to detect when the bush is thick. If the weather is windy, it makes the guides' job harder, as they depend on sound for warning. An unplanned encounter is a situation where walkers are no longer in an animal's 'comfort zone'. The proximity, and how the animal reacts, can be described in growing terms of disturbance: in the 'alert zone' the animal reacts by freezing, or stopping its feeding;

in the 'warning zone' animals tell us not to come any closer. Just about every animal can cause harm if they feel threatened or trapped, particularly if they have young ones, and the warning can range from hissing or snarling, flattened ears and head tossing to a full warning charge. There's a final 'critical zone', whereby the animal feels the best defence is attack, and guide training is focused on making sure that zone is never entered.

In the case of a surprise encounter, the guide will talk quietly or use hand signals to indicate what they want the group to do: stop and stand still, move back or get behind cover. It's important to always stay behind the rifle – in other words, keep the trails staff between you and the animals.

If an animal moves while the group is observing it, it may be necessary for the group to shuffle around a little to keep behind the staff.

Depending on the animal, the guide may ask walkers to squat down. The lower profile of the human body may seem less threatening to a buffalo. However, a smaller profile might make a person look like prey to a big cat. The guide will have experience of many encounters and they are good at reading the body language of animals, knowing when it's safe to stay and when to go. Elephants in particular are very expressive, and are intelligent enough to read human body language, so it helps to show you are relaxed about meeting them. If told to move away by a

Getting down low can keep animals in their comfort zone.

guide, turn and walk steadily as a group. If an animal moves aggressively towards the group, follow the guide's instructions immediately. They can tell a warning charge from a real one and may make a sound that gives the animal a surprise and causes it to stop or change direction; depending on the guide and the animal in question, this could be a gentle word, a shout or a metallic noise.

Safety is not just for us humans, of course, but for the wildlife too. Some people feel uncomfortable about walking with armed guides, concerned that taking part in the activity might lead to an animal being shot. The risk of this is very low when the rules are followed. Guides are trained to use their situational awareness skills and experience in reading the environment to avoid trouble; they

The wordscape of walking safaris

Guiding in Africa is done using English, but guides liberally adopt words from other languages, especially those that describe the landscape walked.

Adam's ale is essential to life, and water sources are invariably a focus. Their seasonality means many are ephemeral and empty during the dry season favoured for walking: when the guide refers to a drainage line, *spruit*, *donga* or *lugga*, don't get excited about seeing water, think sand. On the other hand, there's reason for optimism when walking to a dam, pan or *vlei*. Pans have impervious soils that prevent the water from soaking away, and can hold water well into the dry season, while *vlei* is Afrikaans for marsh. A *dambo* is a term used in Zambia for complex shallow wetlands. They are generally found in higher rainfall plateau areas and have river-like branching forms, which in themselves are not very large but combined add up to a large area.

These watery places all present opportunities for the 'sit and wait' style of wildlife viewing that should be part of every walk. As you contemplate by the Luangwa or Shire or another reliable waterway, remember that you have literally arrived; the words 'arrive' and 'river' come from the same root 'rive'. The other place to sit and wait is upon a vantage point, the world of leopard and hyrax. The word *koppie* (South Africa) or *kopje* (Zimbabwe) is used throughout Southern and East Africa, and literally means 'little head'. Especially attractive are the eroded granite and quartzite outcrops that can be found from the Kruger to the Serengeti. Where a harder layer of rock overlays a softer rock, overhangs or caves form, and these have been used since the beginning of humankind for shelter, shade and exhibitions of art. From such lookouts, it's worth contemplating how wildlife has shaped the landscapes of Africa.

Walking is a fine way to develop dendrophilia, the love for trees, especially when they offer an umbriferous canopy or a thorn-free resting spot. Guides quite rightly will deploy Latin names to identify species, especially for flora, when the same plant can have multiple local names. In this book, the local vernacular names are used, so instead of *Faidherbia*, it will be ana tree or winter thorn. For species, we go with the flow – despite attempts to rebrand the *Lycaon pictus* as Painted Dog or Painted Wolf, the name African wild dog is still the most popular in the guiding community. The same goes for the square-lipped and hook-lipped rhinoceros, which are known to most as the white rhino and black rhino.

don't go bashing about in the bushveld and then rely on the rifle to deal with the consequences. The discharge of a rifle is a highly unusual event, and if it happens it's a big deal. The firearm is the insurance of last resort, and ultimately it's a condition for reserve owners (and their insurers) to allow guided walking in big game areas.

Unfenced camps are the norm in Africa's walking safari haunts and a wildlife encounter at camp is just as likely as one on the trail. The risks can even be higher, as guides may be resting or guests may be inattentive to their surrounds, and after dark it's especially important to follow the staff's instructions. There's no need to be unduly worried – every guide and many a guest has entertaining stories to tell of camp visitors, and it's part of the thrill of being in the wild.

Unfortunately, poaching is a serious issue in some African reserves, and walkers may encounter evidence of poachers, including human tracks, snares and carcasses. In the unlikely event of spotting them, guides will not engage with poachers. Their top priority is to keep walkers safe, and to retreat and report. Trails guides carry VHF radios or satellite phones for use in an emergency. Cell phones are not reliable for safety purposes, as network coverage is poor or non-existent in many African wilderness areas.

Taking a rest

In *Valley of the Elephants*, Norman Carr wrote: 'This tea break on trail, when you are sitting down quietly alongside a stream or lagoon with half a dozen different species of animals in view, exemplifies the difference between rushing around in a vehicle or, as now, when you are on foot among them. In a vehicle you are an intruder, but here we are guests.'

Before a walk starts, the guides have a good idea of where the group will take a break. They have a mental map of the best spots – a shady tree, a rocky outcrop, a waterhole view. It's a chance to cool down, rehydrate, have a snack and ask some questions. Like Carr, you will soon discover that on a walking safari the stops are the main thing, not the walking: it's surprising how much can be spotted while sitting. Sometimes a group can plod in the bush for an hour and see nothing, then sit for a while, and magically animals start to appear.

It's tempting to leave biodegradable waste in the bush as, after all, an apple core or banana skin would be a delicious snack for bird or beast. But it's a bad idea. First, it can build an association between humans and food. Severe problems have been caused where wildlife has discovered this link, notably among baboons and vervet monkeys. Secondly, leaving food waste behind can inadvertently spread seeds. Finally, it violates the 'leave no trace' principle – nobody wants to see eggshells or orange peel left by previous walkers. Smokers should wait until there's a rest stop before lighting up and carry a container to take away the filter with them.

It goes without saying that leaving any litter is a complete no-no. That includes toilet tissue, as in a dry habitat it will not break down and rot for many years. It's best to try to plan so there's no need to go to the toilet when on the trail, but sometimes this is unavoidable. If you need to do so, tell the guide and never sneak off without their knowledge. They will explain where to go – it will usually be back in the direction from which the group has

Guides have a mental map of the best places to take a rest.

walked. The basic procedure is defined in the Old Testament (Deuteronomy 23:12–14) but to save you looking it up, here it is. Find a sandy spot and scoop out a hole with your foot. When you've finished, set fire to the toilet tissue with a lighter, and make sure every scrap is burned. If not, it will quickly be excavated by wildlife and scattered.

Then bury the ashes by pushing sand over them and check that there are no exposed embers – accidental bush fires are a serious hazard in all habitats.

As well as not leaving anything behind, it's equally important to leave objects where you found them. Whether it be a tortoise shell, a pot sherd or merely a lovely feather, don't be tempted.

4 South Africa

South Africa has had formal wildlife reserves for over 125 years and guided walking safaris for 65 years; both are run very well. As a big country with two oceans, it has a rich diversity of biomes and an outstanding range of walking opportunities. In fact, South Africa has the most walking safaris in Africa and also the widest range, with everything from backpacking sleep-outs to super-luxury bespoke trails camps. A consequence of the climatic variation is that there's somewhere to walk all year. The country has a sophisticated tourism infrastructure, good flight connections and is the place most suited to self-drive itineraries.

Like all of South Africa's state-owned entities, the parks organisations have their challenges, but they manage Africa's biggest and most diverse selection of parks and have deep wells of conservation expertise. All conserved areas are fenced, and there's a vast area of privately conserved land in addition to national parks. With the exception of a seemingly unwinnable battle against rhino poaching, wildlife populations are healthy, and the country is at the forefront of programmes to protect endangered species.

The best selection of walks is in the low-altitude savannah to the east of the country, an area known as the Lowveld. This habitat extends from the Zimbabwe border to Zululand in the northern half of the province of KwaZulu-Natal. Walking

Most of South Africa's walking safaris are found in the savannah biome.

is best here when conditions are driest and coolest in the southern winter – April to September. It's preferable to avoid the wet and humid months from December to February. In summer months, the reserves of the Western Cape and Eastern Cape provinces afford perfect walking conditions. Lower game densities are compensated by stunning landscapes and a wealth of flora, and the area is malaria-free. Walks in the South Africa–Botswana borderland reserves on the fringes of the Kalahari present a contrast in landscapes and wildlife and are best from April to June.

To save on conservation fees, there's a Wildcard loyalty programme that's open to all; it grants the holder free access to all state-owned parks but no discount on activity fees. For overseas guests the Wildcard is economic if you spend over seven nights in the Kruger National Park (the park with the highest conservation fees) in a 12-month period.

Walking safaris in South Africa

The wide choice of walking safaris in South Africa is thanks to a long and strong tradition of nature conservation combined with an outdoor culture. It's helped by having high standards in guide training programmes with government-recognised certification and a large pool of professional guides. Uniquely in Africa, many walking safaris are run by the state agencies that manage the national parks: SANParks and Ezemvelo KZN Wildlife. Ezemvelo owns the parks in KwaZulu-Natal, while SANParks operates in all the other provinces and works with neighbouring countries to manage six Transfrontier Parks. These state agencies not only own the parks, but also operate a great number of rest camps and resorts in them and have a mandate to make them accessible to all. State-owned parks allow self-driving and provide affordable accommodation with self-catering facilities. This results in plenty of walking options that are not confined to the higher end of the market.

In addition to its national parks, South Africa has a great deal of conserved lands in community and private ownership. There's a noticeable and welcome trend in recent decades of degraded farmland being consolidated and rewilded to a natural state. These reserves operate a spectrum of activities that include research, hunting, game farming and wildlife breeding for profit. Wildlife tourism is an important component for reserves in the Greater Kruger, Zululand and the Cape, and walking is usually in the activity mix.

The other big asset for South African walking is its large pool of skilled walking guides. Comprehensive training programmes and national recognition of qualifications make it a viable and desirable career choice, and as well as working at lodges and camps, some trails guides run their own private guiding and walks-centric safari companies. For visitors, this means being able to access prime walking areas in the care of professional guides, even reserves that may not have lodges with walking guides on staff.

Throughout Africa, there are two routes to booking a walking safari: contact the walk operator directly or book through an agency, ideally one with specific expertise in walking safaris. These options both apply in South Africa, and a third variation can be added; that is to build your own itinerary and self-drive to the state-owned reserves where walks are available. As this style is unique to South Africa, let's look at it first. Local South African residents, and a good number of international visitors, self-drive in reserves that allow it – the state-owned ones. A standard car is enough to tour the parks and there's no need for the pricey 4x4 that pushes up the cost of self-drive in Namibia and Botswana. A caveat should be added for visitors who choose the self-drive option. South Africa's traffic safety ratings are poor and its roads are literally patchy, and a perfect surface can suddenly deteriorate to a minefield of potholes, even on popular tourist roads such as those of the Panorama Route west of Kruger. Driving after dark is especially dangerous – apart from the risks from road conditions and other drivers, there are pedestrians, animals and badly lit vehicles to consider, as well as some occasional instances of armed robbery. Plan the trip so that driving after sunset is never required.

It's straightforward to book accommodation and walking activities with state agencies SANParks and Ezemvelo KZN Wildlife, who both have dedicated staff to handle multi-day walk bookings. The rest camps in the parks have in-room or shared cooking facilities, and the larger camps have restaurants. A car can be safely left in camp as you venture out for a multi-day trail or a guided morning walk or drive. Making your own bookings and self-driving in South Africa is the least expensive way to experience a walking safari in Africa.

While the self-drive option suits some international visitors, most prefer to let somebody else take care of the itinerary. Starting with a friendly face at the airport to meet and greet, the entire trip logistics are handled with a single booking and payment. Private sector walk operators covered in this chapter are happy to take international bookings directly, just as they do when dealing with their domestic guests. They can arrange transfers by road and air and liaise with other lodges and walk operators for multi-destination itineraries.

Another option is to use a walks-specialised safari company, and thanks to its legion of trails guides, South Africa has plenty of choice in this department, most of them based in the safari hub town of Hoedspruit. Such boutique agencies are knowledgeable about local conditions, with first-hand experience of walking in the areas they recommend. They can spend time with guests on the pre-trip planning, advising on how to prepare for the walks and matching visitor interests with the best locations and most suitable walking guides. As normal, such agencies make income on commission from the lodges, so it does not cost more to use their services than booking direct. They

South Africa has excellent professional guides, such as Cyril Baloyi (front) and Brent Evans, trained under the Field Guides Association of Southern Africa system.

generally use private reserves where they have well-established relationships. The agencies listed on the following pages can plan and book a walking safari in South Africa and some cover other destinations in Africa. In many cases they can provide a private walking guide, who accompanies their guests throughout the journey, which is a wonderful way to spend time on foot with some of Africa's best guides. As well as lodge-based walking tours, many of these guides can run backpacking and slackpacking style trails, often in remote reserves that would otherwise be impossible to walk.

African-Born Safaris

African-Born Safaris organises bespoke and privately guided itineraries throughout Southern and East Africa. Its founders are experienced trails guides who love getting into the wilds on foot, so it's not surprising that walking safaris are a core element of their business. In South Africa, their favoured destination is the Pafuri region of Kruger National Park where African-Born is one of a handful of companies presenting a choice of camp-based walks and Primitive-style backpacking trails. Guests on camp-based trails use the Pafuri Walking Safaris tented camps on the banks of the Luvuvhu River, a comfortable experience that blends morning walks, afternoon drives and fine dining.

Alternatively, the primitive trail is designed for the adventurous. Three- and four-night trails explore areas that are inaccessible to vehicles, sleeping out in a different spot every night. In order to safely manage the night watch rota, the minimum group size is six, accompanied by two guides. On a typical day, the main walking is done early to take advantage of cooler temperatures, with the distance ranging between 6 and 12 km. A suitable camp location, close to a water source and safe from animal traffic, is found at the end of each day's walk. It's a rare and wonderful opportunity to sleep out in one of Africa's great wilderness areas, in contrast to the SANParks Kruger Backpacking Trails, where tents are always used.

To quote Devon Meyers: 'Moving about on foot along ancient animal trails with only your most essential items carried on your back gives you the sense of being an old-world explorer, while putting us squarely back in our place as an indigenous species within our natural environment. This coupled with the fact that you are in a pristine wilderness, surrounded by wildlife, puts Pafuri at the top of any enthusiast's list.'

African Bush Company

The **African Bush Company** organises walking safaris in South Africa, Botswana, Zimbabwe and Zambia. In each destination, the focus is on the best walking zones, such as the Greater Kruger and Zululand in South Africa and Okavango Delta in Botswana. Founder Massimo Rebuzzi has the full suite of professional guiding qualifications, including specialist skills in birding and tracking. He acts as an assessor for new guides and runs mentorship trails that guests can join. Massimo's goal is 'forging profound connections with nature and cultivating personal growth through expertly guided and authentic wilderness experiences'.

In South Africa, the company favours primitive-style backpacking trails, but can also run slackpacking and fly-camping options. The Okavango trails are in sleep-out style, but bookended by nights of comfort in fully catered tented camps. Group bookings are the norm, but the company welcomes enquiries from solo travellers and couples. While there's a

WALKING SAFARIS IN SOUTH AFRICA

Massimo Rebuzzi guiding in the Okavango Delta.

strong focus on walking, African Bush Company has the full mix of safari experiences including traditional lodge-based game viewing and trips focused on photography or birding and wilderness leadership and wellness retreats. Guiding in Italian is available by pre-arrangement.

BHS Safari Company

The 'B' and 'H' in **BHS Safari Company** stand for Brett Horley, a passionate South African trails guide and birding specialist. Since establishing the company in 2013, he has grown it into a boutique safari company that runs trips in an increasing number of destinations in Southern and East Africa.

With a small team of experienced travel experts, BHS now does much more than walking itineraries, but trails are still a strong element, and itineraries offer the full range from lodge-based walks to multi-day slackpacking and primitive trails. Brett's team are in their element when designing bespoke safaris, taking care to listen to guests rather than pushing off-the-peg itineraries. Expeditions with a particular focus are a speciality: searching for a black leopard in Kenya or white lions in the Kruger, getting close on foot to great apes in Uganda, and seeking rare birds and specimen baobab trees.

To quote Brett Horley: 'Rooted in the belief that ecotourism plays a key role in the preservation of our most cherished habitats and species, our work is about curating and hosting personal African experiences and adventures that are true to the individuals who embark on them, true to the ethos of BHS, and true to the nature of Planet Earth.'

Bruce Lawson Trails

Bruce Lawson is one of the best-known trails guides in Africa. A native of the Lowveld, he has logged over 21,000 trail hours and has more than 30 years of guiding experience all over Africa and the world. A formative experience of his walking career was an epic unsupported trek from Cape Town to Cairo. As well as raising funds for charity, the journey cemented a life-long love for Africa's open spaces and its people. Bruce is one of a small number of professional guides on the standards setting committee of FGASA (see page 45), an honorary position that recognises and maintains the highest standards in trails guiding in big game areas. Much of his career has been spent in training, mentoring and assessing thousands of guides, bringing his experience and enthusiasm to new generations.

Each year during the Lowveld walking season, Bruce leads a number of walking expeditions that guests can join. These multi-day trails are run in primitive style, and participants should be fit to carry all they need for a leave-no-trace bushveld immersion. His trails go far beyond a typical guided walk and are ideal for seasoned wilderness walkers. Guide mentoring is usually part of the experience, so guests can expect to share in absorbing knowledge of trails guiding skills as well as developing their appreciation of nature.

Bruce Lawson says: 'The more you spend time in wilderness, the more present you become. The more you learn about yourself, the better connected you become with the world around you. We are all desperate to connect with "The Wilderness Within" and I can help with that facilitation.'

Bush Explorations Africa

John Dixon is a well-known guide in the Lowveld, having been involved in the safari business since 1979. Known as JD, his formative years were in the Sabi Sand Reserve, followed by stints in the Waterberg and Manyeleti, Timbavati and Klaserie Reserves. John owns **Bush Explorations Africa**, and his operations base is on the Olifants River in Limpopo Province.

JD has long been a keen trails guide and he enjoys the immersive nature of guiding on foot and sharing his appreciation for all aspects of the natural world. Guided walks range from morning walks from lodges to trails of three to five days. He mostly guides in the Greater Kruger but also leads privately guided trips in other locations in Southern Africa, depending on guest interests, fitness and budgets, and of course availability and seasonality. Walks are led by John and a

Bruce Lawson guiding a primitive trail.

'second rifle' when required, with the usual maximum of eight guests. With his long experience, he only works with reserves, camps and guides that he has personally vetted, to ensure a high-quality experience for his guests.

Clearly Africa

From their base near the Kruger, **Clearly Africa** leads safaris throughout Southern and East Africa. Their trips focus on prime wilderness walking areas and include the Okavango Delta of Botswana, Zambia's Luangwa River valley, Ruaha, Tarangire and Nyerere in Tanzania, Zimbabwe's Mana Pools and Gonarezhou, and Niassa Special Reserve and Gorongosa National Park in Mozambique. The founders, Marius Swart and Steve Roskelly, have wide experience of guiding travel in Africa, and depending on the destination and guests, all styles of walking safaris are covered from backpack trails to minimalistic fly-camps and more comfortable lodge-based explorations.

Marius and Steve are experienced nature photographers and have been passionately engaged in this art-form from the start of their guiding careers. Photographing nature ethically and sensitively is their priority, and they encourage seeing and photographing wildlife in the context of their lived habitats: their style often means getting down and dirty, venturing away from the vehicle on foot. Through their dedicated photographic journeys, they invite photographers to push beyond their current creative parameters and look at nature through a wider lens.

Fraser Gear

Fraser Gear has been a dedicated walking guide since the mid-1990s. His travels and varied career have led him to guide walking, canoeing, birding and photographic safaris across the continent and beyond; he has worked as a guide in Uganda, Tanzania, Mozambique, Madagascar, Congo, Botswana and South Africa. Fraser was involved in developing some of the first walking guide qualifications in South Africa and continues to train and mentor aspiring walking guides across the continent. He is an expert birder, tracker, plant enthusiast, general naturalist and storyteller. Some of his favourite destinations include Niassa Reserve in Mozambique, Zakouma National Park in Chad and Loango National Park in Gabon.

Fraser guides walking and wildlife adventures across the continent with a focus on conservation tourism, remote and unusual destinations, and wilderness trails. He is a partner guide with African Parks, which allows privileged access to wilderness areas under African Parks' management in Chad, Republic of Congo, Central African Republic, Angola and South Sudan. Fraser is the partner guide for the Niassa Carnivore project and runs conservation tourism to the Niassa Reserve. He also guides for Anderson Expeditions, which operates a range of luxury safaris and wildlife expeditions across Africa.

iLala Safaris

iLala Safaris focuses on wilderness experiences in the Greater Kruger, with the emphasis on no-fuss comfort rather than luxury lodges. Founders Sabrina and Jan Hendrik personalise each safari, offering a mix of guest experiences that go beyond chasing iconic wildlife. Private walking safaris are run in Selati, Timbavati and the Pafuri area in the north of Kruger National Park. An iLala speciality is the combined Yoga and Walking Safari, which blends the serenity of yoga with an immersive safari adventure; and the company has mentorship trails for aspiring trails guides.

Ingwenya Field Guide Training & Consulting

Professional trails guide Phillip Wessels runs **Ingwenya Field Guide Training & Consulting** and has been guiding trails for over 25 years. Known as 'Phil the Drill', his main activity is training, mentoring and assessing upcoming guides under the FGASA system, but he also enjoys taking guests on walking trails and out of their comfort zones to create memorable experiences. His favourite walking areas are Kruger National Park, Hluhluwe-iMfolozi, Nambiti Private Game Reserve and the parks of Zambia. He caters both for guests who favour walks from lodges and those keen on backpacking and primitive trails. Phil loves tracking black rhino and lion on foot, guides specialist walking and birding safaris, and, on special request, does private guiding.

Phil Wessels says: 'Guests who walk with me have comfortable walks where they can connect not just with nature but themselves as well. We all need that. Walking in the domain of big game, sleeping under the stars in nature's embrace, we find our true selves.'

Lowveld Trails Co.

Lowveld Trails Co. (LTC) is operated by experienced guides with a strong wilderness ethos. Founders Brenden Pienaar and Wayne Te Brake each have thousands of trails hours logged and are both FGASA Scouts, the small club of guides who have attained the highest levels in both trails guiding and tracking proficiency. LTC specialises in primitive-style backpacking expeditions, and while primarily operating in the Lowveld, has trips further afield.

On a typical LTC primitive trail, groups spend a minimum of three nights in the wild, totally self-sufficient, entering a world only accessible to a privileged few. Groups set their own pace and explore according to their interests and capabilities; there are no demarcated campsites or routes. Each night is spent under the stars without tents at a pristine location, with participants sharing the responsibility of watch duty. It's hard to imagine a more authentic way to become immersed in the African wilderness.

Lowveld Trails Co. operates primitive trails in Timbavati Private Nature Reserve and Makuya Nature Reserve in the Greater Kruger, both of which have excellent walking terrain and share long unfenced boundaries with the Kruger National Park. Uniquely, LTC runs primitive trails in !Khamab Kalahari Reserve in North West Province, a remote and arid landscape that presents a complete contrast to the Lowveld reserves.

A large component of LTC activity is training and mentoring new guides. Mentorship trails offer spaces for guests who are welcome to join as observers. This provides a fascinating insight into how guides learn to deal with close encounters with potentially dangerous animals, and hone the skills required to guide guests safely in a variety of bushveld conditions. It's a chance to witness how LTC trains with an ethos of learning a holistic trails guide culture and not just building knowledge. LTC bookings are available on both a group and individual basis. Trails take a break between November and March to avoid high temperatures and summer rains. Guests should arrange their own transport to trail meeting points and supply their own hiking kit and food, with packing advice provided in advance.

Brenden Pienaar leading in Timbavati Private Nature Reserve.

Nightjar Training

The head trainer and director of **Nightjar Training** is Charles Delport, who holds the full suite of FGASA qualifications including specialist birding and tracking certificates. He also has a Diploma in Game Lodge Management and has worked a lot in that field, so is as comfortable looking after guests on safari as when training or assessing new guides. Charles runs safaris on request in South Africa's Lowveld reserves, with a particular focus on birding and walking.

Primal Pathways

Brent Harris is an experienced trails guide and runs a walks-focused safari company, **Primal Pathways**. Growing up in rural South Africa, he began guiding with &Beyond in Ngala Game Reserve in 2001 under the apprenticeship of Shangane trackers John Marimane and Eric Mabelane. In 2013, he was gazetted as an honorary wildlife police officer of Zambia, and after guiding trails in South Luangwa he fell in love with the remoteness and solitude of North Luangwa, and today continues to deepen his intimacy with this wild and remote territory.

For select months of the Zambian dry season, Brent leads his walking safaris and nature reconnection groups out of Remote Africa Safaris' Mwaleshi Camp. His personally guided groups can be booked directly with Primal Pathways and focus on camp-based walking experiences that extend to all day walks and sleeping under the stars. Outside his months in Zambia, he leads limited numbers of privately guided safari groups and primitive trails in wildlife destinations across the continent and beyond. Primal Pathways is a full-service safari tour operator company that designs environmentally sensitive travel itineraries with a particular focus on authentic experiences off the beaten path.

Brent believes that nature has a voice of its own, and his style of guiding is to quietly facilitate his guests' innate understanding of their surroundings. Though he began his career with a degree in finance, he left employment with JP Morgan in 1998 for a solo expedition into the Amazon rainforest. Sleeping in a hammock and eating fish he caught in the rivers, he found himself living his true calling: to explore our connection with the natural world.

To quote Brent Harris: 'To me, silence is one of the greatest tools we have to humble ourselves in the wilderness. It lowers the human–nature divide and provides opportunity for creatures to safely include us in their existence. When we embody spaciousness, there's a marked difference in animals' response to our presence. Then, it is profound what starts to enter that space.'

Brent Harris guiding in North Luangwa National Park.

Stones Safaris

Stones Safaris run a variety of interesting trips in the Kruger area, taking in vehicle-based and foot safaris and sightseeing outside the parks. It's operated by two experienced guides, Michael and Lynne Stone, who are familiar faces in the Greater Kruger reserves near their hometown of Hoedspruit. The Stones can recommend and book good walking bases in the nearby reserves, and both can personally guide the walks, whether morning, afternoon or all-day affairs. They organise sleep-out walks, and after dinner by the campfire guests take turns to keep night watch. Camping kit is provided and transferred by vehicle, so the group can walk light. From March to October, three-night walks-focused bush camps are available for self-sufficient campers with their own camping vehicle and kit. These take place inside the Kruger National Park at an unfenced camp and are designed for groups of family or friends of up to eight. Apart from walking safaris, the Stones run nature walks outside the big game reserves that are suitable for all ages, including younger children. Hiking in the Blyde River Canyon is another popular activity, and the Stones enjoy running specialist walks with a focus on Track & Trail, botany and geology. Michael is a marriage officer, and can help to organise unique bushveld weddings; he has a sideline in making and repairing a range of hiking and camping kit.

Tchagra Trails

Tchagra Trails specialises in photographic safaris and the training of trails guides. Founder Noelle van Muiden is one of the select few who has attained the FGASA Special Knowledge and Skills – Dangerous Game (SKS DG) qualification. As such, much of her focus is on training, mentoring and assessing new guides, and guests with Tchagra Trails benefit from this specialist expertise. The experience goes beyond a normal safari, with the ability to observe and absorb the skills that professional trails guides develop. Itineraries typically offer a blend of vehicle and foot as the situation demands. Photographers appreciate the chance to spend time tracking and walking to get shots from positions not possible from a vehicle.

The company uses reserves within Southern Africa that have great game viewing and wilderness walking areas: in South Africa these are Timbavati and Klaserie Private Nature Reserves, Balule Game Reserve and Madikwe Game Reserve; in Zambia, South Luangwa National Park; and in Zimbabwe, Hwange National Park and Mana Pools National Park. While most Tchagra Trails itineraries are lodge-based, backpack and primitive-style trails are available too. Recognising the role that guests can play in conservation, Tchagra's Conservation Safaris present the chance to achieve Track & Sign and Trailing qualifications, as well as working with K9 tracking teams. These safaris expose guests to more of the behind-the-scenes work that goes on in the conservation departments of reserves.

To quote Noelle van Muiden: 'Wilderness guides are a special breed. We prefer bare feet and bird song, with a side of elephants feeding slowly past, over anything that involves too many humans, man-made noise or enclosed walls. Tchagra Trails was built out of a love of wilderness, wide-open spaces, tracking large animals on foot and getting my guests to experience this world.'

Tsala Trails

Formed by a trio of trails guides, **Tsala Trails** presents specialist walks-centric itineraries through partnerships with comfortable safari lodges. The company has full airport-to-airport itineraries, and while the focus is on morning walks, there's always time allocated to getting up close to wildlife in a game viewing vehicle, especially during the afternoons.

The itineraries span South Africa's best walk destinations and feature very comfortable lodges. These include Tomo Safari Lodge in Balule, Rhulani Safari Lodge in Madikwe, Inzalo Safari Lodge in Welgevonden and Madwaleni River Lodge in Babanango. The pricing varies by number of guests: there's no minimum group requirement, and the maximum is normally six. Pricing is fully inclusive of transfers from the major airports and game reserve fees, and just excludes the usual items such as alcohol and tips. Self-drivers are welcome too, of course.

Umkhiwane Sacred Pathways

Sicelo Mbatha is a walking guide with a difference. A Zulu born in Hlabisa, right on the boundary of Hluhluwe-iMfolozi Park, he brings a spiritual dimension to his wilderness walks, an aspect reflected in the name of his company, **Umkhiwane Sacred Pathways**. He guides walks in the wilderness zone of Hluhluwe-iMfolozi Park, in iSimangaliso Wetland Park and the Drakensberg mountains. Walking with Sicelo in Zululand is a chance to share his deep appreciation for nature, which he describes as 'my spiritual home, my medicine and my teacher'.

The walks operate in backpacking 'leave no trace' style, and all the gear and food are included. The group size is six to eight guests, plus Sicelo and a backup guide. In iMfolozi, he believes in spending a week in the wilds and sleeping out, just as it has always been done here. Electronic gadgets are left behind, and as the days pass the walkers fall into sync with the natural world, sharing the trails of elephant and buffalo, tracking cats and African wild dogs, resting in the shade of trees and bathing in the rivers. By night, stories are swapped by the campfire, and then each takes a turn to keep watch until dawn. Sicelo's wilderness name is 'Black Lion', and his story is told in the book *Black Lion: Alive in the Wilderness*.

As Sicelo Mbatha says, 'I invite you to connect with the indigenous wisdom of my people, and with our local communities, and find your soul through the spirit of our collective humanness, our ubuntu.'

Untravelled Trails

Nunu Jobe and Shaun Maitre are the guides behind **Untravelled Trails**, and they perpetuate the long tradition of wilderness walking in Zululand. Multi-night primitive trails are offered year round in iSimangaliso Wetland Park, and morning bush walks are led in the park close to the resort town of St Lucia and from Rhino Ridge Safari Lodge in Hluhluwe-iMfolozi Park.

Wild Wanderer Safaris

Wild Wanderer Safaris specialises in private guided walking safaris within the Kruger area, with a choice of tented trails and primitive style backpacking trails. A typical Wild Wanderer Safaris eight-day itinerary takes small groups of six to eight people into wilderness ecosystems of the private Greater Kruger reserves. Time is spent at a combination of camp-based nights, with two daily game drives for optimal photographic opportunities, and then several days focused on walks, staying either at a mobile tented camp or sleeping out for the more adventurous. This style, the primitive trail, requires walkers to carry everything needed to survive in the bushveld in rugged terrain.

Apart from these week-long itineraries, the company can arrange tailor-made walking safaris, presenting guests with the opportunity to craft a personalised and unique experience. This allows for customisation in accommodations, transfers and optional day trips to nearby attractions.

Wildside Trails

Backpacking style is the speciality of **Wildside Trails**, with multi-day adventures offered in Greater Makalali Private Game Reserve, close to their home base in Hoedspruit, and Pafuri, that 'park within a park' that's one of the best walking venues in South Africa.

In Makalali, Wildside uses Michael Job's Siyafunda camp as a base, with the option to head out into the reserve to camp in tents or just stay at camp and do day walks if preferred. In Pafuri, the backpacking experience can be bookended by a lodge stay, such as at the Outpost, where Wildside can negotiate special rates. Primitive trails – sleep-outs – are an option. It's nice to ditch the tent, but bear in mind that the guests will be the ones sitting up to keep watch, not the guides. Participants should bring their own kit and camp food, and Wildside provide guidance on what to wear and to pack. The maximum group size is the usual eight, and pricing varies depending on the number of guests.

Zululand Explorers

Under the leadership of trails guide and trainer Frederick Aucamp, **Zululand Explorers** is one of the few private guiding companies with a focus on the wild reserves of northern KwaZulu-Natal province. Better known as FP, he has a deep affection for the forgotten wilderness between the mighty Tugela River and treacherous Pongola River, the foothills of the Lebombo mountains where the ocean meets the forest and long green valleys hide wild wonders to explore.

FP and his guides lead multi-day trails in this Zululand wilderness, and guests have the choice to customise their own trails. Each trail starts and ends at one of the exclusive lodges selected by FP. From there, the group heads out on either a slackpacking or backpacking adventure. The lodge option has overnights at one of the many five-star bush lodges and full day hikes into the wilderness. Backpacking style is what it sounds like – carrying everything into the wilds on a leave-no-trace sleep-out adventure.

Zululand Explorers runs a three-day hike along the deep blue ocean of the east coast, disappearing into the coastal forest in search of birds and leopards, and following ancient hippo paths from beautiful coastal lakes to the Indian Ocean. This coastline serves as a migratory route for numerous whale and dolphin species, and guests can literally dive into this marine wonderland and experience some of the best reefs in Africa. It's possible to combine these two trail options, encompassing both beach and bush.

To quote FP: 'At night, when the fire serves as our only light, we become still. We listen to the ebb and flow of the surrounding nature, hearing the stories that the wind brings, of cultures and explorers that walked here before our time.'

The Cape

Western Cape province has the distinction of having the oldest known fossilised footprints of a modern human. Known as Eve's footprints, these can be found on the shore of Langebaan Lagoon and have been dated to 117,000 years old. It reminds us of the long history of human presence in this part of the world, and the province today is a superlative walking destination, its prime natural attractions being the unique fynbos biome and associated birdlife. This vegetation is not the habitat of large numbers of grazing animals and their predators, but walking safaris are not just about encountering the megafauna, and there are some fascinating guided walks that highlight the myriad smaller creatures.

Although there are no multi-day walking safaris in the Western Cape there are a couple of reserves that host small numbers of big game and a wealth of interesting flora that's best appreciated on foot. Both Sanbona and Gondwana can be combined with a tour of the Garden Route, a world-class tourism destination that follows the Indian Ocean coast of Western Cape into Eastern Cape, and has some superb self-guided hiking trails.

The Eastern Cape is wilder, and certainly does have plenty of the African megafauna species including elephant and rhino. The province has a great diversity of terrains and ecosystems, ranging from rugged mountain ranges to endless wind-blown beaches and grassy plains. It's wilder than the Western Cape and has some excellent walking safari options in its national parks and game reserves. Mountain Zebra has a fine selection of day walks, and exclusive trails camps are found in the private reserves of Shamwari and Samara Karoo. A lodge in Amakhala has a unique overnight walk that includes a sleep-out, and there are a couple of other reserves with lodge-based walks, Lalibela and Kwandwe. Both Western and Eastern Cape are malaria-free.

The Cape is a pleasure to visit in all seasons, with the finest walking in summer. The months from October to December provide the best balance of day and night temperatures, combined with the peak flowering season. January and February are high summer and hot by day, but the warm evenings make camping a pleasure. March to April are also good months to visit, while by May the nights are getting cold. The winter months are unpredictable, swinging from pleasant sunny days to driving rain, chill winds and even snow.

Shamwari Private Game Reserve

Shamwari Private Game Reserve has 25,000 ha of protected habitat just an hour's drive north-east of Gqeberha (formerly Port Elizabeth). The reserve is attractive for walking thanks to its diverse vegetation, with five of South Africa's eight biomes present. The dominant habitat is Albany thicket, with its distinctive spekboom and spike-thorn trees. This supports kudu and other antelope species and small numbers of elephant, giraffe, buffalo, and white and black rhino. Lion, cheetah and leopard can be spotted. The rich birdlife is an attraction, and Shamwari is actively working to enrich this aspect, with the successful reintroduction of red-billed oxpeckers followed more recently by the arrival of large numbers of Cape vultures – the first reintroduction programme for these birds in the Eastern Cape. As well as being a

Shamwari Private Game Reserve is a good place to encounter black rhino.

THE CAPE

Quatermain's sleep-out is a rare and special experience.

driving and walking safari destination, the reserve is deeply involved in wildlife rehabilitation, operating big cat rescue facilities in partnership with the Born Free Foundation; and has a volunteer programme, the Shamwari Conservation Experience.

Shamwari has six lodges where guided walking activities are available on request. In addition, the Explorer Camp is located on a plateau amid sandstone extrusions and is dedicated to walking safaris. It operates at weekends in the summer months from September to May, and there's a two-night minimum stay that must include a Friday. Day visits and self-driving are not allowed at Shamwari.

Amakhala Game Reserve

Next door to Shamwari, on Amakhala Game Reserve, there's another fine safari destination to combine with a tour of the Garden Route. **Quatermain's 1920s Safari Camp** is unique in operating the only walking and fly-camping 'Big Five' safari experience in the Cape. Its 9,000 ha have the full range of headline African wildlife, including lion, elephant, rhino, buffalo and leopard as well as cheetah, giraffe, zebra, wildebeest and a good variety of antelope species. It's an excellent birding location. Apart from game drives, Quatermain's offers a guided walking safari that includes a sleep-out in the wilderness. Guests follow game trails on a slow exploration in the care of an expert guide. Overnight shelter is in a small overhang overlooking the Bushman's River basin, an experience as old as humankind. The overhang camp has stretcher beds with sleeping bags and liners, pillows, chairs, a water refill point, and a porta-loo facility. Breakfast and dinner, and a selection of wines, beers and cool drinks are provided and there's not much left to carry on the walk, just water, snacks, and any overnight toiletries. This fly-camping option is available as part of a three-night stay, with the sleepout bookended by nights of pampering at Quartermain's 1920s Camp. The overnight trail is available all year.

Samara Karoo Reserve

Directly west of Mountain Zebra National Park, the private **Samara Karoo Reserve** is a rewilding success story. Since its creation in 1997, reintroductions have resulted in healthy populations of cheetah, elephant and white rhino in a reserve that now extends to 27,000 ha of Great Karoo veld. What makes it fascinating to explore on foot is the reserve's location at the nexus of five vegetation biomes: Grassland, Nama Karoo, Savannah, Thicket and Forest. These are habitats for a rich range of wildlife that includes gemsbok, eland, lion, buffalo and giraffe. There are less often spotted animals present such as aardvark, aardwolf, porcupine and bat-eared foxes, and the birdlife includes specials such as the endangered Ludwig's bustard.

Plains Camp is a light-touch camp that's ideal for slow exploration of a diversity of wilderness and in the summer months it's the base for Samara's three night Cheetah Trail walking safari. Located in a remote corner of the reserve, the camp has four canvas tents inserted sensitively on a fixed site on a low hill and is open from September to May. Each tent has a plumbed en suite and its own fireplace for chilly evenings, while the furniture and fittings have not travelled far, with most sourced from craftsfolk in the nearby historic town of Graaff-Reinet. The camp is the base for the first and third nights of the Cheetah Trail, with the second night spent in the wilds, sleeping under a mosquito net. Guests walk in slackpacking style, covering around 30 km over the four days, including tracking Samara's cheetah. The minimum age for guests is 16 and the maximum number of guests is eight. It takes about two and a half hours to reach the gate from Gqeberha (Port Elizabeth) Airport. Guests self-drive to the reception for check-in, and from there it's a 35–40-minute game drive to Plains Camp.

Cape lodge walks

Driving eastwards from Cape Town on the R60, the most prominent geographic feature is the Great Escarpment, which creates a natural boundary: vineyards and fynbos to the south and semi-arid high plateau to the north. The area immediately north of the escarpment is the Klein Karoo, which extends to the 2,000 m Swartberg Range. Beyond that is the Great Karoo, a near treeless landscape for 600 km to the Orange River and Namibia. A winding road penetrates the escarpment from the R60 to the Klein Karoo and the town of Montagu and about 40 km further is **Sanbona Wildlife Reserve**. Sanbona conserves 58,000 ha of *karooveld* and walks here are an opportunity to appreciate this distinctive ecosystem and the life it supports, which is a contrast to that found in the savannah biome.

At Sanbona, lodge guests on game drives can leave the vehicle at various points for short walks to examine the smaller natural features, including quartz patches and succulent plants, and rock art to remind us that this part of Africa is one of the most ancient places on the planet inhabited by humankind. Sanbona is a three and a half-hour drive from Cape Town, and self-drive and day visits are not permitted.

An hour further from Cape Town, and well positioned for Garden Route travellers, **Gondwana Game Reserve** is very suited to walks, with over 11,000 hectares of undulating terrain, backed by the Langeberg and Outeniqua Mountains. Much of the attraction of a visit is in the appreciation of this timeless landscape and its flora and birdlife and bushwalks are offered to guests at an additional fee.

In the Eastern Cape, the meandering Great Fish River is the central geographic feature of **Kwandwe Private Game Reserve**, its waters feeding 30 km of riverine forest and a broad floodplain. Kwandwe boasts one of the highest land area-to-guest ratios in South Africa; recently expanded to 30,000 ha, the reserve hosts a maximum of just 52 guests, who can choose from two lodges and a handful of private villas. The reserve is inland close to the attractive university town of Makhanda (Grahamstown), and about two hours' drive north-east of Gqeberha. Day visits and self-drive are not allowed.

Kwandwe was established in 2001 through the amalgamation of nine farms. The reserve runs a social development foundation to support local communities and offers guests the chance to volunteer time or make donations. Greater kudu and bushbuck have always been present, and the ongoing process of habitat restoration has seen the reintroduction of big game including large herds of buffalo, as well as giraffe, elephant, hippo, black and white rhino, and brown hyena. Cats present include leopard, cheetah, serval, African wildcat and small-spotted cat; and since returning in 2001, the lion population has grown to the point that some animals have been moved to repopulate other Eastern Cape reserves. The subtropical thicket vegetation is dominated by various types of euphorbias, with riverine thicket along the drainage lines. As well as enjoying close animal encounters on vehicle safaris, guests are encouraged to explore on foot, and the floodplain of the Great Fish River makes for attractive and easy walking terrain. Kwandwe has a couple of options – short, guided nature interpretation walks in the environs of the lodges or making a walk an alternative to a dawn game drive, with the duration and focus based on guests' wishes and interests. These walks take a holistic approach, taking in the smaller things such as tracks, birds, succulents and other plants.

Accessed via the N2 between Gqeberha and Makhanda, **Lalibela Wildlife Reserve** has six lodges set in a 10,500 ha multi-biome landscape. As well as the 'Big Five', it has cheetah, giraffe and a good range of antelope, including red hartebeest, impala, blesbok, nyala, eland, black wildebeest and common duiker. The main lodge, Inzolo, has four chalets, all with expansive bushland views. Walks are guided in two areas, one with the big game, and 'soft walks' in a separate 2,000 ha predator-free area. These are suitable for children, who can expect to see zebra, giraffe, warthog and various antelope.

Mountain Zebra National Park is inland in the east of the Great Karoo region and close to the town of Nxuba. After the Kruger, it has the most walk options of any **SANParks** national park and is one of the best places in Africa to encounter wild cheetah on foot. SANParks provides excellent accommodation at the rest camp in the park, which is set attractively on the lower slopes of the 1,200 m Soetkop, and there are a couple of mountain cottages and a guest house on the Kranskop loop in the southern section.

The main biomes in the reserve are Nama Karoo, grassland and thicket, and its landscape of volcanic outcrops, deep gullies and varied elevations provides splendid scenery, while the extensive open grasslands make game-viewing easy. The park is mid-sized at 40,000 ha and is named for the Cape mountain zebra, the locally endangered sub-species that's larger than the common plains zebra. With several hundred of these animals in the park, visitors will be sure to spot them grazing alongside herds of red hartebeest, black wildebeest, blesbok and springbok. Less easy to find are the small populations of lion and black rhinoceros.

Walks cover a diversity of interests from general wildlife to cheetah tracking, South African War remains, rock art and a climb to the park's highest peak. These excursions take place all year and can be booked via the park's reception office. The dawn walks focus on the park's flora and fauna, and last about three hours. Walkers should be prepared for some steep climbs, albeit with plenty of stops to admire the views. There's a maximum of six guests on these walks and no snacks or water are provided, so walkers should supply their own. Walking safaris encompass human history, and Mountain Zebra is known for its San rock art, which probably dates back 300 years. It depicts what appear to be antelope, baboons, a large cat – possibly a leopard or cheetah – and human figures. Visitors can look out for mountain reedbuck in this area. There's a maximum of nine guests on the guided rock art walks, which children can join.

Cheetah tracking is a special experience, and Mountain Zebra is the only national park where it's available. Although associated more with savannah regions than with *karooveld*, cheetah can be present in all biomes apart from dense forest and at high altitude, and the cats roamed wild here up to the late nineteenth century. They were reintroduced to the park in 2007 as part of a cheetah conservation programme and some of them have been collared, allowing them to be tracked using radio telemetry. Unlike other big cats, cheetah quickly become habituated to humans on foot, and it's possible to approach them up to a close distance without causing disturbance. The cheetah in the park are wild animals, living free, and the experience is tightly controlled by SANParks. Walks only take place during the cheetahs' 'downtime', and the proximity and duration is limited. The initial search for the collared animals is vehicle-based, and the group drives around until the guide picks up a signal. Once a cheetah is located, everyone gets down to track it. Depending on how far away from the 4x4 route the cat is, the walk can be anything from 20 minutes to several hours. A maximum of eight guests are guided on the cheetah tracking walks.

The other interesting walk in Mountain Zebra is the ascent to the peak of Salpeterkop, which overlooks the northern section of the park. This takes about half a day, as an hour is needed to drive the 4x4 track to reach the foot of the mountain. From there it's another one and a half hours ascending Salpeterkop on a scree trail amid invasive prickly pear plants. The climb is worth it for the views, and the relics of the South African War. The area had historical significance as a British lookout point during that war, and some of the soldiers left their mark by carving a chessboard on a flat rock on the summit, along with graffiti of their names and regiments. This walk demands a higher level of fitness than the others, and the maximum number of guests is nine.

Zululand

The province of KwaZulu-Natal has some of the best – and wildest – walking safaris in Southern Africa. They range from sleep-out style primitive trails in Hluhluwe-iMfolozi Park to the heights of comfort at Phinda Private Game Reserve.

The province was formed in 1994 with the merger of Natal and the Zulu self-governing areas of Natal known as KwaZulu; KwaZulu simply means place of the Zulus and is often referred to as Zululand. After the Kruger area, Zululand has South Africa's best range of walks, with options in a number of private and community-owned reserves, and those operated by the provincial

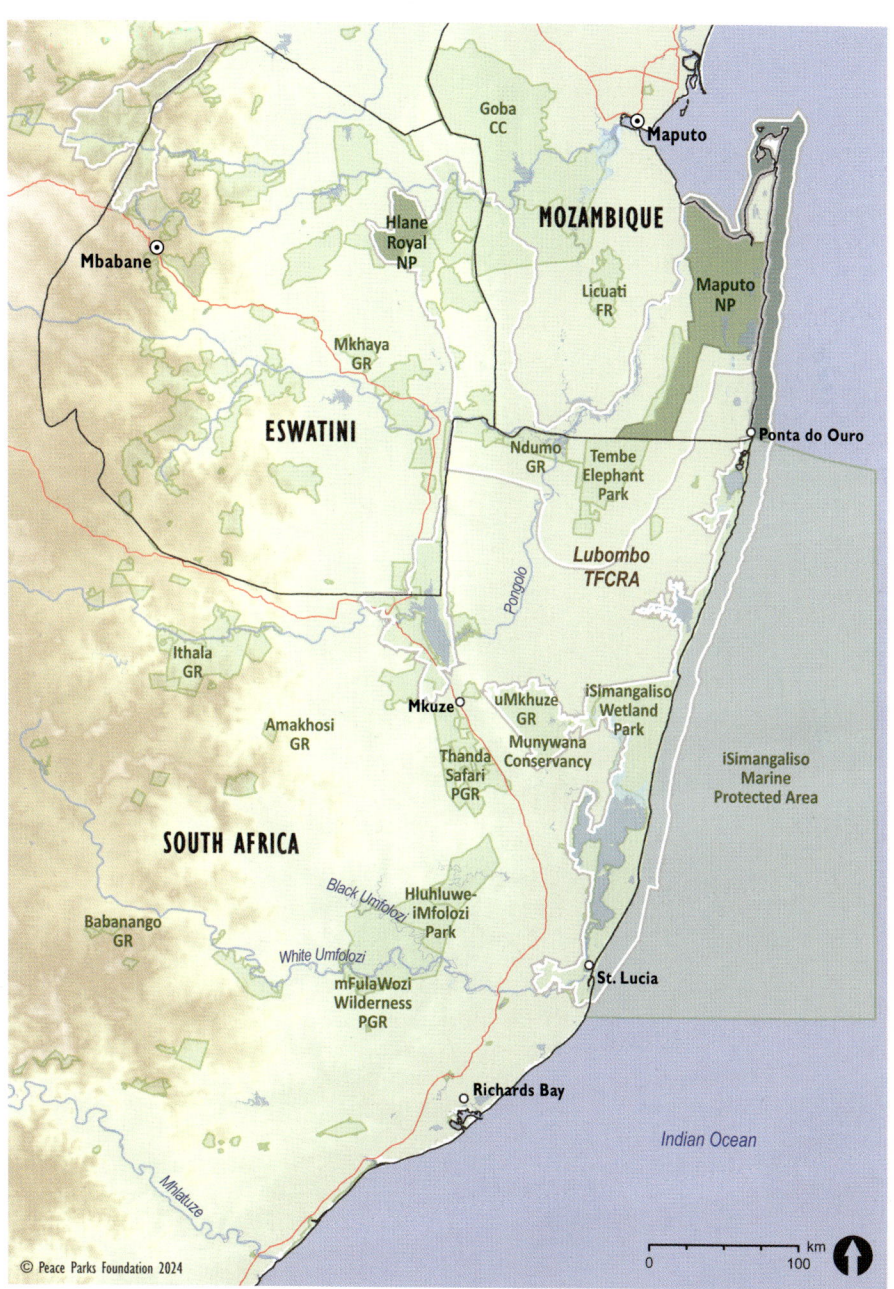

Map 8: Zululand and Kingdom of Eswatini

government agency, Ezemvelo KZN Wildlife.

The country's very first wilderness trails were started in Hluhluwe-iMfolozi Park and are still operated there in the same style by Ezemvelo KZN Wildlife and the Wilderness Leadership School. At the other comfort extreme, Rhino Ridge Safari Lodge is a private concession in the Hluhluwe section that guides day walks. Primitive backpacking trails are run in private reserves in Zululand, and there are a number of reserves that have walks from lodges and rest camps. Self-drive is possible only in the Ezemvelo reserves.

If summer rains are heavy, river crossings may be difficult in March and April. The best walking months are autumnal – May to June. July and August can be chilly at night, while September is another top month. October is getting hot, and November is when the high humidity arrives.

Hluhluwe-iMfolozi wilderness trails

Located in north-eastern KwaZulu-Natal in the heartland of the former Zulu Empire, about 280 km north-east of eThekwini (Durban), Hluhluwe-iMfolozi Park is one of South Africa's pre-eminent wilderness areas. It's a prime walking safari reserve, with a choice of multi-day options and camp-based walks. Hluhluwe-iMfolozi includes the first areas conserved by law in South Africa, with Hluhluwe and iMfolozi having been proclaimed in 1895. Before then, the area was settled by the Mthethwa clan under the Zulu leader Dingiswayo, and in the early nineteenth century King Shaka used the lowlands between the White and Black Umfolozi Rivers as his private hunting ground. Near Siyembeni, at the confluence of these two great rivers, the remnants of his hunting pits, used to trap large numbers of game at a time, can still be found. In the west lies Nqolothi Hill, where the king sat to oversee elephant hunts.

In 1989, the Hluhluwe and iMfolozi reserves were joined to form one park containing almost 1,000 sq. km of wilderness. In 2019, community-owned lands abutting the park south of the White Umfolozi River were designated for conservation as the mFulaWozi Wilderness Reserve, further extending the protected area. iMfolozi, Umfolozi, uMfolozi and Mfolozi are all variants of the names of the rivers that flow through the western section, and park authorities use the Umfolozi spelling for the rivers and iMfolozi for the reserve itself. The name derives from *mfulawosi*, an isiZulu word meaning 'rivers of fibre', which is believed to refer to mountain nettle, a fibrous plant that grows along the banks and is used for making mats. Hluhluwe (pronounced 'klu-klu-wee') is the isiZulu name for Hluhluwe creeper, a thorny, rope-like climbing plant that can be seen alongside the short trail in Hilltop Resort.

The park's soils are derived from eroded volcanic, glacial and sedimentary rocks and allow for a considerable diversity of plants and grasses, which, in turn, provide sustenance and shelter for a great variety of animals and birds. The most dominant trees are knobthorn, sweet thorn and umbrella thorn. Today, the park is synonymous with the white rhino, as it was here that the last of these animals faced extinction by the late nineteenth century. From the early 1960s, under the leadership of Park Ranger Ian Player, the remnant population was saved in Operation Rhino, which saw the development of safe animal darting and transport techniques that led to the distribution of a sustainable population of rhino to other reserves. Only the Kruger National Park has more white rhino than Hluhluwe-iMfolozi, although sadly they are plummeting once again towards extinction, as more effective anti poaching measures in the Kruger has shifted the poachers' attention here.

As well as black and white rhino, elephant, buffalo, nyala, greater kudu, red and blue duiker, bushbuck, impala, zebra, blue wildebeest, steenbok and giraffe are likely to be spotted. Predators present include cheetah, spotted hyena, leopard and lion. More than 350 bird species have been counted in the reserve, making it an excellent birding destination. Noteworthy species include the African finfoot, Narina trogon, Southern ground-hornbill and white-backed night heron.

Hluhluwe-iMfolozi has a wealth of walking options, second only to the Kruger National Park, and overnight trails here are more authentic (or basic) than those of SANParks. It's not possible to do walks as a day visitor, but overnight guests can choose from day walks, wilderness trails and backpacking trails. It's a hilly park, so reasonable fitness is required. The day walks are available from lodgings throughout the park, but all multi-day trails operate in the western part, iMfolozi. There, the river valleys and watershed west of the confluence of the Black Umfolozi and White Umfolozi Rivers form the core of a large wilderness area with no wheeled access. The rugged terrain makes for interesting trails with dramatic viewpoints, and is the spiritual home of wilderness trails in Africa.

Park operator **Ezemvelo KZN Wildlife** operates accommodation at Hilltop Resort and Mpila Camp, as well as a number of bush lodges in both sections of the park. The gateway to all Ezemvelo multi-day trails is the Mndindini Trails Camp on the White Umfolozi River. From here, walkers explore the river valley in both directions. The reed-fringed rivers are broad and meandering and generally easy to cross, unless there has been heavy rain in the catchment.

A particular feature of walking here is the ability to climb to *krantzes* high

Walkers above the White Umfolozi River on an Ezemvelo KZN Wildlife wilderness trail.

Trails in iMfolozi are enriched by interactions with their Zulu guides.

above the river, to enjoy viewing from afar the wildlife behaving naturally and undisturbed. Mahobosheni (the isiZulu name for the puff adder) is a vantage point where the Umfolozi doubles back, forming a shape like a snake's head. A little further upriver is Nqabaneni, which means a fortress, and nearby is a cave with interesting erosion patterns, a good place for a shady rest with a view. Another splendid lookout is known as Shaka's Rock, said to have been used for the execution of enemies during the rule of Shaka Zulu. Walks are led by a trails officer and an assistant guide, and on Ezemvelo walks the assistant usually follows at the tail, unlike the practice in the rest of South Africa, where both guides walk at the front of the group. This is because the thick bush in the park can make it hard for the lead guide to keep all the guests in sight, and the guide at the tail helps to ensure that the group stays close together.

Over the decades, Ezemvelo has developed a selection of wilderness trails formats with a variety of durations and difficulty levels. Trails run on fixed dates and can be divided into three types based on the overnight facility: a bed in a permanent camp, a mattress in a tent or a sleeping bag under the stars.

The most comfortable trail type has walkers based at the Mndindini Trails Camp; this is known as the Base Camp Trail and it runs two or three times a month, each trail spanning a weekend, from mid-February to early December. Mndindini is a fixed and unfenced camp located on the White Umfolozi River. It has tents on wooden decks: each has two beds and bedding, and the camp has a shared fridge for cold drinks. There's a cook at the camp, so the trail is fully catered, with dining at bench tables in the kitchen area. In terms of camp comfort, it's at a similar level to a SANParks Kruger National Park Wilderness Trails camp. Walkers' vehicles remain nearby, so there's no need to stress about something vital being left behind.

Walks take place after an early breakfast and return to the camp by lunchtime, with walkers carrying just a day pack. The trails officer decides on the route, which can range from 7 to 14 km depending on conditions and group preferences. Keen walkers can request another walk in the afternoon. The camp is a pleasant place to relax and watch waterbuck, elephant and buffalo at the river. On the final day, there's a shorter morning walk, and the trail ends before 11:00.

The second type of trail is the standard Wilderness Trail, where walkers are based at a tented fly-camp that is supplied by donkey. Each walk season, a new fly-camp is established, always close to the river. Participants stay in the camp for the duration of the trail and sleep in two-person dome tents furnished with mattresses and pillows. There are no chairs or tables, but camp cushions are provided; these are quite comfortable when propped against a log. Water is sourced from the river and transported to the camp by donkey. There it's heated over the campfire for bucket showers and filtered for drinking and cooking. For toilet needs, a short shovel is provided, and instructions are given about where to go.

There are two variations of the wilderness trail, the only difference being their duration – two nights for the Short Wilderness Trail and three for the Extended Short Wilderness Trail. They both use the same fly-camp, the Short Trail starting on Fridays and Sundays and the Extended Short Trail starting on Tuesdays. The wilderness trails run from mid-February to early December.

For wilderness trails, it's recommended that participants stay at Mpila Resort the night before the trail begins so that overnight gear can be handed over to be ported by donkey. The donkeys leave early on the starting day, and if hikers don't overnight at Mpila they need to backpack in their own kit on the first day. In any case it's wise to keep it light and just pack the essentials needed at the camp – wash kit, camp towel, a change of clothes. Take a day pack for water, snacks and any personal items you may need while walking.

On the first day of a trail, hikers meet the guides at reception in Mpila Resort by 11:00 for departure at 12:00. From there, they follow the ranger's vehicle for 7 km to Mndindini Trails Camp in their own vehicles. The road to the base camp is closed to other park visitors and accessible to non-4x4 cars. At the base camp there's secure parking and toilet facilities, and belongings not needed on the trail can be left in the car. After a snack and a briefing, the walk starts. The fly-camp supply donkeys will already have left, so hikers don't walk with them. The distance walked on the first day varies, as the camp is at a different site each season, and because the guides may take a circuitous route to get there.

Trails are fully catered, with meals prepared by a camp cook. Breakfast dishes include cereal and bacon and eggs. After breakfast, walkers collect their lunch packs, which may contain sandwiches of cheese, salami and tomato, as well as fruit, crackers and biltong. A typical evening meal might be pap (mealie meal porridge) and stew or spaghetti Bolognese with corn on the cob and a side salad, followed by tinned peaches and custard for dessert. Water is filtered at the camp and made available in a canister for refilling personal water bottles.

On the second day walking begins early, each guest taking a lunch bag and water in their day pack. There are some fine lookout points above the river, providing good opportunities for a long lunch break and wildlife spotting. The group returns to camp in the early afternoon, picking up wood on the way back for the campfire. Early on the final day, the donkeys return to take away the guests' bags and camp waste. Meanwhile the group walks back to Mndindini Trails Camp, to arrive by 10:30 at the latest.

The third type of overnight trail is a backpacking trail. Called the Primitive Trail, it's the most demanding and has groups carrying everything needed (except water) and sleeping for four nights under the stars. Hikers take turns to keep watch by a small fire at night, making it one of the most authentic walking safari experiences to be had in Africa. This is how humans have experienced the bush in big game country for aeons. It's wise not to underestimate the difficulty of this experience: distances on the Primitive Trail can be up to 20 km in a day, and hikers must be prepared to carry over 20 kg. Tents are not used and the trail is fully catered, with guides and guests sharing food and utensil portage. If necessary, backpacks, sleeping bags and sleeping mats are supplied, at no additional cost. When booking, participants are asked to indicate what they need, but it's better to bring your own gear if you have it. If rain is forecast, a tarpaulin is carried to be rigged between trees. Water is collected from springs or the river, and guests are advised to bring purification drops. It's a good idea to pack a swimsuit for river bathing.

The wilderness trail camp is basic and close to nature. The spade is for toilet use.

The guides have a selection of favoured camping locations close to water sources and the group may move to a new camp each night or stay in the same spot for a couple of nights. Cooking is done over a campfire by the guides, and participants are expected to help with preparing the food, washing dishes and pots, and digging for water when necessary. Fresh meat is buried in wet sand to keep it cool. The Primitive Trail runs every week from mid-February to early December. Participants should check in at Mpila Resort by 09:30, which is earlier than the other trails. On the final day the group will be back at their cars at Mndindini by 10:00 at the latest, and it's possible to have a hot shower there before departure.

The final option is to combine the Base Camp and Primitive Trail experiences in the four-night Explorer Trail, which operates two or three times per month from late February to late November. This is a good choice for those who have a long drive to reach the park, as the first and last nights are spent at the Mndindini Trails Camp, with all its relative comforts. The second and third nights are spent sleeping in the wild, just as on the Primitive Trail. These nights may be at two different locations or at the same location. As no tents are used, hikers take turns to keep solo night watch by the campfire, regularly patrolling the surrounds with a torch to watch for wildlife. While at the Mndindini base camp, meals are prepared by the camp cook, and on the other nights the trails officers cook with the help of guests.

All of the above trails can be booked directly with Ezemvelo KZN Wildlife. The wilderness trails need a minimum of four participants and the Primitive Trail and Explorer Trail have a minimum requirement of six people to manage the night watch rota. Hikers who book one of the trails and find that the minimum numbers are not reached can request a refund, switch trails or ask the park to try to accommodate them at Mpila or Hilltop where they can go for day walks. For Ezemvelo multi-day walks the minimum age is 14 if accompanied by a parent or legal guardian and 16 if unaccompanied. To preserve the wilderness experience, guests are requested not to bring electronic gadgets and watches with them, and these can be safely left in cars at the Mndindini Trails Camp.

Hluhluwe-iMfolozi holds a special place in the history of African walking safaris, as it was here that park ranger Dr Ian Player and his friend and colleague Magqubu Ntombela led South Africa's first wilderness trail on 19 March 1959. Dr Player succeeded in having an area of 12,000 ha designated as a wilderness zone within the park – a first on the African continent. While working in the park in the early 1960s, Player established the non-profit **Wilderness Leadership School** (WLS) with the goal of incubating a love for the wilderness in future leaders. In the beginning, the WLS brought groups of school children on trails in St Lucia Reserve and what was then the Umfolozi Game Reserve. Headquartered in Durban, the WLS today continues to operate wilderness trails in exactly the same way as Player did, with regular sleep-out trails operated in the park's Black Umfolozi River valley, open to the public. Player believed in the spiritual benefit of the solitary night watch and insisted upon it being part of the routine for all wilderness trail walkers. This ritual continues today on WLS trails, and the experience of sitting alone by a small fire, immersed in the nocturnal sounds of the wild, creates an unforgettable memory.

The WLS operates trails all year, but more frequently in the peak season of May to October. The school supplies all necessary hiking kit, and participants need to be prepared to carry a heavy pack. Food is included, and meals are of a high standard. With no fixed camps, the format is the same as the Ezemvelo Primitive Trail, but more flexible in duration. The most popular WLS trail option is a four-night, five-day stay, and a package is available that includes transport from Durban. Over the years, WLS has extended its operations to reserves in other parts of South Africa and beyond, including Pilanesberg, the Transkei and Okavango Delta. These generally operate on a bespoke basis, and exact locations are dependent on the time of year and group needs.

Hluhluwe-iMfolozi lodge walks

Apart from its multi-day wilderness trails, **Ezemvelo KZN Wildlife** offers dawn and afternoon walks from all resorts and bush camps in Hluhluwe-iMfolozi Park. Walkers meet the guides at designated points, and it's usual to drive some distance in a game-viewing vehicle, varying the start locations. From Hilltop Resort, walks typically explore the bushveld in the environs of the resort and the slopes down to the Hluhluwe River. When the veld is dense and thorny, the walk progresses at a sedate pace, with plenty of time to admire the views as the guide describes the variety of grasses, flowers, shrubs and birds. The park does not take advance bookings for day walks. Guests should make accommodation bookings, then enquire about walks at the reception of Hilltop Resort or Mpila Camp. Ezemvelo KZN Wildlife's rule is 'over 12' for day walks and there's no maximum age stated, but they request that walkers have a reasonable level of fitness.

Rhino Ridge Safari Lodge is a comfortable, privately operated lodge located on community lands that have been incorporated into Hluhluwe-iMfolozi Park. It's part of the Isibindi Africa group,

which has sister lodges with guided walks near to Victoria Falls in Zimbabwe. Walks are a popular activity from Rhino Ridge and are available throughout the year at an additional fee. The lodge location is terrific, perched on a hill on the northern boundary of the Hluhluwe section of the park. There are two ways to reach it; the recommended route traverses the park for 31 km from Nyalazi Gate and takes an hour, as it's partly on gravel road. Dawn walks are led by one or two guides and last about three hours. Afternoon walks are an option and depart after high tea. Although the area around the lodge is hilly, the walks are not too demanding and aim to keep to areas of thin bushveld and grassland. There's a good chance to approach white rhinos on foot.

Other Zululand Reserves

The reserves that sprawl across the Lebombo range in northern KwaZulu-Natal are the epitome of excellent walking safari territory, blending all the key natural ingredients: wildlife, mountains, rivers and a variety of bushveld types. Several safari companies listed at the start of this chapter can organise group trips that include both lodge-based tours and backpacking options suited to self-drive participants who have their own hiking kit. Contact **African Bush Company, Untravelled Trails, Wildside Trails** or **Zululand Explorers.**

mFulaWozi Wilderness Private Game Reserve is contiguous with Hluhluwe-iMfolozi Park to the west and has a couple of lodges with walks. Upriver from there, the White Umfolozi River twists and cuts through rugged loops and valleys watering a variety of wildlife-rich habitats. Some 100 km into the interior, **Babanango Game Reserve** is one of the latest examples of the very welcome trend in South Africa that sees community-owned land shifting to conservation usage. A partnership between landowners, private investors and conservation specialists is creating an area with the potential to be a top-class wildlife reserve. The varied terrain of mist belt grassland, thornveld and Zululand coastal woodlands supports a diverse ecosystem, and the reserve has giraffe, hyena, zebra, rhino and buffalo, and several varieties of antelope. In recent years, the conservation programme has seen the reintroduction of elephant, lion and cheetah.

At Babanango, guests can overnight at one of two comfortable lodges, where professionally guided walks are on the menu at an additional fee. As well as tracking and spotting game and birdlife, the guided walks provide an opportunity to investigate historic copper mine works. Trail snacks are included. Geology is part of the story, with the river erosion exposing rock beds dating from 3.3 billion years ago to modern times, creating a canvas of geological history. For an overnight walk, fully catered fly-camping trails are in the works. It's recommended to request walks in advance, and this will be a requirement for the fly-camping.

Nambiti Private Game Reserve is the only big game reserve with guided walks in western KwaZulu-Natal. It's two decades into an ambitious rewilding project that has seen 12,000 ha of degraded ranch land revitalised into a successful conservation and wildlife tourism destination. Today, it has small populations of elephant, buffalo, rhino and lion, alongside cheetah, leopard, giraffe, hippo, impala, zebra and kudu. There are ten lodges and exclusive-use rentals on the property, several of them converted historic farmhouses. The place to pick for walks is **Cheetah Ridge Lodge**, where both day walks and overnight backpacking trails are available. Backpacking trails guests either bring their own tents or can sleep-out as long as they are prepared to take turns at night watch.

The trails traverse diverse habitats, from sweeping savannahs to dense riverine bush, from the shade of acacia trees to expansive grasslands. Cheetah Lodge is just 30 minutes from Ladysmith. Nambiti is outside the malaria risk zone, and the reserve can serve as a base for tours to the Anglo-Boer War battlefield sites and the Drakensberg Mountains, both reachable by road in an hour or so.

To the north of Hluhluwe-iMfolozi Park are a number of private reserves of interest, all accessed via the N2 highway, itself an ancient elephant migration route. The Munywana Conservancy is an association of private and community lands that together protect around 30,000 ha of land. The conservancy shares a boundary with uMkhuze Game Reserve, which is part of the 328,000 ha iSimangaliso Wetland Park, a UNESCO World Heritage Site. The principal tourism operators are Zuka in the west and Phinda in the east, and both welcome guests to witness a flagship rewilding success story for Africa.

Zuka Private Game Reserve has rehabilitated 10,300 ha that now supports a rich biodiversity across a variety of ecosystems. Elephant, black rhino, white rhino, lion, leopard, buffalo, cheetah and myriad species of reptile and invertebrate can be found. Scientific research is an important element of Zuka, and the reserve is home to the Getty Asterism, a multifaceted ecology venture with researchers, volunteers and conservation students who work on projects spanning wildlife reintroduction, protection initiatives of species, habitat restoration as well as wildlife research and monitoring. Zuka Private Game Reserve has accommodation at **Bayala Private Safari Lodge** or the exclusive sole-use Gladstones. Both run bush walks as well as game drives, with qualified guides and trackers.

Established in 1990 on degraded farmland, the **&Beyond** Phinda Private Game Reserve is today an outstanding destination that's highly regarded for its conservation work, and a wide range of big game, including black and white rhino, is present. Lion and cheetah have been reintroduced, and there's prolific birdlife, with over 400 species recorded. Phinda is strong on exclusive 'experiences' rather than mere luxury lodges and game drives, and this includes walking safaris. The six &Beyond lodges offer guests one-hour nature trails all year and most visitors avail themselves of these short walks, while others set out on four-hour excursions tracking black rhino on foot. An intensive walking safari package is presented for those who favour feet over wheels. This has a minimum two-night stay and, in keeping with the price tag, is tailored to guests' wishes – walkers can stay out in the bush all day if they want. Led by a ranger and a tracker, walks combine viewing of big game and birdwatching with searches for fossils, plants and invertebrates. Trailing big cats is a favourite activity, and in the eastern sandveld zone it may be possible to spot the rare suni, a dwarf antelope similar to the blue duiker.

Thanda Safari is a 16,000 ha reserve west of Zuka on the other side of the N2 road. Accommodation consists of a safari lodge, tented camp and exclusive-use private villas, all set in an attractive hilly landscape with the full range of African wildlife, including elephant, lion and cheetah. Trained walking guides are present, but walks are at the head guide's discretion for the safety of guests and should be booked in advance. The reserve is part of a wider group owned by the Swedish Olofsson family, which includes Thanda Island in Tanzania and the Thanda Classic Cruise in the Mediterranean. Like Zuka and Phinda, Thanda is accessed via the N2 national road, a three-hour drive from eThekwini (Durban). Day visits and self-drive are not permitted in these private reserves.

uMkhuze (also spelled Mkuze and Mkhuze) is a long-established park run by **Ezemvelo KZN Wildlife** as part of the iSimangaliso Wetland Park, and is worth visiting for its guided walks in a mature forest of sycamore figs. Its 40,000 ha lie to the north of Zuka and Phinda reserves, a four-hour drive from eThekwini, and the connecting route from the N2 is via a gravel road that's rough in sections. The south-east area of the reserve that shares a fenced boundary with Phinda Private Game Reserve has extensive wetlands with superlative birdlife and several hides. Following a reintroduction programme, there are a small number of lions in the park, and the kuMasinga hide is a good place to spot them early in the morning. The reserve hosts African wild dog, leopard, cheetah, black and white rhino and elephant.

The must-do walk in uMkhuze explores the sycamore fig tree forest, and this should be requested when booking accommodation. This riparian forest is ancient, with particular trees dated to over 900 years. The trails officer meets the walkers at a nominated spot at either the main Mantuma camp or one of the bush lodges, and the walk begins with a 40-minute journey by game-viewing vehicle to the parking area at Nsumo Pan. From there, the 3 km trail leads through woodland to a suspension bridge over the seasonal uMkhuze River. A highlight of the walk is accessing the canopy boardwalk, which is an excellent bird-spotting location. As well as the fig trees, which fruit all year, there are beautiful fever trees with their distinctive green-yellow bark. Use of mosquito repellent is recommended on this walk, and in the wetter summer months it may be closed owing to flooding. Ezemvelo KZN Wildlife has a choice of cottages and safari tents at the main camp of Mantuma, as well as accommodation at a couple of bush camps in the reserve.

In northern Zululand, Ithala Game Reserve is an Ezemvelo KZN Wildlife venue spanning 30,000 ha of hilly terrain that falls steeply to the right bank of the Pongola River. Established in 1972, the reserve has rewilded former grazing land and restored wildlife populations almost wiped out by hunting and tsetse fly-borne disease. These days it's an attractive park that feels off the beaten track and shelters modest numbers of elephant, buffalo, black and white rhino, spotted and brown hyena, and it's perfect habitat for leopard. There are no lion, cheetah or wild dogs present, and most visible are giraffe, zebra, blue wildebeest, eland and other plains game. Like the other reserves of northern KwaZulu-Natal, the birdlife is prolific, and over 300 species have been recorded at Ithala.

With its mix of steep slopes and grassy plateaus, and the backdrop of the escarpment, erratic boulders and eroded rock formations, it's a pleasant reserve for walking. Alongside guided walks there's an alternative that's unique for any big game reserve in South Africa: it's possible to walk unguided, but only on particular marked trails in a rocky mountainous area with a low possibility of dangerous animal encounters. Most accommodation is at the Ntshondwe Resort, which is nicely situated at the foot of the Ngotshe Mountain amid mammoth-sized boulders, acacias, wild figs and cabbage trees. The camp has a couple of short self-guided trails leading to lookouts, which are recommended for a late afternoon stroll.

The Kingdom of Eswatini

The Kingdom of Eswatini is not a major destination for walking safaris (or safaris in general), but it's a pleasant place to spend time and has a couple of reserves worth a visit. The country has good roads and provides an attractive option when moving between Zululand and the Kruger area.

Broadly, the country lies between two branches of the ancient Lebombo range. Prehistory aficionados should try to drive the fascinating geotrail that connects the South African town of Barberton and the Eswatini border at Bulembu. Among other rocky relics, there's exposed fossil evidence of what is possibly the oldest form of life on the planet, dating to 3.8 billion years.

The mountainous grasslands areas have enjoyable unguided walks, while **Big Game Parks** runs the kingdom's three main reserves. In the Lowveld east, Hlane Royal National Park provides the best guided bushwalking options, with walks for day visitors and overnight hiking. In Mkhaya Game Reserve, overnight walks to a fly-camp have been operated in the past, but in recent years only day walks are available. Hlane allows for self-drive and self-catering, while Mkhaya is restricted to all-inclusive visits.

Weather conditions in eastern Eswatini are similar to the South African Lowveld, with walking less attractive in summer when there's extreme humidity and dense vegetation. From June to September, it's mostly dry, with daytime temperatures in the mid-20s °C, and this is the best season for getting around on foot. The Lowveld of Eswatini is a year-round malaria risk zone.

Between uMkhuze and Ithala parks, **Amakhosi Private Game Reserve** is planning to start overnight walking safaris at the time of writing. In the far north at the border with Mozambique, Tembe Elephant Park and Ndumo Game Reserve are interesting reserves and part of the Lubombo Transfrontier Conservation and Resource Area. Unfortunately, neither has guided walks.

Kruger National Park and Greater Kruger

The Kruger National Park is one of the world's great protected wilderness areas and is South Africa's pre-eminent walking safari destination. Nowhere else in Africa has the variety and quantum of walking options as this park and its adjacent reserves. Established as the Sabie Game Reserve in 1898, the Kruger National Park today straddles the eastern parts of Limpopo and Mpumalanga provinces in the Lowveld and has expanded to almost 20,000 sq. km. Additionally, most of the private reserves to the west share unfenced boundaries and agreed management plans with the national park – and in this book 'the Kruger' refers to this Greater Kruger area. The park is bordered by Zimbabwe to the north and Mozambique to the east, where further conserved lands cooperate internationally as the Great Limpopo Transfrontier Park.

The variety of ecozones in the Kruger, from mountain bushveld to mopane scrubland, savannah and riparian forest, make it a rewarding place for repeat visits to experience a diversity of walks. The underlying geology determines the vegetation type and thus the fauna of each area, so the trail experiences vary from north to south – a distance spanning over 300 km. It has habitat for the full spectrum of Southern African wildlife, including over 500 species of bird and some 1,500 lion – about half of all the wild lion left in South Africa.

South African visitors tend to concentrate in the national park, which allows self-drive, while international visitors are drawn to the upmarket private lodges and camps in both the park and Greater Kruger reserves. The best scheduled air connections and car rental options are at Kruger Mpumalanga International Airport, near Mbombela (Nelspruit), and the airport at Skukuza, the headquarters and largest rest camp in the park.

For overnight walks, there are plenty of trails camps, but Kruger is not the place for camp-to-camp style or truly mobile walking safaris of the type found in Zambia and East Africa. On the other hand, it's the best place in Africa for backpacking walking safaris. The vast majority of walking experiences in the Kruger National Park itself are run by SANParks, with an impressive range of options that span wilderness trails and backpacking trails and walks from rest camps and bushveld camps, and even from the park gates. The walks operated by SANParks are the best value walking safaris in Africa.

The southern park gates are all four to five hours' drive from Johannesburg, while the central Orpen Gate is closer to six hours away. The northern half of the park is accessed via Phalaborwa, Punda Maria and Pafuri gates, all of them six to seven hours' drive from Johannesburg. Owing to a combination of its accessibility and its rich ecosystem, the southern half of the park, between the Olifants and Crocodile Rivers, has the highest density of walking safari opportunities in Africa. As well as having better vegetation and a greater

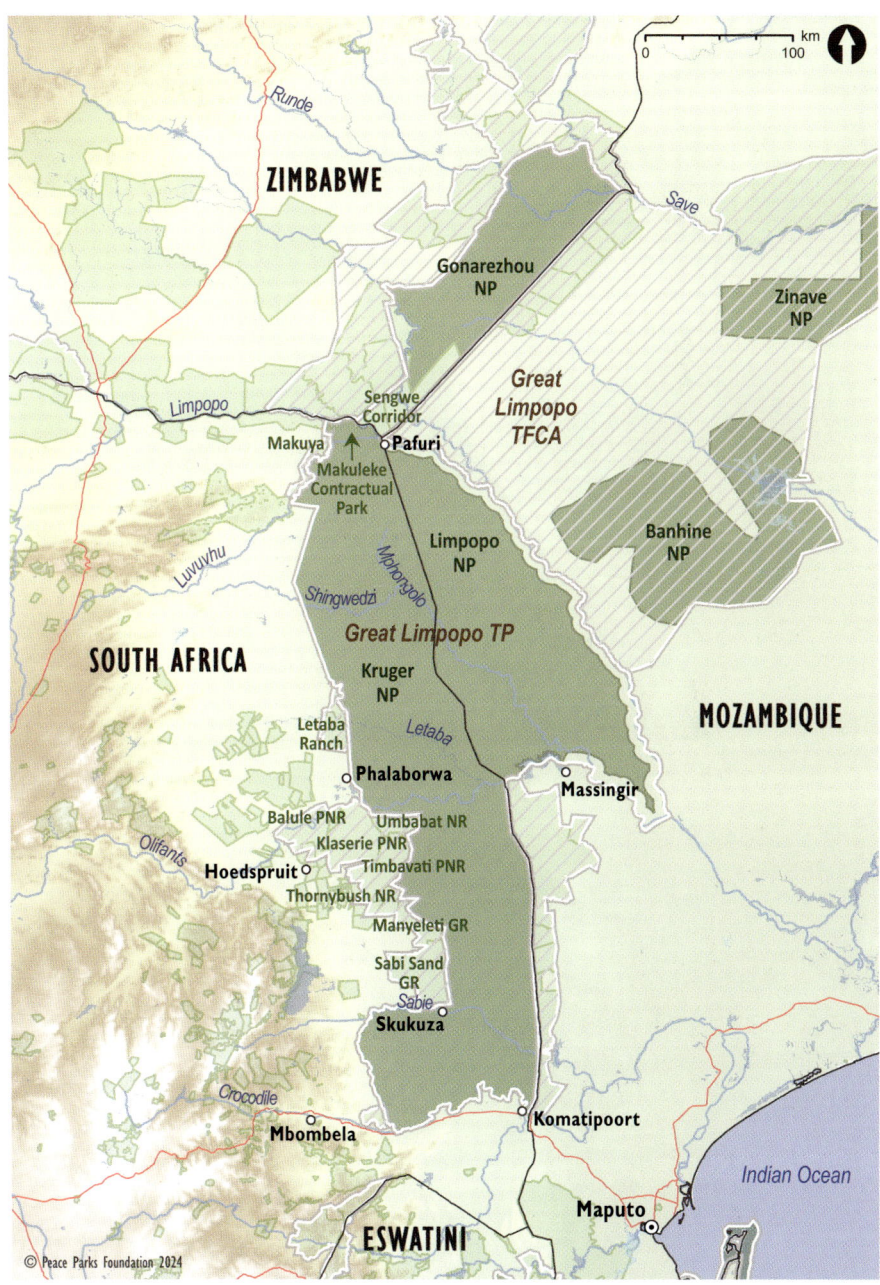

Map 9: Great Limpopo Transfrontier Park

Sabie river in Kruger National Park. The rivers that traverse the Kruger National Park are vital for wildlife and are the focus for wonderful walks.

density of wildlife than the northern parts of the park, the south has far more camps and private lodges, and good access by road and air.

The area south of Paul Kruger gate is mainly granite hills, and it has the best and deepest soils with vegetation classed as sourveld and mountain bushveld. Three of the seven SANParks Wilderness Trails camps are clustered in this area. As the landscape falls gradually to the east, the geology changes to basalts. Soils become much shallower east of the H1 tarred road, and the change in vegetation is noticeable. The upper Sabie River area close to the park headquarters at Skukuza Rest Camp is the locus of excellent walking safaris operated by Rhino Walking Safaris.

The central zone of the park, accessed via Orpen Gate, is less intensively visited, but contains some of its best loved rest camps and private lodges, set close to the Timbavati and Sweni Rivers. The dominant vegetation is knobthorn savannah and mixed bushwillow woodlands. The park's eastern frontier with Mozambique is marked by the volcanic Lebombo Mountains, which rise to almost 500 m. The more open vegetation in the central Kruger Park attracts large numbers of herbivores such as impala, blue wildebeest and zebra – and their predators. In this central part of the Kruger Park, walking safari possibilities are the SANParks Sweni Wilderness Trail, and the day walks operated by a number of private concession lodges and camps.

The north of the Kruger is drier, with poorer soils, and the distinctive vegetation is mopane woodlands and shrubland. These hardy trees survive arid conditions and elephant grazing, but don't make for interesting walking. However, rivers such as the Olifants and Letaba nourish riparian woodlands and attract wildlife concentrations that deliver good encounters: the area is known for its large elephant population and Cape buffalo and nyala are common. The north has huge wilderness zones that can only be accessed on foot, and its rivers are the focus for SANParks' three adventurous backpacking trails.

There are no public access gates to the Kruger Park for some 150 km between Phalaborwa and Punda Maria gates, although one is due to open in 2025 – Shangoni Gate will be near the Shingwedzi River about 50 km south of Punda Maria. The Tropic of Capricorn crosses the park between Mopani and Shingwedzi rest camps, and in the subtropical zone the landscape takes on a different tinge, with a transition to tropical vegetation including baobab trees, and the appearance of birds such as the tropical boubou, Meve's long-tailed starling and the racket-tailed roller. The north has much less tourism infrastructure and receives fewer visitors. For this reason, some people prefer it to the south, and it has some excellent walking options.

In the far north, the landscape becomes more interesting, and the Pafuri region features sandstone gorges, fever tree forests and dense populations of bird and animal life. Here you can find excellent walking on the SANParks Nyalaland Wilderness Trail and at the RETURNAfrica properties in the Pafuri Triangle, the area between the Luvuvhu and Limpopo Rivers.

In the Greater Kruger reserves there's one dedicated wilderness trail operator, Africa on Foot, one seasonal high-end trails camp in Timbavati, and one year-round walks-focused camp in Balule. The Kruger reserves are the stomping ground for the many private trails guides who live in the area, and it's possible to arrange either lodge-based or backpacking trails with some of the best walking guides in Africa (see pages 68–77).

The choice of who to walk with in the Kruger comes down to budget and travel preferences. Regardless of whether walking in the national park or private reserves, guests are in the hands of competent and knowledgeable guides. The national park is best suited to the self-drive style: armed with a map and picnic lunch, such visitors are free to drive the park's 2,000 km of paved and unpaved roads, which (unless there has been heavy rain) are fine for standard saloon cars. It's straightforward to book guided walks and game drives from the SANParks camps, or leave the car for a few days to stay at a wilderness trails camp or head out for a backpacking trail.

The specialist private walk operators who operate camps – Pafuri Walking, Rhino Walking and Africa on Foot – are happy to take direct bookings and can arrange transfers by air or road. These companies are more expensive than SANParks and provide higher standards in lodgings and catering, but are less costly than similar options in other parts of Africa. Otherwise, to include a walk as part of an itinerary booked through a tour operator, it can be arranged at one of the dozens of private lodges on concessions in the park and in adjacent reserves. The lodges are a good deal more expensive than the SANParks camps, but generally come with tasty extras that can include private plunge pools, waterhole hides and fine cuisine.

What about variations in the walk experience? Guides in both the public and private trails are well trained and operate to high safety standards. In general, the trail experience will be similar but private lodges can afford to hire the best-qualified guides, often with additional certification in tracking, birding and other specialities. Private group sizes tend to be smaller and age restrictions are generally lower; and private walk operators enable full flexibility in terms of dates and stay durations, whereas SANParks trails depart on fixed dates for set numbers of nights.

SANParks wilderness trails

The only way to access the Kruger National Park's pristine wilderness-zoned areas is on foot. 80% of the park is zoned in three wilderness levels (wilderness, remote, primitive) and have highly restricted access under the park management plan, in contrast to the leisure-use zones that vehicle-based safaris roam. There are seven **SANParks** Wilderness Trails camps in the park, offering total immersion in nature. Apart from short summer breaks for maintenance, these trails run all year, with departures on Wednesdays and Sundays for three nights. There's a discount in the hotter months from November to February.

The trails are based at special permanent camps with comfortable accommodation and all meals are included in the price. Units are booked on a twin basis and there's no solo visitor pricing. Transfers by game viewing vehicle are included and the access roads to the wilderness camps are not open to other visitors, so whether on

The seven SANParks Wilderness Trails camps

Wolhuter Wilderness Trails Camp is named in memory of one of the first rangers, Harry Wolhuter, and is set under towering trees with a waterhole view in an area of mixed woodlands in the south-west of the park, in a subzone that's classed as a botanical reserve. It's one of two camps still using the older style A-frame thatched huts. This area is perhaps the most scenic of the wilderness trails in the south, with granite outcrops, wooded valleys and areas of flatter bushveld. The walking can be hilly, but walkers are rewarded with opportunities to scale koppies to practise 'sit and wait'-style wildlife spotting.

Bushmans Trail Camp is in similar terrain. Walks thread through mountain bushveld and the highlight of this trail is the chance to examine 25,000-year-old San rock paintings. The camp is nestled among the granite hills, with accommodation in new tents with en suites. The wildlife is similar to that on the Wolhuter Trail – there's a good chance to find rhino. As with the Wolhuter Trail, the base camp is Berg-en-Dal, which is a one-hour drive from the nearest gate at Malelane.

The Napi Wilderness Trail terrain is less hilly than the other trails in the south of the park. Nonetheless, it's interesting walking territory, with granite underlying mountain sourveld and broadleaf woodland in the catchment of the Napi and Bimyati Rivers. There are several seasonal pans that draw wildlife, and it's a good area for approaching rhino and even lion. Camp accommodation is in canvas tents on wooden decks with en-suite facilities.

Sweni Wilderness Trail is in central Kruger National Park, in a basalt area of grassy plains and thorny savannah. Here it's harder for the wildlife to hide than in the thicker bush to the south, so it's possible to tick off quite a few species. The *themeda* grasslands support large herds of buffalo and antelope when feeding conditions are right, and these attract predators. The camp has a waterhole – a pool in the Sweni spruit – so, during the day guests can watch animals come to drink while enjoying a cold one of their own. The camp accommodation was upgraded in 2024 and features air-conditioned 'shipping foot or in the vehicle, guests won't see any others than their group. There's no electricity at the camps, just some solar power for room lighting and device-charging. In the evening, guests dine and relax by the light of a campfire and kerosene or solar lanterns. Each camp has four accommodation units with two beds and mosquito nets, and there are hot water geyser showers and flush toilets. The camps are gradually being upgraded from the older thatched A-frame style and four now have en-suite container'-style units with en-suite bathrooms.

Located on the banks of the N'wanetsi River, south-west of Satara Rest Camp, Mathikithi Wilderness Trail has tents on wooden decking and ablutions are communal. It's named after a 313 m sandstone hill, 500 m away from the camp, which is perfect for sunset views, and the habitat is similar to Sweni – mixed bushveld. Walks are led in grasslands and riparian woodlands, and there are some lovely Natal mahogany trees for shady rests.

The Olifants Wilderness Trail camp is in the central Kruger National Park, amid the low-rising Lebombo Mountains close to the border with Mozambique. Because the rivers here are perennial, there are often great concentrations of animals when it's dry in this region, and it makes for a different experience to the trails in the south. The confluence of the Letaba and Olifants Rivers is about 3 km downriver from the camp, and the waters are busy with hippo, crocodile, fish eagles and waterbuck. The camp was recently upgraded to tents on decks with en-suite bathrooms. The base camp is Letaba Rest Camp, and the journey by game-viewing vehicle to the trails camp

accommodation and three have shared ablutions.

Drinking water, fruit cordial, instant coffee and tea are provided. Guests can bring their own drinks to the camps, and shared gas-powered fridges are available. There's usually a good spot nearby to walk or drive to for a sundowner. In addition to two SANParks guides, each camp has a manager/cook, and the food is of a good standard. Each wilderness trail has a nominated base camp, one of the SANParks public rest camps, where trail can take up to a further two hours, depending on stops.

The only SANParks wilderness trail in the far north of the Kruger National Park is Nyalaland. With gorges, sandstone koppies, rock art and baobabs, it's perfect walking territory. The camp is set on a bend in the Madzaringwe River, about a one-hour drive north of Punda Maria Rest Camp, and being so far from any tarred road, it has a wonderful air of remoteness. The habitat comprises rocky mopane savannah, deep sandstone gorges and riverine forest. It's a great area for birding, with Pel's fishing owl and Verreaux's eagle owl local favourites. The trail presents an opportunity to view dinosaur fossils, hyena caves, San rock art and Iron Age remains, while the sandstone gorges and forests of baobabs make it the most scenic of all the wilderness trails. The camp accommodation is in thatched A-frame huts and ablutions are shared, with suspended bucket showers. Owing to its location and the longer journey time to reach it, Nyalaland is the least heavily booked of the seven wilderness trails. The base camp is at Punda Maria Rest Camp, which is also the nearest gate, a seven-hour drive from Johannesburg.

guests meet at 15:30 on the first day. On the final day, guests are back at the base camp before lunchtime, so it's possible to do a wilderness trail without booking other accommodation in the park; but it's more relaxing to stay in the park the night before starting a trail. Guest vehicles stay at the base camp, and big suitcases may safely be left in the car, so participants can just bring what they need for three nights. On the starting afternoon, guests and their guides travel by game-viewing vehicle to the wilderness trail camp, with stops to see wildlife. The game-viewing vehicle remains with the group for the duration of their stay.

Camps have a *lapa* and camp chairs where walkers can relax in the shade. In the evenings the fire is the focus, a time for stargazing and chats. In keeping with the wilderness spirit, excessive drinking of alcohol is strongly discouraged, and most trailists retire by 21:00. The guides may or may not join the group at the campfire. It's important to note that their primary role is to provide knowledgeable interpretation and safe guiding on trail, and they are not there to serve guests at camp. They are some of the busiest guides in the business, often doing many trails back to back, and their experience can generate some fascinating insights into all aspects of South African wilderness and conservation.

Each morning of the two walking days, guests are woken about an hour before daybreak, and rise to have a hot drink and a rusk. Walks may leave directly from the camp or, more typically, start with a short drive. The walks last four to five hours, covering up to 15 km. The guides carry a snack for breakfast – fruit, sausage or biltong, a packet of fruit juice. Back at camp, there's time for a wash before a late morning brunch. The afternoon walks are much shorter, and often involve driving to a good location to take a short stroll and sit and observe. On the fourth day there's no walk, so there's a slightly later wake-up call and guests return to the base camp after breakfast.

SANParks Backpacking Trails

In the northern half of the Kruger National Park, SANParks operates three backpacking trails, each centred on a different river system. These are demanding trails: hikers provide and carry everything needed for three nights of wild 'leave no trace' camping, and the reward is the chance to explore the deepest wilderness. Water is sourced in nature from rivers or by digging in sandy riverbeds. Tents are used, as given the hot conditions, long walks and sometimes small groups, it's regarded as too much to expect guides and guests to keep night watch in sleep-out style.

Backpacking trails begin on Sundays and Wednesdays only. The group and guides meet at a base rest camp for transfer to the trail by game-viewing vehicle, towing a trailer with the backpacks. The trail tariff covers transfers between the base camp and trailheads and guests provide their own kit and trail food. See 'Packing for Backpacking' (page 38) for advice on what to pack. Note that the shops in Kruger Park camps, while well stocked, are not geared to the meal needs of hikers.

A good level of fitness is required, and hikers need to be prepared to carry a full pack, often without shade. However, it's important to understand that this is not trekking, and the goal is not to hike as far as possible. The daily walking distances vary from 10 to 15 km, and there's plenty of time to stop and observe nature. With the extra effort required for backpacking, the trails are best tackled in the cooler winter months from May to August.

The guides vary the trail start points, routes and camping spots, to reduce the impact on the environment and enhance the experience. The group may camp in a different place each night or may stay in one camping spot for two of the three nights. On a typical day, hikers are up before dawn to have breakfast and break camp. Walking begins by 07:00, probably for four to five hours. If it's hot, a shady spot is selected to sit out the middle of the day. After another couple of hours' walking, the group decide on a campsite. Where there's a suitable river, the guides find a safe spot to bathe and otherwise it's feasible to have at least a 'cat wash' from whatever water source is available. Drinking water is sourced from nature, directly from a flowing river, or by digging a 'gypsy well' to the water table, elephant-style. The sand-filtered water may be safe to drink without any further purification, but check this with the guide. In the evening it's usually possible to light a small fire, but all traces of it must be removed when breaking camp, including any firewood gathered and unused. On a clear night, far from artificial light sources, the star canopy is unbelievable. Tired hikers retire by 21:00; the night air is filled with the sounds of nature, and the tent fabric seems tissue thin.

MANUZUZA WILDERNESS SAFARIS

On backpacking trails, clean sand-filtered water is usually sourced in a 'gypsy well'.

The three SANParks Backpacking Trails

Of the three trails, Olifants Backpacking Trail is regarded as the toughest, as it's the longest in terms of distance covered. The base camp is Olifants Rest Camp, and the trail has several variations, all exploring the catchment of the Olifants River between Olifants Rest Camp and the area where the river enters the park on its western boundary. The goal is to follow the river downstream for 40–50 km. The walking is mostly on the river levees, where there are splendid sycamore figs and marula trees for shady rests. The river is a wildlife magnet, with lots of hippo and elephant and prolific birdlife. From time to time, hikers need to remove their footwear for river crossings, with the water usually deeper in the autumn months of April and May. There's a selection of safe riverside camping spots, and an after-walk dip is generally possible. Although it's not obvious to the eye, the Olifants River is unfortunately polluted by phosphate mining and human settlements upriver, so water purification is essential. The trail meets at Olifants Rest Camp at 08:00 for departure at 09:00. The nearest gate to Olifants Camp is Phalaborwa, 3 hours 20 minutes away, so it's a challenge to stay outside the park and reach Olifants in good time, and preferable to arrange to stay in either Olifants or Letaba rest camps on the night before the trail starts. The Olifants runs from the beginning of March to the end of October; it has a shorter season than the other two backpacking trails because if summer rainfall is good, the waters rise too high to cross the Olifants River safely, making the trail unfeasibly long.

The Lonely Bull Backpacking Trail explores a wilderness area from the H14 Letaba low-water bridge eastwards to Mingerhout Dam. It can begin at several locations in the Letaba River area or be accessed from the east where the Tsendze seasonal watercourse runs south and joins the Letaba. Herds of hundreds of buffalo are spotted in this area, and hikers are sure to meet elephant, hippo and giraffe. There's a good chance of lion encounters. The trail is called after a favourite camping spot of game ranger Bruce Bryden, one shaded by Natal mahoganies; he named it for the lone

Other Kruger backpacking trails

The Kruger area has the greatest concentration of qualified trails guides in Africa, many of them with homes in the Hoedspruit area. These men and women live for the bush and avail themselves of every opportunity to get into the wilderness on foot; some run backpacking style trails in the Pafuri Triangle section in the north of Kruger National Park and various Greater Kruger reserves. These companies are listed on pages 68–77. The private backpacking trail operators have flexibility to run things a bit differently from the SANParks trails, such as doing sleep-outs. Usually referred to as a primitive trail, this is the most authentic style of exploring wilderness, with participants taking turns to keep night watch. They are more flexible in duration and can be tuned to group interests. These private trails are a chance to spend time on foot with some of Africa's most experienced guides, and there's sometimes a chance to observe guide training along the way. Usually, walkers supply their own trail kit and food on backpacking trails, but some operators can help in this area on request.

buffalo and elephant bulls he'd found in the area on his first visits in the early 1970s. There's no set route, and without a fixed distance to cover the guides plan the hike based on the conditions, wildlife movements and any preferences of the group. Some trails break away from the river and delve deep into the mopane and bushwillow veld, sourcing water by digging in the beds of one of the many spruits that run into the Letaba. The base camp is Mopani Rest Camp and the nearest gate is Phalaborwa, a three-hour drive away. Lonely Bull's season is from the start of February to the end of November, and there's a discounted trail fee in the heat of the first and last months of the season.

Mphongolo Backpacking Trail is the northernmost and wildest of the three backpacking trails. It explores the largest section of designated wilderness in the park, an area of about 900 sq. km between the Shingwedzi River in the south and its tributary, the Mphongolo, to the north. The area's geology is mostly granite, with basalts to the east. It has a more varied landscape than the other backpacking trails, including open savannah, mopane woods, sodic

pans and high gabbro koppies in the southern part. There are superior riverine woodlands to those found on the more southerly backpacking trails, and beautiful baobabs. In contrast with the Lonely Bull and Olifants backpacking trails, there's no perennial river on this trail, and the best chance to find rivers in flow is early in the season, from February to April. There may be some distance between a campsite and a water source, so it's good to have at least 4 l of container capacity. Areas of interest include the 400 m-high Phonda Hills in the south-east of the walking zone, war graves at Zari and hot springs at Matiyovia and Malahlapanga. As well as the baobabs, there are many standout jackal-berry, wild fig and leadwood trees to be admired and remnants of Iron Age settlements to be discovered. The base camp for the trail is Shingwedzi Rest Camp, and the nearest gate is Punda Maria, almost three hours' drive from Shingwedzi. The trail meets at 12:00 for departure at 13:00. The Mphongolo Trail season is from the start of February to the end of October, and there's a discounted tariff in the hottest month of February.

The ultimate wild walk in South Africa is the **Kruger Trail**, which traverses the entire park from Crooks Corner in the north-east to Malelane in the south. The distance covered totals 600–650 km, with participants hiking six legs of about 100 km each at intervals over three years. The trail is organised and led by the SANParks Honorary Ranger corps as part of their fundraising role and is designed for groups rather than individuals; the places are strictly limited and can only be booked via an annual auction. This is held each October for walks starting the following year on specific dates from May to September, and once a group wins a starting date, future legs of the trail are charged at a fixed rate. Hikers are accompanied by honorary rangers, and must be totally self-sufficient as the walks are unsupported. The trail traverses extremely wild areas with unknown water sources, so it's best suited for experienced bush walkers capable of carrying heavy loads in hot conditions. Each leg must be undertaken in sequence and comprises six days of walking and five nights of camping in the bushveld. Hikers use their own vehicles to access the trailheads, with the lead guide's coordination. After a night at

Backpacking a timeless landscape
Andrew Booth

The Outpost, the only five-star lodge in the Pafuri Triangle, offered a stark contrast between modern luxury and where we were headed for the next few November days. I could feel the anticipation in my group of six guests, especially Jack, as it was his first time taking on a backpack trail of this nature, in this 'Big Five' country that makes up the north-eastern extreme corner of South Africa. Physical evidence suggests hominids have lived along the Luvuvhu and Limpopo Rivers for at least 1.5 million years; Bushman paintings, stone age tools and Thulamela (a reconstructed village of stone) leave no doubt that humans have been traversing the landscape for a very long time, just as we were about to do.

For a trails guide, a good understanding of your trailists – the group walking with you – is very important; how in touch they are with nature and themselves counts for a lot when walking in landscapes where elephant and buffalo roam in numbers; how people will react to wild animals in close proximity, especially when put under pressure by charging or trumpeting, is difficult to gauge until the situation arises.

My pre-trail briefing covers details about our walking formations, silent ways of communicating and what to do if we do end up in a close encounter. It's not meant to scare, but rather bring to the front of mind what may happen and how we deal with it on trail. For Jack, his imagination could be his worst enemy, and the briefing can add to this as I focus on what to do should a situation arise. I remind the group that the biggest risk they took was getting there by road.

When people get into their cars, they don't think they are going to have an accident, but they know it's possible. When we walk out into the wild, we don't think we're going to get into a situation with a potentially dangerous animal, but it can't be taken off the table. I encouraged the group to become aware of their surroundings, to contribute their observations and what they sense through sight, sound and smell, and even thought. On foot, we enhance our safety by being situationally aware, and while this is largely the job of the guide, our trailists have made valuable contributions in the past.

With all questions asked and answered, we headed out and immediately fell into our single file formation, led by me and my backup, Kai. The first walking session was about half an hour, but it was already getting hot, and a leafy baobab beckoned us in; we dropped our packs to reset our sweaty bodies. I could see that Jack's pack was too heavy and uncomfortable, but he was keeping it to himself. Two others in the group, Roger and Claire, had been on backpack trails often, and I could detect in their faces that they had already started to transform into the wild version of themselves.

I ended our moment under the baobab tree by indicating packs on, and we stepped back out into the sun. Other animals were likely to be standing in the shade or close to water – I needed to be careful we didn't bump into a sleeping animal, picking the most open trails amid the sandy mopane veld.

We heard them first, trumpeting from the direction of a known spring and it was on our route. The fresh spoor and newly broken branches, followed by more elephant sounds, confirmed they were still there as we approached down wind. Creeping in slowly, we found some shade and watched the elephant herd, who were totally oblivious to us, drinking and feeding around the spring. Then as we departed, the wind swirled and they caught our scent; becoming aware of our presence, they fled in the direction we had planned to head next. To allow some time and space, we took up a resting place under a nearby weeping boer bean tree.

Spending time under trees is a very important aspect of backpacking in the wilderness, even more so in summer when the hours of light are long and the temperatures high from about 10:00 through to 16:00. Most of our walking must be done outside this time, meaning selecting places to be still, under trees and preferably close to water. Pafuri has many of these, and my longest lie up to date is six hours, but three hours is more common, especially in the winter months. Before you experience this, it sounds strange to plan to be inactive for so long. But in the bush, it is never too long. Time is never a waste when resting under an African tree.

Mid-conversation, Roger stopped and strained to look, sensing something. A bull elephant in light musth was standing about 70 m away, behind a tree, but watching us, aware that we were there. He was likely following the herd and wanted to visit the water too, but we were in his path. He stepped out and walked at 90 degrees to our position, and I gave the group their first instruction to stand and get behind the tree. The elephant's tail was also at 90 degrees, his temporal glands dribbling – he wasn't happy to find people between him and his drinking hole. My hand moved across my rifle and found the

On trails in Pafuri, we spend time enjoying watching the elephants in the Luvuvhu River.

bolt. Everything felt a bit on edge – that things could easily escalate, or he could turn away. We could only respond to one another in the moment, and it felt like a standoff.

There was a medium sized log in the open space separating us and the elephant, and at the moment the log was in between us he turned and charged. Now elephants cannot actually run, but they can walk very very fast (up to 40 kph), so the ground closed quickly. I instinctively loaded the rifle, wondering for a moment if he was going to stop. Just short of the log he lifted his head and trumpeted, standing back, lifting one foot, showing his big ears. I shouted back, warning him not to come closer. The group had done a great job remaining still behind the tree, leaving the confrontation to myself and Kai, who held a very cool head. The whole encounter couldn't have lasted more than a minute before he stepped away into the bush. Relieved as the intensity of the moment faded, we picked up our packs and moved onward to the Luvuvhu River, where we were to camp for the first night.

Debriefing the encounter that evening around the fire, there was consensus that while it was intense, being well prepared for the moment allowed us all to react together, unified. As guides we had briefed well, and then acted when we needed to. It seemed to accelerate our immersion, and when we climbed into our tents that evening it was difficult to believe we had only entered this primordial world a few hours earlier.

Each trailist who comes on a backpack trail takes a journey that impacts their life and ways of understanding nature, and as guides we do the same, time and time again. No two trails are ever the same, and the space created for a group to interact with nature and with one another varies according to the people and the space. It changes through the seasons and what animals are encountered. The people vary all

Punda Maria Rest Camp, the first stage is hiked from Crooks Corner to Vlakteplaas, with subsequent stages ending in Mopani Rest Camp, Olifants Rest Camp, N'wanetsi Picnic Spot and Lower Sabie Rest Camp, with finally a hike through the scenic Thlalabye hills to complete the monumental journey by adding a stone to a cairn at the Crocodile River, not far from Malelane Satellite Camp.

Rhino Walking Safaris

North of Skukuza Rest Camp in Kruger National Park is a 12,000 ha private concession managed by Seolo Africa that shares 15 km of unfenced boundary with Sabi Sand Game Reserve, a private reserve to the west. The main lodge on the concession is Rhino Post Safari Lodge, where guests enjoy morning and evening game drives. This lodge is the check-in point for Plains Camp, home of **Rhino Walking Safaris**, which is about 30 minutes away by game-viewing vehicle and is the only permanent privately operated trails camp in the Kruger National Park.

At Plains Camp, four well-appointed tents nestle under a thicket of knobthorn trees, providing a stylish camping experience. Each tent is crafted from canvas and wood and features an en-suite bathroom. Two well-qualified guides lead groups on morning walks that typically last for two to three hours but can extend up to five hours depending on sightings, conditions and guests' wishes. The terrain is mainly flat with thorn bushveld and the time, as even returning trailists have changed since their previous trail. As a guide I need to manage this space, make people feel secure enough to engage with nature. I try to do this by demonstration; it's not something that's really discussed, it just happens. It's the one thing we can guarantee: if you come on a backpack experience with an open mind, nature will encompass you and work on and through you. Nothing more and nothing less. The beauty of this approach is that as guides, we are open to the influence of our group of trailists. They each have a story to tell about how they got there, what drew them to the backpack experience, and the way they see and share it grows us as guides.

By the third day the trailists were deeply immersed, and even Jack had found his rhythm. We explored easier terrain across the floodplain, where we encountered many elephants and herds of buffalo. As the season progresses, rainfall and more drinking options result in the animals dispersing, but just then it was buzzing with life. We had timed the trail around the full moon, and the last night was spent up on a rock with a vantage over a spring below; we watched herds of animals come and go throughout the night on a moonlight landscape.

The exit from the wilderness can be the hardest, and as we walked our last kilometre, I wondered how each person would integrate back into their regular routines. For Jack, Roger and Claire, it had only been three nights, but they said it felt like an entire micro-lifetime; it was a brief glimpse into the wild, an experience that exposed the wilderness that still lies within. It's back to the basics to find ourselves, in its truest sense.

ANDREW BOOTH is a trails guide with **Wildside Trails**, and has a particular interest in the mental health benefits of spending time in nature, as well as a love for tracking.

marula woodlands, and every walk is a different experience. As well as looking out for interesting plants, insects and birds, walkers may encounter all the big game, from buffalo and elephant to big cats and African wild dog.

After an early morning walk and brunch, guests relax on the deck overlooking the Timbetene Plain and waterhole or cool off in the plunge pool. In the afternoons, there's usually a shorter walk incorporating a game drive and sundowner stop. A highlight for the adventurous is the chance to spend a night at the Sleep-Out decks, located a 5–8 km walk from Plains Camp, depending on the route taken. Linked by walkways, four individual sleeping platforms are perched above a communal deck; they have flush toilets and hot showers. The decks overlook the Xiteveteve waterhole, a popular wildlife haunt. Dinner is cooked in traditional braai style over an open fire and served al fresco on the dining deck. Then guests climb about 4 m above ground to sleep in safety as animals roam the unfenced camp below: after a day on foot in the bush, nothing but a mosquito net and some canvas separates sleepers from the nocturnal sounds of Africa. Plains Camp operates all year on an all-inclusive basis; the minimum stay is two nights, and it's open to children of 12 years and older.

Africa On Foot

Africa on Foot's headquarters are in the Klaserie Private Nature Reserve where an authentic Lowveld camp has five brick

A night spent on a Plains Camp Sleep-Out deck is a memorable experience.

chalets, two of which are family units. There's a fun treehouse option a little distance away that can be reserved when booking. The camp has an unobtrusive elephant fence, but smaller animals come and go freely. In keeping with its wild credentials, the camp is off grid, but solar power is provided for charging devices and room lighting. From camp, guides take guests on two- to three-hour walks in the mornings and game drives in the afternoons. The walks explore an area with a high wildlife density, and guests often encounter elephant, rhino, buffalo and giraffe. As the drives continue after sunset, it's also an opportunity to spot night predators, including leopard, lion and hyena.

Africa on Foot's sister company, **Africa on Foot Wilderness Trails**, runs mobile fly-camp walking safaris that are unique to South Africa – similar to the types of walking safaris found in East Africa. It's available in winter from April to November and takes place in the Maseke Balule Game Reserve. This reserve is transected by the Olifants River and surrounded by other reserves, including the Kruger National Park to the north, so is just as rich in wildlife as the Klaserie reserve. The dominant vegetation is thornveld and mixed bush willow. The presence of a river system and additional water sources draws a variety of wildlife, and the movement of large herds of buffalo and elephant within this environment signifies a healthy and thriving ecosystem. On the predator front, the coexistence of lions, hyenas, leopards and wild dogs highlights a balanced predator–prey dynamic within the ecosystem; and the birding is top class.

The walking area is topographically diverse and spans both sides of the upper Olifants River, making for a varied experience each day. The wilderness trails run over three nights in slackpacking style, with each night spent in a different location. Guests are woken before dawn to find hot water in a wash basin outside their tent. Once walkers depart, the camp is taken down and transferred to the next location by vehicle. The morning walk is three to four hours, with a picnic brunch taken on the trail, and the aim is to reach camp by early afternoon for a snack, wash and rest. In the late afternoon there's a shorter walk or game drive, and sunset drinks.

It's a comfortable camping experience. Walkers sleep in two-person, stand-up canvas dome tents with real beds and solar lanterns; bucket showers and chemical toilets are provided. The trails are fully catered, with meals taken seated at camp tables before the day winds down around the campfire.

Manukuza Wilderness Safaris

In addition to the seasonal Africa on Foot wilderness trails, Maseke Balule Game Reserve has a specialist trails operator that has walks all year. **Manukuza Wilderness Safaris** is based at a converted farmhouse and presents two flavours of trail, camp-based and primitive-style backpacking. The camp-based trails operate all year, while the sleep-out style is suspended in the hottest months of December to February. The walking area is in the south of Balule, close to the (unfenced) boundary with Klaserie Private Nature Reserve.

Walkers fully loaded on a Manukuza backpacking trail.

The camp-based option is a compromise between adventure and comfort, especially in summer, compared with the backpacking trails. With the convenience of carrying just a day pack, walkers can fully immerse themselves in the experience without the burden of heavy gear. Pricing is on a par with the wilderness trails camps in the Kruger, and Manukuza accepts children from 13 when supervised by parents (compared with the SANParks minimum age of 16), so it's more family friendly. The daily rhythm sees walkers depart at sunrise and return for mid-morning brunch, followed by relaxation in camp before an afternoon walk.

The primitive trail requires walkers to carry all necessities, and this fosters a real sense of self-reliance and adventure. The minimum age requirement for this style is 16, with a need for good health and fitness to ensure that participants can fully engage and enjoy the experience. Nights are spent under the stars, taking turns to keep watch by the fire, offering an incredibly immersive and primal experience.

Standard trails are three nights and longer trails can be arranged. Bookings are on a group basis, with a minimum requirement of six guests and the same price for any group size up to eight. Meals are not included. Travelling time from Johannesburg to the reserve is about five hours and guests meet guides at the Jejane gate by 11:30 on the day of arrival; vehicles can remain at a secure location in the reserve. It's possible to get a free transfer from Hoedspruit. The trail concludes at 09:30 on the fourth day.

Simbavati Trails Camp

Simbavati Trails Camp is a low-impact walking safari camp in one of the richest wildlife habitats in South Africa. It's part of the **Simbavati** collection of safari lodges and camps and is located in the remote northern extreme of Timbavati Private Nature Reserve. The reserve is at the centre of a wide east–west game migration route, and healthy populations of the full range of big game can be found here. As well as open boundaries with other large private reserves to the west and north, to the east of the camp lies a 11,000 ha wilderness-zoned sector of Kruger National Park.

The comfortable camp is established for the duration of the walking season from March to November alongside an ephemeral river, and walks are guided twice daily. There are four Meru-style tents, each with an en-suite bathroom with flush toilet and a bucket shower. Apart from these comforts, the camp is off grid – no power, no phone signal, no Wi-Fi, just the chance to unwind in a remote corner of the Lowveld. The fire-to-plate style of cooking is a highlight, and the cuisine is inventive and hearty. Solar chargers are provided for small devices, and there's a reservoir-style plunge pool for cooling off.

Pafuri Walking Safaris

The northernmost part of Kruger National Park is one of the most attractive walking destinations in South Africa. The Luvuvhu River carves through sandstone gorges amid forests of baobab, ana trees and sycamore figs, and its floodplain has splendid fever tree woodlands. It's in the tropical zone and attracts birds unseen further south. The Limpopo River delineates the northern boundary of the park and the international border with Zimbabwe. The 26,500 ha 'Pafuri Triangle' between the Limpopo and Luvuvhu was restored to its traditional Makuleke owners in the 1990s, and is more properly referred to as the Makuleke Contractual Park.

Conservation management in the area remains SANParks' responsibility and they have recorded approximately 75%

of the total biodiversity of the Kruger here in a space that only represents 1% of the park's total size. Pafuri's wetlands are listed under the Ramsar Convention on Wetlands for their international importance for birdlife. While there are very few rhinos left in the north of the park and a small number of lion have been reintroduced, visitors will definitely encounter elephant and buffalo, and leopard, hyena, nyala and eland are commonly seen.

The Pafuri region is a prime example of how habitat and wildlife conservation can bring benefits to local communities, with representatives of the Makuleke holding important positions in the management structures of the Contractual Park and the community as a whole deriving a share of revenue from tourism. There are just a few concessions in this remote corner of the Kruger. Self-drive access is restricted to the road between Pafuri Gate and the Luvuvhu Bridge, so guests of the concessions are guaranteed an exclusive experience akin to the private reserves of the Greater Kruger.

Habitats in the Makuleke Contractual Park range from deep sandstone gorges on the western boundary to sodic pans on the floodplains. The stand-out walks explore the fever tree forest and Mutale and Lanner Gorges. The first is really special, a large mature forest of elegant fever trees on a floodplain. Habitat like this is rare in the Kruger Park, as trees are under constant attack by everything from insects to elephants. Somehow the scale and speedy growth of the trees here has led to a magical expanse where the walking is level and shady. Lanner Gorge, by contrast, is an ancient U-shaped valley carved over millennia by the Luvuvhu River. It takes an hour to drive to the trailhead for the Lanner, but it's worth it. Another popular option takes walkers to the confluence point of the Luvuvhu and Limpopo Rivers at Crook's Corner, from where Zimbabwe and Mozambique can be seen across the river.

The top walking option is **RETURNAfrica**, which has a selection of properties along the Luvuvhu River and runs Pafuri Walking Safaris in the winter months from April to October. The year-round option is the unfenced Pafuri Camp, which is attractively set on the northern bank of the Luvuvhu River, with 19 large tents shaded by trees. The tents are connected to the multi-level common area by wooden decking. Most guests are happy to have short walks as part of a game drive, and some choose longer walks as an alternative. In addition to the main camp, the nearby Baobab Hill Bush House is an exclusive homestead available for group bookings. Formerly the section ranger's house, it can accommodate up to eight guests.

At the start of each walking season in April, two trails camps are established with minimal impact on the environment. Nkula and Hutwini camps are set within the towering riverine forests a few steps from the Luvuvhu River to the west of the Luvuvhu bridge. Hutwini is the most recently refreshed and has a higher tariff, and both have Meru tents with en-suite bathrooms and flush toilets.

The two camps grant the same experience. On the first day, guests receive a gentle introduction to the terrain with an afternoon walk from the camp. On the following days, they can expect a very early call for the main walk of the day. It's usual to drive to the starting point in order to explore different habitats. Walks last three to four hours and cover anything from 4 to 10 km, depending on the conditions and which animals the group encounters. Back at camp, guests are welcomed with chilled towels before brunch is served, after which there's time to relax and observe the wildlife that frequents the unfenced camp and nearby river. With energy restored,

Nkula Trails Camp is peaceful and well shaded.

guests go on another outing in the afternoon. This can be a walk or a drive, depending on guests' wishes and what wildlife is encountered.

There's a minimum two-night stay for the walking camps, and a typical visit would be for three nights, which is ideal for unwinding and experiencing the variety in the area; longer stays are not hard to justify. Guests may choose to spend a night or two at the main Pafuri Camp before transferring to one of the trails camps. Access is by road via either Pafuri Gate or Punda Maria Gate, or by air to the Pafuri airstrip. Daily seat rate flights are offered from Hoedspruit Eastgate and Kruger Mpumalanga International airports.

Kruger lodge walks

In addition to the overnight walking safaris described earlier, there are dozens of lodges and camps in the Kruger area where a walk can be taken in place of a game drive. These walks can be enjoyed by both the bushwalk enthusiast and those for whom it's a rare adventure.

Dawn walks from **SANParks** camps are available daily throughout the year at all rest camps and bushveld camps. In addition, afternoon walks are offered at Skukuza and Letaba Rest Camps, and Olifants Rest Camp runs a mid-morning walk. As morning walks start early, participants must have accommodation booked in the camp the night before; at the camps where afternoon walks are available, an overnight booking is required, as they return to camp at (or even after) gate-closing time. Walks start with a slow drive in an open-sided game-viewing vehicle, and for chilly mornings the vehicles usually have blankets on board. Driving from the camp allows the walk to begin in a new place each day and reduces the impact on the environment. The lead guide adjusts the pace and distance of walks to suit the group, and a typical dawn walk

Space for nature to thrive

This book uses metric units to indicate the scale of reserves, either in hectares (abbr. ha) or for larger reserves, in square kilometres. A hectare is 10,000 sq. m, or about 2.5 imperial acres. 100,000 ha is 1,000 sq. km – the size of Hluhluwe-iMfolozi Park. This sounds big, but it's a fenced park and requires wildlife management, including transfers to ensure genetic diversity.

The trend in African conservation is to create bigger zones that allow for animals to live and migrate in a more natural state. The Kruger National Park is 20,000 sq. km, the same size as Wales or the state of Massachusetts. Having dropped fences to neighbouring private reserves, it's now part of the 'Greater Kruger', and central to the 35,000 sq. km Great Limpopo Transfrontier Park, along with areas in Zimbabwe and Mozambique. That in turn is in a 100,000 sq. km Transfrontier Conservation Area (TFCA), one of several under development by the Peace Parks Foundation. These have giant ambitions: the Kavango Zambezi TFCA, which spans parts of Botswana, Zimbabwe and Zambia, aims to conserve 520,000 sq. km – an area bigger than Spain.

The fever tree woodlands of Makuleke Contractual Park, part of Kruger National Park, which is in turn part of the Great Limpopo Transfrontier Park.

covers 4 to 6 km over three hours. There's one longer rest stop for snacks and drinks, which are included in the cost and carried by the guides to share with the group.

Uniquely, Olifants Rest Camp runs a two-hour river walk that starts at 09:00/09:30 in summer/winter. This is the only walk that's deep in the park and accessible to day visitors; it's hard to recommend mid-morning walks, but if it's the only option, it's better than no walk. Participants should enter the park via Phalaborwa Gate as soon as it opens to allow three hours for the drive to Olifants. The cheapest way to experience a professionally guided walk in the Kruger (or anywhere in Africa) is to stay outside the park and book a dawn walk from one of the gates. There are private lodges and backpackers close to the southern and central park gates, and they can help to book walks that meet at these gates. SANParks trail guides lead the walks, and the experience is the same as for walks from SANParks rest camps.

The above walks are run by SANParks and cater largely to the domestic and self-drive visitor sectors and are charged at reasonable separate fees. The venues on the following pages are private lodges at concessions within the park and in private reserves that are part of the Greater Kruger ecosystem. In these venues the walks are normally included as an activity in the overnight rates. When planning to include a walk during a visit to a private lodge, caveats apply – make sure the walk is guaranteed (not 'subject to guide availability') and is the main activity of the morning (not 'after the game drive is over'). This list of lodges runs roughly south to north and is not exhaustive.

Jock Safari Lodge is a fabled private concession in the south of the park. It's owned by the non-profit Caleo Foundation, which also has a property in the Western Cape, Sanbona Wildlife Reserve. At Jock's, walks are guided all year in the concession area, which hosts a dense wildlife population that includes rhino, buffalo, elephant and leopard. It's best to request the walk experience when booking.

West of Skukuza, Sabi Sand Game Reserve is one of the best known private reserves in South Africa, and has convenient access via a number of airstrips including scheduled flights to Skukuza airport. The lodges here are all of a luxurious standard, and most have professional trails guides on staff. The only drawback of Sabi Sand is that the relatively high density of lodges and vehicle tracks can make it hard to avoid seeing vehicles while on foot. In the middle of the reserve alongside the Sand River, **Londolozi Private Game Reserve** has a long history of guided walks. Londolozi Varty has welcomed guests for almost a century and is regarded as the first safari lodge in South Africa. As well as Londolozi's five venues, **Mala Mala**, **Notten's Bush Camp**, **Leopard Hills**, **Inyati**, and the lodges of **Singita**, **&Beyond** and **Lion Sands** are all high-end venues with good reputations for guiding standards.

In contrast to Sabi Sand, the 23,000 ha Manyeleti Private Nature Reserve is much less visited. It's owned by the local Mnisi Shangaan community, who gain an income from the concession fees paid by the lodges and camps, and benefit from employment there. It's a well-positioned reserve sharing a long, open boundary with the Kruger National Park to the east, Sabi Sand Game Reserve to the south and the Timbavati Private Nature Reserve to the north. Although there are no perennial rivers, the watercourses are well wooded, and the reserve's geographic situation results in good numbers of game animals in residence and traversing. The extensive palatable grasslands attract herds of buffalo over 300 strong. These and other grazers provide good feeding for predators, and there are at least two large resident lion prides. **Pungwe Safari Camp** has dawn walks of three to four hours throughout the year, with a game drive in the afternoon, included in rates.

A recent addition to the Kruger National Park's safari operations is **Kruger Untamed**, which sets two tented camps during the peak winter months. Both are located in sizeable 15,000 ha concession areas: Tshokwane River Camp has 30 tents alongside the ephemeral Ripane River and to the north, some 40 km away in an area known for its lion population, lies Satara Plains Camp. Their season from May to September coincides with the prime time for walking safaris. A highlight for those keen on tracking is the involvement of Alex van den Heever and Renias Mhlongo. Both are world-acclaimed tracking specialists and form part of the leadership team for the concessions. Their paths first crossed at Londolozi in the Sabi Sand Game Reserve 30 years ago, and since then they've been instrumental in shaping the Tracker Academy and have collaborated on the publication of *Tracker Manual*, sharing their profound tracking knowledge. Tracking walks should be booked via **World Trackers**, and it's possible for groups to specifically request Alex or Renias at an additional fee. These walks can be conducted as a morning activity during a stay at one of the camps, or extended to a three- or four-day tracking safari that includes practical tracking, lectures and use of the metaphor of tracking for business and life.

Singita Kruger National Park is the most exclusive private concession in the actual Kruger park and is located in the east on a hill overlooking the Sweni River, close to the confluence with the N'wanetsi River, which flows into Mozambique a few kilometres downstream. Guided walks are available to guests of both the Singita Sweni Lodge and the nearby exclusive-use Singita Lebombo Lodge. As at the other Singita lodges in South Africa, all guides are qualified to lead trails, and there's 13,300 ha of prime bushveld to explore. The area has a varied terrain of savannah, gorges and rocky ridges, giving a good choice of walking options. Guides decide on the routes in consultation with guests, taking into account the walk duration, weather conditions and animal movements. Some walks explore the N'wanetsi and Xinkelengane Rivers and their riparian woodlands, which feature sycamore figs, fever trees, leadwood and jackal-berry trees. One expedition starts at the Granophyre Ridge, meandering past photogenic rock features to a viewpoint overlooking the N'wanetsi. From there it's possible to descend to the river and return a different way. Other areas to explore include the Lebombo Mountains, the Gudzane Dam and the Central Depression area.

At the same latitude as Singita Sweni but on the western side of the park, the **&Beyond** Ngala Private Game Reserve has the high standards associated with the &Beyond portfolio. Although it's close to some of the lodges in Timbavati Private Nature Reserve, it's actually located inside Kruger National Park. Access is restricted to guests of the Ngala Private Game Reserve lodges, and the concession is most conveniently reached via its own airstrip. The walking area is traversed by ephemeral rivers that flow north, and interesting animal encounters are common.

West of Ngala, Timbavati Private Nature Reserve has a long and unfenced eastern boundary with the Kruger National Park from Orpen Gate northwards. It's a member of the Associated Private Nature Reserves and has 53,000 ha of high-quality walking terrain. Several tributaries of the Olifants River, the largest being the Nhlaralumi, traverse the reserve from south to north through typical Lowveld bushveld habitat. Although they only flow occasionally after summer rain, their waterholes are a major water source for wildlife. Timbavati is the stomping ground for trails and courses run by the Lowveld Trails Company (see page 72) and is the location of a seasonal field camp, Simbavati Trails Camp (see page 110). In addition, several lodges have dawn walks. **Bateleur Safari Camp** is attractively located in dense woodland at a bend in the Nhlaralumi River, with eight comfortable canvas-walled, en-suite units overlooking the sandy riverbed. There are well-qualified guides and trackers in residence, and the lodge has a 10,000 ha walking zone. The format is flexible to accommodate guests' wishes, ranging from a short stroll as part of a game drive to longer three- to four-hour dawn walks in place of a drive. Motswari Private Game Reserve spans a section of northern Timbavati and Umbabat Private Nature Reserves. It has an attractive and varied terrain of bushveld and woodland, and walks from **Motswari Game Lodge** can last from one to three hours depending on conditions and guest wishes. As well as tracking and bird spotting, the guides like to share lore of local traditions and bush survival tips.

West of Timbavati and close to Hoedspruit there are other fine walking reserves that share unfenced boundaries with each other and the Kruger National Park. Thornybush Game Reserve has a few lodges with trails guides on staff, one such being **Royal Malewane**, which has a couple of smaller satellite properties, the Farmstead and the Waterside. A nice option is to walk for a couple of hours between the main lodge and other lodges through a mixed veld of tamboti thickets and open grassland, pausing to spy on any morning visitors at a large watering hole. Breakfast can then be taken at either destination, before return by vehicle.

The addition of immersive guided walks is a recent enhancement to the offerings at **Thornybush Game Lodge** and Saseka Tented Camp. These walks, lasting around three hours, typically follow the course of the Monwana River, an ephemeral tributary of the Timbavati River. Beyond the river, several waterholes are tranquil spots to unwind in the shade, providing opportunities to observe the wildlife coming to drink. The 40-bed lodge has all the expected high-end features, and for a more low-key stay, Saseka Tented Camp is a good alternative. With just six suites, Monwana Game Lodge is an exclusive venue in the centre of Thornybush. Part of the **MORE Family Collection**, its main lodge looks over an active waterhole.

To the north-west of Timbavati is Klaserie Private Nature Reserve, which, at 60,000 ha, is the largest of the Associated Private Nature Reserves. It's less developed than Timbavati and has unfenced boundaries to the Maseke Balule Game Reserve to the west, Umbabat Private Nature Reserve to the east and the Kruger National Park to the north-east. The main geographic feature of the reserve is the Klaserie River, which flows south to north to join the Olifants River. It's dry except in times of prolonged rainfall in the catchment. In addition to Africa on Foot (see page 107), Klaserie has lodges that guide dawn walks. **Makumu Private Game Lodge** is a small venue that overlooks the sandy course of a Klaserie tributary and the lodge derives its name from the Xitsonga language, signifying 'an intangible explanation of an open space, an uncluttered lookout over distant horizons, or endless views'. Notably, evening meals are enjoyed in a 'floating' boma, providing satisfying views of the riverbed and bushveld plains. With capacity limited to 12 beds, the lodge offers an intimate and exclusive atmosphere.

West of the R42 road, there are two reserves that are not contiguous with the Kruger National Park but are regarded as Greater Kruger reserves and are of interest for walking safaris. Both reserves are walked by the private trails companies in Hoedspruit and also have guide training camps that can be accessed by anyone wishing to join a course (see page 48).

Greater Makalali Private Game Reserve protects 25,000 ha of mixed bushveld, and is home to **Siyafunda Wildlife & Conservation**, the initiative of a small group of enthusiastic professional guides. The name means 'To Learn and To Teach' in Zulu, and this tells us about their main focus – the business is not so much about photographic safaris, but more geared to involving conservation-minded visitors in practical work as part of a stay. Siyafunda guests can volunteer to get hands on, helping to monitor wildlife via camera traps, and work on habitat rehabilitation such as erosion control, construction of rock gabions, brush-packing and re-seeding. The bush-volunteering aspect is not compulsory, of course, and visitors can simply come to enjoy a few days of wilderness immersion on the trails. A multi-day backpacking patrol is available, a great opportunity to practise tracking skills, searching for elephant, rhino, buffalo and lion to check on their condition. With three days of supplies to carry, it's a demanding style of trail. Alternatively, Siyafunda offer easier camp-based trails, heading out with just a day pack to carry water and snacks. Guests return to a comfortable bed each day at Job's Halt lodge. Shaded by jackal-berry trees next to the ephemeral Makhutswi River, the lodge is self-catering, with four en-suite twin rooms. A large shaded communal area and a boma with firewood is provided.

The second reserve of interest is Selati Game Reserve, which is north of Makalali and accessed via the R526 south of Gravelotte. Traversed by the seasonal Great Selati River, it has 33,000 ha of prime savannah habitat and hosts a range of conservation and scientific projects. Selati is known for its successful sable breeding programme, and for being the only site in the world to find the Lillie cycad in its natural setting.

At its heart, Selati has 700 m granite hills, and combined with good tree cover and dense wildlife populations, it's excellent walking terrain. **iLala Safaris** run trails with walkers based at a camp in the north-east of the reserve. Normally wilderness trails run for three nights, so iLala's six-night trails will appeal to those who really like to take things slowly and get off grid for as long as possible. The camp is a comfortable oasis between walks, with six large safari tents, each with its own outdoor bathroom. There are a couple of splash pools for cooling off in the warmer months.

In the Makuleke Contractual Park, **Rare Earth's** Outpost Lodge is the only venue in the entire north of the Kruger National Park to combine walks and the luxury lodge experience. The Outpost has twelve open-plan suites nestled on a hillside, each open to the bushveld with 180-degree views. The red sandstone cliffs of the Mutale and Luvuvhu Rivers are important nesting habitats, and the area is rich in plant life, including baobabs, fever trees, ana trees and sycamore figs. Walks are accessed by game viewing vehicle and make the most of the great variation in Pafuri from walking barefoot in the Luvuvhu to exploring the open understorey of the fever tree forests in the floodplain, and wildlife spotting at some of the area's sodic pans.

The Luvuvhu River views from the open-sided suites at Rare Earth's Outpost are a highlight.

Greater Mapungubwe Transfrontier Conservation Area

At the tripoint of South Africa, Botswana and Zimbabwe, there's a conservation area that spans over 5,900 sq. km centred on the historic Mapungubwe kingdom. The Greater Mapungubwe Transfrontier Conservation Area (TFCA) is an emerging project of the Peace Parks Foundation and is one of six such Transfrontier parks on the borders of South Africa and its neighbours. There are a number of parks and reserves with walking opportunities in the TFCA: Mapungubwe National Park and Mapesu Private Game Reserve in South Africa; and in Botswana the Tuli Block reserves that are accessible by road and can be combined well with the South African venues covered in this chapter.

Mapungubwe lodge walks

In north-west Limpopo Province, tucked up against the borders of Botswana and Zimbabwe, Mapungubwe National Park has some of the most scenic walking of any park in South Africa. As well as being of interest for its natural history, the reserve is a listed UNESCO World Heritage Site for its cultural value. The most renowned hill, for which the park is named, is topped with Iron Age ruins from the Mapungubwe Kingdom (c. 1075–1220), and near the park entrance is a good museum. At its height, the city is believed to have had over 5,000 inhabitants, making it the oldest modern capital in Southern Africa.

The park has a heartwarming profusion of baobab trees, as well as fever trees and splendid sycamore fig trees close to the rivers. It's a compact 28,000 ha in size and visitors are likely to spot elephant, giraffe, zebra, hyrax and sable antelope. Animals – including cattle from the communal lands in Zimbabwe – roam freely through the Limpopo River across the international frontier. Mapungubwe National Park is a six-hour drive from Johannesburg and one hour west of Musina. Roads in the area are often potholed, so visitors driving to the park should allow extra time for the journey.

SANParks is the only walks operator in the park. There are interesting early morning explorations, as well as a Heritage Tour to Mapungubwe Hill, which involves larger groups climbing the hill to learn about the area's history and view the thirteenth-century ruins excavated on the hill's plateau. The eastern section of the park is where walks are guided amid heavily eroded sandstone hills, with views down to the floodplains of the Limpopo River. Dawn walks meet at the park entrance at 06:30, and last about three hours. A snack and fruit juice are provided. Although there's big game present, the walks focus on the plant life, including sculptural Transvaal sesame bushes and stands of Ilala palms, which grow here at the southern edge of their range. The park guides share lore on plant uses for traditional medicine and as food sources. For as long as the sun's heat is low angled, it's excellent walking terrain, with vantage points to be reached on koppies and rocky ridges. San rock art and Iron Age stone ruins can be found along the way. As there's little shade while walking, the aim is to be back at the vehicle before the heat of day.

Mapesu Private Game Reserve is a convenient base for visiting Mapungubwe – their entrances are just a few kilometres apart. It's in the process of being rewilded from cattle farming and in recent years has seen the successful reintroduction of elephant, followed by cheetah, sable, giraffe, buffalo and rhino. There's a choice of accommodation at two lodges, the Wilderness Tented Camp and self-catering at the campsite. Walks ae offered all year, with the possibility to track some of the animals that are collared for scientific study and opportunities to see well-preserved San rock art.

Northern Tuli (Botswana) lodge walks

Another component of the Greater Mapungubwe TFCA of interest for wildlife tourism and walking lies across the border in Botswana. The Northern Tuli Game Reserve – commonly called the Tuli Block – is a wedge of savannah between the Limpopo and Shashe Rivers, and is really an extension of South Africa's tourism sector, as it's easier to reach by air and road from that side.

It's a rugged and remote region with habitats ranging from undulating mopane veld and wide-open plains to riverine thickets and craggy sandstone hills. These host a diverse range of flora and fauna, including elephant, lion, leopard and cheetah. The area is characterised by rocky outcrops, dry riverbeds and fine baobab trees. Tuli comprises a number of privately owned game reserves that operate a range of safari experiences, from walking safaris and game drives to horseback riding and birdwatching. In addition to its natural beauty and abundance of wildlife, the Tuli Block has a rich cultural heritage, with evidence of human habitation dating back over 300,000 years.

Lodge-based walks are available in Mashatu Game Reserve, and training company EcoTraining has a camp there too. South of Mashatu, Tuli Wilderness is an excellent walking base on the Limpopo River, and Tswehe Wildlife Reserve is a quiet escape further south.

Mashatu Game Reserve is a 42,000 ha privately owned game reserve that lies within the Northern Tuli Game Reserve. It's bounded by Zimbabwe to the north and South Africa to the south, the border formed by the Limpopo River. The name Mashatu refers to the endemic nyala berry trees, groves of which are found along the banks of the Majale and Limpopo Rivers. The reserve is known for some of the best predator viewing in Botswana, with near daily sightings of lion, leopard and cheetah, as well as hyena, black-backed jackal and the African wildcat. It's one of the few places where there's a chance to see the rare brown hyena. There's a full range of plains game, including giraffe, eland, zebra and the largest population of elephants on any private reserve in Southern Africa. The birdlife is thriving, with over 350 bird species, including the Kori bustard.

Mashatu has a choice of properties, each presenting a distinctive feel. Tuli Safari Lodge Mashatu is one of the longest established lodges in Botswana. Set in lovely, shaded grounds, the roomy tent and stone units are fan cooled. It's close to the Limpopo River, and there's good walking direct from camp in a landscape of eroded sandstone koppies and baobab and shepherd's trees. The cover photograph of this book was taken in the area.

Mashatu Lodge is in the centre of the reserve overlooking a waterhole. The air-conditioned rooms have bush views, and warthogs and bushbuck roam in the camp. Here, guests can add to the adventure by booking a night in the Lala Limpopo Sleep Out Hide, which has all the comforts of a lodge room but has a busy waterhole 2 m from the window. A third venue, Mashatu Tent Camp, is the best option for a more rustic experience. As with the other camps, there's a swimming pool, but the tent accommodation and outdoor showers feel closer to nature. A hide at the waterhole provides close up views on visiting wildlife. These three venues are the best to choose for walking activities, with trails guides available for morning or afternoon outings, which are charged at an additional fee. The other venues on the reserve are the opulent five-star villas at Euphorbia Mashatu and a couple of exclusive-use properties.

More intensive walking safaris are on offer under the WalkMashatu brand. Available from March to October, these are flexible in format and made for guests who want to enjoy the maximum time on foot. This can involve full-day walks, taking a picnic breakfast and lunch and returning to sleep at one of the lodges; or combine fly-camping with a night at Tuli Safari Lodge Mashatu and either Mashatu Lodge or Mashatu Tent Camp. There's even the option to spend three nights out in the wild fly-camping. The fly-camp tents are minimalist, consisting of just enough canvas and mesh to give protection from insects, but furnishing that sleep-out experience. A game viewing vehicle is always at hand to facilitate walking in diverse parts of the reserve and to transfer the camp.

The fly-camp is also available as a 'night under the stars' for lodge guests. In this case, dinner is taken at the lodge before a night drive to the fly-camp. While there, guests may participate in night photography and enjoy fireside stories with drinks and snacks, before sleeping under the firmament. Portable showers and toilets are provided at the fly-camp. The next morning, guests have a light early morning breakfast before departing on a game drive at around 06:00 and then back to camp for brunch.

From South Africa, Mashatu is reachable by road via the Pont Drift border crossing, and it's around six and a half hours' drive from Johannesburg. When the river is not in flood, it can be crossed by a high ground clearance vehicle, which can be parked at Limpopo Valley Airport. If water levels are high, a cable car is used for the crossing, with a rendezvous with the reserve's guide and vehicle on the other side. The airport is reachable via Mashatu fly-in packages from Lanseria airport in Johannesburg.

South African nature training company **EcoTraining** (see page 51) has a camp in Mashatu, established since 2023 near a koppie called Pitsane. Located in a scenic valley and close to year-round water, it's one of a portfolio of EcoTraining camps that span South Africa's Lowveld and the Mara in Kenya. To the west of the camp, the Pitsane River has year-round water pools, and to the east the Shashe River forms the border with Zimbabwe. The camp hosts a number of EcoTraining courses that involve a significant element of walking from short EcoQuest and Track & Trail courses to the 55-day Field Guide. These are targeted at both professional guides and wildlife enthusiasts. The camp consists of ten walk-in Meru-style tents, each with two beds and bedding. There are shared bathroom facilities and a central communal area near a fine leadwood tree. It's off grid so a generator is available for device charging, and drinking water is from a borehole.

Tuli Wilderness is set on a beautiful section of the Limpopo River, the banks sporting venerable nyalas and magnificent sycamore figs. From Serolo Safari Camp, there are game drives all year and walks in the drier winter months from April to October, which is the time when the night sky is at its sharpest. It's fantastic walking country, with sandstone outcrops, similar to those in the Mapungubwe National Park, which make for dramatic photogenic terrain. A popular destination is the Mmamagwa Ruins complex, which is of the same historical period as the ruins at Mapungubwe, and the reserve has San rock art to discover.

There are a number of ways to walk here. The simplest is to just stay at Serolo, which is great value, its prices more akin to South Africa than Botswana. It has a relaxed air and is the family home of the owners, Julie and Stuart Quinn. From

Simion Kolobe guiding with Francois du Toit at Mashatu.

EcoTraining trails guide trainees pause to watch elephants in the Limpopo River during a walk in Tuli.

here, walk the riverine woodlands along the levee near the camp, where there are always elephant around, and perhaps lion or leopard. Alternatively, drive out for a different experience – the easy climb to Eagle Rock is recommended. The summit is a vantage point to overlook the Motloutse River and a major movement route of the resident elephant herds.

There are a couple of other accommodation options that are designed for group bookings. Mohave Camp is an unfenced permanent camp used only for walking trails, while the Eagle View Star Deck camp has a sleep-out deck which provides an even wilder close-to-nature experience. Using a vehicle for part of the journey, it's easy for a group to link the camps and enjoy a three- or four-night walking safari, mixed with time in a game viewing vehicle. Tuli Wilderness is accessed by road via the Platjan Drift crossing, where the Limpopo is bridged and crossable by car all year. It's also accessible via Pont Drift, but a high ground clearance vehicle is needed. The total journey time from Gauteng is around six and a half to seven hours.

South-west of Northern Tuli Game Reserve, **Tswehe Wildlife Reserve** is an 11,000 ha private reserve with an attractive mix of riverine woodlands and mopane *veld* studded with sandstone koppies. Tswehe has a strong sustainability ethos, with low energy usage and zero waste disposal on site. It's a place for escape and quiet immersion in nature – yoga and wilderness retreats are offered alongside bush drives and walks. The northern part of the reserve is a designated wilderness zone that includes Bushman paintings, limited vehicle access and freedom to explore on foot. In the south, Tswehe Hill is the highest peak in central Tuli and grants 360-degree views. There's fine shady walking amid the woodlands of the Limpopo embankment, a place to encounter elephants on their daily watering wanders.

The main camp is Lone Tree Wilderness Camp, which has five tents sleeping a maximum of ten. It's set under

Ghosts of Tuli

It was the middle of October, a time when the midday thermometer nudges 40 C in the Kalahari fringe lands. It was easy to picture a group of early humans taking shade in this overhang, retelling the tale of the morning hunt; passing comment on the ochre rock art, some faded, some fresh – perhaps made by themselves. Today, the cave has only ghosts and the scattered debris of hyena feasts. Knowing the hammer heat that would drop, Jou Mazebedi and I had started early, and it took less than an hour to ascend Eagle Rock. It's a gentle climb from the south, which broadens into a rocky amphitheatre before the summit, from where cliffs drop 300 m to the Motloutse River.

From the cave, we walked onwards, thinking about the barefoot steps of those who passed here before. Even at the top, where vegetation is thin, Jou guided warily – it's not unheard of to find elephant up here. A breeze pushed over the lip of the cliff and raptors rode its wave. At our level, a pair of African hawk-eagles and a brown-headed snake eagle. Higher, the distinctive wedge tail of a bateleur. It was clear why Eagle Rock is so called and why it's a popular walk for guests at Tuli Wilderness. For tens of thousands of years, surely humans have sat here on the textured granite. When homo sapiens started to migrate from Africa, 100,000 years ago, their total numbers were tiny, certainly less than a million, and vastly outnumbered by elephant, by rhino, by everything. What did they see from here?

I liked to imagine they saw what I could see now. A family of elephants browsed in the mopane woodlands beyond the river, half-hidden in foliage. Led by the matriarch, they started to emerge and lumbered one by one onto the wide sandy riverbed. She ignored the stagnant pool below our cliffs and instead picked a spot in the sand and started swinging a foreleg, excavating a deep hole. Another of the adults did the same as the youngsters watched. It was quick work – in five minutes there were two small pools of filtered water to share.

As the elephants drank, five kudus approached below in single file. They were skittish, taking a few steps, stopping, then a few more. They stared up towards us. 'They're not looking at us', said Jou. 'I think there's a leopard on the cliff below.' The kudu warily stepped staccato to the pool to drink. For observers in the past, this might have been the time to start plotting an ambush. For us, it was time to return, as there was little shade on the mountain.

We meandered down the way we'd come. Compared with the action in the river valley, this side of the mountain was church quiet. A pair of bat-eared foxes scampered away – when they stopped to look back, their camouflage was perfect. Jou pointed out interesting bushes and trees in passing, their names evocative, a poetry of the bushveld. Thorny cluster-leaf – also called purple-pod cluster-leaf; zebra-barked corkwood, its rough black stripes oozing resin; rock figs, both large-leaved and red-leaved; brown ivory; small knobwood; sjambok pod; sickle bush and sesame bush and aromatic wild sage. He was still reciting when we reached the vehicle.

That afternoon, we walked from Serolo Camp. The nyala and sycamore fig trees here on the bank of the Limpopo are monumental, full of life-giving fruits and seedpods, habitat for countless insects and epiphytes, bats and birds.

We watched a troop of baboons moving through ana trees, synchronised with impala below, who were eating the discarded fruit pods. The Limpopo levees are a dendrophile's heaven, with a completely different species set to those on this morning's mountainside. Large fever berry, leadwood, weeping boer-bean: all known to our ancestors, who had an intimate familiarity with each. Which would make the best digging stick or supply the wood for a bow, which had fruits to eat in times of drought. Skills and memories kept alive by today's trails guides.

Speaking of being kept alive, that evening's campfire tales were salutary. I sat with the owners of Tuli Wilderness, Stuart and Julie Quinn. Since a childhood tramping in the bushveld of Natal, Stuart has an affinity with wilderness walking, but over the decades has had close calls that have highlighted the risks of sharing space with wildlife and sharpened his survival instincts. He does not sleep out under the stars in Tuli any more – too many lions – and his love for elephants was surely tested to the limit when he crossed paths with a breeding herd on top of Eagle Rock a number of years ago. It was one of those rare unexpected close encounters, a situation made dangerous by sudden proximity and because the animals felt they had no escape route. Badly tusked through the chest, it was a miracle that he lived to tell the tale.

From the terrace of Tuli Wilderness, there's a view of a waterhole on a small shelf that floods if the river is high. Beyond lies the sandy bed of the river, punctuated by still pools in the dry season. The other bank is in South Africa, from where I had travelled. Long before European colonisation, as noted in the works of anthropologist Thomas Huffman, rivers marked boundaries between tribes and kingdoms, but the Kingdom of Mapungubwe was an exception – it spanned the Limpopo and Shashe Rivers. Stone ruins dating to the Iron Age are found on walks in the area, which is now protected in one of Africa's huge TFCAs, centred

a huge nyala tree in the heart of the reserve and has a swimming pool and photo hide nearby. Most guests self-cater, but fully inclusive is available too. A new trails camp overlooking the Limpopo and set beneath ancient riverine trees is being planned. The focus here will be on multi-day guided walking trails exploring the numerous koppies and stunning river scenery. Tswehe is best accessed by road, crossing via the Platjan border post. It's five hours from Gauteng and a high ground clearance vehicle is required for the last section.

The Waterberg, Pilanesberg and Madikwe

North-west of Johannesburg there are large expanses of conserved land, most of it in private hands. Easily accessible for residents of the major cities of Gauteng province – Johannesburg and Pretoria – the malaria-free reserves are popular destinations for either hunting or photographic safaris. In the latter category, there are a few standout reserves that attract international visitors and have walks available. There are no multi-day walking safaris in these reserves, but a decent selection of lodges and camps with guided walks.

In the dry season, the Limpopo River is reduced to pools.

on the Mapungubwe UNESCO World Heritage Site.

Ancient African kingdoms, rock art on Eagle Rock – it's all a reminder that humans are a long-established and natural part of this landscape in Southern Africa. When we walk here, sharing ancient elephant paths, trailing kudu and dodging lion, we walk with the ghosts of people who lived at a time when the human population had little impact on other forms of life. Now that we are billions strong, it's vital that we preserve space for nature to thrive.

Waterberg lodge walks

The Waterberg region, located in the west of Limpopo Province, is one of South Africa's most scenic regions, a landscape of escarpments overlooking sandveld, sourveld and wetlands. In 2001, the Waterberg was designated a UNESCO Biosphere Reserve, with a core area of over 2,590 sq. km and a buffer zone of 4,800 sq. km.

Marakele National Park is in the south-west of the Waterberg massif, three hours from Johannesburg. Managed by **SANParks**, it was established as a national park in 1994 and has since grown to over 67,000 ha. The landscape is dramatic, with bushveld plains backed by sandstone peaks of over 2,000 m. As well as elephants, Marakele Park's big game includes black and white rhino, buffalo, giraffe and lion. It's a good place to spot many species of mountain-loving antelope, including klipspringer, mountain reedbuck and grey rhebok. The rich birdlife includes a large colony of Cape vultures. Lit by a rising sun, Marakele's sandstone cliffs present a stunning backdrop to guided morning walks led by SANParks staff all year. These should be booked in advance of arrival, and guests rendezvous with the guides at the park gate. A variety of starting points are possible: it's usual to drive from the camp reception area to the eastern sector of the park where the elephant, rhino and buffalo roam. There, the bushveld is dense and dominated by small-leafed thorny species, and it's important that the walking group stays compact. As the land rises, the predominant vegetation type is Waterberg moist mountain bushveld. Where possible, the trails explore sandy watercourses amid stands of fig trees, ironwood and waterberry. Overhead there's invariably the silhouette of a Cape vulture or other raptor, with 44 species recorded in the park. SANParks runs accommodation at Bontle Rest Camp and Tlopi Tented Camp; both camps are suited to self-catering, and there's no shop or restaurant in the park.

There are two high-end lodges operated by the exclusive MORE Family Collection group in the **Marataba** private concession, a 23,000 ha contractual park that comprises the northern third of Marakele National Park. From the lodges, walks of one and a half to two hours are possible every day after breakfast. The maximum group size is usually six, but can be eight if the planned route is not too challenging. Walks are available to overnight guests only and should be requested at the time of booking. The walks make the most of the contrasting terrains in Marakele Park. Some stay low, tracking rivers and waterholes, while others penetrate the mountains in narrow gorges, with the reward of finding a pool for a cooling dip. There are sites of historic interest in the trails area, including San cave art, Stone Age artefacts and Iron Age ruins. The group meets at either of the lodges for transfer by game-viewing vehicle to walk starting points. Water and snacks are provided, and there are day packs to borrow if guests need these.

North of Marakele, much of the Waterberg Biosphere is conserved in privately owned lands, including **Welgevonden Game Reserve**, which shares a boundary with the park. Along with **Entabeni Safari Conservancy** and **Shambala Private Game Reserve** to the east, it has a wildlife population that includes elephant, rhino, giraffe, zebra, lion, wildebeest, hippo and many species of antelope. All three of these reserves contain private lodges with trails guides, and walks are available on request. **Lapalala Wilderness** is a 48,000 ha reserve known for its roan antelope and black rhino conservation. Operated by not-for-profit safari company Lepogo Lodges, there are two properties on the reserve, Noka Camp and the exclusive-use Melote House. Guests here can explore the hilly forested landscape on foot, seeking out not just wildlife but Bushman rock art too.

Pilanesberg lodge walks

An enormous volcanic eruption 1.3 million years ago gave North West Province its star safari destination, and a place with excellent wilderness walking. The circular shape of Pilanesberg National Park is a remnant of that seismic event, a series of heavily eroded concentric rocky circles rising some 1,500 m above the surrounding flat landscape. Since its proclamation as a reserve in 1979, a thriving and diverse ecosystem has developed, and it has become a popular wildlife tourism destination thanks in large part to its proximity for residents of Gauteng: it's just over two hours to the park's Bakubung gate from Pretoria. Its rugged jumble of hills and narrow valleys make it interesting terrain for walking, and for a big chunk of the South African population, Pilanesberg's proximity makes it one of the few places to pack a couple of guided trails into a weekend.

The reserve is smaller and busier than Marakele National Park and is in the transition zone from the arid Kalahari desert to the greener bushveld of the Waterberg. Walking here is an opportunity to learn why the area is special, and how its volcanic geology and terrain influence the flora and fauna present. The park contains a wide range of Southern African wildlife, including lion and cheetah, elephant, rhino, hippo, buffalo, African wild dog, hyena and prolific birdlife.

Pilanesberg is referred to as a national park, but that's for historical reasons, and it does not actually have that status. It's owned and managed by the North West Parks and Tourism Board, and unlike SANParks, the board does not operate camps or take bookings directly. Instead, there are lodges run by private concessions within the park, while the large Sun City Resort is adjacent, with other resorts on the fringes. It's possible to stay outside the park and drive in to take a walk. Walks are available all year in Pilanesberg and are more comfortable in the cooler season from April to September. Walking is not a major activity, but as the reserve allows self-drive, wildlife sightings can be busy, so walks offer a pleasant alternative.

The north-west 130 sq. km quadrant of the park is a protected wilderness zone with no vehicle access, so this provides the best walking and can be accessed from the adjacent Black Rhino Game Reserve. This private reserve is integrated into the north-west of Pilanesberg – no fences – and yes, its sweet veld vegetation is perfect for the browsing habits of the black rhino. There's also white rhino, elephant, buffalo, big cats and many other species to be encountered here. For Black Rhino Reserve guests, walks are guided both in the reserve and in Pilanesberg's wilderness zone by **Nare Walking Safaris**.

An alternative to Nare Walking Safaris is to stay at one of the lodges within Pilanesberg and take dawn walks. The three **Legacy Hotels** bush lodges in the reserve have qualified trails guides on their staff and run dawn walks of three to five hours. Walks are provided at an additional fee and a breakfast pack is included, with sandwiches, fruit, chocolate, juice and water. The walks operate throughout the year unless conditions are not suitable, such as in case of rain or when long grass increases the risks. One guide is used for groups of up to four, and two guides if there are more guests. Guide Bennet de Klerk began his guiding career in Pilanesberg with Legacy Hotels and has over three decades of experience of walking in the park. His company **Motsumi Bush Courses** brings guests for overnighting walks in Pilanesberg and runs a fascinating Bush Enthusiast seven-day course (see page 52).

Madikwe lodge walks

Pilanesberg is a volcanic anomaly, and the rest of North West Province is quite flat. Towards the Botswana border, the land becomes increasingly arid, before morphing into sandveld and eventually the Kalahari desert. Madikwe Game Reserve is a large reserve that hugs the border on the South Africa side near the Kopfontein frontier post. Ideally it should be connected to Pilanesberg via a conservation corridor, but plans to do that have been frustrated by mining interests.

In the three decades since the reserve was established, the transformation from 70,000 ha of degraded ranch lands to one of South Africa's prime conservation zones has been gratifying to witness. Visitors can expect to see the full range of savannah wildlife, which includes an elephant population of around 1,000, black and white rhino, African wild dog and all the cats. Over 340 species of birds are recorded. Madikwe is a malaria-free reserve. As stipulated by the park's owner, the North West Parks Board, 16 is the minimum age for walks.

The northern half of the reserve is flatter, dominated by acacias, while the south has bushwillow species and is more rugged. The southern boundary is delineated by the Dwarsberg range, which peaks at 1,228 m, and its cliffs, caves and mountain bushveld provide photogenic walking terrain. There are 200 m inselbergs in the north-west, home to splendid large-leaved rock figs, and these are interesting destinations for walks. Unlike in Pilanesberg, self-drive is not permitted, other than to access a lodge. It's not a budget destination, and there are no wilderness trails camps or backpacking trails in Madikwe, but several lodges have morning or afternoon walks.

Located in the east of the reserve, not far from the perennial Madikwe River, **Molori Safari** is an ultra-luxury lodge, part of the Rora Private Collection. Its guides are highly trained and that includes trails qualifications – which means that guests are not confined to vehicles and can jump down during a game drive to track an animal or appreciate particular landscape features, such as water-eroded dolomitic tufa formations. Short walks are feasible all year, but the best conditions for longer outings are found in the cooler mornings of April to September. If there are more than six guests, two guides go along. A typical walk can last anything from one to four hours, with plenty of interesting stops along the way. Flexibility is the keyword when walk planning, with allowance made for weather conditions, fitness levels and any special guest interests. It's possible to simply set out from the lodge, but more usual to drive to a particular area. Guests just need to carry water and binoculars and can take a breakfast snack prepared by the lodge in a backpack or avail themselves of a full bush breakfast cooked in the wilds – a highly recommended experience.

Kalahari borderland reserves

The south-west of Africa has its climate dictated by the chill currents of the southern Atlantic, which cool the air above the ocean and starve the land of rainfall. The names of the resulting deserts are evocative of adventurous travel: thanks to classic books and nature documentaries we know that the Namib and Kalahari are havens for wildlife that has learned to live in arid conditions. Humans too adapted to these lands a very long time ago, and owing to a climate ill-suited to agriculture, retained a hunter-gather lifestyle into the modern era.

Madikwe Game Reserve suggests a flavour of the terrain and walking conditions characteristic of the South Africa/Botswana frontier. Going west, it's an increasingly barren landscape with little by way of flowing rivers all the way to the Namibian border. The wildlife is better adapted than we present day humans, and the year-round high temperatures can make walks challenging, but cool mornings in the winter months make fascinating explorations feasible in expansive and remote sandveld reserves: !Khamab Kalahari, Tswalu Kalahari Reserve and the Kgalagadi National Park.

Kalahari Primitive Trail

Even a resident of South Africa would have difficulty finding !Khamab Kalahari Reserve on a map, and some would be challenged by the name: the '!' of !Khamab indicates the alveolar click sound common in the Khoisan languages. It abuts the Molopo River that defines the Botswanan border of North West Province and is a very chunky reserve – at 95,000 ha, it's bigger than Madikwe, and one of the largest conserved areas in South Africa. The best thing about the reserve is that there's almost nothing there, with just one pricey exclusive-use eight-bed lodge.

In other words, it's the perfect location for the sort of adventurous self-sufficient trails operated by **Lowveld Trails Co.** (see page 72), who run their Kalahari Primitive Trail here in April and May each year. Participants need to be self-sufficient, and that includes finding their own way to the reserve by road; it's a seven-hour drive from Johannesburg.

Led by the Lowveld Trails Co. guides, who are some of South Africa's best, the trails usually run for three or six nights. There are no set routes or distances to cover: the group simply makes a walking plan on the fly, picking good spots for a break or a siesta, or to sleep-out for the night. The landscape is arid and there are no flowing rivers. A series of calcrete pans mark the route of a paleo river, when the Molopo flowed through the area before changing course 2–5 million years ago. These fill with water in the rainy season and usually hold water for a few months, and this is why the trails run in autumn. These pans attract hordes of plains antelope – eland, gemsbok and springbok – and their predators. Trails groups often run into the large black maned lions that seek out the herds, and brown hyena might be found (much rarer than the common spotted hyena).

The landscape does not have the red dunes characteristic of the Kgalagadi Transfrontier Park to the west, but shares much of its flora and fauna. Even though it's an arid savannah zone, there's good plant cover and it isn't short of shepherd's

An evening rain shower passes through in !Khamab Kalahari Reserve.

trees that offer a shady resting spot. Otherwise, there are camelthorn trees, shrubs such as raisin and puzzle bush and plains covered by bushman's grass. The Kalahari Primitive Trail is open to group bookings, with the same rate for any size group up to the maximum of eight. Booking well in advance is advised, as this is a very rare experience in Africa, with a small number of departures.

Kalahari lodge walks

Northern Cape is South Africa's biggest province by area and smallest by population. As well as endless *karooveld*, it has some of the country's finest national parks, known for their splendid flora. While the walking is good, they don't generally count as walking safari territory, owing to the absence of big game. Of course, walking safaris are not just about the high-profile animals, and a couple of reserves deserve to be included on the basis of their fascinating guided walks.

Kgalagadi National Park and Tswalu Kalahari Reserve are both in the arid north of the province. Here, it's dry all year, with rain most likely in summer, falling in occasional thunderstorms. The climate is not conducive to intensive or multi-day walks, but early morning temperatures are fine for the sort of walks available. Late March to early May is an ideal time to visit, when the heat has eased and any rainfall has quickly translated into greening of the grasslands and blooming of the desert flowers. The mid-winter months from June to August are cold at night, and even frosty. September and October are also good months to visit, with the weather warming and clear, starry nights.

North of the Orange River, **Tswalu Kalahari Reserve** is the largest privately owned reserve in South Africa, conserving 114,000 ha of arid savannah. Tswalu is a conservation project supported by nature-based tourism, with sustainability at its core. By visiting, guests contribute towards Tswalu's regenerative vision to leave the world better than it was found, ensuring that vital habitat is restored so that biodiversity can once again flourish.

This area, on the southern fringe of the Kalahari desert, is the habitat for black-maned lions, black rhino, oryx and African wild dog, and is a rewarding birding destination. Guests can join expert trackers to follow the spoor of brown hyena, aardvark and cheetah, or go on foot to approach a colony of habituated meerkat. Human history is an important part of the story here, and several interesting petroglyph sites can be explored. Tswalu has three high-end safari camps, and with a maximum of 40 guests in the vast reserve, it has the lowest guest-to-land ratio in any privately protected area in South Africa.

North of Tswalu, the even vaster Kgalagadi Transfrontier Park protects 35,551 sq. km of land, most of it in Botswana. It was the first established of Africa's cross-border 'peace parks' and is the only one so far that has achieved the goal of allowing visitors to move freely across the frontier as they explore. The South African side of the park is run by SANParks; it has a wealth of wildlife that includes herds of springbok and gemsbok, lion, hyena and cheetah. The Kalahari desert is a place apart, a treeless landscape famous for big cat sightings, sometimes at close quarters in the unfenced camps. The park is wonderfully remote, with the entrance gate almost three hours' drive from Upington. It's hot and exposed, and best suited to a leisurely exploration by 4x4, but there's one venue with the chance to explore on foot amid the grassy dunes where there's a rich diversity of desert plant life, birds, insects and rodents to be found.

Mans Maasdorp guiding on the dunes near !Xaus Lodge in Kgalagadi National Park.

!Xaus Lodge is on the south-west boundary of the park, a three-hour drive from the park entrance and main rest camp at Twee Rivieren. Access is strictly by 4x4 – a one-way system precludes collisions on the rollercoaster of dunes. Alternatively, guests can be met and transferred from Kamqua Picnic Site to the lodge, leaving their vehicle in a discreet shelter. This private concession is owned by the local Khomani San community and managed on their behalf by a not-for-profit company. The San guides speak English and Afrikaans as well as their own language. The walks provide an opportunity to learn from descendants of Africa's earliest inhabitants, who have a continuous history of survival in one of the earth's harshest terrains.

Walks don't cover long distances, and the emphasis is on ethnobotany, smaller fauna and traditional lore. Almost every plant has a craft, cultural, food or medicinal use for the San. Walks can be taken at dawn or before sunset and are included in the overnight fees. While staying at !Xaus Lodge, a night drive is highly recommended: guests are likely to spot African wild cat, hyena, bat-eared fox, spring hare and spotted eagle owl.

A lion's roar west of !Xaus, a rickety fence delineates a 400 km arrow-straight section of South Africa's border with Africa's emptiest land – Namibia.

5 Namibia

Namibia has the lowest population density in Africa and is one of the driest countries on the planet, with few perennial rivers. Combined with high temperatures, it doesn't sound like a place much suited to safaris, much less walking safaris. On the contrary, the Namibian wilderness supports a remarkable range of wildlife from dew-drinking beetles to handsome gemsbok and desert-adapted elephant and lion. And in the cool morning conditions, going on foot is a great way to appreciate its ecosystems: guided walks are available at the most interesting locations in Sossusvlei, Damaraland, Skeleton Coast Park and near Etosha.

The Kalahari and Namib deserts are year-round walking destinations with a big daily temperature range. While nights in winter from June to September are downright cold, the mornings provide perfect conditions to be out on foot. Summer months bring the possibility of rainfall, and if there's a sufficiency then the desert plains are transformed into lush grassland and any pools of water are instantly full of life. It's greenest from November to April, and April and May are probably the nicest walking months, with the plains attracting grazing gemsbok and springbok, and the temperatures comfortable.

Walking safaris in Namibia

The iconic image of Namibia is that of a gemsbok on the move below the sweeping red dunes of the Namib Sand Sea. But that would be a misleading impression of the country. The dune systems are spectacular, but just one element of a country of splendid landscapes from the Fish River Gorge in the south to the Etosha pans in the north. It's rare to walk on loose sand, with ancient rock more usual underfoot.

It's fair to say that walking safaris are a bit different here than in other countries in this guide. They are mostly lodge based, with just a couple of dedicated trails camps. Risks associated with dangerous game encounters are very low and the only walking area with buffalo present is the Caprivi Strip. If appropriate, guides may carry a rifle, but in some areas, visibility is such that encounters and wildlife viewing are conducted at a safe distance and a firearm is not needed. Apart from the stunning landscapes, the long human history in this part of Africa is of interest, and guided walks with San guides are especially rewarding. These focus on ethnobotany and rock art as well as the natural world.

Professionally guided walks are available in a number of reserves. The prime walking specialist choices are Etendeka Walking Trails in the Kaokoveld and Onguma Private Nature Reserve near Etosha National Park. Apart from these, a number of high-end lodges offer guided walks. The best way to plan a walking visit is to contact the properties listed here directly.

A sundowner at the end of a walking day in the Kaokoveld.

Sossusvlei

The sole natural UNESCO World Heritage Site in Namibia is the Namib Sand Sea, a gigantic dune system that spans the entire coastline of the country. Its only water source is the fog that originates in the chill waters of the South Atlantic's Benguela Current. When the air temperature and wind directions are suited, this moisture drifts inland and is ingeniously syphoned by plants and insects and a bewildering plethora of endemic species. Welwitschia plants and quiver trees are distinctively adapted to conditions in the Namib and can be appreciated on walks. The shifting dunes, which have formed over millions of years and are tinted red by iron ore, can reach to 300 m in height and are a photographer's dream. With luck, some springbok or gemsbok will wander into the viewfinder to give them scale.

The Namib Sand Sea is protected in several enormous national parks and private reserves, including the 50,000 sq. km Namib-Naukluft National Park. Adjacent to that park is the NamibRand Nature Reserve, which at 2,000 sq. km is one of the largest private conservancies in Africa. It's to the south of the famous Sossusvlei and Deadvlei areas, and shares a similar landscape of huge red dunes, gravel plains and rocky mountains.

While this landscape is the star attraction, visitors to the reserve may encounter oryx, springbok, giraffe, Hartmann's mountain zebra, bat-eared fox and a diversity of bird species. Nocturnal wildlife viewing is excellent, and guided night drives present the chance to spot creatures such as aardvarks and desert rodents. Nature walks focus on the desert ecology, and there's no potentially dangerous game present. The reserve is part of the International Dark Sky Association, emphasising the importance of minimal light pollution, and the clear desert skies make NamibRand an excellent destination for star gazing; some lodges within the reserve run astronomy programmes and night sky excursions.

Natural Selection has 26 lodges in Namibia, Botswana and South Africa, and their lodge in the NamibRand Nature Reserve is Kwessi Dunes. It has 12 canvas and thatch chalets, each of which has a separate 'star gazing' room, completely open to the sky – the perfect spot from which to watch the nocturnal celestial show. Kwessi Dunes offers a full menu of activities from quad biking to hot air ballooning, horse riding, guided walks, scenic drives and morning excursions to Sossusvlei, where guests can hike Dune 45, or 'Big Daddy', which takes about two hours to ascend.

Bordering NamibRand to the north are further conservancies with venues that guide walks. Camp Sossus is east of the C19 road in the Namib Tsaris Reserve and is one of the **Ultimate Safaris** company collection. Six shaded and naturally cooled tents feature open-air en-suite bathrooms with flush toilets and hot bucket showers. The solar-powered camp is a base for trips to Sossusvlei and desert swimming pools, biking and walks. In Kulala Wilderness Reserve, close to Sossusvlei, Little Kulala is a comfortable lodge operated by **Wilderness**, from where dawn walks explore the Tsauchab River Trail.

Little Kulala guests on the Tsauchab River Trail.

Celestial Stories
Sivuyile Manxoyi

Dark skies have always served as a source of admiration and wonder for all peoples of the world. The beauty, brilliance and effulgence of the celestial objects not only have an aesthetic value but are also a fundamental part of culture and continue to have a utilitarian and practical contribution to the sustainability of life on our planet, Earth. Most safari guides are trained in celestial Greco-Roman nomenclature. It can be forgotten that indigenous African people have had a deep and profound relationship with the sky and the stars, and that they utilised them for the development of calendars, migration, navigation, storytelling, recreation, hunting, time-setting, naming of children and regulation of ceremonies, among much else.

Venus (second closest planet to the Sun and the hottest in the solar system), being the brightest object in the sky, not only mesmerised the Western World but has also been appreciated and utilised by Southern African people. In the morning skies (before sunrise), the Nguni-speaking people (isiXhosa, isiZulu, siSwati, isiNdebele) call Venus iKhwezi, while the Sesotho, Setswana and Sepedi-speaking people named the planet Mphatlalatsana. Both names denote and emphasise the brightness and radiance of Venus in the early hours of the morning. After sunset, Venus is called uCel' izapholo ('he who begs for milk'). This is based on the fact that in rural communities, boys who fed the cattle after grazing usually milked the cows directly into their mouths, and Venus shining brightly after sunset is seen as begging for milk. Even in other African traditions, the names of Venus in the west have a similar meaning and interpretation as in isiZulu – Venus is seen as uSiCelankobe, in Sesotho/Setswana and Sepedi it is Kopadilalelo, in Xitsonga it is Likwela mkombe and in TshiVenda it is called Khumela tshilalelo – all these names link Venus to begging for food, as Venus was and continues to be used as a signifier for food preparation. In isiXhosa culture, Venus is also called uMadingeni ('dating star'), as for young lovers the appearance of Venus after sunset signified the time to meet near the river banks.

The ancient people used to refer to planets as wandering stars as they appear to be moving against the background of all other stars. You can simply observe planets by the fact that they do not 'twinkle' like stars. Some people tend to think one cannot see the planets with the naked eye. The opposite is true: one can observe the first five planets even without a telescope or binoculars.

The appearance of Venus before sunrise is associated with diligence and industriousness in African culture. In the Nguni tradition, children are also named Khwezi, Kwezilomso and NomaKhwezi. Newly married women are named after Venus as NomaKhwezi, the motivation and the hope being that they will follow the planet and be diligent. The Nama, Khoekhoe, Gqunukhwebe and Gqunuqwa people used the appearance of Venus as a marker for commencing their journeys or hunting expeditions.

The African people appreciated clusters of stars. The Pleiades, colloquially known as 'The seven princes,' 'The seven sisters' or 'The seven daughters', are one such cluster. This open cluster consisting of more than 1,000 bright young stars is

In San lore, the constellations of Taurus and Orion tell the tale of the unskilled hunter Aldebaran.

In the Tswana/Sotho and Pedi culture, the first person to see Canopus would go up a mountain and blow a horn. They were usually rewarded by an offering of a sheep by the chief or king.

The bright stars of the pointers and the Southern Cross were often seen as giraffes, while the /Xam tell the story of a young girl who threw ashes and coal into the sky, making the stars and the Milky Way.

In several African cultures, the Pleiades are associated with either the planting or the harvesting season. Some BaTswana groups believe that the sun is eaten each day by a crocodile, and that it emerges from the crocodile every morning.

known as isiLimela in isiXhosa, isiZulu, isiNdebele, and siSwati, as Selemela in Sesotho, Setswana, and Sepedi, as Shirimela in Xitsonga, as Tshilimela in TshiVenda, as Chirimera in Karanga and Shona of Zimbabwe, as Limela in Nyasa and as Cilimela in Gogo of Tanzania. 'Ukulima' means to plant, and the Pleiades are associated with either the planting or the harvesting season. In the Nguni and in particular in the isiXhosa culture, they are also used to count the years of manhood. Boys at a certain age are required to undergo rituals of initiation either in the bush or on a mountain. Traditionally, this initiation usually takes place during the month of June, and in isiXhosa the month of June is called 'eyeSilimela'

Kunene Region

The homeland of the Damara people in north-western Namibia is renowned for its rugged landscapes and desert-adapted wildlife. The area is characterised by vast, rocky plains, towering mountains and deep canyons, with the Brandberg Mountain, the highest peak in Namibia, dominating the skyline in the south. It's a land with a fascinating diversity of wildlife that includes elephant, black rhino and giraffe that endure in low numbers in an arid habitat. It's the pre-eminent destination ('the month of isiLimela or the Pleiades'). The boys usually celebrate their last days of boyhood (or mourn their last boyhood days) during the month of May, and this is called 'ukutshitsha': Boys go around their villages or townships singing and dancing, signifying their readiness to go to the bush or mountain for their initiation ceremony.

In the Southern African cultures, the month of May is linked to Canopus, the second brightest star in the night sky. In isiXhosa it is called uCanzibe, in isiZulu it is called uCwazibe, in Sesotho, Setswana, and Sepedi it is called Naka and in TshiVenda and Lobedu it is called Nanga. The appearance of this star in May heralds the beginning of winter. In the olden days, in the Tswana/Sotho and Pedi culture, the first person to see this star would go up a mountain and blow a horn. They were usually rewarded by an offering of a sheep by the chief or king. So both the Pleiades and Canopus were closely monitored and observed.

Sirius, the brightest star in the night sky, was given names acknowledging its dazzling brightness. In isiXhosa it is called Qhawe or iNgqaqhawuli (meaning the victor/hero and champion). Other cultures recognised its brightness and dominance of the night sky as well, hence the names Kogagamasigo (Setswana), Kogagamashego (Sesotho) and Khohamustho (TshiVenda).

The Southern African traditions not only acknowledge individual planets, star clusters and individual stars but recognise the constellations. When viewing the constellations Orion and Taurus, the Nama people tell a beautiful story of a hapless hunter (the star Aldebaran) who had seven wives (the Pleiades) and was asked to shoot the three zebras (Orion's belt). However, he missed the zebras and his arrow (Orion's sword) got stuck. He was afraid to collect his arrow because of the raging lion (the star Betelgeuse).

Looking at the majestic Milky Way, the |Xam tell the story of a young girl who threw ashes and coal into the sky, making the stars and the Milky Way we now see in the sky.

As shown by these names and stories, in previous times all people could enjoy a dazzling night sky. In our modern cities, this splendour has been lost to unnecessary light pollution, which not only denies us the opportunity to appreciate the beauty of the night's celestial wonders, but also adversely affects certain animals and birds and has a negative impact on human health. As we walk in the night or early morning, let us look up and observe the stars, planets, the Milky Way, meteors and comets. Let us preserve the sky and its celestial jewels for future generations.

SIVUYILE MANXOYI manages the Southern African Large Telescope (SALT) Collateral Benefits Programme for the South African Astronomical Observatory.

for walking safaris in Namibia and as well as appreciating the landscapes and ecology visitors learn about the history and culture of the local communities. It was in this area, and Kaokoveld to the north, where Garth Owen-Smith pioneered the community-based conservation model that saved the endemic wildlife from extinction through recognition of the role and ownership of traditional custodians.

Etendeka Walking Trails

The Grootberg massif is a distinguishing geographic feature of the Kaokoveld, with its central mountain rising 600 m over the plains. The landscape here is marked by dramatic cliffs and the ephemeral Hoanib River. In the foothills of the Grootberg, the long-established **Etendeka Mountain Camp** is set in a 50,000 ha exclusive-use concession on state-owned land and has ten shaded en-suite Meru tents with outdoor suspended-bucket showers. The conservancy is one of the few places in Namibia to experience a multi-day professionally guided walking safari. From the lodge, guided hikes are run on the Etendeka plateau amid extensive basalt lava flows and flat topped mountains. Although seemingly inhospitable, the area is full of hidden life. The walks here are longer than the average lodge walk in Namibia, with ample time for interpretation and wildlife spotting in the care of well-trained guides.

For the full walking experience, **Etendeka Walking Trails** run overnight walks on the Etendeka Concession. These can be done as a two- or three-night walk, with the option to stay a night or two at the Etendeka Mountain Camp. Walkers on the trail sleep under the stars on raised platforms that have comfortable beds and bedrolls. The platforms feature shades that can be pulled over for an afternoon siesta and removed to reveal the starry sky at night. Each deck has its own bathroom with a toilet and basin and there are communal open-air bathrooms with bucket showers. Meals are cooked on an open fire.

The itinerary starts with a meet-up at Palmwag Lodge, which is on the Uniab River near the gate for Etendeka Concession. A driver collects bags for transfer to the first camp, River Camp, while guests start walking with their guide into the concession. It takes two to three hours to reach camp through a harsh but

Erwin Kasupi guiding on the Etendeka Walking Trail.

splendid rocky landscape, and there's time along the way to investigate the desert flora and keep an eye out for birdlife. The camp overlooks a waterhole next to an established wildlife trail. Although the experience is not built around game viewing, the location allows for safe sightings of animals including Hartmann's mountain zebra, oryx and steenbok, and, if you're extremely lucky, the rare desert-adapted elephant and black rhino.

On the second day, after a full cooked breakfast, it's time to set off again, carrying just day packs with water and snacks. The walk is longer this day, with 15–20 km to cover over six to seven hours, depending on the route taken. The aim is to reach Hill Camp by early afternoon for a late lunch and siesta. The camp has superb views and sits overhanging the cliffs on top of Crystal Mountain, named after the incredible show of crystal quartz and agate that sparkle against its ancient rocky outcrops. In the afternoon there's a short sundowner walk around the plateau.

For those choosing the two-night experience, the third day has either a short morning walk or transfer down to Etendeka Mountain Camp for an overnight or to drive back to Palmwag Lodge. Otherwise, to make it a three-nighter, spend the day on a five- to six-hour walk around Crystal Mountain and down into the valley below.

Damaraland lodge walks

Deep in Damaraland, Camp Doros is located on a high bank overlooking a sandy riverbed and groves of mopane trees. Like its sister Camp Sossus in NamibRand, Camp Doros is a 'wilderness-exploration retreat' operated by **Ultimate Safaris**. It's similar in scale and style, and walks are on the menu here. The 19,000 ha concession area has a number of natural springs providing water throughout the year for desert-adapted wildlife and is a prime area to track and spot black rhino on foot. With a longer stay, it's possible to drive in search of elephant and visit a rock engraving site.

Also in Damaraland to the north of Camp Doros, there are two comfortable **Wilderness** lodges. Wilderness Damaraland Camp is a pioneer of tourism in the north-west and an excellent base for exploring by vehicle and foot. Located in the Huab River Valley, it has dramatic views of mountains fading into the dust haze. A further 50 km north, the vast Palmwag Concession has an austere landscape that's yet rich in nature. Set in a wide valley in the north-west, Wilderness Desert Rhino Camp feels very remote. A very comfortable base for walking, it was completely rebuilt in 2024 and has six Meru-style tents and a main area that overlooks a sweeping plain dotted with Namibia's national plant, the welwitschia. Guided nature walks are encouraged as a way to really appreciate the desert ecology, while the highlight of a stay here is the chance to track rhino on foot. The population of desert-adapted black rhino in Damaraland is thriving, and guests can follow Save the Rhino Trust monitors by vehicle and on foot.

West of Damaraland, the desolate Skeleton Coast is the epitome of Namibian wilderness, a stark landscape rich in nature. The coast is swept by icy currents from the sub-Antarctic, and these give life to seals and cetaceans, while its shifting sandbanks and frequent fogs have brought disaster to countless ships. Despite its harsh conditions, the Skeleton Coast supports a unique ecosystem. Desert-adapted elephants, oryx, springbok and brown hyena are among the wildlife species that have learned to survive in this environment and Cape fur seals inhabit the coastal areas.

Skeleton Coast National Park is not a place to lend itself to long explorations on foot, but short walks in the rocky valleys between the dunes are rewarding. The sandy bed of the Hoanib River wends its way through hills that are bathed in morning mist from the Atlantic. Two remote camps in the valley run morning and afternoon nature walks: Hoanib Skeleton Coast Camp is a **Wilderness** camp, and Hoanib Valley Camp is part of the **Natural Selection** collection.

Etosha

The strongest magnet for wildlife tourism in northern Namibia is Etosha National Park, one of the most astonishing landscapes in Africa. While walking is not conducted in the park itself, it's possible in the Onguma Private Nature Reserve to the east of Etosha and in the Etosha Heights Private Reserve to the west.

There are six camps in the 35,000 ha **Onguma Private Nature Reserve**: Bush Camp, Tented Camp and Camp Kala are gathered around the three natural waterholes and The Fort is at close proximity. Forest Camp and Tamboti Campsite are situated to the south-east. The reserve has been restored from farming use, with a small area in the extreme north-east converted to the Oshivelo farming project to create jobs and help to curb poaching. All six camps guide walks departing at the break of dawn for two hours or so, and these are available all year, with a maximum of six guests led by a qualified armed guide. Most of the guides are Ovambos from Tsumeb or nearby Oshivelo village, some from Windhoek and others from as far as Caprivi Strip. Drinks and snacks are provided and it's best to request walks when booking accommodation.

In 2025, an eight-bed dedicated walking camp will open on the reserve. Set in a prime spot with larger trees for shading and in close proximity to the natural game paths animals follow to get to water, the Onguma Trails Camp offers three-night trails during the winter months from April to September, with guests spending as much time as they wish on foot. During the stay, the reserve's researchers and conservationists come to camp to give talks. The tents feature real beds and en-suite outdoor bathrooms with flush toilets and wood-fired hot tubs. A large communal tent provides shade for the dining area and for relaxing during the day. From the camp location it's likely to spot antelope, elephant and perhaps the elusive black rhino. A game-viewing vehicle at camp allows for a variation in the location of walks that explore the mixed landscape of arid plains, woodlands, riverbeds and shrubby thornveld. If there are more than six guests, a backup guide assists the lead guide. Self-drive guests can leave their vehicles at any of the fixed camps or at a secured parking zone close to the main entrance of Onguma Private Nature Reserve. From there, they are transferred to the walking camp by game-viewing vehicle, a journey of around 30 minutes.

Natural Selection operates two lodges in Etosha Heights Private Reserve, and both guide walks and game drives (including night drives). Safarihoek Lodge is an elegant lodge set on a hill, with 11 thatched chalets and a swimming pool with a view. Nearby, Etosha Mountain Lodge has nine chalets with similar views and amenities. Tracking black and white rhino is a big part of the attraction here.

Walkers in Onguma Private Nature Reserve encounter a relaxed lion.

Kwando River

Thanks to a quirk of colonial era mapmaking, Namibia has a long panhandle that stretches to the Chobe River and the Zambian border. Known as the Caprivi Strip, it runs along the Angolan border, an area where the wildlife suffered during the Angolan war, but since has made a strong recovery, and today the area is an important wildlife migration route. At its eastern extent, the ecosystem blends with that of the enormous Kwando and Chobe river systems of Botswana.

Two former reserves – Caprivi Game Park and Mahango Game Reserve – were combined to create Bwabwata National Park, which protects the section of the Kwando River that flows from Angola south through Namibia into Botswana. It's well off the beaten track, and most visitors are overland travellers moving between Chobe and Etosha national parks. There's at least one lodge along the Kwando that's worth a visit for those keen on a guided walk. **Nambwa Tented Lodge** is shaded by trees on the riverbank and has local guides who lead guests on walks in areas close to the lodge in the cooler morning conditions. Bwabwata has big game including lion, leopard, buffalo and elephant, and as the guides walk without rifles, animal approaches are avoided; indeed, if buffalo are in the area, walks are cancelled on safety grounds. There's a strong focus on ethnobotany, and walks stay on the eastern bank of the river; the opposite side is Botswana.

Downriver, on the Botswana side, are a number of lodges with walks – see page 153 for more on this area. A day's walk to the south – for an elephant – is one of the world's most special natural places, best explored on foot and by canoe: the Okavango Delta.

6 Botswana

Famous for blended walking and mekoro safaris in the waterways of the Okavango Delta, Botswana is a world-class wildlife tourism destination. In the vastness of that renowned seasonal Delta, there are myriad attractive lodges and camps that combine vehicle, boat and foot safaris, and there's a good selection of safari companies that specialise in walks from mobile camps, all based in the Maun area.

The best time for walking in Botswana corresponds with the peak time for wildlife viewing – the cooler drier months from June to October. In the Okavango Delta, the start of the season has the best conditions for safaris that skew to mekoro travel, and as water levels drop, game becomes concentrated and walking opportunities increase. Botswana has summer rains, which typically occur from December through to the end of March, and this is the time to avoid: conditions are likely to be too hot for longer walks, and in the Delta high water can make areas inaccessible.

Walking safaris in Botswana

As a general rule, walking in publicly owned reserves under the management of Botswana's Department of Wildlife and National Parks is not allowed, although there are exceptions, with non-rifle guided walks in Moremi Game Reserve run under a system of permits. But don't worry: there's plenty of land managed in private concessions, and walks are usually available as part of the daily activities.

While the Okavango is the eye-catching headline act, Botswana has other attractions. The Central Kalahari Game Reserve, Makgadikgadi Pans and Kgalagadi Transfrontier Park are magnificent arid wilderness parks – but not walking safari destinations. To the north of the delta, there's good walking in the less-visited Linyanti River system and Chobe National Park has walks from lodges in the buffer zone. Botswana's best kept secret is the Tuli Block at the junction of Botswana, Zimbabwe and South Africa, and good walking can be found there. This area is easier to access from South Africa and is covered in the section on the Greater Mapungubwe Transfrontier Conservation Area (see page 118).

The town of Maun is one of the major safari centres of Africa and the base for a number of companies that specialise in walks, and these are included in the Okavango section (page 143). As well as their own multi-day trips, they can arrange full itineraries, booking lodges and camps anywhere in the country and beyond. Maun is on the southern edge of the Okavango Delta and close to where most of the walking action happens. It's also the gateway to safaris in the expanses to the south – the Makgadikgadi Pans National Park and the Central Kalahari Game Reserve. These areas are better suited to motor safaris, but there are interesting opportunities to get on foot with the Khoisan, akin to the short walks that focus on ethnobotany in Kgalagadi Transfrontier Park. **Deception Valley Lodge** and the **Kwando Safaris** camps at Tau Pan and Nxai Pan are suitable venues to enjoy these.

A walking camp set in the southern Okavango Delta in November, late in dry season.

Okavango River Delta

Inscribed on the UNESCO world heritage list, the Okavango River Delta is one of the planet's great wetlands, a giant oasis that supports a wealth of wildlife – and a thriving tourism industry. It all hangs by a watery thread, the seasonal flow of the Okavango River from the highlands of south-east Angola. In the north, the Delta has permanent water, and in the flood season the wetland area more than doubles in size to around 7,700 sq. km. This annual cycle is vulnerable to manmade interventions in the form of potential damming and water extraction in Angola and Namibia, and the slow-motion catastrophe of climate change, and is becoming increasingly hard to predict.

Vast herds of red lechwe, elephant and buffalo are daily sightings in the delta. Giraffe, eland, lion, leopard and impala are common, and the Okavango protects endangered species such as the African wild dog and brown hyena. Criss-crossed by water channels formed by elephant and hippos, safaris here have a unique flavour, and the quintessential 'Delta experience' is to glide silently within scenting distance of the wildlife in a traditional dug-out mokoro (the singular of mekoro). This is what makes safaris in the Okavango so special. Instead of spending time bouncing on rutted tracks in diesel vehicles, visitors mix exploration by foot and water in a way that feels harmonious with nature. The degree of mix is dependent on the season and the location of the camp, and it's definitely a plus when walking safaris can include some mekoro time, as it adds a dimension – the ability to get close to animals without disturbing their natural behaviour. It's a dynamic system, and visitors should be prepared to adapt: when water levels are high there's more water travel, and when low more walking. In recent years, Botswana has suffered from a prolonged drought, which has had a severe impact on the wildlife. The terrain is flat, traversing grasslands and islands, making walks very accessible. It's not unusual to have to wade through water, so it's ideal to wear trail shoes or trainers that can be kept on, rather than heavy boots.

The Delta is a patchwork of reserves and concession areas, usually referred to as 'blocks'. The eastern part is protected in the community owned Moremi Game Reserve and managed by the Department of Wildlife and National Parks and permits walks without rifles. In other concession areas to the west, south and north of the core delta, rifle-guided walks are very much part of the experience. Camps are deliberately kept small in scale, and they host about 100,000 visitors a year. The size of the camps, and a policy of targeting low-volume high-revenue safaris, makes the Okavango the most expensive destination in this book. There are options other than staying at the fixed camps, and several specialist walk operators run trips from mobile tented camps; these are generally lower in cost than the fixed lodges.

Beagle Expeditions, David Foot Safaris, Endeavour Safaris, Okavango Walking Safaris and Walk Botswana all run multi-day walking trips in the Delta, using their own mobile camps. Ker & Downey Botswana have a dedicated trails camp, and a few lodges offer a fly-camping/walk combination including Moremi Crossing, Oddballs and Delta Camp. Not a safari camp, but of interest for a deeper dive into nature, Kwapa Camp is the base for the African Guide Academy.

Beagle Expeditions

Beagle Expeditions runs its Kweene Trails in a remote and wild corner of the Okavango Delta alongside the Kweene River. There, it operates a mobile tented camp that's set exclusively for each group of guests. The owners, Simon and Marleen Byron, have long experience of designing bespoke safaris in the Delta, and have settled on an attractive format that's supported by a well-established team of staff and guides.

The isolated location adjacent to the 'sandveld tongue' in the western Delta makes it most practical to access by helicopter. Once there, guests are in a world of their own and unlikely to encounter other visitors. The camp is relocated by vehicle and is first set along the southern section of the Kweene River. This area floods infrequently and has an aridity and palatable grass species that support large herds of grazers and the predators that follow them. The second camp is to the north in the Kweene River system at Magwegwe. This is a seasonal swamp habitat where the Kweene is inundated annually in the flood season. It has the quintessential Delta landscape of endless floodplains with well-wooded islands and year-round surface water drawing in an abundance of wildlife.

When moving between camps, a full day is spent in wilderness, travelling by a combination of vehicle, foot and mokoro. A picnic lunch and bush siesta is taken in the wilds. A lot of comforts are designed into the mobile camp, where bedrolls are laid out on padded carpets in large Meru tents. Each tent has a real bed and an en-suite bathroom with a bucket shower, a compost toilet and all the necessary amenities to ensure comfort and privacy. There's a common dining area and a carpeted relaxation corner scattered with cushions, while the campfire is the focus in the evenings and mornings.

David Foot Safaris

Born in Africa, David Foot has over 35 years of experience running safaris and conservation projects. After time working in Zambia and Malawi, he and his family are now based in Maun and run mobile safaris with a strong focus on walking and horseback riding in the community reserves of the Okavango Delta; they work closely with these communities and have a student sponsorship programme.

Walking safari guests are accommodated in a low-impact mobile camp that's comfortable and well equipped with walk-in tents and full bedding. The shower is under a tree and the toilet is a bush loo. The camp location is dependent on water levels and wildlife movements; when water levels are low, the group can walk from island to island and when water levels are higher, a mekoro flotilla is used. **David Foot Safaris** walking itineraries are ideal for those with an adventurous spirit, and many of the walks are led by David himself.

The company presents fixed date departures throughout the year. The maximum group size is six and three nights would be the standard duration, but it's possible to extend the itinerary for up to a week, in which case the camp is taken down for transfer to a new location.

David Foot guiding walkers in the southern area of the Okavango Delta.

Endeavour Safaris

Endeavour Safaris operates walking safaris in the western, central and eastern Okavango. The name behind the company is Mike Hill; originally from Cape Town, he has been guiding in Botswana for over 30 years, and as a citizen guide, he knows the Delta inside out. He is committed to raising the profile of the area as a walking destination, and enjoys working to pioneer new routes with the various operators in their concessions and community areas.

For Mike, the concept of his walking trips is to be totally immersed in the Delta's environment, mimicking humankind's early ancestors. He organises itineraries that blend days on foot in the wild with overnighting in selected classic to luxury lodges. The walking terrain is a combination of dry or wet floodplains and variously sized Delta islands. Walking speeds are generally slow and attentive, making the walks very accessible. Endeavour does not have an upper age limit for walking trips, but walkers need to be adventurous at heart. The distance covered is tuned to guests' abilities as the trips are private and tailormade.

All the walking takes place in either private concessions or community areas. The use of lodges rather than mobile camps opens up the possibility to incorporate activities other than walks in the itineraries – game drives, boat and mekoro trips – offering a different aspect to wildlife spotting. It's feasible to stay at a particular lodge for two nights to facilitate this. Usually, the lodges are not booked exclusively, but Endeavour reserves whatever accommodation is needed for the walking party. Trips are a minimum of three days and go up to 18 or even longer. A walking day starts with a healthy breakfast, before setting off with a day pack carrying a packed lunch and enough water to satisfy individual needs and temperatures for the time of year. The wildlife often has an influence on the walk – if there are interesting encounters, it can be fun to spend time and observe their natural behaviour and end up not covering a lot of distance. Other days, walks can cover anything up to 25 km or more if everyone is up for it. In the summer months, it's possible to find safe places to swim and relax during the hottest part of the day.

Endeavour is notable as a company dedicated to inclusive travel, and walking safaris for people with visual disabilities are achievable. There's no better way to experience the Okavango Delta for a person with a visual disability than on a walking safari. As the trips are all tailormade, they can be developed around individual needs, with a focus on touching the African bush to better understand the environment where the wildlife exists. The company has a multitude of inclusive travel destinations including Cape Town, Victoria Falls and the Kalahari. Endeavour runs walking safaris from April to the end of November, with peak season from July through to October.

Mike Hill says: 'As humans, we have been designed to walk, it's in our genes. If society could walk more, there would be a lot less health issues, and more awareness and conservation of our natural areas.'

Okavango Walking Safaris

Founded by Okwa Sarefo, an experienced guide born in the Okavango Delta, **Okavango Walking Safaris** runs adventurous itineraries for walkers in the Okavango and Moremi as well as the dry pans of the Makgadikgadi. A variety of formats is available from lodges and camps to fully mobile, with the latter giving the best wilderness walking experience as guests overnight in catered camps at locations chosen by Okwa. The safaris

A group guided by Mike Hill pauses by a water seep in the Okavango Delta.

begin with a 'meet and greet' in Maun, and a typical four-night itinerary would proceed as follows. The first day has a drive into a remote community area of the Okavango Delta arriving at the mobile camp in time for lunch. After a rest, there's a choice of a short walk or, depending on water levels, a mokoro safari. Dinner is served by the campfire, and guests retire early to be ready for a pre-dawn start. The dome tents feature en-suite bathrooms with a simple toilet and a bucket shower, with the water heated on the fire. From then, there are three full days to explore the area, with twice daily activities. Mostly, this is on foot, but with short mekoro crossings to reach other walking areas. Morning walks are generally four to five hours. Every walk is different, and, with a high concentration of wildlife, there's the possibility for all sorts of encounters. On the fifth day, the itinerary ends in Maun, or there's the option to continue with further exploration, such as a visit to an isolated island to meet the Bayeyi people at Jao Village. Okavango Walking Safaris offers a combined itinerary with Beagle Expeditions.

Walk Botswana Safaris

Owned and operated by Maun residents Gareth and Robyn Flemix, **Walk Botswana Safaris** has an interesting selection of itineraries. Most have a strong walking element, with a variety of styles to accommodate different budgets and walking style categories. A series of mobile camps are established in remote locations, and guests walk with light packs as the camp is relocated by vehicle. Alternatively, guests walk from the camp daily for a set number of days, exploring different areas and then moving, with guests driving or flying on to the next location. The camp facilities come in different formats – Adventure, Classic and Luxury – with the main difference being in the accommodation comforts: Adventure guests get two-person dome tents and shared ablutions, Classic Style guests have en-suite bathrooms, while the Luxury Style has larger tube-framed en-suite tents.

Walk Botswana Safaris expeditions are led in community-owned wildlife concessions in the Okavango Delta, with areas adjacent to the Central Kalahari Game Reserve (CKGR) and Kgalagadi National Park also covered. Depending on budget and preferred style, guests can pick from a number of standard itineraries or design a custom one. 'Lechwe Languish' is a six-night walking and vehicle safari mix, while the seven-night 'Sitatunga Special' is a boating and walking combination that's dependent on water levels. 'Kudu Kicker' is a dedicated walking itinerary that focuses on the Delta, with an option to swap the first location for the CKGR or the Kgalagadi. Given the distances to remote corners of the CKGR and Kgalagadi, a helicopter or fixed-wing charter transfer is an option.

Regardless of the itinerary, the walking day is tuned to the guests' walking preferences and abilities, with anything from a couple of hours on foot each morning to full days in the bush for the most energetic. The walking itself is focused on not just seeing the landscape but also on tracking animals for sightings. A typical six-night itinerary with Walk Botswana Safaris starts in Maun with an airport pick-up in a game drive vehicle. The journey to the first camp location takes a couple of hours, before crossing through the 'Buffalo Fence' and into the wildlife area. Camp is set under a canopy

A Walk Botswana camp set under a glorious starry sky.

of trees on a big lagoon fringed with water lilies and covered in ripples from the ever-present hippos.

On the second day, the walking safari begins with a quick breakfast and early start to explore while conditions are at their best. Lunch at camp is followed by downtime and enjoying whatever birds and wildlife appear in camp. In the afternoon, it's time to head out again on foot, the route depending on what was spotted earlier in the day.

On the third day, guests enjoy a shorter walk as staff take down the camp in preparation for moving to a new location. After returning for brunch, the group transfers by vehicle, and during the flood season it's necessary to retrace the arrival route to Maun and from there cross to the next destination. Along the way, there's a picnic lunch or a stop in Maun if preferred, and once back in the concession area, there's a slow game drive to the camp location, then a short leg-stretch walk while staff set camp. Dinner is served by the fire under the Southern African starscape. The beauty of the camp location is especially evident at dawn, with its yellow-barked fever trees reflected in another magnificent lagoon.

On the fourth day, there's less walking and more boating. Guests leave camp slightly later for a game drive to rendezvous with a little flotilla of mekoro. It's a marvellous way to get close to wildlife in silence and guests can expect to see plenty of waterbirds and the more water-dependent species of antelope such a sitatunga and lechwe. Following lunch there's time to relax after the busy days so far, and at sunset take an early dinner and go out on a night drive. The fifth and sixth days are filled with exploring on foot, island hopping and tracking animals. Along the way, there's a bush lunch followed by hammock time. On the last evening, dinner is served early so there's another opportunity for a night drive. On the final, seventh, day, guests enjoy a lie-in and late breakfast as camp is taken down, followed by a transfer back to Maun.

Shinde Footsteps Camp

All **Ker & Downey Botswana** camps have a focus on walking, including from the newly rebuilt and rebranded Shinde Footsteps. Located in a remote private concession in the Delta's central east, Shinde Footsteps is a year-round camp that's ideal for couples or small groups, with three twin-bedded canvas tents and one family tent. Each tent has an en-suite bathroom with wash basin, porcelain flush toilet and hot water bush shower, and there's a daily laundry service.

While walking is the main focus, other possible activities at Shinde Footsteps include game-drives, mokoro or fishing trips (subject to water levels). The walking experience from here combines well with the other Ker & Downey Botswana camps, which are Shinde, Dinaka, Kanana and the newly refurbished Okuti. The camps can also be used for overnighting on a mobile walking safari with a specialist walking company such as Endeavour Safaris.

Kwando Safaris

Moremi Crossing Safari Lodge is one of a number of lodges in Botswana operated by **Kwando Safaris** and one of the few lodges in the Delta to run a fly-camping experience. It's located in Gunn's Private Concession on the boundary of Moremi Conservancy overlooking Chief's Island. Walking here is usually combined with water activities when the water level is high or game drives when the level is low. The walking and adventure camping combination is available to guests who book a minimum of two nights at the camp and is only possible in the dry

Late afternoon at the Kwando Safaris 'adventure camp'.

season from April to October. Guests walk to overnight in a rustic type of camp set up a short distance from Moremi Crossing. Depending on water levels, it might be necessary to take a mekoro or drive for some of the way.

Nature walks are available at all of the other Kwando Safari camps all year except Tau Pan and Nxai Pan. In the Kwara Private Concession in the northern Delta not far from Shinde Footsteps, 4 Rivers camp is the newest Kwando Safaris venue for walks, and these explore Maboa Island, a short walk from camp. The island's name means 'mushroom' in Setswana, so called owing to its density of termite mounds, which cover about 40% of the land. There's low-growing couch grass and a thin cover of trees – mopane, jackal-berries, leadwoods, rain trees and Kalahari star apple – that make year-round walking possible. In summer months, the island's fruiting trees attract elephant, baboon and monkeys, and it's a good location to see sable and African wild dog.

Lodges of Botswana

Delta Camp and Oddballs' Camp are independently owned camps located in a prime position on the Okavango River on the edge of Chief's Island not far from Moremi Crossing Safari Lodge. Oddballs' has a nearby satellite camp called Oddballs' Enclave, and all the venues cooperate as the Lodges of Botswana group, with **Footsteps in Africa** providing marketing and reservation services. These camps are special in that there are no motorised activities – neither vehicles nor noisy boats. Instead, guests are invited to immerse themselves in a slow safari, exploring on foot and by handmade mekoro, just as humans have done here for thousands of years. Not only is it an enjoyable way to travel, but it's also good for the environment – no fuel to port in, no boat wakes disturbing nesting birds.

As always in the Delta, the degree of time spent on the water is dependent on the season, and when waters are high, guests arrive at the camps by mekoro.

The guides are local and invite their guests to appreciate the entire ecosystem as they glide through the channels and walk the floodplains and islands. It's a cultural experience too, an opportunity to witness another way of life in a true wilderness. For shorter walks, camp guests can venture out in the early morning, returning for a late breakfast, and head out again in the afternoon after the midday heat has dissipated. Another option is to take a picnic lunch and spend all day out in the wilderness with the guide.

Footsteps in Africa offer a multi-night 'Mekoro Trail' that blends camp stays with fly-camping while moving on the water and on foot. These only operate from April to September, when the water levels are higher. On a Mekoro Trail, guests spend their first and last nights in one of the camps and at least two nights wild camping, and everything needed for the camping travels by mekoro. The fly-camp format and cost vary depending on the base camp. Oddballs' has the most basic amenities with the smallest dome tents, and guests pitch in with the camp set up and food preparation. A mattress and sleeping bag and towels are provided, and drinks are not included in the rate. Oddballs' Enclave fly-camp tents are a bit bigger and have linen, soaps and shampoos. Guests can help out if they want to, and drinks are inclusive. Delta Camp has the highest service level: it includes a larger dome tent with bedrolls, linen and a chef to cook meals. The staff set camp, which normally stays in place for the duration of the trail.

Campsites are chosen for their beauty and remote qualities, and usually stay put for two nights; if there are additional nights booked, then the camp can be moved. All trails provide long-drop loos, hanging bucket showers and privacy provided by canvas shading and shower blocks.

Okavango lodge walks

Many camps and lodges in the Okavango Delta can guide walks. These vary in intensity depending on the terrain of the location, season and guest wishes, and a typical morning on safari at one of these camps might combine a vehicle, walking and mekoro travel. In wet season, water-based safaris are favoured, while in the cooler winter months from April to September, expect to spend more time in vehicles and on foot. For a walks-focused trip it's best to check in advance what can be arranged. African Bush Camps, Great Plains Conservation, Machaba Safaris, Natural Selection and others have multiple camps, and typically visitors would hit at least two on a trip, presenting the potential to walk in different parts of the Okavango ecosystem.

Great Plains Conservation has two camps deep in a private reserve in the northern section of the Delta. Duba Plains and Duba Explorers camps both have excellent walking opportunities, remote from any other camps. The walks are dependent on water levels and on what animals are around – the islands here can have high predator numbers, and if they are present, it's best to move with the mokoro or game-viewing vehicle.

A newcomer to the Delta is Karangoma camp, located in the northern NG12 Wildlife Management Area, sometimes known as the Mapula or Magwegqana Concession. It's the first venture in Botswana for **Wild Expeditions Africa**, a company that designs adventurous wildlife travel itineraries in Ethiopia and Madagascar and took over operation of a famous walking base in Zimbabwe, Camp Hwange. Karangoma runs walks all year, although they can be tricky from August to October if water levels are high and big elephant herds concentrate along the intersection between the woodland and water. The six-tent camp is located at the meeting point of the Okavango floodplains with the northern woodlands and originated in partnership with the local Bukakhwe San community. A typical walk starts with a short drive from camp to the water and then transfers to a mokoro or boat (depending on water levels) to reach islands in the Magwegqana waterway. The group explores the larger islands there, before either boating/poling back or being collected by vehicle. Karangoma, in partnership with Beagle Expeditions (see page 144), has a seven-night walking trip focused on a combination of Karangoma and the Kweene Trails camps, including a helicopter flight between the two areas.

&Beyond have a couple of elegant camps, Nxabega Okavango Tented Camp and Xaranna Okavango Tented Camp, both in a concession bordering Moremi Game Reserve. Nxabega has nine suites on raised platforms under ebony trees, while Xaranna is the same scale and looks out onto a lagoon. Both camps run walks in a mixed terrain of grasslands and cathedral mopane woodlands, and when water levels are suitable these can be combined with safaris by mokoro or motorboat.

Machaba Safaris is Botswanan-owned and has a collection of ten small scale camps in Botswana and Zimbabwe. Machaba is the Setswana name for the sycamore fig tree. All five Okavango camps provide guided walks, as does their Ngoma Safari Lodge on the Chobe River. Kiri Camp is the nearest to Maun, and has walks on the Kiri floodplains, combined with mekoro safaris when the water levels are up. A pair of camps on the Gometi River offer similar terrain and have the

When conditions are favourable, mokoro safaris are a serene alternative in the Delta.

classic mekoro/walk combination on plains dotted with palm trees. Machaba and Little Machaba are neighbours in the Khwai Concession at the eastern fringe of the Delta. The 1,900 sq. km concession is managed by the Khwai Development Trust on behalf of the local Khwai community and is a model for community-focused wildlife tourism in the Delta. Situated on the edge of the Monachira channel in the north-east region of the Moremi Game Reserve, the newest venue, Monachira Camp, opens in May 2025. Excellent walking is also available from the Machaba camps in Hwange and Mana Pools, and the company can put together attractive itineraries that combine their Botswana and Zimbabwe properties.

African Bush Camps was founded in 2006 by Zimbabwean professional guide Beks Ndlovu, and has since expanded from his home country into Botswana and Zambia, with a total of 17 camps. In the Khwai Community Concession adjacent to Moremi Conservancy, Khwai Lediba is a recent addition to the portfolio, and it runs walks in the dry season as its sister camp Khwai Leadwood does. The company has a couple of other fixed camps and the seasonal Linyanti Expeditions camp in the Linyanti area, and all guide walks. The newest camp is Atzaro Okavango Camp, surrounded by lush palm islands and vibrant Delta vegetation.

In Khwai Private Reserve, **Natural Selection** offers walks during the winter months from its two camps in the southern part of the concession. Tuludi and Sable Alley are year-round camps where a mix of land-based and water-based activities are available, including guided walks. In the central area of the concession is Hyena Pan, set next to a remote pan surrounded by mopane woodland; it operates from April to December.

About two hours from Maun in the southern Delta, Kwapa Training Camp is the base for the **African Guide Academy**. As well as training guides for the Botswanan safari industry, it's open to anyone who wants to join a Trails Guide or Wilderness Trail course out of general interest (see page 49).

Northern Botswana

It operates in the shadow of the Okavango Delta, but the north of Botswana has excellent reserves centred on the Kwando and Linyanti Rivers. This area is known for its diverse ecosystems, including riverine forests, open grasslands and seasonal floodplains, all of which is habitat for a wide variety of wildlife, including elephant, hippo, crocodile, buffalo, lion, leopard and a rich array of bird species. North-east of Selinda, the Kwando River marks the border between Botswana and Namibia's Caprivi Strip. At 2,320 sq. km, Kwando Reserve is an enormous conservation zone, and the river flows south and largely disappears into the vast marshland outside Kwando Reserve. What's left flows east to join the Linyanti River.

Linyanti Wildlife Reserve has some excellent walking options, and the Linyanti River is a vital water source that attracts a concentration of wildlife, especially during the dry season. The river delineates the border between the reserve and the Chobe National Park, and flows east to join the Chobe, a perennial river that's substantial by the time it in turn joins the Zambezi at the tripoint of Botswana, Zimbabwe and Zambia. For its final 100 km, the Chobe forms the northern boundary of Chobe National Park.

Blue wildebeest give Selinda walkers a curious gaze.

Remote and wild, the north is at the extremity of the Great Rift system. It's less visited than the famous reserves to its west and east in the Okavango and Chobe National Park, and a number of companies that have lodges and camps in the Okavango have venues in Selinda, Kwando and Linyanti, which makes it easy to plan a one-company tour with a diversity of safari locations. These include Kwando Safaris, African Bush Camps and Great Plains Conservation.

In the private 118,000 ha Selinda Reserve, **Great Plains Conservation** give guests the opportunity to explore this conservancy on foot with expertly guided walking safaris alongside open vehicle and boat safaris. Selinda links the waters of the Okavango Delta in the west with the Linyanti and Savuti waterways of the east via the Selinda spillway, which flows in the winter months. There are two Explorer collection safari camps, Okavango Explorers Camp and Selinda Explorers Camp, as well as two Réserve-Collection safari camps, Selinda and Zarafa.

There are two remote camps with walks on the Kwando River, bordering the eastern end of Namibia's Caprivi Strip. Like the **Kwando Safaris** camps in the Delta, the Kwando Lagoon and Kwando Lebala camps both run walks as long as conditions allow. The camps are set on the floodplain of the river before it flows east to disappear into the enormous marshlands that divide this area from the Zambezi basin. The landscape here is quite open in comparison with the mopane woodlands further east, and walkers will spot the full range of plains game as well as elephant, hippo and buffalo. There's always a good chance of big cat encounters.

Three **African Bush Camps** venues along the Linyanti River guide walks. Linyanti Bush Camp and Linyanti Ebony are neighbours, while Linyanti Expeditions Camp is about 12 km downriver. All three are well placed to walk the floodplain and its marshes between the Chobe National Park and the border with Namibia.

The Linyanti River winds slowly 1,000 km to the north-east to meet the Chobe River in Chobe National Park. This legendary safari destination is known for its wonderful game concentrations along the river, best viewed by boat. In common with other national parks, walking is not permitted in the park itself, but there are interesting walks in the mix at a couple of venues in the adjacent Chobe Forest Reserve. Both are located south of the Ngomo bridge.

Ngoma Safari Lodge is one of a number of **Machaba Safaris** lodges in Botswana and Zimbabwe. It's perched on the escarpment above the floodplain of the Chobe, and the view changes with the seasons as the waters rise and fall. Game drives run into the Ngoma section of Chobe National Park, which is less busy than the eastern Kasane section. All day outings to cruise the river and drive back via the park are very popular. Chobe's roads can be bumpy and tiring, so a morning walk makes an attractive alternative during a stay. These are led by a professional guide, and as elephant, buffalo and lion are all frequently seen, the guide carries a rifle. Walks depart from the lodge and explore the floodplain directly below amid fine knobthorn trees and umbrella acacias.

Walking distance from Ngoma, and with an identical aspect facing west across the Chobe River, **Muchenje Safari Lodge** is a charming base for visiting Chobe National Park. It has an informal atmosphere, with communal dining, joined by guides and management, the norm. The 12 thatched cottages and

Muchenje head guide K.B. Motshwarateu examining a giraffe skull …

… and Johane Matengu from Ngoma Safari Lodge tracking lion.

common areas have decks with river views that are connected by pathways lined with verbena, which attracts clouds of butterflies. Walks are led directly from the lodge down to the floodplain of the Chobe, where it's not unusual to find the tracks of lion that have passed through in the night. There are six guides on staff, which means there's usually one available for walks while other guests go for game drives and boat safaris in the park.

As we sit on the decks of Muchenje or Ngoma, the water glistening below is surging eastwards, and will soon blend with that of one of Africa's mightiest waterways; a river with countless tributaries that nourishes some of the continent's finest wildlife habitats and many magnificent walking safaris; one whose waters are destined to tumble over a fault line and into a cavernous cleft: the Zambezi.

7 Zimbabwe

Don't let its history of poor governance put you off a visit to Zimbabwe. For the visitor, it's a marvellous, warm-hearted country, with good tourism facilities and incredible guides. The disastrous economic situation that makes life hard for the majority of the population is all the more reason to give Zimbabwe some time and love. It has one star attraction, Victoria Falls, which should be on the wish list for every world traveller, and some top-class national parks that range from the well-known Hwange and Mana Pools to the less trafficked Matusadona and Gonarezhou.

The walking season is from April to November. At this time the weather is dry and vegetation is less dense, making it easier to spot wildlife as it gathers at remaining water sources. The wet 'green season' is not a time to be on foot, and multi-day walks do not operate.

Walking safaris in Zimbabwe

Zimbabwe is rightly proud of its strong wilderness guiding tradition, and combined with an excellent selection of national parks and reserves, this makes it one of Africa's most enjoyable walking safari destinations. Its guides qualify through Africa's toughest assessment (see page 46) and come from a diversity of backgrounds, including Shona, Matabele and those of European descent, and all bring their experience to bear to make walks about much more than nature.

Often Zimbabwean walking guides work solo, which makes walking in Zimbabwe a bit different from neighbouring countries. It means that impromptu walks can be part of the experience, in contrast to places where more planning is needed, the ones that have a policy of two rifle-carrying guides or a park ranger escort. It's common to set off in the game-viewing vehicle and get down for walks multiple times depending on the location and what wildlife is around and the combination of expert guiding and habituation to seeing humans on foot can result in very close encounters with elephant. Multi-day walking in Zimbabwe is generally mobile camp based. The national parks have allocated spots that can be exclusively booked by the walk operator, and everything is brought in by vehicle for the duration of the visit. The camp may stay in one spot or move, depending on the duration of the visit, and there's usually a good mix of walks and game drives.

Hwange National Park is the country's biggest and most visited park, and its proximity to Victoria Falls makes it a visitor favourite. The park has no shortage of lodge-based walks and walking guides from Bulawayo and Victoria Falls run mobile camps. In the north-east, Mana Pools is a renowned and beautiful destination and the country's second most popular walking safari park. It has a few good overnight walks alongside lots of lodge-based walking. The fact that so many lodges in these two parks have walking guides makes it feasible to do lodge-to-lodge walks with vehicle support to transfer bags and pick up and drop off if needed.

Matusadona National Park is emerging as one of Zimbabwe's best walking venues.

Zimbabwe is a country that offers a lot of potential for finding new areas to explore on foot, and several companies are more than happy to organise trips into untrodden zones of Chizarira, Matusadona, Gonarezhou and the seldom visited parks of northern Mozambique. As in South Africa, many Zimbabwean guides operate independently, combining stints at lodges with private guiding tours and safari planning and booking services. Some run mobile camp-based walking safaris in Hwange and Mana Pools, while others favour adventurous backpacking safaris in the remoter parks. They can put together lodge-based walking itineraries and include private guiding services if requested. A selection of Zimbabwe's private guides and walks-focused safari companies is covered here.

Discover Safaris

From his home base in Victoria Falls, Charles Brightman's **Discover Safaris** has an interesting selection of activities in Zambezi National Park and Hwange National Park. An accomplished guide and birder, he runs the anti-poaching unit in Zambezi National Park, and also schedules regular guided walks there. He or his selected guides pick up guests in Victoria Falls for the short drive into the park. Departures are at 06:00 and 14:50, and the whole trip lasts around four hours; light snacks and drinks are included. There's a minimum booking requirement of two guests and a minimum age of 16, and walkers should be fit to cover 10 km on foot. Full day walking/driving safaris in Zambezi National Park – and in Hwange – are available on request, for a minimum of four guests.

Doug McDonald's Safaris to Africa

Born in Zimbabwe and still based there, Doug McDonald is a product of Zimbabwe's demanding professional guide qualification programme and still helps with the assessment of new guides coming through the system. In addition to his status as a guide, he is trained in hotel management, with years of experience in running safari camps in Zimbabwe and Tanzania.

Doug has a dedicated team working with him behind the scenes at **Doug McDonald's Safaris to Africa**, and all have extensive experience so they can design and plan safaris throughout Southern, Eastern and Central Africa as well as having expertise in offbeat destinations such as Chad, Gabon, Mozambique and the Republic of Congo. Every safari is bespoke and designed to the level of adventure, comfort and walking style that guests prefer. This may mean walking from camp to camp with your own backpack; climbing one of the peaks and ranges; or walking for shorter distances to track a pride of lions or herd of buffalo, while staying in one of the high-end lodges in a private concession.

As Doug Macdonald says: 'To me, being able to get out on foot with an experienced guide is the best way to truly experience Africa. All your senses will be alert, which gives you a totally different perspective of your surrounds and slows everything down. Walking along with a big elephant bull is a very different experience to sitting in a safari vehicle watching the same.'

Inzila Mobile Safaris

Inzila Mobile Safaris is led by Zimbabwean Adam Jones, who is an experienced professional guide and guide trainer. Based in Victoria Falls, Inzila runs mobile fly-camping safaris to Hwange National Park, and these are usually led by Adam himself, who is a keen tracker. Guests are based at exclusive-use unfenced campsites, with the essential comforts including hot bucket showers and large mesh tents. Each campsite has one flush-toilet, with en-suite short-drop loos for night-time use. The locations are off grid with solar lighting, and device charging can be done in the vehicle. In Hwange,

The Inzila Mobile Safaris camp set above a spring on Hwange's Lukosi River in May.

the standard Inzila format has walkers spend three nights at each of two locations to provide a variation in terrain and habitat. The duration of walks is decided in consultation with the group, and the game-viewing vehicle is always at hand to provide a mix. The trails are open – solo guests are welcome to join scheduled group trips – and the maximum number of guests is six.

John Stevens Guided Safaris Africa

John Stevens Guided Safaris Africa has a long pedigree in Zimbabwe, as its eponymous founder was warden of two of the country's most important reserves, Matusadona National Park and Mana Pools National Park. In Mana Pools, his love for the area is recognised with the name of John's Camp, jointly owned by John's daughter and son-in-law and Robin Pope Safaris. Now based in Harare, John and his wife Nicci have managed the company for over 40 years, and design and operate bespoke safaris, both guided and independent, throughout East, Central and Southern Africa. Although all sorts of safari styles are accommodated, John encourages guests to walk whenever possible. His favourite walking areas include Mana Pools, along the Zambezi River, through forests and across floodplains awash with wildlife, or up in the more rugged landscapes of Matusadona. He advocates for his guests to put down their cameras and phones and to pause, listen, smell and really feel the wonder. No matter their age, physical ability or focus, John wants guests to experience Africa the way he does, with full attention, joy and energy.

More recently, the John Stevens Expeditions Africa collection gives intrepid guests the opportunity to explore Africa more actively and profoundly with a select few of John's guiding colleagues in the more unexplored parts of Africa, from Niassa in Mozambique to Zakouma in Chad.

Khangela Safaris

Mike Scott is the professional guide and seasoned explorer behind **Khangela Safaris**, headquartered in Bulawayo. Rooted in the heart of Zimbabwe, Mike specialises in leading walking safaris and covers all of the country's main wilderness reserves and beyond. Mike and the Khangela team cater to any level of travel style – from trail walking and backpacking to comfortable vehicle-based camping trips. In Zimbabwe, walks are run in the popular parks of Mana Pools and Hwange and the less visited parks of Gonarezhou and Chizarira. Beyond Zimbabwe, Mike's exploration ventures encompass neighbouring Southern African countries: in Mozambique, particularly in Niassa and Gorongosa, the possibilities are boundless.

Mike runs trips throughout the year, but recommends backpacking between April and August when the conditions are optimal, as it gets hotter and drier in the months of September and October. January, February and March tend to be the wettest months, so depending on the trip style and area, caution is advised. Apart from walking safaris, Khangela Safaris offers more challenging hiking trips, kayak river tours and bike expeditions. Mike is always open to offbeat adventures and is known as 'the go-to guy for *rekkie* trips'. In Zambia, Mike accommodates special requests for North Luangwa while Namibia has vehicle camping predominantly, with opportunities for hiking and biking from April to August. In Botswana, Khangela Safaris runs motor safaris in the Central Kalahari Game Reserve, Khutse Game Reserve and Kgalagadi, but not walks.

Off the Track

Off the Track is a destination management company (DMC) headed by a Zimbabwean local, Robyn Whaley. As a DMC, its main business is handling the logistics on behalf of overseas tour agencies, but they expertly deal with individual travellers too. Trips are all tailor-made to match visitor tastes, interests and budget, and Off the Track know which lodges and camps have the best combinations of walk guiding, service, locations and wildlife viewing. The small team of safari specialists not only know their own country comprehensively, but are also continually on the move to check up on places, visit new destinations and learn about the practicalities of travelling around Southern Africa. Robyn has close links with the Zimbabwean operation of Mack Air, and this is an advantage in ensuring seamless transfers between the best walking destinations in Zimbabwe.

16° South

A small, owner-run adventure tourism company, **16° South** creates specialist expedition safaris in some of Zimbabwe's wildest and most remote destinations. Each trip is designed around guests' interests and brings elements of luxury and exploration to the traditional mobile safari experience. The company name references its favoured destinations of Mana Pools, Matusadona and Chizarira National Parks, all of which lie on the 16° South line of latitude in northern Zimbabwe. Multi-day walks are vehicle supported, ensuring guests can walk in slackpacking style and arrive to their pre-set camp and all its comforts. The vehicle allows for flexibility in the daily plans, as the guides like to venture on unexplored routes, scouting for remote water sources and ancient trees. The walks tend to unfold based on what is found, and the radio is then used to arrange a vehicle rendezvous. Particular

Guests on 16° South mobile trails overnight in comfort.

attention is paid to rest-break cuisine, which can feature freshly cooked pancakes and filter coffee or soup and toasted sandwiches in winter.

In Mana Pools, 16° South has access to the escarpment as well as the shoreline, which allows walkers to experience the full diversity of terrain and ecology from narrow spring-filled gorges and baobab-studded foothills to the large winter thorn forests and riparian woodland of the shoreline. Meanwhile, in Matusadona the company has been granted an exclusive 25-year private concession to an area of the interior that is a base for both walks and game drives from a seasonal fly-camp.

Co-owner Graeme Sharp says: 'We see our offering suiting those who want adventurous comfort, who want to explore off the beaten track destinations with passionate and knowledgeable guides who love to leave the confines of a lodge behind and take their guests into a unique and truly incredible mobile safari that brims with adventure, discovery and authenticity. And at the same time, know they are safe, appreciated and well looked after with an environmentally sensitive and light footprint.'

Tented Expeditions

Tented Expeditions is focused on walking safaris in Hwange National Park. Guiding on foot is just one aspect of owner Ian Batchelor, who has a fascinating background that took him from childhood in Kenya and Zimbabwe (then Rhodesia), to university and the army in South Africa before attaining his Zimbabwe Professional Guiding qualification. He then worked in some of Africa's most interesting wild places, guiding on foot and by vehicle and managing lodges in Sabi Sand Reserve in South Africa, with Wilderness Safaris in Zambia and Malawi, Ker & Downey in Tanzania and then back home to Mana Pools in Zimbabwe. His latest venture is a partnership in Daka Plains, a new lodge on the Botswanan frontier in Hwange National Park. As such, his walking itineraries are concentrated in that north-western area of the park, mixing nights at Daka Plains and fly-camping.

As a private guide, Ian not only has an encyclopaedic knowledge of the natural world, but is an accomplished photographer, and enjoys helping his guests to get the most from this aspect of their safari. As well as Hwange, he has a special affection for the wilds of Gonarezhou and itineraries there blend walks, drives, lodges and fly-camping.

Umdingi Safaris

Founded by local Clint Robertson, and based in the town of Victoria Falls, **Umdingi Safaris** specialises in mobile camping experiences in some of Zimbabwe's best walking national parks, including Hwange, Zambezi, Chizarira and Matobo. These 'Exclusive Wilderness Safaris' can incorporate as much or as little walking as guests wish. Zambezi National Park is convenient for those with limited time, while Hwange brings a greater mix of terrain and more wildlife. Umdingi aims to maximise guests' wildlife encounters and experience an authentic African adventure. After the walks and game drives are over, evenings are devoted to campfire storytelling and stargazing.

The Umdingi style is a mobile tented camp, which comes in two flavours of comfort, one using dome tents and the other the larger Meru-style tent. This is a format available in Zambezi, Hwange and Chizarira National Parks. For visits to Matobo National Park, where dangerous game encounters are unlikely, it's even possible to sleep out on the rocks with nothing but a mattress. Umdingi is one of the few companies running backpacking trails in rugged and remote Chizarira. As well as offering customised itineraries, Clint or one of his selected guides can provide private guiding services and accompany guests on their travels, not just on the Exclusive Wilderness Safari but on lodge-based itineraries in Zambia, or further afield in Botswana, Zambia or even Uganda.

Victoria Falls area

No visit to Zimbabwe is complete without seeing Mosi-oa-Tunya, or Victoria Falls, where the Zambezi thunders into a chasm, its perpetual spray creating a micro-rainforest. Apart from the headline feature, the falls are a good hub for safaris, close to some of Africa's biggest and best national parks – Hwange to the south in Zimbabwe; Chobe to the west, in Botswana; and Kafue to the north, in Zambia. Above the falls, the Zambezi River runs through protected areas on both the Zimbabwean and Zambian sides, and these parks are worth a visit, both having walking opportunities.

Victoria Falls lies within the Kavango Zambezi Transfrontier Conservation Area (KAZA TFCA), which is a monumentally ambitious conservation effort spanning five countries and 520,000 sq. km including 36 proclaimed protected areas such as national parks, game reserves, forest reserves, community conservancies and wildlife management areas. Like the Great Limpopo, Greater Mapungubwe (see page 118) and other TFCAs, it's a project of the Peace Parks Foundation and has been in development since 2004. There's a lot of cross-border behind-the-scenes activity, and a tangible benefit for visitors is the KAZA UNIVISA – a joint visa for Zambia and Zimbabwe. If you plan to cross the bridge between Victoria Falls and Livingstone, then request this visa when arriving in the country. The visa covers Botswana crossings via Kazungula, but only for day trips for some reason.

The best time to see Victoria Falls is in the months of April to June, as the cascade water volume will be high, but not at the peak levels when spray obscures the view.

Zambezi National Park (Zimbabwe)

On the Zimbabwean side, the town of Victoria Falls has developed into an important safari and adventure tourism centre, yet retains a charming low-key atmosphere. Although it has many hotels and guest houses, and a bewildering range of activities, it's still an island in a sea of bushland. Elephant, buffalo and warthog are frequent pedestrians in the quiet streets, and the waterfalls are managed in a sensitive way, with only natural bush material for the fences that keep visitors safe from the churning gorge. The town is sheltered from the economic challenges of Zimbabwe, with a noticeable absence of potholes or power-cuts and a fine international airport terminal.

The gate to Zambezi National Park is accessed directly from the town of Victoria Falls, and many visitors enter the park to enjoy an evening boat cruise on the river. The park extends a further 56,000 ha to the frontier with Botswana and protects a variety of wildlife, including elephant, buffalo, lion, leopard, giraffe, zebra and numerous species of antelope. The Zambezi River itself is rich in aquatic life, including hippo and crocodile, and the birdlife is prolific with over 400 species recorded. There are a few lodges within

The end of a day on safari in Zambezi National Park.

the park that serve as bases for walking, driving and river safaris, and several safari companies in Victoria Falls can organise overnight camping and walking visits (see pages 157–162). The minimum age for canoeing and safari walks in the Zambezi National Park is 16.

Part of the Isibindi Collection, **Tsowa Safari Island** is sited on a forested island in the Zambezi River, about 35 km upstream from Victoria Falls. It has eight tents with en-suite indoor and outdoor showers, with each tent carefully positioned in the shade of the forest to ensure guest privacy and maximise the river views. The island itself is safe to walk with a guide as long as elephants are not present – they often swim out to feed on its dense tree cover. Here guests can find ancient baobab trees, a vibrant array of birdlife and a secret river that traverses the island. The blend of forest and water makes for superb wildlife viewing, and morning walks back on the 'mainland' are very special here.

Not far upstream from Tsowa, **Matetsi Victoria Falls** is a family-owned high-end escape set on the bank of the Zambezi in a 55,000 ha private concession within Zambezi National Park. Accessible by road or via its own airstrip and helipad, its 18 suites and private villa are presented to groups on an exclusive use or part exclusive use basis. As well as boat and vehicle safaris, walking safaris are guided in the concession area.

Further upriver, Chundu Island is at a similar level of comfort to Tsowa. Part of the South African **Seola Africa** portfolio, the lodge is on a picturesque and densely wooded private island. The island is safe to walk by day, and staff brief guests if any elephants are visiting. As well as plentiful birdlife, walkers can expect to spot some of the small resident animals such as bushbuck, warthog and vervet monkeys.

The island is home to a variety of stunning trees, from winter thorns to baobabs and palms. Bee-eaters nest in the banks of the island and a variety of waterbirds and waders spend the day on the white sand beach or rocky outcrops (depending on the seasonal water level). For a professionally guided walk, guests are taken by boat across the river, and then by vehicle to the chosen walk location. Walks usually take place in the early morning or late afternoon, to take advantage of the cooler hours of the day. A sister lodge to Chundu Island, Masuwe Lodge, is in the eastern end of Zambezi National Park. While it does not have the river location, it's a good base for walks, and convenient to both the falls and airport. Walks take place in the Chamabonda area close to the lodge.

Mosi-oa-Tunya National Park (Zambia)

Adjacent to the town of Livingstone, Mosi-oa-Tunya National Park protects 12 km of the Zambezi River and is a good base for visiting Victoria Falls from the Zambian side. It's the only park in Zambia where white rhinos can be found, and although there are no predators such as lion or hyena, the park has plenty of other wildlife to keep walks interesting, including elephant, giraffe, buffalo, hippo and a range of antelope and birdlife.

Within the park and overlooking islands in the river, Toka Leya is a **Wilderness** property that offers an attractive blend of vehicle, boat and foot activities. The luxurious camp has 12 en-suite safari-style suites, all with expansive decks and river views, and connected to the common area by raised boardwalks.

Upriver and outside the park, **Green Safaris** runs a couple of alluring lodges. Tongabezi has a collection of cottages and private houses on the riverfront about 12 km above the falls. Nearby, Sindabezi is even better located, set on a tiny island in the Zambezi. Guests at both can arrange day trips to walk with the rhinos in Mosi-oa-Tunya Park. A selling point for Green Safaris is that they have lodges in all of Zambia's walking safari destinations, which makes for a smooth itinerary for those who want the full Zambia experience.

Hwange National Park

Hwange National Park is located in western Zimbabwe and is the country's largest national park. Walks have long been guided here and it's an excellent walking safari destination where visitors can see the full range of African savannah wildlife, including elephant, lion, leopard, buffalo, giraffe, zebra and various antelope species. The park is habitat for over 400 bird species.

Hwange can be accessed by road from Victoria Falls via a three-hour drive to the gate. It has a good network of airstrips, and Mack Air has a daily schedule with both charter and 'seat rate' options. The eastern sector of the park accessed via Mbala Gate has been blighted by opencast coal mines, and Sinamatella Camp, a long-time favourite of park visitors in a splendid location, is all but abandoned. The approach via Main Gate, or Nantwich Gate, in the north-west is less depressing. There are 14,600 sq. km of semi-arid wilderness to explore, and the park's best walking is to be found in the north in proximity to the Deka and Lukosi Rivers and their tributaries. The dry season from July to October is the best time to walk in

Hwange, with a good chance to encounter large concentrations of wildlife.

Most walking in Hwange takes place from the many fixed lodges and camps, the alternative being to book a trip with one of the specialist safari companies based in Victoria Falls and Bulawayo (see pages 157–162) who run seasonal walking safaris from mobile tented camps. There are designated camping sites in the park, which can be booked exclusively, and everything needed is brought in by vehicle. Typically, the camp is set for a few days, and walks can go directly from camp or guests can be driven somewhere with interesting terrain. These companies can also arrange itineraries that mix their mobile camps with fixed lodges and camps in the park.

Hwange Bush Camp

The most walks-focused camp in the national park is **Hwange Bush Camp**, a low footprint camp established each April for the dry season. Located not far from Robins Camp in the west of the park, there are seven en-suite tents hosting a maximum of 14 guests. It's a genuine escape – off grid, no decks, no Wi-Fi, no pool. The camp is owned by professional guide David Carson, and his company Kazuma Trails runs vehicle-based mobile safaris in Botswana. For an even wilder dive into nature, the camp has a fly-camping option. A four-night itinerary has the first and last nights at the bush camp and a couple out at the fly-camp. The camp can be set in a number of locations in the Sinamatella and Robins areas, depending on the time of year and which area has the best wildlife viewing at the time.

These trips mix game drives and walks in a flexible way in harmony with guests' wishes, weather conditions and wildlife movements. It means there can be a series of short walks, with game drives in between. A suitable spot in the shade is picked for a lunch stop, ideally overlooking a water source. In the heat of the day, it's good to pass a few hours just resting and seeing what turns up. Before sunset, the group reaches the camp location to find the dome tents set up by the camp crew.

An afternoon walk from Hwange Bush Camp.

Cold drinks, a warm suspended bucket shower and campfire-cooked dinner follow.

The second day typically begins with a light breakfast preceding a more extensive walk and possible game drive combination. The areas walked have an interesting topography of woodlands, rocky outcrops, natural springs and ephemeral rivers. A light picnic lunch is set up under the shade of a tree around midday, after which guests are given the opportunity to enjoy a siesta before going out again in the afternoon on a walk or drive. As the sun sets, the group will stop to enjoy a sundowner at a waterhole before heading back to the fly-camp for the night. The final day of the safari begins with a snack in camp before leaving for the morning walk. It finishes at Hwange Bush Camp around lunchtime, when guests can enjoy a well-earned meal and afternoon siesta. The afternoon's game activity is tailored to suit the guests but is likely to include a short game drive to a waterhole to enjoy chilled drinks while watching animals come down to quench their thirst. Both Hwange Bush Camp and its fly-camp operate for the season from April to November, and the fly-camp is open to bookings from two guests to six.

Hwange lodge walks

Many lodges in Hwange have trained walking guides on staff, and walks are a popular alternative to game drives. It's normal to have a guide carry a rifle in the vehicle, which facilitates impromptu walks during a game drive. Recommended walking venues are Camp Hwange, Bumbusi Wilderness Camp, Camp Chitubu, Daka Plains, Deteema Springs, Robins, Verney's, The Hide, Sable Valley, Somalisa, the Wilderness camps and the Imvelo lodges.

In a remote location in the northern end of Hwange National Park, lies Hideaways' **Bumbusi Wilderness Camp**, formerly run as a Zimbabwe National Parks and Wildlife Management Authority (Zimparks) venue. Today it's a stylish camp with seven stone chalets in a grove of mature trees and a waterhole that's a focal point for wildlife. Walks are a big part of the experience here, thanks to its interesting terrain of river gorges and lookouts. In addition to the flora and fauna, there's human history to explore: it's possible to walk to Bumbusi National Monument, an archaeological site and ruins from the Nambya tribe that hail from the Great Zimbabwe area, and there are rock etchings to be found. The camp is available for exclusive use, with the rate including accommodation for up to three guests; additional guests incur a nightly fee. Alternatively, visitors can book individual rooms and mingle with other travellers, paying per room.

On the north-western edge of the park, **Daka Plains** is a recently rejuvenated camp with chalets of stone, canvas and thatch. It's part-owned by Kenya-born Ian Batchelor, an experienced walking guide who has spent years running both mobile tented safaris in Tanzania and Zimbabwe and permanent camps (see page 162). The camp is a 40-minute transfer from Robins airstrip and it has all the expected comforts, including a plunge pool. Ideally, visits should be planned so that walks can be guided by Ian himself, as it's a fascinating privilege to spend time with such an experienced guide, who has a deep knowledge of some of Africa's finest wilderness areas. The Deka River and its valley has a long and interesting history, which includes being traversed by many of the early European explorers, among them Frederick Selous and Thomas Baines. While rugged, the walking area is not too challenging, with much of the walking taking place along the Little Deka and Deka Rivers and the seeps and springs that attract a lot of game in the dry season, including roan antelope. It's possible to arrange walks around the Tsamhole Pan to the south of the Daka Plains concession, an area with a different aspect including a mix of teak forest and miombo habitats.

Some of Hwange's best walking venues are in the Robins area. **Robins Camp** itself is a fine walks base, a former Zimparks camp now upgraded and run by Machaba Safaris. The camp dates back to times before the area was conserved, and was the homestead of rancher Herbert Robins in the early decades of the last century. Some of the original buildings from that period survive, including the lookout tower that Robins constructed. Today, the camp is one of the more affordable places to stay in the park, and everything has been refurbished since its days under park management. There's a good selection of chalets, some thatched and some in a modern design, all nicely decorated in traditional styles. Walks are guided in the attractive landscape of marshes, grasslands and rocky kopjes, and can last for anything from one to three hours, with a fee charged per person per hour.

Close by Hwange Bush Camp, Deteema Springs occupies a prime position on a former Zimparks picnic site. There's less of a focus on walks here, so it's advisable to make the walking request when booking. The tents and common area overlook the natural springs, and elephants and other animals are frequent visitors. There's a pumped dam nearby, where it's possible to approach the wildlife safely on foot below a spillway wall. Drives take in nearby salt pans and Big Tom's and Little Tom's dams. Deteema Springs is part of the **Machaba Safaris** collection, and for a variation in walk experience it works well with another of their camps, Verney's, which is in a private concession area in the sandy south-eastern area of the park. It has ten spacious tents overlooking a large waterhole, and animals move freely through the camp to reach the water.

Between Deteema Springs and Sinamatella camp, Camp Chitubu is run by locally owned **Mutondo Safaris**. A newish unfenced camp set on a ridge with six large well-appointed tents, it makes a good base in an area with a topography that keeps walks interesting. Walks are guided by owner and professional guide Julian Brookstein, who is a big fan of tracking; he has been known to stay on the trail of a black rhino for up to 25 km. One area he favours is around the rocky outcrops between Masuma and Shumba, as the terrain provides good cover and vantage points. On occasion this has resulted in incredible sightings of lions feeding and close encounters with leopard and elephant. Mutondo has a relationship with Inzila Safaris (see page 159), and can organise walking itineraries that combine nights at Chitubu with nights at the Inzila mobile camp.

In central Hwange, south-east of Robins and west of the well-known and productive Shumba Pan, Camp Hwange was formerly a sister camp to Hwange Bush Camp but is now part of the **Wild Expeditions Africa** portfolio. It retains its focus on walking, which is an activity common to other Wild Expeditions venues in Ethiopia, Madagascar and Botswana. All of the guides have walking qualifications, and the terrain has a good variety to keep things interesting – granite kopjes, grasslands, a number of pans and woodlands of teak and mopane. Several waterholes have log hides making it possible to get up close to animals. The eight-tent camp overlooks a pan, and since 2024 has had a new airstrip called Shumba, which means it's just a 15-minute game drive to the lodge.

Although the north provides the best walking terrain, there are walking opportunities at lodges throughout the park. Some operators have lodges in other parks, making it convenient to build a multi-destination itinerary with walks at each camp.

Sable Valley is the largest private concession in Hwange, located east of Camp Hwange on the road to Main Camp. It has 11 thatched rondavels, and the common area has a view over Dete Vlei, about 9 km of which is exclusive to the concession. Walks here can explore wonderful teak forests, and there's the chance to encounter some of the 'Presidential' elephant herd, a super-herd of over 450 animals that's divided into around 20 family groups. Part of the family-owned **Amalinda Safari Collection**, the camp can be combined with a sister lodge in the Matobo Hills where there's a guarantee to find white rhinos on foot.

African Bush Camps operates three camps along the same drainage line east of Verney's. Somalisa is the company's original camp, opened in 2006, and is a seven-tent solar-powered bush camp tucked away under the shade of an acacia grove, along the edge of an ancient seasonal floodplain. Somalisa Expeditions nearby is a 'glamping'-style camp, while Somalisa Acacia is designed for families. All three camps have walking guides, and walks are inclusive in the rates.

A ground-level view hide and a tree-level view sleep-out 'nest' are two signature features of **The Hide**, a family-owned lodge on the eastern boundary of the park. It's an hour's drive from Hwange Main Camp or a shorter drive from the airstrips at Main Camp or Umsthibi. Morning and afternoon walks are on offer, always focused on guest interests – for example, birding, looking for elephants to approach on foot, or simply walking from waterhole to waterhole, resting, sitting and observing with a flask of tea. It's an option to book a private guide for the day and go out with packed lunches, either walking directly from camp or driving to a spot and going from there. This is the normal routine if guests book their stay in one of the exclusive-use options, Tom's Little Hide or The Private Hide. Walks take place in both the concession area and the surrounding park, which gives a good variation of terrain including open savannah plains and *vlei* lines to more wooded areas.

Further east again, the Linkwasha Concession preserves 14,600 sq. km of woodlands and savannah; it's in an area rich in wildlife with a variety of habitats, which makes for interesting walking at any time of year. With a choice of three camps clustered in the exclusive concession, **Wilderness** is a good choice to mix game drives and walks at more than one camp in a single visit. Wilderness Linkwasha has nine tents shaded by trees and views of Ngamo Plains. Little Makalolo, 10 km to the west, is smaller but in a similar style and setting. A third option is Davison's, situated in a glade of false mopane trees overlooking a busy waterhole that's popular with elephant and buffalo. The camps are open all year, and the best walking time is in the dry season from April to August.

South-east of Linkwasha in the Ngamo Plains area, the **Imvelo Safari Lodges** run guided walks. Camelthorn Lodge and Bomani Tented Camp are located on private concessions that share an unfenced boundary with the national park and provide an important source of employment and revenue to the Tsholotsho community. Two other Imvelo camps are located in the park: further west is Jozibanini in a remote and undeveloped wilderness, while in the north is Nehimba, combining sandveld and rocky basalt ecosystems. The most experienced guides do the walking safaris, which are tailor-made to the guests, from short approaches to wildlife for photography, or longer hikes for more strenuous exercise. Most guests focus on game drives or spending time in one of the hides, while a unique experience is the railcar ride from Dete to Ngamo. For guests at Bomani and Camelthorn, there's the possibility to walk with Hwange's only white rhinos, reintroduced in 2023. The rhino project is the latest step in involving local people in conservation in the area, with the Cobras anti-poaching unit financed by the fees visitors pay to see the rhinos. These walks are short, with the group driving to find the rhinos, and then making an approach on foot to a safe distance. The animals are calm in their natural environment and habituated to seeing people.

Matobo National Park

On a tour of Zimbabwe, an essential stop is the UNESCO World Heritage Site of Matobo Hills, approximately 30 km south of the city of Bulawayo. The hills are known for their unique geological formations, including balancing rocks, onion-skin weathered granite outcrops and caves that contain thousands of examples of traditional rock art. The area is rich in other cultural heritage, with evidence of human settlement dating back over 2,000 years. Colonial-era magnate Cecil John Rhodes chose it as his grave site. For walking safaris, the prime attraction of Matobo Hills is the combination of a stunning landscape and the presence of rhino. It's also a twitcher haunt, with over 200 bird species recorded in the area. There are a handful of recommended venues to overnight and enjoy activities – Big Cave Camp, Camp Amalinda and Matobo Hills Lodge. Umdingi Safaris and Off the Track have overnight trips to the park with walking.

Big Cave Camp is a short distance from the tar road that borders the Matobo National Park. The camp runs sundowner game drives to Lightning Rock on its own property as well as the Matobo National Park recreational area. Early morning and afternoon game drives often include short (or longer) walks to view rock art in overhangs. White rhinos can be approached on foot in the care of a trained guide and anti-poaching scout. These walks are available all year, and the usual practice is to drive until they are spotted, then get down and walk the final approach, which can be up to 1 km. Apart from rhino walks, Big Cave has nature walks on its own property. These focus on birdlife, flora and smaller things, and the chance to spot various plains game. Longer walks in the national park are an option as a full day activity.

A few kilometres north, Amalinda Lodge nestles in a lovely location below a cluster of the rocky kopjes typical of Matobo. It's part of the **Amalinda Safari Collection** and a sister lodge to Sable Valley in Hwange, offering a convenient two-destination itinerary. Facilities include a pool and spa treatments, and sunset walks to lookout points are especially enjoyable. Naturally, rhino tracking walks are the most popular, but walks to view San rock art are worth doing as well. A half-day excursion involves departing early with a packed breakfast for a one-and-a-half-hour game drive to the base of the Inanke Cave in the middle of the park. There follows a 7 km hike, with the chance to spot kudu and possibly leopard.

Rock art appreciation is a favourite element of Matobo walks.

More moderately priced than these lodges, **Matobo Hills Lodge** is the top accommodation option that's actually in the park. It has an excellent range of activities, and walks are more or less mandatory. As with the other lodges, these can be guided walks of two to three hours that focus on the entire ecosystem, as well as rhino tracking walks and cave exploration.

Gonarezhou National Park

Gonarezhou National Park is made for adventure on foot. A huge reserve of over 5,000 sq. km, it has a terrain marked by rugged and rocky hills, sandstone cliffs and deep gorges carved by the Mwenezi and Save Rivers. The park encompasses miombo woodlands, mopane forests, baobab-studded plains, riverine forests and open grasslands. Miombo is the local name in several languages for a biome of subtropical woodlands and grasslands dominated by the *Brachystegia* and *Julbernardia* that are widespread in the Zambezi basin. Unlike the acacias, they grow close enough to form a canopy and don't have thorns – so make for an enjoyable walking habitat.

The park is known for its elephant population, and walkers can spot a wide range of Southern African wildlife including buffalo, lion, leopard, cheetah, giraffe, zebra, wildebeest, hippo and various antelope species such as impala, eland and sable. Black rhino was reintroduced in 2021. It's heaven for birders, and notable residents among its 400 recorded species are the martial eagle, Lilian's lovebird, Pel's fishing owl and the rare African skimmer.

On foot in the woodlands north of Gonarezhou.

Visitors to Gonarezhou National Park can enjoy game drives, walking safaris and camping. The park is a major element of the Great Limpopo Transfrontier Conservation Area, along with the Kruger National Park, but has a tiny fraction of Kruger's visitors, making it a great destination for those looking to get off the beaten path and experience the African wilderness in a more remote setting. Walking in Gonarezhou is possible all year, although during the December to May 'emerald season', when the bush is thicker and greener, walks are slightly shorter and take place in different areas, in order to give guests the best and safest experience.

A walking adventure in Gonarezhou can be arranged via one of the walking guide companies such as Khangela Safaris, Tented Expeditions or Doug McDonald's Safaris to Africa (see pages 158–162). Chilo Gorge Lodge is in the north of the park near the border with Mozambique, and can facilitate walks from both the lodge and fly-camps, while Singita Pamushana Lodge is another high-end venue with guided walks. The park can be accessed by road or by air.

Bush Bound Gonarezhou

Doug McDonald's Safaris to Africa runs tented mobile camps in the park under the name Bush Bound Gonarezhou. These trips are always with a qualified walking guide, so guests can mix walks and driving freely as they explore the park. Groups overnight at a series of semi-permanent camps, bespoke fly-camps and sleep-out decks.

The Massasanya Camp is in the north; it has four chalets overlooking a large waterhole – very rustic but with the essential comforts. This is an excellent walking area, and there's no shortage of wildlife in the vicinity of the camp – herds of elephant and buffalo are a common sight here, along with the resident hippos, zebra and antelopes. Walkers can discover tracks of African wild dog, leopard, lion, caracal and spotted and brown hyena, and this camp is in the black rhino area of Gonarezhou. Mwenezi camp is a similar style in the south of the park, with views overlooking the Mwenezi River. This is often a base for full day outings, which set off with a picnic lunch to explore along the river or some of the seasonal pans in the vicinity. The remote south is known for its great herds of buffalo, along with giraffe, nyala, elephant, bushbuck, steenbok and wildebeest.

A third camp utilised is at the Chilojo Cliffs, which are an unmissable feature of the park. These towering walls of sandstone were formed by millions of years of sediment deposition, followed by millions more of erosion by the Runde River. The private tented camp is set on the bank of the river, looking towards the cliffs, and again is in an excellent game viewing area. Large walk-in safari tents with en-suite bathroom facilities provide the necessary comforts.

Between nights at these fixed camps, fly-camps are established at interesting spots either along the Mwenezi and Runde Rivers or at one of the seasonal pans away from the rivers. These camps use 3 × 3 m canvas dome tents with two stretcher style cot beds, an extra mattress on top and proper linen. The shared ablutions have a screened-off suspended bucket shower system with preheated water and a long-drop toilet. Depending on the number of nights and location, the dining area may be in the shelter of a large tree or under a canvas gazebo.

Finally, there's the option of using one of the sleep-out platforms built by the

Doug McDonald uses breeze-catching mesh tents for trails in Gonarezhou.

park management. One is at Bhenji Weir and the other is at Malugwe Pan. These are great for families or groups of up to four people to spend the night out under the stars overlooking a seasonal water point; they are especially wonderful on full moon nights. The set-up is similar to the fly-camping in terms of the sleeping arrangements, except that a mosquito net is used in place of the tent. Meals and drinks are taken at the platform and the ablutions are as those for the fly-camp, set up to the side of the platform and easily accessible.

Khangela Safaris

Khangela Safaris offers a week of wilderness walking in Gonarezhou. In a small group, guests are professionally guided in remote areas of the park including along the Pombadzi, Mwenezi and Guluweni Rivers. A highlight is the approach to the dramatic red sandstone Chilojo Cliffs, which provide a stunning backdrop to the wilderness.

The walks are designed for experienced hikers, and guests should supply their own kit including lightweight tent, sleeping mats and sleeping bag. Food is provided, but it's nice to bring some additional energy treats. Full packing guidance can be given before travel. The typical walking day is about three to four hours in the morning. A suitable campsite with a water view is selected, and the remainder of the day can be spent resting and wildlife-spotting in the vicinity of camp before enjoying a campfire meal. Walks are guided personally by Mike Scott of Khangela Safaris, one of Southern Africa's most experienced walking guides, and a Zimparks ranger escorts the group. The maximum group size is six and participants need to be fit and experienced in backpacking. As well as backpacking trails, Khangela can arrange mobile camp-based walking safaris in Gonarezhou.

Chilo Gorge Safari Lodge

Chilo Gorge Safari Lodge is an eye-catching venue in the Jamanda Conservancy on the northern boundary of the park. The main lodge overlooks the Save River and has ten thatched twin-level chalets, while its satellite seasonal Chilo Tented Camp Experience at Mahove has four Meru-style tents. There's a mobile option too, the Ivory Trail Adventure, which combines fly-camping, game drives and walking safaris. The ideal way to enjoy walks in a diversity of areas is to blend nights at the lodge with either the tented camp or Ivory Trail fly-camps. The maximum group size for walks is six.

The walking area has a good variation in terrain, with walks tracing riverbeds and the big natural pans such as Tembawahata, and traversing open plains. There's a beautiful walk following an elephant path up to the Chilojo Cliffs, which is a fine morning activity when doing the Ivory Trail fly-camping experience. Ivory Trail operates all year, but June to November are the recommended walking months, when the grass is short and more areas are safe to explore. One vehicle is dedicated to guests, facilitating walk drop-offs and pick-ups, while another looks after camp relocation. The fly-camp comprises two-person dome tents with stretcher beds, bedding and a bedside table. A wash basin is provided for each tent and there are shared bush camp style ablutions.

A sample itinerary sees guests fly into Chipinda Pools airfield close to the park reception, and spend four nights camping, mixing walks and drives, ending with two nights at the lodge before departing from Mahenye airstrip, which is next to the lodge. Apart from enjoying the park's natural attractions, walks can take in battlefield sites and human history. Outside the park, Chilo Gorge guides walks in the Jamanda Conservancy to Chivilia Falls – a nice afternoon experience followed by sundowners overlooking the rapids of the Save River.

Gonarezhou lodge walks

Bordering Gonarezhou to the north and close to the town of Chiredzi, Malilangwe Wildlife Reserve is a private conservancy managed by the non-profit Malilangwe Trust. It has an attractive landscape of sandstone outcrops and baobabs and a rich collection of historic rock art sites. Within its 500 sq. km wildlife includes black and white rhino, lion, elephant, African wild dog and many bird species. It has an effective anti-poaching operation, and income from tourism operations benefits the Trust. Exclusively, accommodation is at the **Singita** Pamushana Lodge or the villa Malilangwe House, set high on a sandstone ridge overlooking the Malilangwe Dam. The lodge has eight opulent suites, all with plunge pools. Apart from drives and boat cruises, guided walks are available, and the guides are adept at tracking rhino and other beasts.

Chizarira National Park

Off the beaten track and delightfully difficult to access, Chizarira National Park is situated in the Zambezi Escarpment, west of Lake Kariba and near the town of Binga. It's one of Zimbabwe's least-developed and little-visited national parks, offering a remote and untouched safari experience. Several NGOs are engaged in rehabilitation projects in the park, and it would be a good candidate to fall under the management of African Parks, who have shown the way in Matusadona. The park is characterised by rugged and hilly terrain, with deep gorges and valleys. The name comes from the Tsonga word *sijalila*, which refers to the escarpment cliffs. It's part of the Zambezi Rift Valley and affords stunning panoramic views from the escarpment. A good birding destination, it has elephant, buffalo, lion and various antelope species.

It's not a venue to find a lodge with guided walks, but rather a destination for adventure backpacking through one of the private walking guides (see pages 157–162). It's a drive-in rather than fly-in destination, and 4x4 is essential. There are a number of nominated unfenced camping sites in the park, and everything needed should be brought in. The animals tend to be skittish around humans, so don't expect the Mana Pools experience.

Matusadona National Park

In northern Zimbabwe, Lake Kariba might conjure up images of fishing and house boats, but it's gradually becoming known as the lake with the park – Matusadona National Park. This is located on the southern shore of the lake and since 2019, under the management of the Matusadona Conservation Trust, a partnership between Zimbabwe Parks and Wildlife Management Authority and the non-profit conservation organisation African Parks, Matusadona is regaining its former status as an important protected wilderness. Its lush and varied 1,470 sq. km of terrain is perfect for exploration on foot, with habitats containing a large diversity of savannah and woodland species. The park itself has two parts: the valley floor that's hemmed in by Lake Kariba, which makes up about one-third of the area, transected by meandering rivers that flow through the thick *jesse* bush and down into the lake. The northern boundary's kilometre-wide drowned forest dates from the creation of the vast Lake Kariba in the 1960s. The other two-thirds of the park rise into the Matusadona mountains, which form the southern escarpment of the Zambezi Valley.

Matusadona is benefiting from wildlife reintroductions and improved protection, and the valley floor has a dense population of elephant, buffalo, hippo, lion, leopard, zebra and a host of antelope species. There are plans to reintroduce cheetah and black rhino and the park has logged over 240 bird species, from the aquatic birds of the lake shore and estuaries up to the big raptors that nest in the escarpment. It's a beautiful walking area with a terrain of rugged mountains, extensive grasslands and forests of mopane and mahogany trees. Accommodation options in the park range from tented camps to a selection of lodges, with most of them located along the lake shore, presenting peaceful views of the lake.

To access Matusadona, there are a few options. The recommended route is to travel by air; apart from charter flights, seat-rate flights are available with Mack Air to airstrips at Fothergill Island, Bumi Hills, Kanjedza and Tashinga. Overlanding, it's a tough access route for experienced 4x4 drivers. It's easier to drive to Kariba town, a six-hour drive from Harare or three hours from Lusaka, this latter route passing through Siavonga and across the Kariba Dam wall at the border. Vehicles can be left at a safe parking location in Kariba, and it's a 45-minute speedboat charter journey from Marina Harbour or three to four hours on a chartered car ferry.

Matusadona overnight walks

Matusadona is emerging as one of Zimbabwe's most attractive walking venues, thanks to its combination of good management and low volume of visitors. The **Matusadona Conservation Trust** (MCT) gives visitors the full package of accommodation and professionally guided walks and game drives, and in recent years they have developed a selection of camps that can be used as bases. For walking, the ideal choice is Matusadona Bush Camp, which is a mobile camp designed to relocate seasonally as dictated by wildlife movements. It sleeps 12 in six large tents in the East African style, all with en-suite bathrooms with hot and cold running water. The camp is fully catered and is booked on an exclusive basis with a minimum charge for four guests, who can choose from walking, driving and boat safaris.

Alternatively, there are chalets at Tashinga beside the park headquarters, where guests can either self-cater at a fully equipped kitchen or use the services of a cook and meal plan. In addition, there are two campsites with shared ablutions – one at Tashinga, the other at Maronga. Visitors can either bring in all their own kit or arrange with MCT to supply and erect a tent; MCT can even provide a cook and camp attendant for laundry and other camp duties. Finally, an interesting alternative is to sleep out on one of a couple of game viewing platforms that overlook inland springs. All of these accommodation options are open all year, and guided half- or full-day walks can be led by MCT professional guides.

For the fit and adventurous, overnight backpacking trails are available by advance arrangement. These are guided for anything from one to seven nights, and mostly target the remote escarpment of the park; springs on the valley floor can also be explored. Backpacking groups determine their own routes and camp locations and must be fully self-sufficient. Kit should include camp stoves, food, lightweight tent and sleeping bags, and at least 4 l of water carrying capacity.

Apart from taking advantage of the MCT resident guides, it's possible to arrange a visit with 16° South (see page 161), which runs vehicle-supported overnight trails in an exclusive-use area of the park's interior; and private guides from Victoria Falls and Bulawayo bring guests to the park for lodge-based and backpacking trails.

Matusadona lodge walks

One of the attractions of Matusadona is the small number of lodges and visitors. Apart from the African Park options, there are just half a dozen lodges, ranging from venues that have a mostly local clientele such as Spurwing and Rhino Camp to upmarket camps Changa Safari Camp and Fothergill Island. Several have qualified walking guides on staff, and guided walks are available alongside game drives, boating and fishing activities. Walks can explore the open areas near the lake shore, but to avoid the (few) vehicles around, they tend to go inland to track the twisting drainage lines that meander through the hills where there are year-round springs and elephants dig wells in the riverbeds. The watershed bush is thick, but can be traversed with care – jumping between drainage lines.

In the late 1950s, Lake Kariba's creation set the stage for a new island to emerge as a popular fishing destination among Zimbabweans. Since then, **Fothergill Island** has undergone a remarkable transformation, and in 2021 it was reborn as a high-end tented camp, now among Zimbabwe's most exclusive destinations and part of the positive trajectory of Matusadona.

The camp prioritises sustainability, evident in its design and features. A protective fence surrounds the area, safeguarding over 450 newly planted trees that are quickly growing and effectively preventing sand encroachment. Powered by a large solar plant, Fothergill Island has seven Lake Suites, each with their own plunge pool and viewing deck. Secreted away at one end of the island, Little Fothergill is an exclusive-use camp with three tented suites and its own pool and private dining. During a stay at Fothergill, a boat trip to Sanyati Gorge is a must; you can fish while watching dozens of crocodiles just metres nearby. Another highlight is the evening sundowners on the lake shore, a time to spy kingfishers hunting and then bats emerging from a hollow tree after sunset.

Not far from Fothergill, **Changa Safari Camp** is a less expensive but high-quality venue with walks. It has eight tents and a swimming pool. In the west of the park, **Rhino Safari Camp** is an affordable venue that can guide walkers by prior booking and is used as a base camp by private walking guides. Outside the park's western boundary, Bumi Hills Safari Lodge is part of the **African Bush Camps** collection. It has ten airy suites set on a ridge overlooking Lake Kariba. The full set of Matusadona activities are on the menu: game drives (including night drives), walking safaris, boating, fishing, village visits, sunset cruises and a unique boat sleep-out on Lake Kariba. The walks are guided inside the park in the Ume to Tashinga area, with a park ranger escort.

Mana Pools National Park

There's a lot of fondness for Mana Pools from those who have visited repeatedly. Famous for a rich proliferation of classic African wildlife, it's a top walking safari venue with landscapes that include riverine forests, floodplains and monumental baobab trees. The combination of Zambezi waters and photogenic (and shady) woodlands makes it attractive for combining drives, boating and canoeing with exploration on foot. It's blessed with some of Africa's best walking guides, who know how to interpret the full ecosystem.

Mana Pools National Park is a UNESCO World Heritage Site and part of one of Africa's transnational 'peace parks' along with Lower Zambezi National Park on the northern side of the river in Zambia. In 2023, the Zimbabwean government and the Peace Parks Foundation agreed a 20-year Greater Mana Pools ecosystem co-management plan. Visitors find a diversity of wildlife, including elephant, lion, leopard, cheetah, hyena, zebras, and various antelope species and the waterways are habitat for a large population of hippos and Nile crocodiles. The park is a popular destination for birdwatchers, with over 450 bird species recorded, including numerous African fish eagles, kingfishers and storks.

Most international visitors to Mana Pools travel on an organised trip and are in the safe company of professional guides during their stay. In common with other Zimbabwean national parks, it's possible to self-drive, although the busy A1 road is not for the faint of heart. For those who are fully self-sufficient, there are a number of public camping spots that can be booked with Zimparks. It's essential to follow guidance on safety when camping in Mana Pools, especially after dark.

Mana Pools has the distinction of being the only big game park in Africa where visitors are permitted to get out of vehicles and walk unaccompanied by guides. This practice evolved in the decades when the park was largely the preserve of local residents who for generations came to camp, fish and enjoy the wilderness; being confined to a vehicle was not practical or desirable. However, because something is permitted doesn't mean it's a good idea, and it's hard to overstate how important it is only to walk with an escort. Self-drive visitors who want to go on foot can get a permit to do so at the park reception, and are strongly advised to book a park scout for safety.

The park is a popular safari destination, and in recent years has seen the introduction of more lodges. As the best game viewing is on the floodplain near the river, amid fairly open woodlands, that area tends to be busy with vehicles, which makes it increasingly hard to walk without spotting one. For this reason, some walking guides now favour walking in the park interior, especially near Chitake Springs, a site renowned for its resident pride of lions, which ambushes buffalo that come to take water. During the rainy season, the spring at Chitake is in flow and feeding into the Ruckomechi. By the time the walking season begins in April the river is dry, but the spring continues and becomes a vital water source for this part of Mana Pools. The valley floor, with its mix of mopane, combretum and acacia woodlands, buzzes with wildlife, and the concentration grows as the dry season intensifies. Numerous elephant and herds of over 1,000 buffalo can be found at the springs and these and the smaller game animals attract predators and scavengers including lion, leopard, hyena, African wild dog and vultures. The 'sit and wait' style of safari at Chitake can be very rewarding as one gets to observe wildlife behaviours not possible when walking.

On foot on the shaded floodplain during Natureways' Mana Shoreline Walking Safari.

Walking safari options in Mana Pools range from multi-day camping to full-service lodges. The main operators of overnight walks are Natureways and Bushlife Safaris, and other walking safari specialist companies (see pages 157–162) run camping and walking combinations in the park. There are a couple of dozen lodges and camps in the park, the majority located along the Zambezi River, giving fine views of the river and the wildlife that inhabits its banks. Bushlife's Vundu Camp is one such, and others include Kavinga, John's Camp, Goliath Camp, Camp Mana, Mana River and the camps of Wilderness and African Bush Camps. There are some interesting venues in quiet areas away from the river, such as Kavinga, Ingwe Pan and new arrival Mashuma. East of the park lies the Sapi Game Reserve, which has lodge-based walks in an area remote from other visitors.

Bushlife Safaris

Bushlife Safaris is a well-known Mana Pools safari operator with a private concession area east of the confluence of the Zambezi and Ruckomechi Rivers. All of the Bushlife guides are walking-qualified, which means guests are able to get down from the vehicle to really appreciate the full Mana Pools experience. For example, if African wild dog or lion tracks are spotted on the road and there are vultures going to ground in the distance, that's the signal to investigate on foot. Likewise, an elephant bull might be spotted through the acacia woodland, and it's then possible to approach him in the natural way. It might even be Boswell, a large bull who is well habituated to walkers and is renowned for his ability to stand on his back legs to reach a high winter thorn branch and its tasty scarlet seedpods.

There are two Bushlife camps in the concession, Vundu and the smaller seasonal camp, Little Vundu, both unfenced. The main camp is set directly on the Zambezi and has eight canvas and thatch chalets, one of which is a family room. Wildlife is attracted to both the river waters and a small pan behind the camp, and it's an easy place to pass hours sitting on the veranda of the chalet or on the raised deck of the common area. Little Vundu is on the river about 1.5 km upstream and is a smaller tented camp with five Meru-style tents. Like a number of lodges in Mana Pools, Vundu can run canoe safaris on request, and uniquely has its own pontoon boats. The boats allow guests to go for fishing trips or on a hot day to take a trip out to a sandbar in the Zambezi for a paddle in the shallows. Bushlife is owned by Nick Murray, a Zimbabwean professional guide with life-long experience in conservation and wildlife tourism. He guides many walks personally, and ensures all of his guides are trained to the highest standards. A career highlight was guiding Sir David Attenborough and his team from the BBC during the filming of features on elephants and on the African wild dogs in the Mana Pools area. If a wild dog pack can be found, walking with them is a highlight for the lucky guests, as the animals are very relaxed with humans and carry on their fascinating daily routines.

Apart from the drive and walk combinations from the camps, Bushlife runs camping trips to Chitake Springs, an area with few roads that's well suited to walking. There's a resident lion pride of around 20 individuals, which often splits up into two or three groups scattered in different areas around the spring; Bushlife guides enjoy tracking them on foot. On request, the Chitake mobile camp can be used to create a multi-day shoreline walk, using either of the two Vundu camps for a night and mobile camps at the Chessa and Ilala sites for two nights.

Natureways

Natureways has brought adventurous visitors to Mana Pools for over 40 years, where it specialises in active safaris, both canoeing and walking. Headquartered in Kariba town, it's a prime operator of authentic mobile safaris in the park, with guests moving on foot or on the water from camp to camp. The Natureways Mana Shoreline Walking Safari is a three-night journey that begins near the confluence of the Ruckomechi and Zambezi Rivers and continues along the Mana Pools shoreline to Ilala Camp across from Chikwenya Island in the Mana Pools wilderness zone.

It's recommended that guests spend the first night at Camp Zambezi to ensure a restful night and time to organise kit before the walking begins. Each day, the group departs camp at dawn to walk to the next camp at a gentle pace, with plenty of time for sitting to watch wildlife along the way. The first night is spent at Vundu Point, then Chessa and finally Ilala. At camp, a cold drink and hot shower awaits, and dinner is served at the campfire. The Shoreline Walking Safari departs Mondays, Tuesdays, Fridays and Saturdays between 15 April and 15 November, and the minimum age is 14.

Natureways run trips to Chitake Springs too, making use of the Zimparks campsite. They bring in all the camping gear and establish large stand-up tents with en-suite chemical toilets (for use at night). In the winter months, from May to the end of August, longer walks are taken from the Springs area up into the different habitats of the hills. When it's hot from September to November it's preferable to stay near the springs through the heat of the day and wait to see what turns up, and

Natureways provides a bush hide to help keep out of sight. Walks early and late in the day are enjoyable in the sandstone gorge and surrounding woodlands.

A three-night Chitake itinerary begins with a rendezvous with the guide at Nyamepi, the park headquarters close to Mana Main airstrip. From there it takes around one and a half hours for a game drive to Camp Chitake, arriving in time for lunch. The camp crew go on ahead, and the fly-camp set-up is the same as that used for the Shoreline Walk. The afternoon walk is a short one, taken in the area of the camp. Next day, after an early wake-up call, there's hot water for washing, with tea, coffee and muffins or home-made biscuits waiting by the campfire. The day's itinerary depends on what guests have planned with the guide – perhaps an early morning walk to watch the sunrise. These walks are customised to each group with regards to preferences, fitness level and interests. Walking options may include exploring the course of the Chitake River as it flows to the Ruckomechi River, hiking upstream towards the escarpment or visiting other waterholes in the woodlands. Alternatively, it's possible to visit some dinosaur fossils or discover the inside of a hollow baobab that's the old lair of a leopard (and still has bones inside it).

Guests return to camp for lunch, and may set off on another walk afterwards or simply sit back and enjoy whatever wildlife is around the camp. In the evening, by the campfire, the plan for the next day is discussed. This could be an early start for a morning walk or a full breakfast before going on a longer outing. Alternatively, if there's a lot of action at the Springs, it can be good just to stay close and watch. On the fourth day, depending on guests' departure time, or if guests are moving on to do a canoe trail or an alternative camp, they may either take another early walk before breakfast or have a lie-in. After that, there's a game drive to the airstrip or back to Nyamepi.

Mana Pools lodge walks

Just about every lodge and camp in Mana Pools has good walking guides on its staff and includes walks in the activity mix during the dry season. The best options are described here, starting with some camps in the remote interior of the park, and then going west to east, downriver.

Overlooking the sandy bed of the Ruckomechi, about 1 km upstream of its confluence with the Chiwuye River, **Kavinga Safari Camp** has seven comfortable raised tents built on the edge of a cliff. With the backdrop of the nearby Zambezi escarpment, it affords a more isolated experience than the busy river area. The riverbed is frequented by elephant, and morning walks near camp reveal the tracks of leopard, civet, genet and porcupine around the pan below. Walking from Kavinga is a chance to explore areas away from the usual game drive areas. It has a different aspect from the more open woodlands of the main river valley. Here, there's riverine bush – Natal mahoganies, raintrees, acacias and combretum – and away from the dry riverbeds are some open grasslands with the odd pan dotted about depending upon the time of year. The Ruckomechi gorge is a challenging walk as it's very rocky and sandy, but the reward is finding beautiful leopard orchids, pink jacaranda, cassias, American propeller trees, tamarinds, euphorbia and aloes hanging off the cliffs. Behind the camp is a mini terraced floodplain and a thick *jesse* bush belt with numerous big baobabs, woody pears, an ebony forest and a Zambezi bell-bean forest. Kavinga is open from April to November, with game viewing and wildlife at the waterhole at its peak from August onwards. The camp can be accessed by

Wandering and wondering by the Zambezi

The Zambezi is mesmerising, surging and swirling, a steel grey sheen in the pre-dawn light. The bank below Mana River Camp is sheer to the water, too steep for hippos to climb. Their guttural sounds, and the plaintive call of the African fish eagle, are the signature sounds of the riverfront. I watched as a small bow wave pushed towards a sandbank – a crocodile on the move. Upriver, an elephant forded the river from the Zambian side, the water lapping its belly, the tips of his tusks ploughing the water. 'Looks like Pretty Boy,' said Richard Yohane, referring to one of the bigger tuskers of the park. 'Maybe we will meet him today.'

Richard was dressed for walking: a bush hat with tales to tell, a pressed shirt and khaki shorts held up by a belt that had a chunky revolver alongside the usual essentials – a precautionary backup to the rifle for some Zimbabwean guides when they guide alone. Short gaiters over his boots, binoculars of course, and a backpack full of reference books and spare water. A simple whittled cane of wild olive wood completed the ensemble – not a walking stick but useful for pointing.

We turned our backs to the water and set off inland. Ten minutes later, the cane was put to use, circling a fresh print. He looked at our little group, to see who would have a guess. It was not too distinct in the soft sand but looked like a cat, or maybe hyena. The fact that Richard had circled it made me think cat, and to cover my bases I said 'Leopard … or a lion cub.' He nodded and said 'Leopard. If it was a young lion, I'd expect to see more tracks, but this animal is alone.'

We scanned the winter thorns. Maybe the leopard had made a successful hunt in the night and was now high in a favourite tree with its catch. The scene was classic Mana Pools – the low morning sun casting a rich russet glow, filtered through the trees and lighting up a well-cropped understorey. Above the winter thorn – known as the ana tree in South Africa – the air tinged azure; Richard explained how the oils exuded by the leaves create the tint, and how their long tap roots mean that the tree can leaf in the dry season when most others are bare.

We walked on, following the leopard track, the air fragrant with the hint

Richard Yohane of Machaba Safaris admires the flower of a sausage tree.

We scanned suitable trees in search of the leopard.

of wild sage. From a distance, a black cuckoo call competed with a duet from the ever-present Cape turtle dove and emerald spotted wood dove. Our destination was one of the bigger lagoons, Long Pool. Mana means four, and these pools are old channels of the Zambezi River, created eons before it was tamed by the Kariba dam. At the lagoon, African openbills dominated. We circled back, stopping to admire a sculptural strangler fig, rising in thick braids around a void, the ghost of the tree it consumed. A metre-long monitor lizard, confident in its camouflage, adhered to the bark.

In the end, we found evidence of our quarry — an impala carcass stashed in a tree. But it was an old one, just skin and bone. Richard explained how a leopard will kill an impala about every three days. And this area has a high density of leopard. As he talked, he scuffed his boot on shards of brown pottery. It's not long since humans were present in what is now a national park. A natural presence living sustainably, as Richard explained. This was the land of the Korekore, whose Chief Chimombe was entombed in a hollow baobab at Sapi River.

After the walk, we took a slow drive inland, passing Chisasiko pool — another of the Mana. A dozen marabou storks stood stoically, their white legs ankle deep. In contrast, African jacanas were in perpetual motion, seeking insects amid the pond plants, appearing to walk on the surface of the water. The bush became dense — it's referred to locally as 'jesse bush', after the dominant species, a sort of bushwillow. Almost all Mana Pools lodges adhere to the river and the open floodplain woodlands where wildlife is easy to spot. In the central area of the park, there's only a kilometre or so between riverfront camps. So it was interesting to travel inland towards the southern escarpment and explore a less-trodden part of the park.

We drove a winding track to Ingwe Pan camp, which has its own little concession area and private game drive loop. The camp name means leopard in Zulu and related languages, and it has a real feel of bush immersion – surely there are leopards to be tracked here too. The dining area is under a fig tree, home of bats. Their occasional droppings are a small price to pay for the incredible job they do of hoovering up insects, aided by the frogs; for a bush camp beside water, there were remarkably few mosquitos.

The sounds of Ingwe Pan were different from those of Mana River. In the night, an African scops owl repeated its gently rolling call from close by, probably in that sycamore fig; the morning alarm was the harsh cry of Egyptian geese passing overhead at first light. As porridge cooked in the potje over the campfire embers, I listened to the soft splash of an elephant wading into the water hyacinth on the other side of the pan, disturbing a hippo that surged away. A grey-headed bush shrike call carried across the water, a mix of plaintive low whistles and impatient ticks. Next a red-eyed dove began its endless dance-music loop. It's moments like this, amid the sounds of natural Africa, that linger in the memory and draw me back.

road via Chimutsi Gate or by air via Ruckomechi airstrip, which is a 20-minute game drive from camp.

Kanga Camp is an **African Bush Camps** venue set on high ground on the eastern side of the Ruckomechi River valley about 15 km from the Zambezi. It's attractively constructed with tents on decks that feature outdoor showers with a view. Kanga Pan is one of the few water sources in the area and attracts plenty of game in dry season. In this remote south-western zone, walks explore *vlei* lines, mopane woodland and riverine forests. Kanga is accessed via Dandawa airstrip. The company has another pair of camps – Nyamatusi Camp and Nyamatusi Mahogany – in a prime position on the Zambezi in the centre of the park, allowing for a contrast in walking habitats.

Wilderness has three camps that present the full range of safari activities, including guided walks. At the western end of Mana Pools, Ruckomechi is located in a large private conservation area and affords a similar service level as the high-end lodges across the river in Zambia's Lower Zambezi National Park. Its ten rooms are shaded by winter thorn trees, and their seed pods are favoured by elephants who wander freely through the unfenced camp. Nearby and downriver, Little Ruckomechi is a smaller camp that offers a similar experience. Further downstream, at the other extreme of Mana Pools, Chikwenya is another Wilderness camp; it's nestled in a forest of winter thorn and Natal mahogany trees overlooking the river. Raised walkways link seven rooms to the main lounge and dining areas, and the pool and deck are perfect venues to pass the middle of the day, enjoying the views and passing wildlife.

Camp Mana is an owner-operated and traditional style 12-tent camp set on the edge of a floodplain near the Zambezi, a few kilometres east of Bushlife's Vundu Camp. It has the full set of Mana activities – game drives, walking and canoeing. The setting allows for walks directly from camp onto a very productive terrace, and these can be anything from one to three hours in duration, or longer when exploring southwards into the park's interior. This option is especially rewarding, as walkers traverse several different ecological zones in quick succession and move away from the roads and other visitors who are concentrated near the river. It's also common to drive from camp to enjoy the sunrise in the winter thorn woodlands and walk there. Walks are usually led by professional guide and lodge owner Steve Bolnick, who has particular affinities for tracking lion and appreciating the magnificent trees of Mana Pools. Overnight walking excursions to Chitake Springs are possible, for a recommended three nights.

Continuing downriver, there are fewer camps, and John's Camp, operated by **Robin Pope Safaris**, has a quiet concession area about an hour's drive from Mana Main airstrip. It's named after former park warden John Stevens. The camp is not directly on the river but has a view of a wide expanse of floodplain, usually with plenty of wildlife. There's a raised deck that can be used for wildlife spotting by day and as a sleep-out location by night.

The largest of the four Zambezi paleochannels that give their name to the park, Long Pool, has year-round water and extends to 11–14 km during the wet season. Nearby are Chisasiko Pool and Chine Pool, between Mana Main airstrip and the Zambezi in the central zone of the park. In this area are a few fine waterfront choices for walking bases – Mana River Camp, the African Bush Camps venues and Goliath Camp.

Mana River Camp, operated by **Machaba Safaris**, is a classic-style tented camp sleeping 12 guests. The sound of hippos comes from the river by night and day, but the bank is too steep for surprise visits. Dining is outdoors under a winter thorn tree. Walks here are interesting not just for the flora and fauna, but for the human history associated with the area. Machaba Safaris has a second camp in Mana Pools that's in an isolated location in a private concession. Ingwe Pan Camp is about an hour's game drive via woodlands of cathedral mopane and thick *jesse* bushlands. It faces directly onto a pumped pan, home of crocodiles and hippos – and is a birdwatcher's heaven. Walks from here have a different flavour to those in the more open woodlands of the floodplain.

Zambezi Expeditions camp is a little to the west of Mana River Camp and is similar in scale and location on the water's edge. It's part of the growing network of **African Bush Camp** properties. To the east are another pair of their venues, side by side. This area does not have public access, so has an exclusive feel. Nyamatusi Camp is quite fancy and even has a wine cellar, while nearby Mahogany Camp is designed for family use.

Downriver from Mana River camp, Goliath Camp is the home base of **Stretch Ferreira Safaris**, which is run by a well-known character in Mana guided walking for over 40 years. The camp is open from May to mid-November and accommodates up to 12 guests in eight Meru-style tents, with solar lighting, fans and en-suite bathrooms. There's a minimum stay requirement of three nights, and it's not hard to justify longer stays to really absorb the Mana Pools walking experience. Guests are guided personally by Stretch and his equally experienced professional guide Alistair Hull, together with a team of learner guides. Walks are often combined with drives, with the opportunity to start the walk to approach wildlife spotted in the distance when driving. In his long years of guiding, Stretch has come to know the park's bull elephants very well and is familiar with personalities that can be safely approached on foot. Goliath Camp is not far from Long Pool, which affords photographers excellent opportunities to capture the wildlife in the perfect light. Walking and other activities, including afternoon canoe trails, are included in the rates. Goliath Camp is normally accessed by flight transfer into Mana Main airstrip, but transfers by road and river are available from Chirundu via Nyamepi harbour.

Beyond Mana Pools are great expanses of wilderness stretching to the Mozambique border, much of it allocated as Game Management Areas, with controlled hunting activities. However, **Great Plains Conservation** has taken one large – 128,000 ha – former hunting zone and converted it into a photographic conservation area. Sapi Private Reserve is a model of rewilding in action, with investment in wildlife reintroductions, anti-poaching and tourism facilities. The only accommodation options are the Tembo Plains camp and the two-bedroom Jahazi suite nearby. This is part of the Great Plains Réserve-Collection of camps, which includes several Okavango camps and others in Kenya. It's the only member of Relais & Châteaux in Zimbabwe. Sheltered in the riparian woodland, the solar-powered camp operates seasonally from April to November. Guests enjoy game drives, guided walks, canoeing and boating on the Zambezi. The walks allow for exploration of the river, the fine woodlands of the floodplain nearby and, for variety, the reserve's interior, where mopane and *jesse* bush dominate. The lodge can be accessed by air via Chikwenya airstrip.

In the evenings, from the Tembo Plains boma, lights can be seen twinkling across the sandbanks, like an African will-o'-the-wisp. They are the lanterns at Old Mondoro, a magical camp in a marvellous park in a magnificent walking safari destination: Zambia.

8 Zambia

As a safari destination, Zambia has a lower profile than other countries covered in this guide and has to fight for its place: the government has helped by eliminating pesky tourist visa fees in recent years. Yet as a walking safari destination, Zambia is top tier, and this is thanks to a long tradition of guided trails and some superlative destinations on the Zambezi River and its northern tributaries.

The safari season in Zambia is confined to about half of the year. Some lodges stay open for the green season, but the walking really begins in April. At the start of the dry season, bush is dense, and game tends to be in the interior. It's hard to predict when water levels will drop to levels that make walking feasible, but it's best to plan from mid-June, as rains may leave waterways high and hard to cross on foot.

July to September has excellent walking conditions in the whole Zambezi basin. From September it starts to get hotter, but these months are popular with photographers, who like the combination of sunlight, dust and the blue hue from the secretions of the winter thorn trees (*Faidherbia albida*, known as ana trees in South Africa). By November, most walking has ended for the season.

Walking safaris in Zambia

Unlike Zimbabwe or other destinations in this guide, Zambia does not have independent walk specialists that can run mobile walking safaris in the parks. Walks are operated by companies that have presence – a concession or a privately owned lodge or camp. More so than other destinations, Zambian lodge and camp owners cooperate to make it easy for visitors to put together multi-park or multi-camp itineraries; rather than booking through a safari agency in your home country, pick one of the companies from the following pages. Chiawa Safaris, Classic Zambia, Green Safaris, Remote Africa Safaris, Robin Pope Safaris and Shenton Safaris are walks-focused companies with their own camps that can build a full itinerary with transfers and cross booking with other safari companies.

Zambia is known as the Home of the Walking Safari because the first wilderness trails were created in the Luangwa River valley (in the east of the country) in the 1950s. Today, that area is protected by three national parks – South Luangwa, Luambe and North Luangwa – which together have one of the highest concentrations of wilderness walking options in Africa.

The Luangwa joins the Zambezi River at the tripoint of Zambia, Mozambique and Zimbabwe, and the Zambezi valley to the west of there is another walking safari hotspot. The entire area is an emerging 17,700 sq. km cross-border conservation zone known as the Lower Zambezi-Mana Pools Transfrontier Conservation Area. Mana Pools National Park (see page 178) is mirrored on the northern bank of the Zambezi in Zambia's Lower Zambezi National Park and shares a similar landscape and habitat – a floodplain threaded with channels suited to canoeing and backed by a wild escarpment. Lower Zambezi has superb woodland walking – albeit at a higher cost than Mana Pools and

Luangwa valley – and it's not a place for overnight or camp-to-camp walks.

Apart from these two world-class wilderness areas, Zambia presents enticing lodge-based walking in the wetlands of Liuwa Plain in the remote west and backpacking and lodge walks in the vast central reserve of Kafue National Park. A must-see while in Zambia is the mighty cascade of Mosi-oa-Tunya (also known as Victoria Falls), where shorter nature walks and rhino-tracking are available (see page 165).

Wildlife police officers – sometimes referred to as scouts – from the Department of National Parks and Wildlife provide a rifle escort for all walks in big game areas.

Liuwa Plain National Park

In Zambia's far west, Liuwa Plain is a pristine 3,600 sq. km wilderness area with outstanding expanses of savannah teeming with wildlife. It covers an extensive floodplain that was once home to the Litunga, or king, of the Lozi people. The terrain of Liuwa Plain is characterised by vast grasslands, punctuated by seasonal wetlands and wooded islands. Protected for over a century and now under the co-management of conservation non-profit African Parks, the landscape is transformed by the seasons. During the rainy period, from late October onwards, the floodplains become shallow lakes, attracting thousands of waterbirds and water-loving wildlife. The conditions attract large numbers of blue wildebeest – the second-largest wildebeest migration in Africa – and their predators, including growing numbers of lion, and the park is a cheetah stronghold. Liuwa hosts large numbers of zebra, antelopes such as red lechwe and common tsessebe, as well as hyena, jackal and a variety of smaller carnivores and herbivores.

Liuwa Plains can be accessed by road from the Chobe area of Botswana by travelling via Namibia's Caprivi Strip to cross the Zambezi via the bridge at Katima Mulilo. It's a long drive that can be broken with a stopover at **Lumbe Pools**, where short walks to the Ngonye Falls are available. The park reception is a 45-minute drive north of the town of Kalabo, and for self-drivers a 4x4 is required in the park. Alternatively, there are air charters with Proflight to Kalabo Airport, from where guests are transferred to the park lodgings.

April, May and June are wonderful months to visit if it has been a normal rainfall year, and in July the park starts to dry out and wildebeest begin to migrate north. September and October rains generally come in the form of showers or afternoon thunderstorms after the day's walk is completed. The rains transform the plains to a riot of wildflower colour, and over the following months the floodwaters rise and the birding is excellent. In October, the wildebeest move south again, and from then onwards is predator season, the open landscape making it possible to witness hunting activity. For walking, the wet season from November to March is better avoided.

Liuwa Camp is the latest piece of tourism infrastructure developed by African Parks; it's in the south-west of the park, around 45 minutes' drive from the headquarters. Overlooking a waterhole and attractively set in a grove of mobola plums and jackal-berry trees, the camp has seven en-suite tents and a family unit, sleeping 18 guests in total. It's a low footprint off-grid camp, and the décor showcases Lozi culture.

It's the most affordable fully catered option in the park, and operates from March to December. Game drives and walking are included in rates, and the walking terrain is generally flat and open. Self-drive guests staying at Liuwa Camp are transferred into camp from either Kalabo airport or Liuwa Headquarters and private vehicles can be left at either location.

Ker & Downey Zambia (a sister company to Ker & Downey Botswana) has recently announced that it is to take over operation of the 6-tent King Lewanika Lodge, and walks will be available there too.

Kafue National Park

Zambia's largest and oldest national park, Kafue National Park, conserves over 22,000 sq. km of prime wilderness, which, like Liuwa Plain, is co-managed by pan-African conservation organisation African Parks. The terrain ranges from dense woodlands and savannahs to grassy plains and riverine forests. The park is situated in south-central Zambia in the Kafue River basin, and the meandering river and its tributaries nourish a wealth of wildlife; habitat for elephant, lion, leopard, cheetah, African wild dog, hyena, buffalo, zebra and numerous antelope species.

African Parks have imminent plans for black rhino reintroduction. Kafue has recorded over 500 bird species, including the endangered wattled crane and the African finfoot.

An adventure backpacking trail operates seasonally in a gigantic wilderness zone, and lodges with walking guides include those operated by Classic Zambia, Green Safaris, McBrides, Mukambi Safaris, Nanzhila and Northern Kafue Safaris. The best time to walk in Kafue is during the dry season from June through to mid-November.

The view across the Kafue River into the national park from Mukambi Lodge.

Malala Wilderness Trail

The **Malala Wilderness Trail** is a backpacking trail for the truly adventurous, an opportunity to explore a vast wilderness in leave-no-trace style. The area walked is west of the expansive Itezhi Tezhi lake, a designated wilderness zone of over 4,360 sq. km that dwarfs the similarly zoned areas in the Kruger and Serengeti national parks. The wilderness trail is an initiative of African Parks in collaboration with the Department of National Parks and Wildlife and South Africa's Lowveld Trails Co., and runs for groups of four to eight hikers from June to the end of October. The trail base is the new Malala Campsite on the remote western shore of the lake, which has five pitches, each with its own ablutions with hot showers and enviro-loos. The rise and fall of the lake creates extensive lawns that attract a variety of grazing animals including buffalo, puku, impala, Kafue lechwe and hippo. Guests should arrive fully equipped for their stay and packing advice is provided in advance.

There are trail options for three or six nights, both priced on a group basis. Departing from Malala, trailists are guided by a Department of National Parks and Wildlife police officer alongside Lowveld Trails Co. mentors. The trails take place in the hinterland, where the sheer size and diversity of geology and soil provides for a variety of landscapes and vegetation that offer endless variations for exploration. The granites, slates, quartzites and limestones ensure a varied and rugged landscape in the southern portion of the wilderness area, while the clay soils that overlay this rock in the west create *dambos* in the Luansanda River system that are largely surrounded by miombo, with *munga* and mopane woodlands found on the deeper clay. The drainage lines that separate the rugged formations create multiple riverine tributaries, the primary being the Musa, Luangandu and Luansanda, and it should be feasible to find safe flowing water for bathing during a trail. The area also hosts Zambezian Baikiaea woodlands, climatic relics that add biodiversity to the landscape.

Malala can be accessed via the scheduled one-hour Proflight link from Lusaka to Chunga Airstrip, which runs Mondays, Wednesdays and Fridays. From the airstrip, it's around two and a half hours' game drive to Malala Campsite. Guests with high ground clearance vehicles can self-drive; it takes at least five hours from either Livingstone (via Dundumwezi Gate) or Lusaka (via Main Gate). It's best to plan to spend the first night at the campsite or one of the lodges in the park along the way.

Kafue lodge walks

In the southern half of Kafue, **Nanzhila** is an owner-operated company with two camps that have walking safaris in the activities mix. Plains Camp is a 12-bed venue with a choice of safari tents or chalets, well located overlooking a *dambo* on the floodplain of the Kasha River. The camp operates from May to November with the walking season from the start of July to the end of October. The year-round water and interlinking grasslands generate a constant stream of game and birdlife. Walks explore the plains and move between bands of miombo that provide shade and the chance to spot birds of that habitat, with the woodlands giving cover to get close to grazing antelopes that can include sable, roan and eland.

Lake Camp has a longer season, opening in March and closing at the end of December. It's well set overlooking the Musa River at the point where it enters the southern end of Itezhi Tezhi lake.

It's in a very active wildlife belt that's a predator hotspot, especially late in the year. Walks are guided from mid-August until the end of season and tend to follow the Musa River and/or lake shoreline, spotting waterbirds and grazing game along the way; with luck, there's a chance to encounter African wild dogs on foot. Both camps are usually accessed via road transfers and can be included on an overland itinerary between Livingstone and Lusaka. Self-drivers should note that a high ground clearance vehicle, ideally 4x4, is needed on the sandy roads in the park. From Livingstone it takes three and a half hours to reach the park gate at Dundumwezi, from where it's a 90-minute game drive to Plains Camp. Guests usually take in nights at both camps, with the transfer via a morning game drive of around two and a half hours.

Mukambi Safaris is family owned and long established in Kafue. There's a choice of two locations in very different parts of the park – Busanga Plains camp in the north, and a pair of camps in the central east, accessible by road from Lusaka. Walks are available in both areas, offering a diversity of habitats and landscapes. Headquarters is Mukambi Safari Lodge, set overlooking the Kafue River. The main area has multiple levels of decks set around a tumbling stream; it's especially attractive in the evenings as the sun sets over the park on the opposite side of the river. Accommodation is either in thatched rondavels or more well-appointed safari tents, or in a riverside villa designed for families. In all, the camp can accommodate 32 guests, and has a relaxed atmosphere with a dining deck where guests sit in their own groups with the owners usually present. The unfenced grounds are popular with elephant, lion, leopard, hyena, puku, impala, baboons and vervets. All safari activities from Mukambi Lodge start with a short boat hop across the river to where the game viewing vehicles await. Guests are led by a walking guide and escorted by a wildlife police officer. Mukambi can be reached via a low-traffic road from Lusaka, and much of the four- to five-hour drive leads through a Game Management Area. Chunga airstrip is a 40-minute game drive from the lodge, and is accessed by charters and thrice-weekly scheduled flights.

A good walking option is to choose the smaller seasonal camp, Fig Tree Bush Camp, located in the park less than an hour via game drive from Mukambi. This very special place is open from May to November and sleeps just eight guests in four tents on high platforms; three overlook the Shishamba River and the fourth has a view of a waterhole and grasslands. Like the main camp, it has an infinity pool for relaxing between activities. Its signature feature, a magnificent sycamore fig, provides shade for the dining and lounge area. If the tents are not wild enough, a 'Star Bed' is the answer – just a bed on a platform, safe from any nocturnal wildlife visitors, with a bathroom below. As from Mukambi, walks are enjoyed as an alternative to drives, generally going out for about three hours and returning for brunch.

In the north of the park, Mukambi's Busanga Plains Camp operates from July to October when the water levels have dropped. It's really in the heart of the plain and the walks explore the flat terrain, a mix of grasslands and wooded habitats. Busanga Plains can be accessed by air charter via Busanga airstrip, which is 40 minutes by game drive from camp. In any case, Kafue is not a place to rush, and it's recommended to allocate time to reach the north via a rewarding day-long game drive through the park from Mukambi Lodge or Fig Tree Bush Camp.

On foot in Kafue, guided by Malcom Phiri of Mukambi Safari Lodge.

Also in the north, and not far from Busanga Plains Camp, Chisa Busanga is remarkable for its unique tree-height sleeping 'nests' that are crafted from aluminium, canvas and twigs. Operated by **Green Safaris**, Chisa Busanga is a place to combine game drives (in an electric Land Cruiser) and walks to appreciate the entire ecosystem. The area is flat and dotted with wild date palms, sausage trees and fig trees, and fine for easy walking. It has high numbers of antelope, including Defassa waterbuck and red lechwe – and their predators. It's a birding hotspot. Walking in Busanga Plains is confined to the dry season and best enjoyed from July until September. In October rains are more likely, and by mid-November the camp closes and the plains are given over to water and wildlife for the duration of the green season. The camp, which is bookable for exclusive use, sleeps eight, but walking groups have a maximum of six guests.

There's a discount rate for three nights or more.

Green Safaris has a second lodge between the Kafue Hook Bridge Gate and Mukambi Lodge. Following a fire, Ila Safari Lodge was completely rebuilt on its riverside site and reopened in 2024. It has a striking design, with 'nest' rooms inspired by Chisa Busanga. There's a large solar bank to power its electric game viewing vehicles and boat. Activities, including walks, begin with a boat transfer across the river into Kafue National Park. Ila is accessed via the Chunga airstrip or by road from Lusaka, and can be combined with Chisa Busanga via a 20-minute flight or a long game drive. Green Safaris also have lodges near Victoria Falls and in Lower Zambezi and South Luangwa national parks. Ask about offers that include free air or road transfers.

Classic Zambia Safaris has a heritage in walking safaris, formed through the merger of Jeffery and McKeith Safaris, originally based in the Kafue National Park, and Tusk and Mane Safaris, based in Lower Zambezi National Park. The company runs traditional seasonal bush camps in the deep interior of Kafue and in Lower Zambezi and North Luangwa National Parks. With their own aircraft and flexible departures on shared charters, providing seat rates from Lusaka and Livingstone, Classic Zambia is a good choice to combine a Victoria Falls visit with walking in these parks.

In Kafue, Musekese Camp is open from the start of May to the end of November and Ntemwa-Busanga Camp from July to the end of October. Musekese is set on the Kafue River, while Ntemwa-Busanga is a bush camp in the north with views of the grassy expanses of Busanga Plains. It has a shorter season because of the annual inundation of that part of the park. Musekese is completely off grid and off network, and has just five stretched-canvas chalets. It's accessed by air to Lufupa, and from the airstrip transfer to camp is by boat across the river and then a short drive into camp. It's a three-hour drive north to Ntemwa-Busanga Camp, or longer if there are a lot of game stops along the way. There's a maximum of six guests for activities at both camps, and two of Zambia's rare female guides work here. Musekese is the choice for guided walks.

Northern Kafue Safaris guide walks from two of their camps, Kafue River Lodge, which is in the Game Management Area on the edge of the park, and Kikuji Camp, which is inside the park on the Lunga River not far from Musekese. They are open between June and November, and walks must be booked in advance to allow for a game scout to be in camp to accompany the guide during the walk. The walks can be organised to start from camp or after driving to a selected location.

In the same area as Kikuji, the campsite at **McBrides Camp** is popular with self-drive visitors, and it also has seven moderately priced double chalets overlooking the Kafue River at its main camp and a self-catering bush camp 14 km away. It's open from March to December, and as well as drives and river safaris, walks are guided in the park. A slackpacking-style walk between the two camps can be arranged, a flat route that tracks the river for some of the way, before crossing miombo woodlands and open pan areas.

Lower Zambezi National Park

Lower Zambezi National Park is in the south of Zambia along the Zambezi River, which forms the park's southern boundary. Overshadowed by the Luangwa valley for walking safaris, the 4,000 sq. km park is nonetheless a superb destination to explore on foot. For wildlife, its scale is enhanced by the even larger Mana Pools National Park on the opposite side of the river in Zimbabwe, and animals – especially elephants – move freely back and forth. It's a place for lodge-based walks, with no fly-camping or mobile walking safaris of the type that are found in Luangwa or Mana Pools. It has the advantage over Mana Pools in having fewer camps, but prices are higher here. There are excellent small family-owned walking venues from Chiawa and Classic Zambia, and walks are available from the luxury lodges of Time + Tide, Anabezi, Amanzi, African Bush Camps and Green Safaris. Outside the park, self-drivers favour Mvuu Lodge Campsite.

The terrain of Lower Zambezi comprises floodplains backed by

A space for nature

Stepping off the boat onto the bank of the Kafue River, there was a sense of landfall on a wild and ancient shore. To the west, south and north lay a park bigger than Kruger National Park in South Africa. Kruger gets over 1.5 million visitors a year. And Kafue? We were among just 16,000 who make it here annually. It's a place in which to get lost, to walk or drive without seeing other visitors, a wilderness where the natural world has priority over ours.

This part of Central Kafue is heavily wooded, in contrast to the open grasslands and marshes of the north of the park. Even before we started walking, there was a remarkable feature to appreciate – a termite mound the size of a house, with a baobab tree on top. I had to check with guide Malcom Phiri: was this huge tree, hundreds of years old, growing on top of the termite hills, or had the termite hills developed around the tree? He said it really grew on top – these termite colonies can be thousands of years old.

It was an astonishing fact to ruminate upon as we set off, led by Department of National Parks and Wildlife scout Michael Mwanza. This wild place in western Zambia endures at its own pace, measured in millennia, not years.

Malcom Phiri showed us some porcupine droppings.

It was curious to see how the baobab, leadwood and candelabra euphorbia grow in a cluster.

It was here, in the late 1950s, that the park's first Wildlife Warden Norman Carr made his name, and it was under his management that it became one of the first areas in Africa to begin the shift from extractive usage to conservation. Since that time, it has become more accessible and our lodge, Mukambi Safari Lodge, was an easy four-hour drive from Lusaka on an empty road. It feels like an important reserve, a place with the scale to allow wildlife to thrive.

Some of these animals were now in view, a puku ram and its leggy harem, the thick-coated antelope most associated with Zambia. Among them was a couple of waterbuck – 'mukambi' in the Kaonde language – that towered over their smaller cousins. Otherwise, it was all quiet on the wildlife front, and Malcom drew our attention to the trees as we walked away from the river. We were in a miombo woodland, dominated by four-leaf combretum. He pointed to the mud tracks created by termites on a leadwood tree. These foraging tubes are constructed to protect the insects from the sun and predators. It was interesting that the leadwood kept company with two completely different trees – a candelabra euphorbia and a baobab. As Malcom showed us the mud nest of an African swift, artfully attached in a shady groove of the tree, I wondered about the science of that – presumably evidence of successful seed dispersal strategies.

Malcom had moved on and was still dipping into the walking guide repertoire used when there's little wildlife around: focus on the things that don't move. We stopped for some fresh porcupine droppings and tried to pick up its track, without success; and broke up a dry ball of elephant dung as Malcom explained how it can be boiled to make tea to treat asthma. We admired a sausage tree, and he told how the wood was favoured to make mokoro, the vernacular canoe of Africa. The ground beneath was scattered with red blossoms that had fallen in the night. 'Careful where you stand,' Malcom warned, as he picked up one of the fruits so we could weigh it in our hands. Nearby, another termite mound – a baby compared with the first – was polished smooth at warthog height: the fresh mud is always a sign that there's water nearby.

We walked on, and there was a flurry and flash of fur to the side. We'd disturbed a white-tailed mongoose, which had been passing the daylight hours in a shallow bunker. Feeling a bit guilty about that, I was glad when we returned to the river, knowing it would deliver interesting sights. Not just hippos and crocodiles, but birds – a tawny eagle in a tree; openbills eating jackal-berry fruits; an African harrier-hawk patrolling the airways. It was a fine spot for a water break. As we counted birds, Malcom picked up the flight feather of a helmeted guinea fowl. They are so common as ground birds, we forget they are decent flyers when they need to escape, and of course every evening when they bustle up to roost in their favoured trees.

Rested and rehydrated, we looped back inland. Michael stopped and signalled for us to do likewise – a sound had got his attention. He and Malcom consulted quietly, then motioned for us to follow. Using a termite mound for cover, we managed to spy on a small group of elephants, a female and her young. 'There will be more behind in the deeper bush,' said Malcom, and told us we should retrace our steps to avoid running into them.

A couple of hours later, I chatted with Malcom amid the aromas of the pizza oven at Mukambi. He is originally from Chipata and has good memories of guiding in the Luangwa valley, close to his hometown. He started out as a teacher and feels that nature guiding lets him use the same skills. Malcom is Ngoni, a people widely scattered in Southern Africa and related to the Zulu Nation of South Africa. He is proud that Zambia's many tribes – 73 it is said – have created a republic that is on a good trajectory and has avoided the tumultuous history associated with most of its neighbours. I asked him what he likes best about Kafue. 'It's the feeling that so much is unexplored here,' he said. 'I love that there are new areas to discover, and so few vehicles here. And walking – that's how I feel attached to nature.'

escarpments and mountains to the north. Wildlife and tourism is focused on the Zambezi, which is flanked by a mosaic of habitats, including shallow side channels, grassy plains, woodlands, pans and riverine forests. As well as being known for walking safaris, one of the best features of Lower Zambezi National Park is the opportunity to view wildlife from the water. Riverine ebony and fig trees grow thickly along the water's edge, bordering inland floodplains with towering winter thorn and acacia. Boat safaris (and fishing) are popular, and side channels provide safe conditions for canoe safaris. The ideal time to walk here is July to September.

West of Lower Zambezi National Park, there are a number of lodges along the river in the Game Management Area. They have the advantage of being easier to access by road from Lusaka, but for walking, it's recommended to stay in the park itself if this is within your budget.

The western boundary of the park is delineated by the Chongwe River, where a couple of **Time + Tide** properties sit. Both Chongwe House and Chongwe Suites have river views and can be accessed by air from the nearby Royal Zambezi airstrip. The season runs from April to mid-November. Walks are a popular choice in an activity mix that includes night drives, canoeing, fishing and a sleep-out on fancy hammocks. More intensive camp-to-camp walks are available from Time + Tide's venues in South Luangwa National Park.

The much-loved **Chiawa Safaris** Camp is the original safari camp in Lower Zambezi National Park, still owned by the founding Cumings family. In the 1980s it was chosen as the site of a tented camp that was reset for each season, and now has a more substantial presence, with its tents and common areas raised on eco-friendly bamboo decks. Each of its nine expansive tents has a hammock and plunge pool that overlook the Zambezi River, and there's always something interesting in view, such as elephant wading or swimming the river. The camp is accessed via Jeki airstrip, and the one-hour road and boat transfer sets the tone for the stay: a river full of life, hundreds of hippos, crocodiles on the sandbanks, fish eagles perched on their favourite trees. As a safari base, it offers an attractive balance of vehicle, walking and water based activities that's rare to find in Africa. As well as the motorised

The first coffee of the day before setting off for a walk from Chiawa Camp.

Old Mondoro is a small camp, ideal for walking safaris.

boat trips, there's a channel that's safe for a canoe safari – which is a must-do while at Chiawa. It's possible to navigate the shallow channel and get remarkably close to wildlife without disturbing it – giant herons perching, baboons feeding, water bucks browsing, crocodiles doing what crocodiles do.

Thanks to the combination of river and woodlands, Chiawa Safaris operates in some of Africa's finest walking habitat, and it has the guides to make the most of it: they benefit from annual upskilling training that includes tracking, photography and bushcraft. The canopy of the winter thorn and mahogany forests have a thin understorey, making unexpected close encounters with big animals unlikely. The elephants have a pattern of movement, going inland to the escarpment at night, where it's warmer and there are less predators. So, walks have a natural evolution – perhaps starting following the tracks of lions and African wild dogs, encountering the occasional bull elephant; and, by the end of the walk, threading a route through herds of elephant arriving at the river for water.

35 km downriver, its sister camp, Old Mondoro, is a place cited by experienced travellers as their favourite camp in Africa. A smaller five-chalet camp set in open woodlands, it's in an area that always seems bustling with wildlife – animals browsing on seedpods, and their predators prowling by night. Its outdoor bathrooms with views on the river are a highlight. It's arguably even better as a walking base than Chiawa, as it has the smaller scale associated with walking camps. Old Mondoro is a one-hour transfer from Jeki by game drive, and, like Chiawa, it's open from May to mid-November. Combined itineraries are available from Chiawa Safaris in South Luangwa National Park. Direct flights between Jeki airstrip and Mfuwe airport are available, so it's possible to have a walk in Lower Zambezi in the morning and an afternoon game drive in the Luangwa valley – or vice versa.

A couple of other lodge options are close to Jeki in the central zone of the park: Lolebezi is a relatively new lodge operated by Zimbabwean company **African Bush Camps** and **Mwambashi River Lodge** is at the confluence of the Mwambashi and Zambezi Rivers. Both run morning walks, with Mwambashi specialising in birding walks.

Two local companies operate camps in three of Zambia's best walking safaris areas of Kafue, Lower Zambezi and the Luangwa valley: Green Safaris and Classic Zambia. This makes them suitable for seamless multi-park itineraries. In Lower Zambezi, **Green Safaris** runs Sausage Tree Camp and Potato Bush Camp, while Classic Zambia operates Chula Island and Kutali. The Green Safaris lodges operate from April to November, and both have luxurious tents with river views. The heavy tree cover and Zambezi side channels make this one of the nicest walking sectors in the park.

Chula Island and Kutali camps are low-impact seasonal **Classic Zambia Safaris** camps that contrast with the fixed structures of the high-end camps in the park. After the river levels subside, around April, both camps are set on islands in the quiet eastern zone of the park, across the river from Sapi Private Reserve in Zimbabwe. The lodges run game drives and walks in enchanting and varied riparian woodlands. From Chula Island, which is west of Old Mondoro, walks explore the river channels, the Natal mahogany woodlands and the grasslands of Jeki plains. From Kutali Camp, east of Old Mondoro, it's winter thorn as far as the eye can see, often with elephants munching seedpods in their shade. From either camp, it's superb walking habitat.

Chula is located on a large island, Katengahumba, and is reached by boat from the mainland; while there are two vehicles on the island, there's no access for anyone else, so this is a private island experience. The wildlife, including elephant and leopard, is not deterred by the water and can be seen in camp. The sandy beaches are at their best at dawn and sunset, and it's not unusual to see elephants wading or swimming. Kutali is equally well situated under the tree canopy by the river. Both camps operate highly recommended canoe safaris, which take place on narrow channels that wind through the interior of the park and sometimes on the main Zambezi River too. There's a maximum of six guests on walks, and as both camps are on islands, it means there's no likelihood of spotting vehicles while walking, something that can happen in other parts of the park. Each camp has five well-spaced tents on the river, which are pleasantly Ruritanian – no Wi-Fi, no charging points in the rooms and bucket showers. When the season is over at the end of October, all traces of the camps are removed. The nearest airstrip is Jeki and Classic Zambia has its own aircraft to facilitate transfers from Lusaka and to its camps in Kafue and North Luangwa and other destinations.

Downriver from the Classic Zambia camps, **Anabezi** is a five-star tented camp that opens from Easter until mid-November and features a raised boardwalk that connects the tents and common areas, allowing guests to move freely in safety by day and wildlife to roam by day and night. As well as individual plunge-pools at each of the 12 tented suites, the camp has two swimming pools. Safaris by vehicle, boat and canoe make for an enjoyable variation of experiences alongside guided walks in the winter thorn woodlands. Anabezi is accessed via a 40-minute game drive from Jeki airstrip, or by private charter to Kulefu airstrip, which is closer.

The last camp in the park is the remote and exclusive **Amanzi**. It has just four classically styled safari tented suites, all overlooking the river and its wildlife. As well as offering game drives, boat safaris and fishing, Amanzi has a trained walking guide on staff, and the walks are led through the gorgeous woodlands and along the braided river channels. The camp is open from the start of April to mid-November, with the access airstrips the same as those for Anabezi.

South Luangwa National Park

Defined by the seasonal ebb and flow of its watercourses, the Luangwa River valley is Africa at its wildest. The natural cycle of inundation has played a big part in protecting the valley, and today it's one of the continent's pre-eminent walking safari destinations. The genesis was in 1961 when the wildlife warden Norman Carr recognised the potential to take visitors for a truly immersive safari experience and began to operate his wilderness trails. Today the valley is protected in three national parks, and the largest, spread over 9,000 sq. km, is South Luangwa National Park.

Most of the park is west of the river, but there's a chunk on the eastern bank called the Nsefu sector. The park lives to the rhythm of the undammed river and its tributaries, and its wide floodplains, dominated by mopane woodlands, are inhabited by great numbers of herbivores and their predators. The Luangwa's paleochannels form oxbow lakes and are referred to in the valley as lagoons (in the American sense rather than the Pacific salt-water sense). As these shrink through the dry season they are utilised by all sorts of wildlife, and provide for much of the walking focus.

In the main channel, the river has sheer sandy banks that provide perfect nesting habitats for spectacular colonies of bee-eaters which take up residence from September. The river continues to change its course, eroding these banks, and sometimes a big flood can sweep away entire camp locations. It's not unusual to hear the phrase 'that's where the camp used to be', with the speaker pointing at a sandbank in the river. The best trail conditions are in the dry season from May until October. After then it gets hotter, and the rainy season usually starts in mid-November. The majority of camps close for the duration of the wet season from then until April.

During the dry season there's a very strong focus on walking in the park, and visitors can choose from an excellent range of lodges, camps and mobile walking safaris. Most of the lodges and camps are located along the Luangwa, facilitating marvellous views of the river and the wildlife it sustains, and others are tucked into tributary valleys with river courses that are a mix of sand and pools in the dry season.

A particular feature of South Luangwa is the camp-to-camp walk, and several walk operators have multiple camps within the park including Remote Africa Safaris, The Bushcamp Company, Shenton Safaris and Time + Tide. Robin Pope Safaris is known for its range of walk options, including the only truly mobile walking safari in the park. The itinerary building possibilities are limitless. The walk operators listed here will generally put together trips throughout the valley and in other parks in Zambia, managing booking with other companies and arranging seamless transfers. Traversing the valley from south to north, the following sections cover all the specialist walking operators and a selection of lodges with walks.

SOUTH LUANGWA NATIONAL PARK

Wandering amid the leadwood trees of South Luangwa National Park.

The Bushcamp Company

With two permanent lodges and six bush camps in South Luangwa National Park, **The Bushcamp Company** has Zambia's largest selection of walking bases. Most guests include walks as part of their stay, and these are available from both lodges all year and seasonally from the camps. The bush camps are in the south of the park, remote from other camps, and this has some great advantages: inter-camp coordination means you can spend the entire day without encountering any other visitors, and guides can discreetly share information on wildlife sightings, making finding elusive animals easier.

The bush camps are intimate in scale – most have four tents or chalets, designed to fit the maximum size of a walking group. They are constructed in sympathy with tradition and the landscape, nestled unobtrusively on sites overlooking rivers or lagoons. It's not obligatory to walk, and game drives are at least part of the experience. There's no need to devote too much time to deciding which bush camp to pick – they are all charming and splendidly located. The decision will likely come down to what is available, as they have different operational months, and opening times can be disrupted by flood conditions.

Chindeni and Bilimungwe are first to open in May, followed in June by Kuyenda and Chamilandu, and these four close by the end of October. Kapamba and Zungulila operate the longest season, from April to January, as they are both located on the Kapamba River and are less subject to flooding than the main Luangwa valley. Zungulila had a complete redesign and rebuild for the 2024 season. At Kuyenda, tariffs are a bit lower than the other camps. The newest lodge is KuKaya, an exclusive-use villa located close to Mfuwe Lodge. Even in the 'green season' from January to April, it's possible to find places suitable for walking when staying at either of the lodges.

Luangwa – a little recent history

The Luangwa valley is a microcosm of the African wildlife tourism business and a good example of how it originally developed: pioneering individuals welcoming intrepid travellers to remote camps that continue today as second- and third-generation family-owned safari operators. In 60 years, the valley has shifted from a landscape exploited by hunters and poachers to one enjoyed by a multitude of nature lovers, and one person is given most of the credit: Norman Joseph Carr (1912–97).

Apart from a few years as Wildlife Warden in Kafue, Carr spent his career in the valley, from an elephant control officer in the 1930s to the establishment of some of today's best loved camps. The first half of that career was spent in game management, including efforts to combat tsetse fly, a serious vector for cattle disease. It was a time when 'safari' referred only to 'hunting safari'. He was then a pioneer in the shift to photographic safaris, and in the recognition of the necessity of involving local communities in conservation. As Warden for the Zambian Game Department in what was then the Luangwa Game Reserve on the western side of the river, he established Nsefu camp in 1950. This was the valley's first tourism camp, set in an area of abundant wildlife on the eastern side of the river on the land of Chief Mwanya. In 1954, a permanent camp was added downstream in the territory of Chief Nsefu. The area reserved for photographic safaris straddled the land of both chiefdoms, and the naming of Nsefu Game Reserve, as well as the fact that Chief Nsefu gained control of the revenue, are bones of contention to this day.

Each year during the 1950s, the Nsefu reserve attracted an average of 440 tourists and generated £1,000 for the community owners. Hunting and photographic safaris continued side by side in the area for some years, so it's hard to pin down exactly when Carr led the first of his 'Wilderness Trails'. Certainly, by the time he retired from the Wildlife Department in 1961, he was devoted to walking safaris, and his company Norman Carr Safaris established a series of camps in the following years, starting with Kapani, which he shared with two lions. They had been adopted as cubs following an unfortunate incident in Kafue when a ranger approached their hiding place and shot their mother.

Of course, Carr was not alone in developing Luangwa into the marvellous

A typical six-night itinerary would start with a couple of nights at the main base of Mfuwe Lodge, which has 18 air-conditioned thatched chalets. From there, drive south to Chindeni and use it as a walking base for two nights. Then transfer by vehicle (or walk part of the way) to Kapamba for two nights, to experience a different river valley. On the last day, take a slow morning game drive back to Mfuwe Lodge, and onward travel. Alternatively, it's a nice idea to book at bush camps that are close enough to transfer on foot (while the bags go by vehicle). Chamilandu to Chindeni is about four hours; Chindeni to Bilimungwe three and a half hours; Bilimungwe to Kapamba three hours; and from there to Zungulila two and a half hours.

walking safari destination that it is today. Barry Shenton (1929–2007) worked alongside him in the Game Department in the early years in both Luangwa and Kafue, including when Nsefu was established. After a varied career he returned to the valley and helped his son Derek establish Kaingo camp near Nsefu in 1972, still run by the Shenton family.

Old Chibembe was set by Carr in 1964 inside the park, and he guided with Phil Berry, a fixture at Kuyenda camp (now part of The Bushcamp Company set) until his passing in 2022. To accommodate walking guests, they built seasonal camps of grass and other bush materials, a practice that continues today with some valley operators. In 1971, the Nsefu Game Reserve was absorbed into South Luangwa National Park. Carr built Chibembe Lodge on the eastern bank in 1974, soon joined there by Robin Pope, who became senior guide. From there, the wilderness trails were led in the park, utilising various locations including Lukusuzi, Kasansanya, Old Chibembe and Chikoko and later Mwamba bush camp. Carr's Chinzombo camp was established in 1977 as a place to wait out the 'wet season' followed by Kakuli and then Kapani Lodge near Mfuwe, Carr's final home (not be confused with the now gone Kapani camp 60 km upriver, where he lived with the lions). His last set of lodges and bush camps are now operated by Time + Tide, who use Kapani as their local operational camp.

Nsefu was run by the Zambian Tourism Board until it was privatised in 1979, along with the 'old' Lion Camp and Big Lagoon (now, like Chikoko, a Remote Africa Safaris bush camp). They were bought by Zambia Safaris & Wilderness Trails, who also acquired Carr's company. Robin Pope took on the rebuilding and management of Nsefu from 1980 to 1985 and John Coppinger (see page 221) joined him as a guide in 1984. Guests who stay at today's Nsefu camp are sleeping close to the site of first permanent camp in the valley.

John and his wife Carol took over management of Nsefu in 1986, when Robin started his own safari company. The Coppingers subsequently ran wilderness trails from Chibembe Lodge, before starting Remote Africa Safaris and, with Chief Mwanya's blessing, building their home camp at Tafika, close to Carr's original Kapani camp location. They, and others, continue to share the wonders of wilderness walking in the Luangwa valley with new generations.

For those who manage to extend their Luangwa visit with a trip to Lake Malawi, Carr's former holiday home is now a lakeside guest house idyll called Norman Carr Cottage.

Robin Pope Safaris

The well-known guide Robin Pope has retired, but his style of walking safari continues with **Robin Pope Safaris** under the ownership of the de Rooy family. The name has a long association with walking safaris, and the company continues to place a strong emphasis on walks that include the valley's longest mobile walking safari. Apart from South Luangwa, Robin Pope Safaris has expanded to run lodges in Malawi and Zimbabwe, and operates as a full itinerary provider for the region through partnerships with other lodges.

Robin Pope Safaris has six properties on the eastern bank of the river in South Luangwa, and all are small scale, with no more than six tents or chalets. The western bank is accessed by boat or vehicle (via a pontoon, or just fording when water is low). Headquarters is at Nkwali, 40 minutes' drive from Mfuwe airport, which has six chalets and is open all year, as is its nearby private-use Robin's House (built by Robin and Jo Pope). A second private house nearby, Luangwa Safari House, is available from mid-March to mid-January. Not far north of Mfuwe bridge, Luangwa River Camp is restricted to opening when the river level is low, from April to November, and it's the smallest camp – with just five suites overlooking the water.

Further north again are two attractive camps in the Nsefu sector of the park – Tena Tena and Nsefu, both six-room camps. This area is inaccessible in the wet season owing to the heavy cotton soil of the access road. Nevertheless, Nsefu opens to boat and walking safaris from late January to the end of March. This is unusual for the valley, and while most other camps are closed it lets guests enjoy a completely different season, with superb birding and a possible visit to a large stork colony in the area. Nsefu then closes for a couple

An elephant skull gives John Mphasi of Robin Pope Safaris an opportunity to show his knowledge on the way to the Luangwa Bush Camp.

of months and reopens from late May to mid-November, while Tena Tena operates from May to October. Nsefu has history (see pages 202–203) and a unique, classic ambience. Its grounds have been reshaped over the years by the shifting river, but its six rondavels endure, all now updated with en suites and featuring a low energy 'evening breeze' air-conditioning system, whereby a specially designed mosquito net is cooled for comfort.

All of the Robin Pope Safaris venues run walks, with guests accompanied by a knowledgeable professional guide and a wildlife police officer. Most guests choose to visit two or three camps and mix walks and game drives. For more intensive walking safaris, Robin Pope Safaris has two options – to link up Nsefu and Tena Tena via a couple of nights of fly-camping at the Luangwa Bush Camp, or to embark on South Luangwa's only true mobile walking safari, a vehicle-supported expedition that lasts for a week or more.

Operating from June to the end of October, the Luangwa Bush Camp is set for the exclusive use of a maximum of four walkers, with two stand-up Meru-style tents. The tents are furnished with mattresses on the ground, sheets and blankets, and each has a wash basin. There's a shared bucket shower and long-drop bush loo. The camps do not skimp on food, and there's full service, including bar. The walks are in one of the most lagoon-rich areas of the Luangwa, and hence the game is prolific. There are about three leave-no-trace camp locations utilised, all attractive spots to pass the day with binoculars at hand.

It's normal to mix the bush camp nights with nights at one of the fixed camps, and the experience can be booked for any number of nights, but two is a popular choice. A seven-night walking package billed as the Luangwa Trail gives guests two nights at Luangwa River Camp, one at Tena Tena, two nights at the Luangwa Bush Camp and finally two more at Nsefu Camp. The vehicle is used when walking from Luangwa River Camp, but the entire way from Tena Tena to Nsefu via the bush camp nights is walked.

Robin Pope made a huge contribution to making the Luangwa valley a renowned walking safari destination, and the present day company continues his decades-old practice of leading walks in the remote wilderness along the Mupamadzi River. These 'mobile walking safaris' are unique in Zambia and rare in Africa: an authentic week-long wilderness journey on foot. Like the Bush Camp, they run from June to October and are led by the company's most experienced guides.

This is a classic-style mobile safari where the camp is packed every other day to move ahead of the walking party by truck, with five to seven nights spent on the walking trail. Each day around 10 km is covered at a modest pace, and it's best enjoyed by regular walkers with a reasonable level of fitness. Guests bookend the trail with nights at one of the fixed camps, and normally start with a night at Nkwali. It takes about five hours to drive from there to the trailhead, so enclosed vehicles are used; there's a pop-top roof to use for sightings along the way. The route crosses the Luwi River, and mostly traverses miombo woodlands. The camp set-up is the same as that used on Luangwa Bush Camp walks: large Meru-style canvas tents, with short-drop toilets and suspended bucket showers. There's a mess tent and a gas-powered refrigerator – an essential luxury.

The walking follows the Mupamadzi downstream in a remote area in the north, unvisited by game drive vehicles. The river defines the northern boundary of the park, with a Game Management Area on the other side, and it eventually joins the Luangwa north of the Nsefu sector of the

Leopard lairs and aardvark tracks

I've never seen an aardvark in the wild, but this was nearly as good – fresh tracks, three unmistakable big toes on each print, dew-sharp in the dawn's first rays. We were only 100 m from Tena Tena camp, and it was tantalising to know how close we were to the elusive animal. It was a good start, and things were soon to get even better.

We were on foot on the way to Robin Pope Safaris' Luangwa Bush Camp – a fly-camp set up just for us somewhere in the wilds of South Luangwa National Park. It would take a few hours and there was no particular hurry, other than to make it before the day became too hot. We stopped for anything that caught our eye – tracks, seed pods, the skull of an elephant, the shell of a leopard tortoise, a mutable sun squirrel living up to its name, basking on a pod mahogany branch.

Our guide, John Mphasi, knows the area well. He started as a general worker, then housekeeper for Robin Pope, before studying guiding and working his way up to the highest level – the walking guide. His patch lies between Tena Tana and Nsefu Camp, a land of ebony, jackal-berry and leadwood, ox-bow lagoons and open plains. He knows the ideal shaded spots to set camp for a night or two.

John led us towards a tree where he'd seen a predator's meal stashed recently, and we found a desiccated baboon carcass wedged in a fork. 'Leopard kill,' he said, and then, as if on cue, we heard baboons alarm-calling in the distance. These sounds blended with impala barks, confirming something was around. We left the remains and headed towards the hullabaloo across a grassless area of hardpacked soil, a dried-out lagoon. Two giraffes turned their heads to look at us, then swivelled back to gaze in the direction of the alarm calls. The impalas stood like statues, focused, telling the leopard 'we see you'. John scanned with the binoculars and, following the impalas' lead, quickly found the cat. It was sitting on a termite mound in shade and as we watched, it moved off, tail flicking the air languorously, pursued by baboon barks. This is the life of a leopard by day – whenever on the move, surrounded by warning cries. The cat was no threat to us, and it was electrifying to meet one on foot.

Walks in South Luangwa are sociable affairs. In Zimbabwe, it's usual to set out with just a guide, but here, alongside John, we had park scout Wallace and assistant guide Lameck Mbao. Lameck was serving his long apprenticeship to guide on foot: he acted as another pair of eyes to spot wildlife and as a sweeper at the back to make sure we stayed close. He was also responsible for looking after us when we stopped for a break, which we took on some perfect natural seating – a fallen tree overlooking a lagoon.

Here, there was more drama. As we sipped tea, we watched spoonbills at work until one stabbed into the shallow water and came up with a bream. Perhaps it should have eaten it immediately, but it made the mistake of taking off with its catch. In an instant, an African fish eagle dived, a fleeting tumult of wing feathers. No contact was made, but it was enough to make the spoonbill drop the fish, and the eagle did an elegant tight circle and landed to grasp it. 'Typical fish eagle hunting,' said John with a knowing smile. He pointed across the lagoon, to the white blazes in the trees, one every couple of hundred metres.

'Lots of them here, and each has its own territory. They steal more food than they catch themselves.'

After another hour of walking, we found ourselves back on the Luangwa above a sheer section of bank. These outside bends are favoured nesting sites for carmine and white-fronted bee-eaters, and it was clear that October is the time of year to find them in great numbers. It was a mesmeric display of colour, of movement, of sound. Months later, it's still my most vivid memory of Zambia's wilderness.

The fly-camp came as a welcome surprise – at this time of year it gets seriously hot by mid-morning – and we were greeted by Dominic Banda and a box full of bottles on ice. Camping does not mean discomfort, and apart from the cold drinks, I was pleased to find a fan in the tent, powered by its own small solar panel, essential for a comfortable post-prandial nap.

We, and our guiding trio, were ready for more by four o'clockish. This would be a gentle stroll near camp, mostly in the shade of sausage trees, crossing metre-deep hippo highways. It was evident how their habits create water channels, and ultimately how one animal can mould a landscape; the Luangwa valley is estimated to have 20% of Africa's entire hippo population, perhaps 25,000 animals. As we examined a bleached hippo skeleton in a clearing, John picked up a wad of woven vegetation. 'People call this hippo spit,' he said. Pointing at the teeth in the skull, he said 'Hippo's incisors and canines are adapted for defence, so they sometimes lose what they are chewing from the side of its mouth.'

We admired a hamerkop nest, and mourned a tree, ringbarked by elephant and doomed. But this too was part of the natural process: the tree would stand dead for many years and become a habitat for fungi, wood-boring insects,

An African fish eagle swooped in and stole the bream.

and provide nesting holes for owls and bush babies and snakes. A sudden loud rustling in an area of thicker bush made us stand to attention – was it warthogs, or, worse, a buffalo? No, a troop of banded mongoose, not capable of moving quietly on the dried leaves that littered the ground.

Back at camp, we carried directors' chairs down to the beach below, overlooking the receding Wafwa lagoon, an oxbow of the Luangwa River. In the water, three saddle-billed storks stalked steadily, and behind, above a steep sandy bank, we could see elephant feeding in the dense bush. As time passed, the setting sun behind us was counterbalanced by a rising full moon in front. Dominic magicked up a very impressive meal, and then confessed that the main preparation was done at Nsefu, the camp that would be our destination after the nights at bush camp. Having eaten too many freeze dry meals straight from a packet while camping, I was enjoying the pampering, including dessert and an Amarula on ice.

'Awooo uh! Awooo uh!' The night belonged to other creatures. It's tempting to picture hyena with their heads thrown back like wolves, but in fact their call is directed at the ground and resonates far and wide. Lion sounds reverberated too – their low tones travelling on the cool night air, declaring their territory. Somewhere close by, the darkness surely cloaked the silent progress of an aardvark. Maybe we would find its tracks in the morning.

John Mphasi, Dominic Banda and Lameck Mbao at the Robin Pope Safaris Luangwa Bush Camp.

park. On the last day of the walk, guests are transferred by vehicle to a crossing point for transfer by boat to Tena Tena (or Nsefu camp if preferred). The minimum age for the mobile expedition is 21 years – it's 16 for other Robin Pope walks – and the maximum group size is six.

Time + Tide

In a long and interesting career as wildlife warden and safari operator, Norman Carr is credited with the introduction of walking safaris to Zambia, and today, visitors to South Luangwa can still walk in his footsteps following animal trails from camp to camp. **Time + Tide** is now the operator of the camps Carr developed in the 1970s on the Luangwa and its tributary, the Luwi River, the area with some of the best wildlife viewing in the park. A selection of five small-scale camps offers the epitome of the Luangwa walking experience.

Each camp has a unique setting, from a small lagoon frequented by wildlife to a lofty perch along a sweeping curve of the Luangwa River. There's one year-round camp, Time + Tide Chinzombo, which is located close to the main gate of the park and easy to access via Mfuwe airport. The other camps are all further north in the Luwi area. Time + Tide Kakuli camp is near the confluence of the Luwi and Luangwa and opens early in the season, in January. The walks season does not start until late May, with the opening of the other camps: Time + Tide Mchenja, Time + Tide Nsolo and Time + Tide Luwi. These four camps operate vehicle safaris but are close enough for camp-to-camp walks. From Mchenja to Kakuli is about 7 km, or two hours, and to Nsolo is longer at 12 km or four hours. Kakuli to Nsolo meanders 14 km over four to five hours, and from Nsolo it's 9.5 km or three hours to the remotest camp, Luwi.

Flexibility is the keyword, and depending on conditions and the group, vehicles can be used to cover the routes in part or to vary the experience. The prime walking season runs from June to October, and the camps close again in November. There's a maximum of six guests for walks and drives. Time + Tide is owned by the Dalais family, and as well as a presence in two of Zambia's great parks, the company has in recent years established a camp in northern Madagascar.

Shenton Safaris

Shenton Safaris is long-established, locally owned, and has a strong tradition of guiding on foot. It operates two camps on the western side of the Luangwa River inside the National Park and guests can walk from (or between) the camps, ideally adding a night's 'camp out'. Kaingo Camp is the flagship Shenton property, established for over 30 years on the bank of the Luangwa. During the season, it has six chalets that open to the sunrise, each with spacious verandas and outdoor bathtubs. Guests at Kaingo have an opportunity to sleep out on the 'Elephant Hide Star Bed'. Alternatively, the smaller Mwamba Bush Camp had a complete rebuild in the 2024 off season. It maintains its style of comfortable simplicity with four chalets set above the channel of the Mwamba River, which dries out as the season progresses.

Shenton Safaris are known for their collection of game viewing hides, some fixed and some mobile, and they are appreciated both by photographers and nature lovers who simply want to relax and enjoy watching the wildlife up close in a serene location. The company has a large plot in Mfuwe where fruits, vegetables and herbs are grown, and the kitchen is proud of its fresh and healthy cuisine. Both camps are walking bases, and it's possible to walk between the camps, with kit transported by vehicle. Walking activities allow a maximum of six guests along with a scout and walking guide. Morning walks are generally around three hours in duration and taken at a slow pace to enjoy the varied landscapes of mopane and ebony woodlands along the tributaries of the Luangwa, and to make time to linger at the waterholes. Shorter afternoon walks are enjoyable, and these depart after tea and end with a sundowner in the bush and a game drive back to camp in the twilight hour.

Ideally, a stay will combine walking with a night of sleeping out in the wild. The Shenton Safaris Camp Out is available to private groups of two to four guests from May to August, and requires a booking of seven nights (which can be spread across the two camps). It has the typical simple ambience of a fly-camp, but is quite comfortable: sleeping mat, mosquito net, a wash basin; naturally, cold drinks from a cooler box and dinner served by the campfire. The usual routine sees departure by vehicle following afternoon tea to head north-west towards the baobab forest. There's a choice of good locations with the camp either set on an embankment overlooking the Luangwa, in the midst of Numbu Plains or in deep wilderness at Kapanda Lagoon. The last hour of the day is spent on foot to the fly-camp, and after a night immersed in the night sounds of Africa, there's an early morning walk before returning to the fly-camp for breakfast.

Remote Africa Safaris

Remote Africa Safaris has walking in its DNA. Its camps hark back to the earliest tourism camps in the Luangwa valley, a time when each chalet was crafted anew at the start of the season using only local bush materials. The main camp at Tafika is the family home of the Coppinger family and is on an idyllic riverside setting; a new camp is due to open a little to the south in 2025. Across the river are two walking camps accessible only on foot, via Tafika Walking Trails. As well as this set of camps, Remote Africa is the leading operator of safaris in North Luangwa National Park, thanks to having two camps there and its own aircraft to access them (see page 218).

Tafika camp is the first to wake to the new season, usually in May. It's perched on a high section of the eastern riverbank just outside South Luangwa park, near the Chikwinda Gate – the northern entrance to the Nsefu sector of South Luangwa National Park. During April, each of its six chalets is rebuilt by local craftsfolk using material sourced in the area – grass reeds, bamboo, wood and woven mats. All of the Remote Africa camps have this style, which is unchanged in half a century and feels very natural; the camps are unfenced and have regular wildlife visitors. Beside Tafika, there's an extensive *munda*, a garden that supplies fresh produce for the camps. Tafika is accessed by road from Mfuwe airport, with the journey taking around two hours and passing through the Nsefu area of the park. Alternatively, it's minutes from Lukuzi airstrip, and many guests arrive via the RAS aircraft from Mfuwe or other airports.

Tafika camp presents a choice of walks or drives, or a combination of both. For keen walkers, it's definitely worthwhile allocating a few days to walk Tafika Walking Trails, which utilise two foot-access only camps, with guests taken by small boat across the river into the national park. Chikoko Tree is the northerly camp, and the crossing point takes about half an hour to reach from Tafika by vehicle. Once across, the camp is a 15-minute walk. This is the valley's original seasonal walking safari camp, on

Tea break time on Tafika Walking Trails with guides Stephen Banda and Sasu Mwanza and Wildlife Police Officer Jones.

a site selected by Norman Carr. It's set in a grove of trees near a year-round pan, which oscillates from a lagoon in the rainy season to a marsh in the dry. The common area and three rooms all have a two-storey construction, which helps to capture a cooling breeze as well as providing viewpoints over the acacia woodlands.

The second trails camp, Big Lagoon, is south of Chikoko Tree camp, across the river from Tafika and also about 15 or 20 minutes' walk from the boat landing point. As the name suggests, it's set with a view of a sweeping lagoon, an oxbow of the Luangwa that shrinks and swells with the season, and always an attraction for wildlife. The rooms, shaded by ebony trees, are large and open to the lagoon; at night a bamboo screen is used to guard against unwanted room guests. For decades, Big Lagoon was the location for a camp constructed in 1987 and subsequently run by the national Wildlife Department, and one of the few tourism facilities in the park. Some remains of those brick buildings can be found there, now used for storage and the camp kitchen. Guests can walk in either direction between the Tafika Walking Trails camps, and may choose to spend more than one night at either camp and explore further. It's more pleasant to walk south-west from Chikoko to Big Lagoon, as the morning sun is then behind one's shoulder.

South Luangwa lodge walks

Apart from on the foot-only Robin Pope Mobile Walking Safaris and Remote Africa's Tafika Walking Trails, guests at camps in the sections mentioned thus far are always free to swap in a drive instead of a walk. There are many other lodges and camps where walks can be enjoyed – indeed, it's hard to identify a camp that does not have guided walks.

Sungani Lodge is notable for its remoteness in the far south of the park. It's a family-owned lodge and has a sister camp Kulandila, which is located 6 km upstream. Access to both properties is by a short transfer flight from Mfuwe airport to Luamfwa airstrip. They have very experienced walking guides who explore both sides of the Luangwa River and its floodplains and ox-bow lakes. The habitat's open understorey is interspersed by towering ilala palms, winter thorns and Natal mahogany trees.

Kafunta Safaris is a long-established Luangwa safari operator with its main base, Kafunta River Lodge, set on the eastern bank of the river, a 50-minute drive from Mfuwe airport. It has access to the park via either the main gate or a seasonal pontoon crossing near the lodge. The lodge is home to the owners, Anke and Ron Cowan, and has ten chalets and a new exclusive-use three-bedroom house. About 40 km to the south, Three Rivers Camp and Island Bush Camp are the recommended walk bases, both of them ten-bed camps that open from late May until the end of October. Three Rivers Camp is named after its location at the confluence of the Luangwa, Kapamba and Lusangazi Rivers. The five stylish tents sit under shady sausage trees, each with its own sleep-out 'star-bed', which turns into a daybed for relaxation and game viewing over the lagoon or river. The rooms are set far apart, with the wildlife passing freely through the camp, and the dining area has views of both the river and a waterhole.

Inside the national park, set under a canopy of mahogany trees on the Luangwa River, is Island Bush Camp. The site was selected to capture both sunrise and sunset, with views that extend from the Chindeni Hills in the east to Muchinga Escarpment in the west. This rustic camp has five reed-walled chalets set on platforms high above the ground, each open to the front and overlooking the Luangwa. The en-suite bathrooms feature the traditional warm-water bucket shower.

At Island Bush Camp, the chalets are fashioned of grass reeds in the traditional Luangwa valley style.

There's a hide at the waterhole toward the back of the camp, a fine way to pass a few hours during the day, observing activity. It's possible to walk between the two camps, which takes around four hours: luggage is transferred by vehicle. Kafunta Safaris run extended safaris that can include South Luangwa, Lower Zambezi, Kafue, Lake Malawi and Livingstone.

Chiawa Safaris has two impressive lodges in South Luangwa, and loyal repeat guests often pair a visit here with the Chiawa camps in Lower Zambezi National Park. The lodges are operated in partnership with Chichele Safaris and are located close together about an hour's drive south of the park entrance. Puku Ridge has eight safari tents with excellent views, sleep-out towers for a night under the stars and plunge pools. Tents have both fans and air conditioning. Chichele Presidential Lodge has an even more elevated location. Long established, in recent years it has had a complete rebuild, and is now one of the most well-appointed venues in the Luangwa valley. Both lodges have all the amenities associated with high-end lodges, and a highlight is the art and craftwork on display in the rooms and common areas. Puku Ridge and Chichele are both excellent venues to combine the lodge experience with guided walks.

Nkonzi Camp is in a remote location away from the Luangwa River, about 45 minutes' drive from the main gate. Overlooking the sandy bed of the Mushilashi River, the five en-suite tents are in the classic canvas style, easy to take down when the season closes at the end of October. It features a dining area under a Meru-style tent and a couple of hides to enjoy during free time. Walks are led by owner Gavin Opie, who has over 25 years' experience guiding, and Shadreck Njobvu. These usually go directly from camp and depart early in the morning or as a walk/night drive combination in the afternoon. Game drives from camp have the advantage of exploring remote parts of the park that few others visit. Gavin has a safari company, Gavin Opie Safaris, which can organise multi-park walking itineraries in Zambia.

In the central zone close to the main gate, **Msandile River Lodge** has a fine location on a stretch of the Luangwa that always has plenty of water. It's on the eastern bank in a Game Management Area and has direct access to the park by boat, so it's possible to quickly enter the park at dawn to take a walk instead of a game drive. Msandile is one of more affordable lodges in the valley.

A little north of Msandile River Lodge, Shawa Luangwa Camp is also on the eastern bank of the Luangwa River in the Game Management Area. It connects with the park via boat, and walks and drives are conducted in an area without other lodges or their vehicles. It's owned by **Green Safaris**, which is one of the few companies to run walks in three Zambian national parks – Kafue, Lower Zambezi and South Luangwa. The camp itself has tents in an idiosyncratic style, pyramid-shaped on wooden decks. It's solar-powered, and each tent has a bath, toilet and outdoor shower. Shawa is named after its head guide and co-owner, Jacob Shawa, who selected the site; he has a big personality and is well known for his trail guiding in the valley.

North of Shawa, **Chikunto** is a small independently owned camp located inside the park on Big Bend, where the Luangwa doubles back on itself. Everything is set on raised decking, which makes the unfenced camp safe to negotiate and protects it from the annual inundation, a time when the camp is closed. It's a camp that strikes a balance between rustic and opulent and features a unique saltwater counter-current swimming pool; one of the suites has its own elevated sleep out platform. Chikunto works as a destination in itself or as a place to end a camp-to-camp walking safari: it's in the same area of the park as Robin Pope Safaris, and vehicle link ups are possible to more distant operators such as Remote Africa Safaris and The Bushcamp Company. The lodge partners with Classic Zambia to offer a three-park itinerary that includes Kafue and Lower Zambezi.

In the north, the highly regarded **Lion Camp** is located on an oxbow between the Shenton camps and Remote Africa's Tafika base. It's about two and a half hours by road from Mfuwe airport. This is one of the most wildlife-dense areas of the park and known for its resident pack of African wild dogs. Independently owned, Lion Camp has ten tents and five walking guides. The maximum number of guests on a walk is four.

There are no budget options within South Luangwa National Park, but this does not rule out affordable walking. There are a number of lodges located on the eastern bank of the river outside the park gate that can arrange walks.

Wildlife Camp is downriver from Mfuwe Gate in an isolated location surrounded by bushland. It's a popular stopover for self-drive overland travellers, and guests can use their own tents or stay in one of the camp's en-suite chalets or tents with shared ablutions. There's a restaurant on site. Walks are operated from June to October, usually utilising the Zambia Conservation Society land on the eastern side of the river. There's no great difference in the experience, as wildlife is present on both sides, but walking on the private side is cheaper as no park fees are payable. It also avoids the drive to reach the park, which would waste the first hour of daylight. Tea and coffee are provided, and walks depart at six o'clock for four hours at most. The best option from Wildlife Camp is an overnight walk to a bush camp. This too is conducted on the eastern side of the river, and guests usually walk out of the main camp at dawn and arrive at the bush camp for a cooked brunch. Hot bush showers, long-drop toilets and nicely sized tents with cots and duvets await. It's comfortable, quiet and remote. Then an afternoon walk is led, followed by dinner and drinks by the fire; and next day, there's a walk back to main camp (by a different route) after breakfast. Wildlife Camp's Bush Camp experience is the most affordable overnight fly-camping/ walk combination in Zambia, and can be extended to two nights.

Flatdogs Camp is a popular choice outside the park that is also used by self-drive overlanders. It has large bright chalets with cooking facilities for self-caterers and an all-day restaurant. It's very close to the Mfuwe Main Gate, which means it's possible to get into the park for drives and walks early in the morning.

In similar proximity to the gate, **Track and Trail River Camp** has chalet and camping options at a good rate. A little upriver, overlooking the Luangwa north of Mfuwe gate, **Thornicroft Lodge** is a more upmarket venue, but still in the moderate bracket. As well as having game drives and guided walks in the park, Thornicroft runs cycle safaris and village visits.

Luambe National Park

Luambe National Park is a special place, a little-visited reserve located between South and North Luangwa National Parks. Once a premier Zambian safari destination, human encroachment took its toll on habitat and wildlife, but today it's on the way back to a healthy ecology thanks to a privately funded conservation project that's focused on community engagement, ecotourism and anti-poaching measures. Guests will witness recovering wildlife populations, which include the endemic Thornicroft's giraffe, Cookson's wildebeest and endangered African wild dog.

Uniquely, **Luangwa Valley Safaris** offers guests a triple national park walking itinerary that covers South Luangwa, Luambe and North Luangwa. This follows the expansion of their collection to include Painted Dogs Lagoon and North Luangwa River Lodge, both of which offer a contrasting walking environment to that of Luambe National Park. Luambe Camp is the sole camp in Luambe park and provides a choice of lodge-based walks, fly-camp walks and two forms of mobile walking, one of which is a rare sleep-out-style primitive trail. The camp directly overlooks the Luangwa and has four comfortable and spacious en-suite tents; it's open from June to November. There are huge pods of hippo on the river here, and the unfenced camp sees regular visits from leopard and elephant.

Two seasonal, walk-intensive itineraries are available. The Luangwa Wilderness Walking Trail runs in backpacking and sleep-out style – a format popular in South Africa, where it's referred to as a primitive trail. Guests need to be fit and experienced walkers, prepared to carry everything they need to camp in the wilds, sleeping under the stars. The Luxury Luangwa Walking Trail is easier, mixing lodges and

Early season walkers on the Luxury Luangwa Walking Trail.

fly-camping in slack packing style. The trails operate as five-night itineraries, with the Wilderness Walking Trail starting in June and the Luxury Trail from July, and both run until the end of October.

The trails cope with the logistics of reaching Luambe by starting (or ending) with nights at Painted Dogs Lagoon camp, the latest addition to the Luangwa Valley Safaris portfolio. It overlooks the river about 30 minutes from Mfuwe airport. This means that the second day can start with a slow game drive through the Nsefu sector of South Luangwa National Park before proceeding to Luambe Camp, arriving in time for high tea and the trail briefing.

Guests on the Wilderness Walking Trail then sort out their gear, top up their water and head out directly to begin with a gentle introduction in the rich light of late afternoon. This second night and the two subsequent nights are spent in the wilds of Luambe, sleeping under the firmament. On the fifth day the group returns in time for a bush brunch under Luambe's trees, with the rest of the day to relax at camp, share stories and enjoy dinner. That night is spent at Luambe Camp, and on the sixth day there's an early breakfast followed by a road transfer back to Mfuwe. Participants on the Luangwa Wilderness Walking Trail must be 16 or older and fit to carry a full backpack in sometimes hot conditions. The group size is six to eight, and a packing list is provided in advance.

For guests on the Luxury Luangwa Walking Trail, the second night is spent at Luambe Camp and the third and fourth nights at a comfortable sleep-out camp. The camp is moved by vehicle while the guests are walking. The fly-camp features camp cots set under mosquito nets, warm water bucket showers and short-drop toilets. On the fifth day there's an early walk and then a bush breakfast before returning to Luambe Camp. On the sixth day guests drive back to Mfuwe. On this trail, the group size is four to eight and guests just carry a small day pack.

Apart from these two walks-intensive itineraries, Luambe has a single night sleep-out option, as long as it's part of a four night stay at Luambe Camp. Guests who have made the journey to Luambe can extend the adventure with walks at a sister lodge in North Luangwa National Park (see page 217).

North Luangwa National Park

If South Luangwa National Park is remote from the mainstream safari circuit, North Luangwa National Park is off the map. The south has easy access via scheduled flights and a tarred road, and dozens of camps and lodges; as for the north – it's either a back-numbing drive, or, more practically, a stunning low-level flight upriver. With few drivable tracks in the southern half of the park, wildlife viewing is primarily on foot, and there are a handful of seasonal safari operations run by Remote African Safaris, Classic Zambia and Luangwa Valley Safaris.

The park protects around 4,600 sq. km of the western bank of the upper Luangwa River valley, with terrain that includes plains, riverine forests, escarpments and mountain ranges. The Mwaleshi and Luangwa Rivers flow through the park, creating a network of channels and lagoons. The wooded areas make for especially enjoyable walking, and feature a variety of tree species including ebony, mahogany, winter thorn and sausage tree.

North Luangwa is a place apart, a remnant of Africa's historic wilderness. Its remoteness has been its main protection,

The Mwaleshi camp chalets are crafted anew each season and are open to nature.

although like most of the valley its wildlife was decimated in the twentieth century. In the 1980s, the first walking safaris here began with Major John Harvey and his wife Lorna. At the time, poaching was rife, and Frankfurt Zoological Society began a partnership with the Department of National Parks and Wildlife to help manage it. Controversial anti-poaching tactics under the stewardship of Mark and Delia Owens, famous for their book *Cry of the Kalahari*, put the reserve in the news for the wrong reasons. In this century, it's on a much more positive trajectory, and anti-poaching and wildlife reintroduction initiatives have transformed its fortunes. The park hosts Zambia's only population of black rhino, and their fenced area has been greatly expanded. Known for its high density of lions, it's habitat for the endemic Cookson's wildebeest as well as the full range of African big game animals including elephant and buffalo. There are over 450 species of birds recorded.

North Luangwa is difficult to access by land, and most visitors fly into its airstrips; both Remote Africa and Classic Zambia facilitate this via their own aircraft. Self-drivers who have fully equipped 4x4 vehicles and experience in remote travel can access the park from the west at Mpika or from Chifunda chiefdom, from the south via Luambe National Park and from the east via Chama or Lundazi. There's mandatory GPS control of vehicles traversing the black rhinoceros sanctuary. The park is a special place that justifies the extra effort and expense in visiting. It has almost no tourism facilities – just four active camps, all open from June to October.

North Luangwa River Lodge is a seasonal camp located on the upper Luangwa River, about 20 km north of the Mwaleshi confluence. It's operated by **Luangwa Valley Safaris** and, like the other options in the park, is at walking group scale, sleeping a maximum of eight guests. The thatched huts are on raised platforms located at the confluence of the Lutaba and Luangwa Rivers. In addition to sweeping views, nightly visits from lion and hyena make the elevated position of the bungalows exciting.

In 2024, the camp came under the same management as Luambe Camp and was refurbished. The two venues have joint walking-focused itineraries, with two or three nights at both. It's about three hours' drive from Luambe to the pontoon used to cross the Luangwa for access to North Luangwa National Park, and from there a further 30 minutes to the River Camp. A drive-in, fly-out package is available. Walks are guided on the Luangwa's well-wooded floodplain, and the area is within reach of the fenced area of the rhino sanctuary. There are over 50 black rhinos in the park – the actual number is a secret – and while they are difficult to spot, there's a good chance of least finding their tracks.

Mwaleshi and Takwela camps are **Remote Africa Safaris** properties that are established from mid-June, once the rivers have dropped, and close again at the end of October, as the first thunderstorms of the green season build. Takwela Camp is on the confluence of the Mwaleshi River and the Luangwa, where there are hundreds of hippo in the rivers close to camp, and their sounds are ever present. Mwaleshi Camp is set on the southern bank of a scenic bend of the Mwaleshi 10 km upstream and is wonderfully low key and crafted in the Remote Africa signature style – simple rooms of grass reeds, with woven mats and split bamboo matting. Bucket showers are filled by hand with water heated on the fire. The main concessions to guest comfort are flush toilets in the open-air bathrooms and solar powered fans. Unusually, Mwaleshi has no single supplement; there are four chalets but only six guests at a time, which accommodates solo travellers. Takwela is similar in style but has a few extra comforts, akin to the Remote Africa home camp in South Luangwa, Tafika.

At the beginning of the walking season, the landscape is green, and the lagoons provide great birdwatching. As the season goes on, vegetation becomes sparser and animals are easier to spot. It's possible to walk between the two camps, in an experience similar to Tafika Walking Trails (see page 210) and campouts are an option by prior arrangement. It's more usual to combine the camps via a vehicle transfer as a morning game drive. In either case, walking is not obligatory at the Remote Africa camps, and both have a game viewing vehicle to hand.

Kutandala Camp is in a wonderfully remote location in the upper Mwaleshi River. After some years of dormancy, it has recently been reopened by **Classic Zambia** and during the walking season has four chalets of canvas and thatch, each with en-suite flush toilets and bucket showers. Kutandala is a one-hour drive from Mwaleshi airstrip, which – unless you are an overlander – is the only practical way to reach camp. Classic Zambia has its own aircraft and can bring guests in at seat rates.

North Luangwa National Park is included in the boundaries of one of Africa's vastly ambitious Transfrontier Conservation Areas, with the Peace Parks Foundation working to conserve montane grassland habitats between the park and the Nyika National Park in Malawi. This is a challenging prospect, given the fast growing population, especially in Malawi. Nonetheless, that country has some outstanding conservation success stories, and these are topics of Chapter 9.

Remote conversations

It was late in the dry season and the hippos were grumpy, squabbling night and day, jealously guarding the best spots in the remanent pools of the Mwaleshi River. The brown wallow in front of where we stood was a hippo soup, three dozen mud-crusted lumps claimed by spotless egrets. The hippos had got our scent, and a couple of heads popped up, jaws gaping. We respectfully gave space and departed as our guide reminded us of the charging speeds of these hefty herbivores. This was a routine encounter for guide Brent Harris and park scout Davy in North Luangwa National Park, but familiarity breeds respect, and one of the goals when walking is to enjoy the wildlife without disturbing them. Especially cantankerous hippos.

In the case of the puku herds, this was difficult, but Brent showed us how. He explained how prey animals can tune in to the behavioural language of potential predators. A group of humans marching with a single-minded agenda is threatening. We could reduce our impact by simply approaching at an angle, mulling about and avoiding staring at the antelope. It seemed to work. The puku saw us from afar, skipped off a little and resumed grazing as we meandered and closed the distance unobtrusively. A natural encounter: perfect.

Just then, Davy, at the front of our little line, did a sidestep, interrogating the ground: fresh tracks of a black rhinoceros. This was exciting – Brent explained how once the entire Luangwa valley was a black rhino stronghold before their local extinction in the 1980s. Thanks to a successful reintroduction program and ongoing sophisticated protection measures, he said that their numbers are increasing, and the success of this program has served as a blueprint to subsequent rhino reintroductions such as in Gonarezhou in Zimbabwe.

We trailed the rhino to a nearby midden, a territorial dung heap. It was interesting how the tracks meandered and crossed back over themselves: It's the skill of a tracker to visualise the animal's behaviour, to infer its intentions from the evidence, to try to adopt the mindset of the animal. From the scrapings in the leaves, it looked as if this was a male focused on marking his territorial boundary.

We headed for the tree line, seeking shade. In October, there are about three hours of pleasant walking conditions in North Luangwa before the heat descends like a heavy blanket; a mature mutaba tree (common wild fig) provided relief. We switched from walking to watching as assistant guide Kennedy Nkhoma unpacked the tea and biscuits. Stopping like this is a great way to appreciate the birdlife, which can be missed while on the move: we listened to the unmusical shrieking of Lilian's lovebirds and watched a showy aerobatic display of a lilac-breasted roller.

Our walk had taken us upriver from Mwaleshi Camp across the floodplain, threading through light woodlands. It would be an exposed return walk, so it was a relief to hear the vehicle engine – we'd be driving back. The camp is wonderfully organic – to the point that we awoke that morning to find an elephant had eaten the thatched roof of the riverside pergola. Each season, the camp is entirely reconstructed with bush materials – no nails, no wire and certainly no plastic. At night, a bamboo trellis is erected to prevent a leopard or hyena entering the room.

Our rest stop under a mature mutaba tree.

The next morning, the plan was to walk under a forest canopy, so we drove east from camp, passing the airstrip, to reach the Luangwa River. This area is well wooded, and we walked immediately in the shelter of figs. The ground was dappled with interesting tracks – civet, genet, hyena, snake. And leopard. We followed a track, and as we approached an especially large sausage tree, there was movement and a fleeting blur of a rosette coat. In the fork of a branch, an impala carcass dangled.

It would be futile to try again to sneak up on a leopard already aware of us in this terrain. Brent said that the cat would be close, watching us from deep cover. If it had moved further, we would hear the alarm barks of impala and vervet monkeys. Leopards trust their camouflage: guides tell tales of walking almost within touching distance of a leopard crouching in grass, and by pretending not to see it, passing without incident. As we walked, I gave sideways glances under the thickets.

The understorey gave way, and we stood speechless under the canopy of the most magical winter thorn woodland. Shafts of sun dappled the ground and a Verreaux's eagle owl dropped from a perch; with a single beat of its wings, it relocated to another tree. I felt as if I'd found what I was looking for, the epitome of African walking. It was a moment that did not need interpretation, and we simply stood for a while in silence and soaked it up.

Later, we picked a spot overlooking the Luangwa to rest, watch fish eagles hunt, and chat. Brent, originally from Cape Town, comes here to guide each year. Having travelled and worked around the world, in a very diverse career, he is well placed to evaluate why this particular river valley deserves one third of his year. He believes that nature reminds us how to be human, and finds that this rings true in his work with people as a life and business coach. 'If you want to understand the way an animal thinks, just put yourself in their predicament and you will see that you make very similar decisions,' he said, as we watched a bull elephant excavating on the other bank. 'Our primary needs are no different from that elephant. Beneath our perceived complexity is just another creature standing face to face with their surroundings.' As the elephant started to inhale sand-filtered water, I took a swig from my bottle of water from the same river – filtered at camp – and nodded.

* * *

I was soon to discover that the winter thorn forest is not at all antique. Sitting with Remote Africa Safaris founder John Coppinger at his home at Tafika camp, he says that when he first visited North Luangwa in the late 1980s, it was scrubland, subject to burning by humans every year, and those woodlands were just seedlings. Few people have been in the valley as long as John, who has the perspective to testify to a positive transformation over the decades. He is especially enamoured with North

We stood speechless under the canopy of the most magical winter thorn woodland.

Luangwa. 'Mwaleshi has a magic. I don't know if you felt it?' he asks me. 'I like it when there are no roads.'

His path to Tafika deserves a book of its own. 'I remember sitting on a miserable oil platform in the North Sea in a storm, reading a book by Iain Douglas-Hamilton, asking what am I doing here?' It triggered a life change, and John came back to spend a year travelling Africa with his brother, the naturalist and author Mike Coppinger, and through happenstance ended up as a guide in Kenya. A few years later, armed with a pilot's licence, he came back to Zambia thinking of life as a bush pilot, but was recruited as a guide by another pioneering guide, his friend Robin Pope, and four years later, he and his wife Carol moved from Nsefu to Chibembe, a little to the north of where we sat, and ran wilderness trails.

'The valley was already known for walking, which really originated from Norman Carr's passion,' says John and he naturally inherited that style of safari. 'In the early days, the roads and camps kept getting washed away, so walking was the ideal way to do things.' Having developed a good relationship with the community in the area, he received permission to build Tafika on raised ground on a wide bend of the river. 'I knew it would be in danger of erosion on an outside bend, but the view was so perfect.' He knew which trees were evidence that the site would not flood, and indeed Tafika's vegetable and fruit gardens have always stayed above water. Remote Africa Safari's natural style of camp was the one used widely in the early days, and the Coppingers have kept it unchanged. 'I've always preferred grass, I just like it. It's cooler than canvas. And it's good to keep local skills alive.' The only concession to modernity has been the addition of flush toilets, demanded by his American guests.

John's life in the valley has a pleasing trajectory. His mother in particular enjoyed the remote bush travel, and he soaked it up, visiting the government-run

John Coppinger at Tafika.

camp at Big Lagoon in what was then South Luangwa Reserve. 'My brothers and I loved it; the place was full of elephant. I remember being charged by one.' Fifty-six years later, his next night at Big Lagoon was as owner of the camp, now used for his Tafika Walking Trails.

John and Carol had already been running safaris in South Luangwa for a decade when they were invited by the Owens to set up tourism facilities in the north, and picked a site for Mwaleshi camp, followed later by Takwela. In those days, it was a six- or seven-hour drive in a Unimog – the only vehicle that could ford the river – an adventure relished by a very niche class of guests. John recalls how the wildlife knew humans only as poachers, and how aggressive the lions were compared with the south. Today, the RAS Cessna makes access simple, but the park's remoteness and short season don't make it profitable; however, he is determined to keep operations there, and in recent years as the Frankfurt Zoological Society has assumed new powers of management, it has renewed his optimism for the park.

John's enthusiasm for adventure has not waned. In 2020, he walked part of the 'Walk Luangwa' expedition organised by his son-in-law Nick Riddin, who runs operations for Remote Africa Safaris. This began at Marula Puku ranger station in North Luangwa National Park and continued all the way to the most southerly camp in the valley. 'On my leg of the walk, we spent three nights sleeping out and on two occasions we had lions in camp.' When we met, he was about to set off up towards the river's headwaters to explore an area with no roads, thereby completing an entire exploration of the river course on foot or by canoe. His microlight aircraft, once a tool to track poachers, is still used for fun; and the whole family was planning an off-season visit to the Central African Republic.

While the valley and its national parks are on a good conservation path, John sees the effects of climate change in the seasons. 'It has become so unpredictable. We used to run by the calendar, and now early rains come in November. And not just thunderstorms – we had a massive storm five years ago, and had to evacuate our guests from the camps in the north.'

What makes him optimistic? On a personal level, it's the involvement of their two daughters, Jen and Christine, and many other young people, in conservation efforts. For Zambia, he sees fantastic work from NGOs, none of which existed when he came here first. Not just the Frankfurt Zoological Society, but African Parks, Conservation South Luangwa and others. And for the Luangwa valley? 'It's very rare to find poached elephants or snared animals. Visitor numbers are good, and I feel that getting people to come is the best way to protect Luangwa for the future.'

9 Malawi

Malawi is not well known as a safari destination, much less a walking safari destination, which makes it all the more wonderful to discover. Helped by its proximity to one of Africa's walking safari hotspots – the Luangwa River valley – the country attracts visitors interested in active safaris or looking to relax at Lake Malawi. Malawi's national parks are on a promising trajectory in recent years, thanks to expert co-management by African Parks, a non-profit conservation organisation that works on holistic rehabilitation of areas at risk.

The peak walking season is from May to November. The hot and wet months of December to April are to be avoided, when the country is at risk of cyclones.

Walking safaris in Malawi

Liwonde National Park is the best destination for guided walking safaris, as it has the full range of African animal life, and it's where Central African Wilderness Safaris operate the country's only overnight big game area walking experience. Robin Pope Safaris has lodges in Liwonde and Majete Wildlife Reserve and is a walk operator in Zambia's South Luangwa National Park and Zimbabwe's Mana Pools National Park. As such, the company is well placed to organise full regional itineraries that can include partner properties in Victoria Falls and other places.

Nkhotakota Wildlife Reserve is a little-visited but attractive reserve on a good conservation path, and two lodges guide walks there. In Nyika National Park there's good hiking to be found, but it's not a place for walking safaris in the sense of big game encounters.

Liwonde National Park

Liwonde National Park is a stunning protected area located in southern Malawi, which together with the adjacent Mangochi Forest Reserve protects about 88,000 ha. The park is mostly on the eastern banks of the Shire River (pronounced 'Shirry'), which drains from Lake Malawi south to the Zambezi and provides a reliable and vital source of water for the region's wildlife. Managed by African Parks, Liwonde has benefited from recent wildlife reintroductions, and now has a good range of animals that includes elephant, cheetah, lion and black rhino that were transferred from South Africa in 2019. In 2024, a new African wild dog pack was brought in, after the previously introduced animals succumbed to poisoning. It's a superb waterbird habitat and they share the river with crocodile and a great many hippo (possibly too many). Visitors can explore the park on game drives, boat safaris and guided walks.

Central Africa Wilderness Safaris

As a walking safari destination, Liwonde matches the best in Africa, and is the only park in Malawi with an overnight walking safari/fly-camp combination.

This, the Shire River Trail, is available from **Central African Wilderness Safaris** (CAWS) when the river water levels are low, generally from June to November. As well as this seasonal trail, walks from the CAWS venues in Liwonde – Mvuu Lodge and Mvuu Camp – are run all year.

The lodge is delightful, organically integrated into the shoreline woodlands with pathways of decking and sand connecting the elements. Eight fan-cooled suites with en-suite bathrooms overlook the marshy confluence of the small Nangondo River and the Shire, a glade alive with birdlife from pre-dawn. There's Wi-Fi at the raised lounge and bar area next to the campfire 'beach'. It can be reached by road via the park's main gate, but it's a shorter journey to enter through the park gate to the west of the Shire, accessed from the M2 highway via a drive through a picturesque series of villages. Once in the park, it's a short hop by boat from a little jetty to the lodge – a magical approach. Not far from the lodge, Mvuu Camp offers a lower cost alternative; it has eleven cottages and its own dining area and swimming pool. The owners of CAWS, the Badger family, live nearby, and are good sources of information for not just Liwonde but all of Malawi. They operate Chelinda Camp in a remote area of Nyika National Park in the north of the country and also run Heuglin's Lodge in Lilongwe, which is convenient for arrivals or departures and for combining Malawi with Zambia's Luangwa valley parks via road.

The Shire River Trail operates on a bespoke basis for a minimum of two, and its walkers explore 20 km of bush along the east bank of the river, overnighting

Guide David Mkandawire at Mvuu Lodge.

All the walking ingredients

When I heard the excitement in the guide's voice, I knew it was something special. It's always fun to see an animal for the first time – a first for me at least, and a rare sighting for David Mkandawire, a guide with Central Africa Wilderness Safaris in Liwonde National Park. 'Meller's mongoose,' he said quietly. But there was no need to be quiet, as in the twilight we could see a mating pair, who had no intention of being distracted from the business at hand. I consulted the African mammals app on my phone, where it said that Meller's is the 'least known of the mongoose family', a shaggy and shy animal found in Zimbabwe, Zambia and evidently here on the Shire River in Malawi.

It was a pleasing end to a day that had started at 04:30 with a wake up at Mvuu Lodge and a pre-dawn gathering. The night watch warned me of elephants in camp – it was comical to see them carefully threading the trees on narrow sandy paths, asserting a timeless right of way. It created a little delay in walking out of camp, but we made it just as the sun broke the horizon. We walked south from camp, a little inland from the river, crossing a bone-dry floodplain amid palms and baobab. The best of the baobabs are protected by wire mesh, and it was a bit sad to see the state of some of those that were not, in various stages of elephant destruction.

Soon, we were to meet more of these lovable villains, and it took some delicate manoeuvring to avoid them in a riverine thicket, trying to stay downwind and struggling to walk quietly – impossible in a deep cyan pot pourri of sausage tree leaves. David, and the African Parks scout Alan Mwitho, seemed to enjoy the challenge. We squatted down and could discern a small breeding herd just 30 m away. The elephants were making more noise than we were, which no doubt helped us to avoid detection, and as soon as it was safe, David motioned for us to move on and out of the thicket.

As we walked back towards the water, we bisected herds of antelope – water buck and puku to the right, kudu and impala to the left. This walk was developing nicely, and we came upon fresh lion tracks and then the scrapings and midden of a black rhino. All the ingredients that make for walking safari perfection were in the mix: the river backed by Borassus palms lit by the rising sun, its waters thick with hippos. The baobabs of course, the profusion of animals. Now the tracks. Not just the big animals, but delicate prints of civet and porcupine dappling the sand.

We moved from grasslands into the shade of mopane woodlands – a variation of habitats is another alluring feature of the best walks. David's sharp birding eye directed us to a Livingston's flycatcher and a Böhm's bee-eater, and he found the bee-eater's nesting hole in the ground beneath a cucumber tree. In a place of such biodiversity, there was something of interest every few steps. A termite mound that doubled up as an elephant scratching post. A scattering of dead grass detritus that showed the entrance to a harvester termite colony, 2 m below our feet. David paused by an innocuous bush that would be easy to dismiss – a red mustard – and explained how it's a little pharmacy, with the branches boiled to make an infusion to combat headache and other ailments, and its twigs useful to make antibacterial toothbrushes.

It was four hours of fascination on foot to the fly-camp. There, we found

We squatted down and could discern a small breeding herd just 30 m away.

Doreen and her camp crew with a full kitchen tent nestled under fever trees and Natal mahogany. The dome tents looked fairly standard from the outside, but inside were fully furnished. A discreet distance from the tents, the bucket shower was screened from camp, but open to the river – splendid.

After a siesta, Doreen appeared with cake and banana and chocolate roulade – Chef Christopher was determined to make sure that the dining standards at Mvuu Lodge are maintained at his bush kitchen. We drove south, taking rutted tracks across the dry-season floodplain and only encountered one other vehicle along the way. The afternoon walk was shorter – October is the hottest month of the year in Liwonde – and the highlight was meeting a herd of buffalo in the open. Back in the vehicle, we came upon two snoozing lions near the Shire, and retreated to a safe distance to get down for sundowner drinks. As the sun moved behind a perfectly shaped tall sterculia, a glossy ibis glided to roost and a porcupine trotted on urgent business across the plain towards the river, nose to the ground. Prime roosting spots were already filling – dozens of open bill, sacred ibis and great white egret sharing branches. Away from the water, guinea fowl and red-billed quelea doing the same. It was on the twilight drive back to camp that we saw the Meller's. While that was the highlight, we also came across three civets, a side-striped jackal, another porcupine and countless sengi. Liwonde is a very productive park.

The next morning's walk was again full of wonders. At times, we just moved in silence, appreciating the temperature, the light, the sounds, and simply being in this wild and lovely place. Then, something would catch David's eye, and we would go into classroom mode. A hippo whisker on the ground. The smooth corky texture of the bark of a toad tree. The bulb of a red spider lily freshly excavated in the night by a porcupine. He picked up a well-preserved warthog skull and showed us its preorbital gland grooves, part of their scent-marking anatomy.

Back at Mvuu Lodge, the elephants had moved on, with no evident damage. Sitting quietly on the deck of my chalet, I had a wild menagerie for company. A metre-long monitor lizard scampered below and into the outdoor shower area. A solitary yellow baboon sat under a tree, concentrating on a seed pod; they don't raid the rooms and are more likeable than the bigger and more aggressive chacma baboons. Under the deck, a female bushbuck browsed in its shade. Almost within touching distance, a cardinal woodpecker landed.

Later, on the river, David turned off the boat engine and we drifted with the current. We passed our fly-camp spot, recognising the trees – the tents gone, of course. The lions were still where they had been a day and a night before. A pair of goliath heron stood sentinel, and behind them were waterbuck in numbers more usually associated with impala. A black skimmer was chased by a pied kingfisher and, to the west, a skein of glossy ibis transected an amber sky. A few days before, I was only vaguely aware of Liwonde National Park and the Shire River. Now, it's one of my favourite places.

We walked by the Shire River in the shade of fever trees.

in a fly-camp. The distance may vary depending on game movements and local conditions: if water levels are high in the side channels, it can be necessary to go a little more inland to cross them. The terrain is generally flat on the floodplain, which is well endowed with shady woodlands. There are frequent stops to learn about tracks, habitats, birds and flora, and for spotting wildlife. The first night of the trail is spent in Mvuu Camp, followed by two nights in the bush – longer stays can be arranged. The fly-camp is one of the better equipped, with well-furnished tents and bush ablutions with a view. It's set up by vehicle in readiness for the walking group; there's a full crew and camp kitchen to prepare meals that match those of the lodge in quality. A game viewing vehicle is provided at camp, which allows for drives rather than walks in the afternoon, seeking out the lions or rhinos, or exploring southern reaches of the park.

Liwonde lodge walks
There are three **Robin Pope Safaris** lodges in southern Malawi, and as well as making attractive add-ons to visits to the company's camps in South Luangwa National Park in Zambia, they are good destinations in their own right. The company has itineraries that take in Liwonde, Majete, Lake Malawi and the attractive tea estates south of the city of Blantyre.

In Liwonde, Kuthengo Camp is an intimate camp of just four tents located on a plain not far from the Shire River, in an area that features exemplars of Liwonde's signature trees – baobab, Borassus palm and fever tree. The tents are all en suites with outdoor showers, and the camp has a plunge pool for cooling off during the midday downtime. The unfenced camp has regular wildlife visitors, including lion, so adherence to safety guidance is important. Walks are available as an alternative to game drives, led by an experienced guide and escorted by a park ranger. Boat safaris are highly recommended during a stay here. Kuthengo can be reached by road transfer in the same way as Mvuu Lodge – to a crossing point on the Shire River for transfer by boat, or by road via the main gate in the south of the park. Charter air access is via Makanga airstrip.

Majete Wildlife Reserve

In the south of Malawi, the lower Shire River flows through a deep valley on its course to join the Zambezi in Mozambique, one of the most southerly manifestations of the Great Rift Valley, and Majete Wildlife Reserve conserves 70,000 ha on the western side of the valley. The reserve was established in 1955 and the late twentieth century was not kind to it, with the utter depletion of its wildlife. But like Nkhotakota Wildlife Reserve, Majete has been transformed in the custody of African Parks, and is now a good news story for conservation.

Majete is a favoured escape for residents of Blantyre and also a destination for visitors on a tour of southern Malawi. It's about five hours by road from Cape McClear and four from Liwonde National Park and the Zomba Plateau, and tea plantations are often included in such itineraries. Since taking over in 2003, African Parks has established effective protection of the reserve and developed the road infrastructure and tourist facilities. An ongoing reintroduction programme has seen the restoration of locally extinct species including elephant,

Breakfast with a view of the Shire River at Mkulumadzi Lodge.

lion, black rhino, giraffe and African wild dog. It has a good bird list that includes racket-tailed roller, Böhm's bee-eater and Livingstone's flycatcher.

The hilly terrain is covered in miombo woodlands, punctuated by mahogany and ghostly large-leaf star chestnut trees. There are areas of thinner savannah, but wildlife spotting is challenging, especially when the bush is thicker. From a walking perspective, it's good terrain: like Nkhotakota in central Malawi, conditions are shady and mostly thorn free. June to August would be the season for walking, when it's dry and the bush has thinned, but at the time of writing in 2024, walks are not operating; it's anticipated there will be options in the future.

Mkulumadzi Lodge is in a 7,000 ha private concession, about an hour's drive from the reserve gate. Approached via an elegant, suspended footbridge over a rocky tributary of the Shire River, Mkulumadzi matches the standards associated with other **Robin Pope Safaris** venues in Malawi, Zambia and Zimbabwe. A cathedral-like thatched roof shades the communal area, with views of the tumbling Shire below. The eight large chalets are spread far apart, and it's a decent walk to the furthest units with the lowest room numbers. The valley has a reputation as a heat trap and conditions are usually a good deal hotter than the escarpment; an attractive feature of the rooms is the low energy 'evening breeze' air conditioning system. The thick bush can make wildlife spotting tricky during a drive, and it's more rewarding to spend time at one of the concession's two waterhole hides. Night drives are conducted on the return from bush sundowners, and these can be productive. The lodge closes from January to mid-March.

Nkhotakota Wildlife Reserve

Nkhotakota Wildlife Reserve is little visited and well off the beaten track, and is quietly going about its conservation work. This, under the management of African Parks, is proceeding very well, most notably with the reintroduction and protection of elephant: over 500 were transferred in recent years from Liwonde and Majete in a huge feat of conservation logistics. It's a big reserve with over 1,800 sq. km of rugged wilderness spanning the Bua River, most of it under miombo woodlands. As in Majete, there are some open areas of savannah, but in general the density of vegetation precludes seeing large quantities of wildlife while driving; there are a few productive hides at solar-pumped waterholes, which are good locations to spot sable antelope.

Wildlife travel is not always about numbers of species ticked off, and visitors who make the effort to visit Nkhotakota are contributing to a conservation success story and will see plenty of evidence of thriving biodiversity, especially by going for a walk or two. Apart from those well-travelled elephants, there's the chance to spot forest-loving antelopes and bush pigs, and there are over 280 species of birds recorded. Since taking on the park in 2015, African Parks has focused on behind-the-scenes infrastructure, staffing, anti-poaching and the restoration of a healthy ecology. The location means tourism will never overwhelm the reserve, which is an attraction for those who like to feel alone in the African wilderness. There are two comfortable lodges for visitors, both located on the Bua River.

Deep in the reserve, **Tongole Wilderness Retreat** is well named. Multiple levels of decking provide places to simply soak up the natural ambience of the woodlands and do some birdwatching

The Bua River is the lifeblood of Nkhotakota.

against the background music of the Bua River waters tumbling over rocks. The central area is a towering construction of thatch and beams, with its highest deck a place to take a private meal or read a book. There are four fan-cooled thatched rooms and a family cottage, each with an enormous bath and a mosquito net bigger than most tents. The cottage decks all overlook the river, where elephants can often be seen taking water. Walks are led by a Tongole guide and escorted by a reserve ranger. The woodlands are shady and the trees are not thorny, so it's enjoyable to thread the trails created by elephants and hippos. Expect to see tracks of civet, leopard and other nocturnal prowlers, and plenty of birdlife, including Böhm's bee-eater. Take time to sit and observe at the river, where it's possible to spot five species of kingfisher. The mountain in view across the river from the lodge is Kasukusuku, and this makes for an interesting longer hike, best done in the cooler months from May to August.

A few minutes' drive from the park entrance, **Bua River Lodge** is spread across the southern bank of the river and a wooded island accessed by a suspension footbridge. The tents are well spaced out, affording a genuine immersion in nature. Priced as a mid-range boutique lodge, it's a lower-cost walking base to Tongole.

Directly east of Nkhotakota and across 60 km of freshwater lake lies a wild and mountainous region calling for adventurous travellers – northern Mozambique.

10 Mozambique

Despite having vast areas of suitable habitat, Mozambique has never become a major safari destination. In part this is because of the poverty of its infrastructure, which takes a battering every year in the cyclone season. It suffered under decades of civil war, when nature protection was non-existent and destruction of wildlife rampant. The twenty-first-century story is more positive, and there are large scale conservation initiatives underway, especially in the development of Transfrontier parks in cooperation with South Africa and Zimbabwe and the inspirational privately funded restoration of Gorongosa National Park. Mount Mabu is a similar forested 'sky island'; it, and the large southern national parks that are part of the Great Limpopo Transfrontier Park, have future potential as safari and walking safari destinations.

Mozambique's wild places are best visited between May and September. Gorongosa closes during the wet season from mid-December until late March or April, when the risk from tropical storms is highest.

Walking safaris in Mozambique

The prospects for future walking safaris in Mozambique are bright, but for now there are limited options. The choice is between expeditions organised by adventure safari companies from Zimbabwe and South Africa or a visit to Gorongosa.

Gorongosa National Park

North of the city of Beira in Sofala Province in central Mozambique, Gorongosa National Park has attained almost mystical status among devotees of African wildlife travel. It was difficult or dangerous to reach for much of the twentieth century, but in recent decades both ecologists and tourists have enjoyed the opportunity to explore the park's 4,000 sq. km of grassland, savannah, wetland and rainforest, and its central geographic feature, the 1,863 m Mount Gorongosa.

The Gorongosa Restoration Project, a collaboration between the Mozambican government and the Carr Foundation, has been working for over 20 years on rehabilitating the park's previously devastated ecosystems and wildlife. Part of the project involves bringing back wildlife tourism, and **Gorongosa Safaris** facilities a steady trickle of intrepid visitors to experience its forests and wildlife. Between protection of remnant populations and reintroductions, the park is now a thriving habitat for elephant, lion, African wild dog, Cape buffalo and numerous antelope species. Its waterways teem with hippo and crocodile, and there are over 400 species of birds recorded.

Visitors can access Gorongosa by air or by road. For international visitors, the air routes are via Johannesburg or Maputo to Beira. For those who arrive on scheduled flights to Beira, it's a four-hour (200 km) drive from there to the park HQ at Chitengo. The most attractive option is to fly from Beira directly into the park's airstrip with the park's partner SafariAir, where both seat rates and charter options are available. There's another air route from Maputo via Chimoio, from where it's just a two-hour drive to the park; alternatively, SafariAir charters can also be organised from Chimoio. Gorongosa Safaris can arrange pick-ups at either Beira or Chimoio, bearing in mind the park gate closes at 18:00.

Once in the park, there's a choice of camps. For walking, the prime options are Gorongosa Wild Camp and Mount Gorongosa Community Camp. Wild Camp is a seasonal camp designed to provide access to remote lowveld sections of the park in a low-impact way. While comfortable and well kitted out, the camp leaves no trace once removed, and it's re-established each season. It has six stand-up canvas guest tents with proper beds and en-suite outdoor bathrooms with flush toilets. Solar power is provided for lighting and USB device charging. There's an outdoor dining area and the obligatory campfire for evening drinks and chats. The Wild Camp facilitates both game drives and walks, and boating and canoeing during the months of April and May.

Excursions to Mount Gorongosa are possible at an additional cost. These day-long trips involve a drive of about three hours and then a hike to the waterfalls. Here, a hot picnic lunch is cooked while guests bathe in the natural pools. Keen birders will want to overnight on the mountain and, in response to visitor demand, the park started the Mount Gorongosa Community Camp experience in 2024. This fly-camp is highly recommended as a way to get on foot on the mountain instead of the rather long day trip.

Apart from the Wild Camp and Community Camp, guided walks are available from Muzimu Lodge and the Activities Centre at Chitengo. Muzimu was the first lodge established in the park; it's an unfenced camp set amid shady purple cluster-leaf trees on the banks of the Mussicadzi River. It has six comfortable canvas chalets, each with its own deck and en-suite bathroom; like the other camps, it's solar powered. The park has trails guides qualified to Field Guides Association of Southern Africa standards, and in the lowveld section the practice is to walk with one rifle-carrying guide for a maximum of four guests and two for groups of up to eight. In addition to guides with the Field Guide and Trails Guide qualifications, the park has a number of trackers trained by South Africa's Tracker Academy, and these add greatly to the experience.

Niassa Special Reserve

Gorongosa is for now the best equipped wildlife tourism destination in Mozambique, but other large areas are in various stages of conservation recovery. One such is in the far north along the border with Tanzania. Niassa Special Reserve covers about 42,000 sq. km, and can be accessed from the west via Lichinga, close to Lake Malawi. Alternatively, Niassa can be reached from Pemba in the east, but make sure to check government sources for security updates. The easiest access, if not cheapest, is via air charter from Nampula. The ideal time to visit is during the dry season from May to September. There's a rich choice of habitats to explore spanning miombo woodlands, montane forest, riparian

Each season, Mike Scott brings adventurous groups to Niassa Special Reserve.

woodlands and open savannah. It has the biggest population of African wild dog in Mozambique, as well as lion, elephant, zebra and various antelope of course.

Niassa Special Reserve is a target of walking expeditions run by Zimbabwean-based companies such as Khangela Safaris and John Stevens Guided Safaris Africa, and Fraser Gear's Niassa Expeditions.

Niassa Expeditions

South African wilderness guide Fraser Gear leads week-long trips to Niassa National Reserve that are based at a trails camp in the reserve or can be run in self-sufficient primitive trail style. These **Niassa Expeditions** are available on a bespoke basis from June to September. Access is via scheduled flight to Nampula from Johannesburg, followed by a charter propeller flight into Niassa's Mariri (L5S) airstrip, which is where guests link up with Fraser. From there, the week is spent in the L5 South concession area of the reserve in an open game-viewing vehicle, on foot and in canoes.

There's no shortage of empty and unspoiled wilderness to explore, with an interesting variety of terrain. A focus is the Lugenda River, which is undammed and wild and has sandy beaches and braided channels during the walking season when water levels are low. Beautiful riverine forests with incredible birdlife are a feature of this part of the river. Beyond its floodplains are endless woodlands punctuated by dramatic inselbergs. During a trip here, visitors will not cross paths with any other tourists, and only local fishermen on the river.

The base for walks is the Mpopo Trails Camp, which is operated as part of the conservation partnership agreement between Niassa Carnivore Project and Mbamba Village. It's a simple camp with water sourced from the river – boiled and filtered for drinking – and meals are cooked on a fire at the camp using locally grown vegetables and food sourced from the nearby 'livelihoods programmes' – rabbits, ducks, goats and chickens, and honey from 'beehive fences' that are designed to protect crops from elephants. Trips are inclusive of meals and accommodation, fly-camping, canoeing and all activities. For those keen on primitive trails, it's possible to head into the wilds for several days. In this case guests need to bring all their own kit and be prepared for some demanding walking and shared night watch.

Khangela Safaris

Zimbabwean company **Khangela Safaris** runs walking safari trips to Niassa, with the typical guest being a traveller who has been to Africa a few times and is looking for more space and wilderness. For more information about Khangela Safaris, see page 160. The normal access route is via a scheduled flight with LAM from Maputo to Lichinga for a rendezvous with the guide and vehicles; and then a full day road transfer to Niassa on a road that's partially tarred towards Marrupa. The trips are bespoke, with the duration and activities planned in consultation with guests. The style can be backpacking, mobile fly-camping or lodge based, or a mix. Driving, walking and canoeing are all part of the experience: the potential for an African adventure in the reserve's Lugenda Wilderness zone is limitless.

The Lugenda flows east and then northwards through Niassa, eventually joining the Rovuma to demarcate the border with another land of great rivers and enormous wilderness areas – Tanzania.

11 Tanzania

Tanzania is a land of superlatives: Africa's highest mountain, the world's greatest large mammal migration, the 'endless plains' of the Serengeti, the vastness of Ruaha National Park. Over a quarter of the country is protected in national parks and reserves, which span everything from alpine moorlands and tropical rainforest to mangroves and coral reefs. Safaris are concentrated in the areas of savannah grasslands, miombo woodlands and wetlands, and in particular those in the north of the country. Apart from in the renowned Ngorongoro Crater, and during 'great migration' river crossing events in the Serengeti National Park, it's an easy place to escape the crowds, especially by taking opportunities to safari on foot.

Tanzania has a subtropical climate, and its monsoon rains come in the form of 'short rains' in November and December and 'long rains' from March to May. The hottest months are December to March and coolest are June to August. These periods do not disrupt the safari season in the north, which runs all year, but walks are better in the dry season – ideally June to November. The 'southern circuit' parks such as Ruaha and Nyerere tend to become difficult to access in the rainy seasons, and many camps close, only really being feasible for walking from mid-June to October.

Walking safaris in Tanzania

As wilderness walkers, we like to feel that we leave no trace and that our footprints will soon disappear on the game trails. Yet in northern Tanzania there's a remarkable reminder that our ancestors have walked these lands for many years: the hundreds of human prints preserved in the mud at Engare Sero, on the southern shore of Lake Natron, have been dated to 5,000–19,000 BCE. Of course, modern humans are a recent species, and these prints are youngsters compared with those discovered south of the lake at Laetoli, which are believed to have been created by the human ancestor *Australopithecus afarensis* and are an astonishing 3.6 million years old.

Yes, walking in the land that's now called Tanzania is as old as time, and in its parks we can go on foot and share this ancient experience. While most safari visitors are focused on chasing the wildebeest and zebra migration herds, expansive wilderness zones are there for exploration on multi-day walking trails. Walking safaris are a more recent development in Tanzania than in other East African destinations, but a growing number of safari operators have guides trained to lead trails, and lodges and camps have overnight walks to fly-camps.

Safaris in Tanzania tend to focus on either the northern or southern circuit, and if there's enough time, to take in western circuit parks, famous for their primate populations, or incorporate the coast and islands for relaxation. The north has some of East Africa's best wildlife reserves and is the heartland of the Maasai people; in addition to its walking safaris in big game areas, there are treks in the Crater Highlands and ascents of

In peak walking season in August, dawn greets walkers in the Ruaha grasslands.

Kilimanjaro and other volcanoes. In park buffer zones, walks are guided in Wildlife Management Areas (WMAs) such as Randilen WMA and Burunge WMA. The community-owned areas near Lake Eyasi are notable for having some of East Africa's last traditional hunting and foraging peoples, and walks here are especially fascinating.

The southern circuit has a couple of truly huge parks ripe for exploration on foot: Ruaha and Nyerere. Walks in the south are more seasonal, and with much fewer visitors there's less choice of walking options than in the north. The ability to dive into little-visited wilderness on foot compensates for the extra expense and logistical challenges. Apart from big game walking safaris, primate-focused walks are guided in Gombe Stream and Mahale Mountains. Other less-visited national parks with guided walks are Mkomazi, Katavi, Saadini and Ugalla River.

The town of Arusha in northern Tanzania is a major centre for safari operations, and like Hoedspruit in South Africa, Maun in Botswana and Victoria Falls in Zimbabwe, it has walks-specialised and locally owned safari operators, who should be high on the list for any visitor seeking a walking safari in Tanzania: African Environments, Dorobo Safaris, Mark Thornton Safaris and Wayo Africa. In addition to these, Nomad Tanzania has a wide spread of camps and lodges, with seven national parks covered, and operates a high-end mobile walking camp in three of them; and Entara Lodges & Camps has a strong tradition of guided walking. A notable walking specialist in Ruaha is Kichaka Expeditions.

The parks authority, TANAPA, provides armed rangers to escort walkers in big game areas, and while all the multi-day walks are privately operated, these rangers can be booked by individual visitors for day walks. Private walking guides are not numerous in Tanzania, but many of those listed in the chapters for South Africa, Zimbabwe and Kenya can organise and lead walks-focused itineraries in Tanzania. Apart from booking a walking safari via the specialist companies listed here, lodge-based walks are widely available, especially in the Serengeti, Tarangire, Nyerere and Ruaha national parks.

African Environments

African Environments is a pioneer of East African walking, and is as much a trekking company as a safari company. Alongside its mountain ascent activities, it's one of a handful of companies to run multi-day mobile walking safaris in the Serengeti wilderness zones, as well as walks in the Ngorongoro Conservation Area, Arusha National Park and the Eyasi basin.

For over 30 years, African Environments has been integral to the development of safe and sustainable walking in Tanzania through the work of its directors Richard Beatty and Wesley Krause. Richard's training and leadership skills developed during his work for Outward Bound in Asia and America, while Wesley was the Director of international wilderness school NOLS in Kenya. A large part of its business is organising and leading ascents on Mounts Kilimanjaro and Meru, but it has an array of activities for every duration and budget from day trips to exclusive use tented camps that are excellent walk bases, and longer expeditions in the Serengeti wilderness zones, all with a focus on unusual and adventurous activities with a light environmental footprint. The camps are Pembezoni in the Serengeti, Itikoni in Arusha National Park and the seasonal Mysigio Camp in the Ngorongoro Conservation Area. Apart from walks in big game areas, the company runs trips to walk with the Hadzabe people in the Eyasi basin, and has a selection of activities in the Arusha area; these include short hikes with a bush lunch and multi-day walks.

Dorobo Safaris

Dorobo Safaris is a long established walking specialist with a fascinating collection of guided walks throughout the country. Their founding philosophy is based on how it feels right and natural to walk in the environments that shaped our early ancestors, and the Dorobo walking experiences range from remote wilderness walks with wildlife to cultural experiences where guests can learn from a synergy of scientific and indigenous knowledge.

The company does not operate permanent camps but establishes private mobile tented camps that are set up and moved for each bespoke trip. The prime Dorobo walking safari destinations are the Serengeti, Tarangire, Ruaha and Katavi National Parks. Outside these major parks there are guided walks in the Ngorongoro Conservation Area, the Yaeda Valley near Lake Eyasi and the Nou Forest west of Lake Manyara. Walking is a core aspect of Dorobo's activities, but over the years the company has grown to facilitate a variety of travel styles in Tanzania, including vehicle-based wildlife safaris, mountaineering, mountain bike trips, rock climbing and kayaking, specialist birding and photographic safaris, and trips to find primates in the western parks near Lake Tanganika.

The Dorobo tented camps leave a light footprint, and have a format honed over many years of trial and error. They are functional but comfortable, and are kept to a scale easy to pack up for relocation each day. Guests sleep in two-person dome tents, which are big enough to stand in. There are simple solar showers, which are effective and much appreciated after a day on the trail. Water can be scarce in the locations walked, and in this case sufficient water for a daily shower is transported with the camp. Environmentally friendly pit-latrines are dug at each site. A large tent serves as a gathering spot, a sheltered place to rest or for table dining – although mostly guests prefer to eat at the campfire.

Ethan Kinsey Safaris

Ethan Kinsey was born and raised in Tanzania and began his safari career running a camp in remote and wild Ruaha National Park over 20 years ago. From there, he moved to the Serengeti's periphery, managing and leading the guiding from a camp before breaking out on his own to design and guide safaris throughout East Africa. Always up for challenges, Ethan tends towards organised unconventional safaris, with a keenness for being adventurous. A partner of the activity-based Entara Lodges & Camps, he is focused on making immersive safari experiences accessible. While primarily occupied with designing and guiding private safaris throughout East Africa, he also actively leads training and development of guides, and is no stranger to the big name (and smaller) safari companies in Tanzania, including many in this book. A defining moment of his career involved organising walking safari-focused training for Tanzania National Park rangers over a five-year period, allowing walking safaris to reopen in Ruaha National Park.

Ethan's love and curiosity of nature and wilderness are evident, and he is a reassuring and inspiring presence when walkers find themselves sitting in the midst of a herd of elephants. He is equally comfortable stalking buffalo on foot, looking for scorpions in desert environments or birding in rainforests. He can plan and guide all sorts of experiences, which include walking out of his Entara camps in Serengeti and Tarangire, exploring the Ruaha River with Kichaka Expeditions, walking safaris in Katavi with Dorobo, and Mahale's chimp experience. He is ready to lead to less-visited destinations too, such as Nyiragongo in the Democratic Republic of Congo and Ethiopia's Bale Mountains.

Mark Thornton Safaris

Mark Thornton Safaris (MTS) specialises in multi-day walking safaris. Since the company's inception in 1998, its focus has been on taking guests to the remotest areas of Tanzania's reserves, places where few others go. Walking safaris are led primarily in the wilderness zones of Serengeti National Park and Tarangire National Park, but MTS also conducts walks in other parts of northern Tanzania's Maasailand as well as Ruaha and Katavi National Parks in the south. Some walks are two-day 'tastes' and others are extensive walking safaris, such as its signature **Great Serengeti Traverse**, a ten-day, 100 km foot safari across the largest wilderness zone of the Serengeti National Park.

Almost all MTS itineraries have a mobile walking safari focus. During this part of the trip, lodges or fixed camps are eschewed in favour of mobile wilderness camps, which are lightweight and facilitate movement to new locations each day. The camps have hot solar showers and sit-down loos, and while comfortable, they are low impact. After the walking safari days, there are usually further days of game drive safari, with the chance to see the wildebeest migration in the Serengeti, while staying in private camps or boutique lodges. The company offers post-safari travel to Zanzibar, Rwanda and other Tanzanian national parks.

MTS Serengeti walking safaris are led by its own team of professional walking guides, all of whom have over a decade of experience leading treks; they go through rigorous training and a lengthy apprenticeship programme. An attractive

WALKING SAFARIS IN TANZANIA

feature of MTS is that guests can plan their trip directly with owner Mark Thornton, and he guides many trips personally. Over the years he has established a loyal following of repeat travellers, who range from couples to families and groups of friends keen on active safaris. Whether two guests or a dozen, each party is escorted privately with its own professional walking guide, safari vehicle and mobile camp. For families with children, the company has options outside the national parks for eye-opening and educational wildlife walking, cultural and adventure safaris.

Nomad Tanzania

While it mainly runs vehicle-based safaris, **Nomad Tanzania** is a big advocate for including walks in the activity mix and runs them from almost all of its camps, which have the widest geographic spread of any safari company in Tanzania. This focus is best appreciated in the Nomad Expeditionary Walking Camp, which is a newish venture. Designed to be a 'back to basics' experience for those that wish to dial down the distractions of fixed lodges, it compels guests to simply absorb the wilderness experience: no plunge pools, no Wi-Fi, no spas, no need for a fitness centre. It's still pretty comfortable and features large A-frame tents with cot beds and cotton linen. There are two bathroom units with bucket showers and short-drop toilets. The camp caters to a maximum of six guests and three tents. As always, walk intensity is tuned to the particular guests, with anything from three to six hours on foot daily.

The Expeditionary Walking Camp is mobile in two senses. It moves between parks – Serengeti, Ruaha and Ugalla River – and also shifts at least once during a particular guest booking, which is normally three nights. In the Serengeti, it relocates with the seasonal migration, spending a couple of months in each

Nomad uses mesh tents for fly-camping, such as here in Katavi.

sector from November to July. From July to October, it heads to southern Tanzania and to settings on the Ruaha River. The remote and little-visited national park of Ugalla River operates the camp from August to October. It overlaps with Ruaha as there's more than one set of camp kit.

Apart from the Expeditionary Camp, Nomad has lodges in seven Tanzanian parks, and so is very well positioned to provide seamless multi-park itineraries, with as much walking as guests want to experience. In the north, there are a number of lodges in Tarangire and Serengeti National Parks and an excellent selection of walks in Ngorongoro Conservation Area. In Katavi, Nomad Chada operates from June to November, while in Mahale Mountains National Park, Nomad Greystoke is open from June to mid-March. In the south, Nomad has Kigelia camp in Ruaha, and in Nyerere there are two camps, Kiba Point and Sand Rivers, with a walking and fly-camping option.

Tanzania National Parks Authority

The **Tanzania National Parks Authority** (TANAPA) is responsible for the management of the country's 22 national parks, and plays a role in regulating walking activities and providing armed ranger escorts for walking safaris. While most tourism facilities and activities in the parks are delegated to the private sector under concession agreements and permits, TANAPA provides tourism facilities directly, including campsites and cottages.

In some less-visited parks, TANAPA may be the only option for accommodation and activities. If there's big game in the park, visitors are not allowed to walk without an armed ranger, and it's best to enquire about guided walks when booking accommodation. The guides will keep you safe and can provide nature interpretation. The standard varies from park to park, depending on individual guides and their training, but this option is a budget-friendly alternative to walking from private lodges in the main parks. In the Serengeti, park staff are trained to guide short interpretive walks from points of interest, such as special natural or historic features, or just to give visitors a chance to escape their vehicles and spend an hour on foot. This type of walk is also available from Tarangire main gate, and Lake Manyara has longer trails guided by TANAPA staff.

Wayo Africa

Wayo Africa is a walking specialist with a focus on northern Tanzania. It operates a number of seasonal camps in the Serengeti and Lake Manyara national parks, and has a smorgasbord of activities outside these parks that include nature walks suitable for children, mountain biking, canoeing and picnic lunches in the wild. Their camps come in three flavours: Wayo Green Camps in the Serengeti and Manyara run both game drives and walks; the Wayo Little Green Camp is a smaller seasonal camp set in the Serengeti, and likewise offers game drives and walks; and the Wayo Walking Camp is a Serengeti mobile fly-camp, relocated each day by vehicle and dedicated to walking.

The force behind Wayo is Jean Du Plessis; he has a particular love for the Serengeti wilderness zone walks, those from the Wayo Walking Camp. These camps operate on a bespoke basis with the guest experience, dates, location, duration and intensity of the walks tuned to the guests. The camp can be booked exclusively for anywhere between three and fourteen days, and they either relocate each day as the guests walk or stay in the same location with shorter walks. The routes are chosen close to departure

Lit by the rising sun in July, a group from Wayo Serengeti Green Camp walks near the Bologonja River.

time to take into account wildlife movements and weather conditions. The Wayo Walking Camp works well as its own experience or at the start of a longer safari itinerary. While most of its business is bespoke for groups, Wayo operates a number of itineraries on fixed dates that individuals can join. These are moderately priced, and an eight-night itinerary combines stays in Manyara and the Serengeti and has walks, game drives, canoeing, swimming and village visits.

Ruaha National Park

Ruaha National Park is one of East Africa's largest national parks; it's located in central Tanzania in the Iringa and Mbeya regions. With the addition of the Usangu wetlands, and including the surrounding game reserves, over 45,000 sq. km of land is conserved, approximately three times more than the Serengeti. It's known for its healthy population of elephant and many endemic species including oribi, roan and sable. Ruaha's topography is very varied, rising from an elevation of 700 m in the east to 1,800 m in the west, with a mix of dense miombo woodlands and open plains broken by granite outcrops and baobab trees. The Great Ruaha River is a major source of water for the park's wildlife and there are many seasonal rivers, creating a dynamic ecosystem. Guided walks have been run in Ruaha for decades, and it's a park with endless possibilities to explore areas where few, if any, folk have walked before. In particular, the interesting terrain of the park's river valleys is ideal for exploration on foot. The best time for walks is in the June to October dry season, and options are much reduced from November to May.

Kichaka Expeditions operates year-round lodge-based walks and a week-long seasonal expedition, and Dorobo Safaris and Mark Thornton

Safaris run on-demand multi-day walking expeditions from their mobile camps. The upmarket Nomad Tanzania Expeditionary Walking Camp rotates seasonally around Tanzania and is available in Ruaha from July to August, and Nomad has a fixed bush camp in the park called Kigelia. Asilia, Hodi Hodi, Ikuka and Laba Jongomero camps all run walks and seasonal walking/fly-camping combinations. The park is best accessed by air via Msembe airstrip, an hour and 40 minutes from Dar es Salaam. With the right vehicle, it's possible to self-drive and camp in or near Ruaha. In this case, a TANAPA scout can be booked at the gate to escort walks.

Hodi Hodi Bush Camp

On the eastern edge of Ruaha, **Hodi Hodi Bush Camp** operates from June to January, closing during the rainy season. The unfenced camp is set in a private concession that shares an open boundary with the national park, and the wildlife is the same as that found in the park. It has five double and two quadruple tents spread along a high ridge that overlooks a large expanse of acacia woodland and savannah all the way to the far edge of the Great Rift Valley. The start of the season is popular with specialist botanical, ornithological or entomologist groups and short walks are possible, but the prime walking season begins in July, as the vegetation thins, and runs through to December.

Hodi Hodi presents a selection of walks designed to suit different abilities and interests. The easiest is a two-hour morning or evening walk to a hide: a short stroll to a spring through woodlands of acacia, baobab and miombo. For a longer outing, looped walks from camp can take anything from half a day to a full day. The river walk involves a short drive from camp and a half-day on foot along a semi-dry riverbed. Birds and monkeys, perhaps roan and sable antelope, and even big cats can be spotted.

A more challenging walk traverses a high ridge following elephant trails, before dropping down to the plains for refreshments, followed by a return to camp via the excitement of a short night drive. This can be turned into a two-day trek, turning around at a small satellite camp near a substantial and busy waterhole, and walking back through the plains the next day. Hardcore hikers can tackle the mountain, a four-hour ascent in steep and forested terrain. The reward is a fine view over the park, and with binoculars it's fun to pass some time spotting from the summit. Walkers are likely to encounter klipspringer, baboon and bushbuck, and there are resident leopards. Most guests fly into Iringa town or Msembe park airstrip, both two hours' drive from the camp, and it's accessible to self-drive visitors, being about 50 km from the main TanZam highway that connects Zambia and Malawi to Dar es Salam.

Ikuka Safari Camp

Overlooking the Mwagusi River, **Ikuka Safari Camp** is an owner-managed camp with seven large tents. Walks are on offer all year at an additional fee in place of a morning game drive. They may set out directly from camp or begin with a short drive, and during the wet season from January to March it can be necessary to drive further to access more open areas for safety. Walkers are guided by co-owner Mark Sheridan Johnson or one of the other specialist guides and accompanied by a TANAPA ranger. There's an excellent variety of terrain to explore, and walks follow the rivers, scramble up kopjes, investigate Stone Age sites, wend through baobab forests and always leave time to sit by a waterhole to see what turns up.

RUAHA NATIONAL PARK

The golden hour at Ikuka Safari Camp.

Guests at Ikuka can request a fly-camp experience, and this is done just a short walk from the main camp. Called the 'rock house', a mesh tent is set in a well-chosen location on a wooden platform between two enormous boulders. It has a real bed, and a bucket shower and toilet are set up on the deck. Guests can enjoy a candlelit dinner by the fire under the stars before sleeping with a view of a brilliant night sky, and then walk back to base in the morning light.

Kichaka Expeditions

Kichaka Expeditions is a walking specialist, and its main Zumbua camp is home to owners Andrew Molinaro and Noelle Herzog. It's sited on a ridge in the Lunda zone in the eastern corner of Ruaha with a fine view of the Great Ruaha River – often the scene of animal crossings – and accommodation is in three safari tents or three new *bandas*. The large tents are on raised platforms and have shady thatched roofs. Each has its own plunge pool and their en suites have flush toilets, bathtubs and outdoor showers. Walks are available all year for guests at Zumbua and can be combined with game drives. There's a good variety of terrain to explore within reach of the camp, including riverbanks, low hills and rocky outcrops.

The ideal time to visit is in the dry season from June to the end of October, a time when Kichaka has two overnight walking options – Kichaka Kidogo and Kichaka Wild. Kidogo is a lightweight fly-camp designed to let guests escape into the bush for a few nights, camping by the river and exploring on foot. It has three dome tents, bucket showers and short-drop toilets. There are a couple of suggested itineraries, with 'Trailblazer' combining three nights at Zumbua and two at the Kidogo camp, and 'Swashbuckler' adding an extra night at each camp. In either case, guests will experience as much walking as desired.

Kichaka Wild takes that fly-camp into remoter reaches of the park for proper adventures. This is the perfect way to discover the beauty and diversity of Ruaha's truly wild ecosystem, with walks led personally by Andrew. Typically set up along the banks of rivers or nestled into the nearby forests, the camp is a base for walks, game drives and night drives. Each expedition is booked on a private basis and is customised to clients' specific

Kichaka Expeditions fly-camp by the Ruaha River in August.

interests. Given the logistics involved, it's wise to plan it as a week-long experience. Kichaka Wild has a choice of four remote locations, and guests should come with a spirit of exploration. The Ruaha River area is available to walk from May, at the end of the rainy season, when the park is almost empty of visitors. A week of walking here allows for a heroic transect following the Great Ruaha River through pleasant acacia forests and palm groves, and over gentle rolling hills and intersecting sand rivers. From Jongomero in the west to Lunda in the east, walkers pass through the prime viewing sections of Ruaha.

From June, a couple of other options open up. Mpululu is about as remote as it gets in the park, and has towering kopjes, inselbergs and monoliths on the park's northern boundary. Walks explore Mzumbe River, strewn with lava flows and rocky pools which provide plentiful water well into the dry season and support huge hippo numbers. Meanwhile in the southwest, the Usangu area is swampy, and the floodplains can be walked as it dries out in June. Its waterways are teeming with birdlife, and attract herds of topi, roan and hartebeest. As the dry season progresses and vegetation has thinned out, a fourth area can be targeted. Kilola Star is in the highest western extent of the park, and is marked by the junction of four high altitude streams atop the Isunkaviola plateau. The area is prime mature miombo woodland and offers a stark contrast to other parts of the park. An expedition here is not easy, but the reward is to experience something few other visitors to East Africa can achieve.

Laba Jongomero Camp

Laba Jongomero camp is part of the **Laba Laba** group, which has lodges in Serengeti National Park, Nyerere National Park and the Songo Songo archipelago. Unfenced, it's set in a remote area on the Jongomero River, a tributary of the Great Ruaha River. The camp has ten en-suite tents and the adjoining exclusive-use Laba Jongomero Private Bush Manor. From the end of June to the beginning of December, walks are available as an alternative to game drives, and these can be combined with fly-camping during the prime walking season.

Outings can be gentle nature walks, which last one and a half to two hours and stay near camp, getting close to flora and animal tracks and smaller things not easily spotted on a game drive. These walks are nice to combine with brunch served in the bush. More intensive tracking walks are offered too. To make things easier, trackers are sent out early to search for fresh prints of elephants, big cats or other interesting wildlife. Once found, the group will follow the trail, learning age-old tracking skills. With luck, the animals can be found and approached safely on foot.

During the walking season, from mid-July to mid-November, a fly-camp option is available. At this time, wildlife is concentrated near water sources, and the thinning vegetation allows for good viability and safe walking conditions. One or two nights are spent at the fly-camp, with a night at the main camp before and after. Guests can expect to cover 8 to 10 km per day, so should have a reasonable level of fitness. The camp is set up by a team via vehicle, so the group can walk with just light day packs. After a few hours of walking, they arrive to a prepared camp with hot showers and three stand-up dome tents made of mosquito netting, allowing guests to sleep under the stars. It's set with a good view, so is a pleasant place to pass the rest of the day spotting wildlife.

Comfortable camp beds with linen are provided, and outside each tent is a washstand, while warm bucket showers are set up suspended from a tree. For the fly-camp there's a minimum booking of two and maximum of six. To ensure safety, walking guests are accompanied by the camp's head guide, an armed ranger and a Maasai staff member. Laba Jongomero camp closes from March to May during the core rainy season.

Nomad Tanzania

Nomad Tanzania Kigelia has six tents in a bush camp style under magnificent sausage trees. The tents have 'star beds' attached for a sleep-out experience, en-suite facilities with warm suspended bucket showers and flush toilets. This low-key camp is typically combined with other Nomad camps of the southern circuit, such as those in Nyerere. Walks are guided from Kigelia from June to January. From July to August, the Nomad Expeditionary Walking Camp is offered in Ruaha. This is a high-class fly-camping experience, normally run over

Laba Jongomero camp presides over a sandy riverbed in the July dry season.

three nights, and when combined with a couple of nights at Kigelia makes for an excellent Ruaha adventure. See page 241 for more about this option.

Usangu Expedition Camp

Asilia Africa operate several camps in Ruaha; for walkers, the Usangu Expedition Camp is the perfect base, operating from June to the end of November. Located at the edge of the seasonal high water mark in the Usangu wetlands, the camp is in an area well suited for walks, with a mix of wetlands, woodlands and grasslands that thin out as the season progresses, giving good visibility. The six-tent camp feels remote and pioneering. Wildlife is still in the process of becoming habituated, but walking safaris are interesting and exciting through both the wetland and woodland terrain. The duration of walking safaris can be tailored to meet the fitness levels and wishes of guests. Ideally, walks should be combined with a night of fly-camping. Rather than canvas tents, guests sleep in 'star cubes' – just mesh that provides protection from insects but allows the moonlight and starlight through. The tents have a comfortable mattress and proper bedding. A handwashing basin is provided, and a shared short-drop toilet and shower are available in separate tents.

Further north, Jabali Ridge is a luxurious base from which to explore the wilderness of Ruaha. Nearby, on the banks of the dry Mwagusi River, Kokoko Camp opened in 2024 on the site that was previously home to Kwihala Camp and now presents a pared-back – but very comfortable – safari experience. Located in the prime wildlife region of the park, the exclusive-use camp has just three tents and is designed as a safari experience that focuses on the essentials. The exploratory feel of the camp lends itself well to walking safaris, but a vehicle is always available for

game drives. Asilia runs about 20 high-end camps in Tanzania and Kenya and can design marvellous multi-park itineraries. As well as Ruaha, walks are available from camps in Nyerere, Tarangire and Serengeti National Parks and the Ngorongoro Conservation Area. Rubondo Island has nature walks and chimpanzee trekking in a non-big game area. For guests who book seven consecutive nights, with a minimum two nights per camp, Asilia include the road or air transfers for free, subject to terms.

Ruaha mobile walking camps

Dorobo Safaris does not have a fixed presence in Ruaha but runs multi-day fly-camping trails during the dry season on demand. These are focused on the most interesting walking habitats along the river systems in the remote areas of the park. Itineraries are flexible, with a minimum of three nights up to five or six nights. For the adventurous, it's possible to explore a different ecozone, taking time to walk away from the rivers in the miombo woodland and, with more time, to take an excursion to the remote Isunkaviola plateau. Another recommended option is to add days before or after the walking to game drive in the Jongomero or Msembe areas.

Mark Thornton Safaris targets remoter areas of the park via its mobile camp safaris. Trips are usually four to seven nights and have a walking focus, often finishing at Laba Jongomero Camp or another tented camp, or taking in Nyerere National Park on the tour. Their walks in Ruaha typically focus on the rivers. Each morning after coffee by the campfire and breakfast, guests and their guide set off to slowly meander through the classic landscape of jackal-berry and paperbark acacia, looking out for hippos, crocodiles and Pel's fishing owl. The water attracts wildlife from afar, including rarer species such as sable and roan antelope and African wild dog – always an exciting sighting. Mornings are spent on foot walking to a new camp location, with water and snack breaks along the way. When the sun is overhead, guests stay in the welcome shade of camp, which is relocated each day as guests walk. Afternoons are enjoyable, with time devoted to gentle walks or game drives to explore the new location, to add to the bird list, spot some wildlife or take in the view over the water.

Ruaha lodge walks

Apart from the overnight walking operations in Ruaha described earlier, a number of wilderness camps run guided morning walks, and one such is Mdonya Old River Camp. This is operated by **Essential Destinations**, a Tanzanian company created by a team of ecologists and biologists, which has a sister camp in Nyerere. An early start is required for walks, as the group must drive the one and a half hours to park headquarters to pick up a ranger. From there, the usual walk is about two hours at a gentle pace along the Ruaha River. Walks are at an additional fee.

The name of **Ruaha River Lodge** describes its location, overlooking the Great Ruaha River in the centre of the national park. Its 24 stone chalets are unique to Ruaha in style, and game drives, fly-camping and walks are all available. Walks are a dry season activity and tend to focus on the river valley, which provides opportunities for safe encounters as animals come to drink in the mornings and evenings. The camp is spread out for over 2 km along the river, allowing for one-hour Maasai-guided walks within its footprint, and these are suitable for children as well as adults.

Nyerere National Park

Nyerere National Park is Africa's largest national park, protecting some 55,000 sq. km of wilderness; before its formation in 2019, it was part of Selous Game Reserve. Tourism is concentrated in the most accessible areas of the north along the Great Ruaha and Rufiji Rivers. Little visited compared with other parks of East Africa, it's ideal for a genuine remote adventure on foot. The park was listed as a UNESCO World Heritage Site for its biodiversity, but is nevertheless beset by challenges, including a new dam that has inundated a large area, and ongoing poaching. The safari operators in the park deserve support in their efforts to maintain its conservation status.

The park terrain includes hardwood forests, open plains, rocky hills and volcanic springs, and visitors can expect to see the full range of East African animals and their predators: elephant, buffalo, lion and various plains game. There's a good opportunity to spot African wild dog and leopard but rhinoceros and cheetah are rare. The rivers and lakes are a major draw, offering the chance to mix boat safaris with drives and walks. There's a large population of crocodiles, hippos and fish, and it's a premier park for finding waterbirds among over 400 species of bird recorded. Given its size and remoteness, most visitors fly in to one of its airstrips. A number of lodges in the park guide day walks, and a couple run overnight fly-camping, combining boat, vehicle and foot travel. The dry season from June to the end of October is the ideal time for walks. During the long rains, from April to the start of June, the lodges are closed, and some are inundated.

Nomad Tanzania

From June to November, **Nomad Tanzania** operates two camps side by side at a fine well-wooded location on the Rufiji River. Kiba Point has four open-sided cottages with thatched shelters. Each has its own plunge pool and en-suite bathroom with inside and outside showers. Sand Rivers is directly on the river: it has five open cottages in the same style as Kiba Point and three hillside suites. As well as vehicle safaris, boat safaris are popular from both camps.

Nomad was a pioneer of walking in Nyerere and has well-trained guides on its staff. It's possible to combine walks with overnight fly-camping, which is charged as a supplement. Guests sleep under mosquito net cubes, while a bucket shower with hot water and short-drop toilets are set up behind camp. A full complement of staff provides a cooked breakfast, light lunch and three-course candlelit dinner.

Selous Impala Tented Camp

Located overlooking the Rufiji River, **Selous Impala Tented Camp** is a comfortable nine-tent camp and an ideal venue for combining safari styles. It's in an area with extensive wetlands and you can drive, walk and take a boat on the same morning, maximising the wildlife spotting opportunities. Camp guests avail themselves of morning or afternoon walks all year, and these start from camp and last around two hours, the morning walks ending with a bush breakfast. For more intensive walking safaris, fly-camping is on offer in the dryer months from June to November. This is the time when walks are safest as vegetation is sparse, and wildlife is drawn to the water sources. The fly-camp comforts are equal to those at the main camp, with large walk-in tents.

A four-night itinerary sees guests arrive at Mtemere airstrip in the morning, and head straight out on a boat trip with a picnic lunch on the Rufiji River. The first night is spent at Selous Impala, where there's a trail briefing with the professional walking guide after dinner. Walking starts

The Selous Impala fly-camp is simple yet comfortable.

early the next morning in the company of an armed TANAPA ranger, Selous Impala guide and Maasai tracker. The walk explores the area alongside the Rufiji River to Lake Siwandu, where it ends with a bush lunch. After lunch, the game viewing continues with a drive to Lake Tagalala for dinner and overnight stay at a fly-camp set at a private remote location by the lake.

The third morning is devoted to walking, with another early start and meander through the bush to the Beho Beho hot spring. In this area, the waterways are surrounded by open grassland, acacia woodland, riverine forest and rocky hills. The grave of explorer Frederick Selous is at the foot of the Beho Beho mountains. As on the previous day, lunch and a siesta take place in the bush, and the afternoon is given to a game drive. A second night is spent immersed in nature at the fly-camp.

On the fourth day, there's an easier start, with a full breakfast before leaving the fly-camp for a game drive back to Selous Impala Tented Camp in time for lunch. The camp pool is always tempting to fill the hours until the afternoon boat safari, which stays on the water until sunset, passing through the Rufiji River to Siwandu Lake. Dinner and the final night are at Selous Impala Tented Camp before onward travel after breakfast the next day.

Nyerere lodge walks

Rufiji River Camp has an idyllic location amid riparian woodlands near Mtemere airstrip. Perched on a high section of bank on a promontory, guests are treated to lovely sunsets over the water. It's a good venue to mix vehicle, boat and walking safaris, and these are available all year apart from in April and May when the camp closes. The usual plan is to drive some way from camp to begin the walk and return after a couple of hours before the day heats up. Favoured areas are near to the banks of Lake Mzizima, where walks have the lake as the backdrop, and exploring the small open patches that occur in an otherwise bushy and woodland park. Fly-camping is available, but not combined with walks. The maximum number of guests on an activity is seven and walks are inclusive in the rate. Rufiji is part of the Foxes Safari Camps group, which has other lodges with guided walks in Mikumi, Ruaha and Katavi National Parks.

Laba Siwandu was the first camp to be established in Nyerere, and has a distinguished list of former guests. Part of the small **Laba Laba** collection, it's a similar scale to its sister camp Laba Jongomero in Ruaha National Park. It has 13 lakeview tented suites set on the eastern shore of Lake Nzerakera; a pontoon lunch, boating safaris and catch and release fishing are popular on-water activities. Walking is encouraged, with an emphasis on spotting birds along the lake shore. Laba Siwandu can be reached by light aircraft – around 45 minutes from Dar es Salam or around 1 hour and 20 minutes from Laba Jongomero.

Roho ya Selous is an **Asilia Africa** camp, its name meaning 'heart of the Selous', reflecting its central location on the western shore of Lake Nzerakera, opposite Laba Siwandu and close to the Rufiji River. Its eight tents are equipped with low-energy air-conditioning systems. As well as game drives, walks and boating safaris are available. Walks generally focus on the small lake in front of the camp and its prolific diverse birdlife.

Lake Manze is a 12-tent camp operated by **Essential Destinations**, who run a sister lodge in Ruaha National Park. It has a fine lakeside location, and the tents have en-suite bathrooms with solar heated water. Morning walks are an option all year apart from April and May, when the camp is closed. In the cooler months from June to September, afternoon walks are an option. The walks are at a gentle pace and last around two hours, covering up to 3 km in the vicinity of the camp. Game drives, boat safaris and fishing are on the activities menu too.

Makubi Safari Camp is deep in the park in an area with a good mix of woodlands and water. Operated by local company **Isyankisu**, the camp offers more than safaris; through its nature education programmes, guests can deepen their knowledge and understanding of the natural world. From lectures and workshops to guided walks and hands-on activities, the programmes have something for everyone, from the seasoned naturalist to curious beginner. The camp can run walks and other activities for self-drive visitors who use the public Tagalala campsite, as it's not far from Makubi camp.

Beho Beho is a long-established safari base that makes the most of the variety of ecosystems in its area; these range from riparian forests to miombo woodland and open plains. The main walking areas are in the Msine River valley and the (usually sandy) Beho Beho River valley. Morning walks can run for anything from two to five hours depending on conditions and guest wishes. Usually, a picnic breakfast is part of the walk. The norm is to walk directly from the camp, and there are several routes depending on time of year and conditions. Afternoon walks end with a good spot for sundowners, and a half-day Lake Tagalala boat safari is popular too. Walks are rifle-guided, and the guides are trained to the Field Guides Association of Southern Africa Trails Guide qualification system. If there are six guests, then two guides are used. There's a minimum three-night stay, and the camp closes from mid-March to the start of June.

Sable Mountain Lodge is located just outside the north-western boundary of Nyerere National Park and guides walks in the buffer zone close to the lodge. With the presence of elephant and buffalo, and sometimes quite thick bush, an armed ranger escorts the group. A typical walk departs from the lodge in the early morning walk and descends to a nearby waterhole where there's a hide. Snacks of tea and cake can be taken there, and breakfast is served at the lodge after the walk. It takes about two to three hours and requires some hilly walking. Sable Mountain is part of the collection operated by **A Tent With a View**, which has other lodges in Saadini National Park, the Serengeti and Zanzibar.

Mikumi National Park

The isolated mountain range protected in Mikumi National Park is more accessible by road than Ruaha and Nyerere are, being close to the A7 section of the TanZam highway. Though smaller than those two giants, the park still has over 3,000 sq. km of conserved lands, which are a mix of grassy plains, acacia and miombo woodlands. The Mkata River, which flows through the park, provides a water source for the wildlife. South-west of Mikumi, Udzungwa Mountains National Park makes for interesting forest walking, with at least ten species of primate present. It's more demanding than other Tanzanian walking safari venues.

Mikumi Safari Lodge is located in the park's buffer zone and runs walks in the park during the dry season. These typically start with a pre-dawn coffee or tea and then a drive in the game viewing vehicle to collect an armed ranger escort and onwards to the walk departure point. The vehicle meets the walking group elsewhere, and a bush breakfast is had before dropping off the ranger and continuing with a game drive. The lodge can arrange walks outside the park, including to Udzungwa Mountains National Park.

Deep in the park, **Vuma Hills Tented Camp** has 16 en-suite tents, each comfortably furnished with its own shaded deck. Game drives and walks are available in Mikumi, and there are excursions to the Udzungwa Mountains National Park. It's part of the Foxes Safari Camps group, which has another smaller venue in the park, Stanley's Kopje. This is in a prime location overlooking the Mwanamboga waterhole; the tents are spaced around the lower perimeter of the hill, with stunning views across the plains. Walks from both venues are an option during the dry season when conditions are safe, and are carried out on the Mkata plains, a very flat area, with walks weaving between acacia trees and passing the occasional rocky kopje.

Ugalla River National Park

Safari visitors to Tanzania are often directed to one of two park circuits – the northern for the famous migration scenes and the spectacular volcanic landscapes; and the southern for those who prefer the safari road less travelled. There are other alluring parks that are worth the effort, and while they are not major walking safari destinations, there are rewarding opportunities to go on foot.

One such venue is the Ugalla River National Park, centred on the Ugalla River that flows west into Lake Tanganyika. It's very remote, and that's a large part of the attraction: visitors can feel they have the place to themselves. It has a mixed habitat of woodlands and savannah that supports elephant, buffalo, giraffe, lion, leopard and a wealth of bird species. The river serves as a crucial water source, attracting a concentration of wildlife, especially during the dry season. It's a tough place to reach, and the most practical way is to fly in and stay at **Nomad Tanzania's** Expeditionary Walking Camp (see page 241), open from August to October. There's a Nomad air charter loop that includes Katavi and Mahale Mountains Parks, and it stops at Ugalla River on certain days during the season.

Katavi National Park

Katavi is situated in western Tanzania, near the eastern shore of Lake Tanganyika, and covers about 4,400 sq. km of vast plains, woodlands and seasonal lakes. June to October is the time to visit for walks, and the birding is especially rich. It has a similar range of wildlife as the other large parks and is said to have the highest concentrations of game in the country. In practice it's a fly-in destination, and the best options for multi-day walks are via mobile camps arranged through Arusha-based specialist companies Dorobo Safaris and Mark Thornton Safaris.

Of the park's three lodges, two run dry season walks: **Nomad Tanzania's** Chada camp, which has the typical Nomad small scale of just six tents, and the nine-tent **Katavi Wildlife Camp**, part of the Fox Safari Camps collection that spans four national parks on the southern circuit. From here, walks are led on the margins of the Katisunga floodplain, with the Katuma River and Ikuu Springs in the background. Otherwise, there are lodges to be found outside the park gate, and the park headquarters can provide a TANAPA escort for walks.

Dorobo Safaris operates multi-day fly-camping trips to Katavi on a bespoke group basis. These trips are proper wilderness experiences, exploring areas where no other humans will be seen once the headquarters is left. The walks skirt open wetland/grasslands (*mbugas*), which are often hives of wildlife activity, and for variation they can delve into the hills and their miombo woodlands. See page 239 for more about the Dorobo fly-camp experience.

As with its mobile walking safaris in Ruaha, in Katavi **Mark Thornton Safaris** (MTS) runs bespoke trips that are conducted in the areas more secluded from the main tourism routes. Trips here combine walking and game driving, with camp set up for two nights at a time in dramatic locations. A typical MTS Katavi walking safari is four to seven nights, during which time guests experience a good range of habitats; one day camping alongside palm tree-lined floodplains, then in a shaded forest by a clear stream, and others by a boulder-strewn river. Walks can be gentle flat-ground walks or challenging hikes up the escarpment or into the hills. It's possible to combine a walking trip here with walking in Ruaha or a visit to Mahale Mountains to see the chimpanzees.

Mahale Mountains National Park

North-west of Katavi, Mahale Mountains National Park is located along the eastern shore of Lake Tanganyika. Like Gombe further north, the park is synonymous with chimpanzee viewing, as there are several habituated groups that can be approached. This is a very beautiful park, with peaks rising to 2,460 m, and can only be explored on foot. Walking conditions are tricky owing to the forested and mountainous terrain, and so the area is best visited between June and October when at its driest.

While walks tend to be very chimp-centric, there's plenty more of interest to see on foot, including other primates such as red- and blue-tailed colobus monkeys, and a wonderful selection of bird species. Accessed by boat, **Nomad Tanzania**'s Greystoke Camp is directly on the lake and has six traditional thatched *bandas* open from June to mid-March. Its walking guides are keen to show guests the full natural panoply and not just the primates. A visit to Mahale Mountains works well with Nomad's venues in Katavi and Ugalla River as they are all on the same western Tanzania charter flight loop operated by Nomad.

Gombe National Park

Gombe National Park is Africa's best known sanctuary for chimpanzees thanks to the many years of research conducted by Jane Goodall in what was then Gombe Stream Chimpanzee Reserve. It's a tiny park, just 56 sq. km, and very scenic. It attracts a steady stream of primate-loving visitors, who normally arrive by boat from the nearby town of Kigoma. The best time to walk in the forest is June to October, and the rainy months of March and April are to be avoided. The only accommodation option in the park itself is Gombe Forest Lodge, and most visitors stay in Kigoma. which is accessible by road or air.

Saadani National Park

Saadani National Park is located some 100 km north-west of Dar es Salaam and is one of the country's smaller parks, with an area of 1,100 sq. km. It's Tanzania's only coastal park and is unique in East Africa for its combination of freshwater rivers, salt water and mangroves. Wildlife present includes elephant, lion, leopard, buffalo, giraffe, hippo and various antelope species. Its location opposite Zanzibar makes it a convenient stopover, and a couple of lodges in the park offer guided walks.

A good choice for walking is Simply Saadani, part of a set of lodges operated by **A Tent With a View**. The main camp has nine en-suite rooms on raised decks under the forest canopy facing a white sand beach. Within the camp grounds there are four colour-coded nature trails of varying lengths, and these can be walked independently or with a guide. There's a chance to spot duiker, bushbuck, elephant shrew, mongoose and warthog. There's a second two-bed property called Babs' Camp, which is a 20 m-high tower next to the salt flats. Guests at either camp can avail themselves of walks with a Simply Saadini guide and park ranger escort. These focus on the salt flats, which show a myriad of animal prints, painting a story of what went before. The flats surrounding Babs' Camp can have fabulous elephant herds passing through – and staying around, as they feel safe near the tower. The walking is easy here on the salt flats rather than through thick bush, and usually lasts for around two to three hours before returning for 'brunch with a view' in the tower at Babs' Camp. Simply Saadini can be accessed in four hours by road from Dar es Salaam or by air to Saadani airstrip, which is 30 minutes from camp; there are daily schedules from Zanzibar. The camp is closed in April and May. Sable Mountain is a sister lodge in Nyerere National Park, and there are other properties in the Serengeti and Zanzibar.

Mkomazi National Park

One of the newest parks in Tanzania, Mkomazi National Park is in the Eastern Arc Mountains on the northern border adjacent to the Tsavo West National Park in Kenya. The park is recognised for its efforts in black rhino conservation and has been involved in conservation initiatives, including the reintroduction of African wild dogs, community-based conservation programmes and efforts to protect and rehabilitate the habitat for endangered species. The park is accessed through the town of Same and there are a handful of camps inside that can arrange guided walks; while for those staying outside the park, TANAPA can provide a ranger for escort from Zange Gate.

The scenery is one of the star attractions of **Mkomazi Wilderness Retreat**, which makes the most of its hilltop location with views southwards to the Ibaya Plains and northwards to the Dindira Plains and a hazy Mount Kilimanjaro, some 100 km away. The dominant trees are acacia, myrrh, combretum, figs and shepherd's trees. Guided walks are highly recommended during the dry season when the grass is short and the wildlife abundant. There are a couple of favoured routes each lasting about three hours, and a hike up the 1,620 m Maji Kununua is a possibility. In the walking season, guests are likely to see elephant, giraffe, buffalo

Mkomazi Wilderness Retreat overlooking an unusually verdant Dindira waterhole and plain.

and zebra, while resident antelopes include eland, hartebeest, waterbuck and dik-dik. Walks are accompanied by a knowledgeable guide and escorted by a park ranger.

A lower cost alternative is to stay at **Babu's Camp**, a peaceful tented camp with views of Kilimanjaro. It has six en-suite tents set amid baobab and acacia trees, and its bar/dining area is set on a rocky outcrop with views of the Dindira valley. The camp does not guide on foot, but can arrange for a park ranger to take guests on walks that range from gentle one-hour strolls near camp to more demanding and hillier three-hour outings.

Burigi-Chato National Park

Gazetted as recently as 2019 through the amalgamation of several game reserves, Burigi-Chato is a 4,707 sq. km national park in the extreme north-west of Tanzania close to the borders with Uganda and Rwanda. It has a number of lakes, the largest being Lake Burigi, and prolific waterbird numbers. The landscape has rolling hills with a mix of savannah grasslands and scrub, marshes and riparian woodlands. Habitat rehabilitation is an ongoing project, and a small number of lions have been reintroduced. Tourism facilities are scant, but TANAPA can escort walks in the park. Wildlife is likely to be skittish.

Tarangire National Park

Tarangire National Park is located in northern Tanzania, and is named after the Tarangire River, which flows through the park. In terms of big game walking safaris in northern Tanzania, the park is second only to the Serengeti, with options from lodges in the national park and the surrounding buffer zones, and multi-day bespoke trips. Tarangire conserves the full panoply of East African wildlife, including elephant, lion, leopard, cheetah, hyena, wildebeest, zebra, giraffe and diverse antelope. The park is habitat to over 500 bird species, including the endemic yellow-collared lovebird and the kori bustard, one of the world's heaviest flying birds. Tarangire hosts one of the highest densities of elephant in East Africa, with an estimated population of 3,000, so there's a great chance to encounter them on foot.

During the dry season, which runs from June to October, the Tarangire River is one of the few sources of water in the area, attracting large volumes of wildlife to the park, and is a focus for guided walks. In addition to the wildlife, Tarangire is known for its stunning landscapes and picturesque views of the surrounding hills and mountains. The terrain is characterised by a mix of open grasslands, acacia woodlands and tall baobab trees. These ancient trees are especially impressive and provide a unique and iconic backdrop to the park's walking safaris. The dry season is the time to walk, with a possibility to extend into November if the rains are late. After the rains, the grass gets too long to safely walk.

The park has multi-day mobile camping itineraries with Dorobo and

The end of the day, under a star-filled sky, at Olkeri Camp.

Mark Thornton Safaris, while Entara runs overnight walks to a fly-camp from its lodge. Walks are available from a number of other lodges in the park and buffer zone.

Olkeri Camp

Olkeri Camp is an **Entara Lodges & Camps** property in the 31,000 ha Randilen WMA adjacent to Tarangire National Park; it can be reached by road from Arusha in three hours. Here, along with game drives, walks are an option all year subject to conditions. Whether walking in the WMA or across the river in the park, it's splendid walking terrain, with an attractive blend of woodlands, rocky outcrops and grasslands. Two of the giants for which Tarangire is renowned – baobabs and elephants – are bound to feature in every walk.

In keeping with Entara's 'active safari' philosophy, fly-camping is in the mix, as it is at most Entara camps. It's possible to walk to and from the fly-camp, normally setting off in mid-afternoon either from camp or via a short game drive to the starting point. Following a slow and meandering walk, the sun is low on the horizon when the camp is reached. Guests enjoy hot showers and cold drinks as dinner is prepared on the campfire. The tents are comfortable but minimalist, with a mesh design that excludes insects and admits moonlight. A visit to Olkeri can be combined with walks and fly-camping from Entara's Kisima Ngeda Camp on the shores of Lake Eyasi or in the Serengeti from Olmara Camp; and, from June to October, walking from Esirai camp.

Tarangire mobile walking camps

Dorobo Safaris runs walks in Tarangire and, as with its walking safaris in other parks, the mobile camps operate on a bespoke group basis, with walks adjusted to the ability and interests of the guests. The typical daily rhythm sees the group set out at dawn, returning to camp for brunch and relaxation, and then taking a shorter late afternoon walk. The itinerary can be anything from two to eight days, and longer stays make it possible to relocate the camp and drive to other wilderness zones to experience a different terrain. See page 239 for more about the Dorobo fly-camp experience.

For two decades, **Mark Thornton Safaris** (MTS) has led multi-day walking safaris into the wilderness zones of Tarangire National Park. These are supported by a mobile tented camp that moves every day or two, offering a chance to explore the variety of terrain in the park. The camp is low-impact and provides the essential comforts, while being lightweight enough to access the remote areas. The walking safaris are conducted in the deep interior parts of the park, far from the main tourism routes, allowing for several days in the backcountry without encountering other tourism activities. Trips are conducted from July to October, when wildlife from the adjacent WMAs moves into the park's wilderness zones. In addition to big cats and large numbers of buffalo and elephant, the wilderness zones of Tarangire provide the wildlife enthusiast with a chance to see seldom-sighted species such as gerenuk, lesser kudu, fringe-eared oryx and vulturine guineafowl. Trips run from two to six nights as part of a package that can include the Serengeti migration. MTS runs a special seven-day Elephant Experience in Tarangire's wilderness zones, a walking-focused safari based on observing and learning about elephant behaviour and conservation. Mobile walking safaris often end with a few days in a private camp for game drives.

A bush breakfast is the perfect conclusion to a walk from Elewana Treetops.

Tarangire lodge walks

Oliver's Camp, Kuro and Tarangire Safari Lodge run walks inside Tarangire National Park, while Elewana, Nimali, and Entara all have walks from their lodges located in the Randilen WMA adjacent to the national park. For those staying at the campsite or outside the park, walks with TANAPA guides can be arranged at the main gate. There are additional lodge-based options in the Burunge WMA west of Tarangire.

Tarangire Safari Lodge is a family-owned property on the northern edge of the park; there's a choice of classic safari tents and bungalows built in the circular style of a Maasai boma. In the dry season, morning and evening bush walks are guided along the river beyond the lodge, and these usually last around two hours. Night drives within the park boundary are another lodge activity.

Deep in the park, **Nomad Tanzania** Kuro has six tents under a canopy of acacias and sausage trees. It's one of the few lodges in the park itself that runs walks, and the best time is June to September, when wildlife numbers in the area are at their peak. The camp is normally included in a circuit of Nomad venues in the northern reserves.

Operated by **Asilia Africa**, Oliver's Camp is in the far south in the park, close to the Silale Swamp. It's closed in April and May when water levels are high, and at other times walks are available alongside day and night game drives. The camp is named after its original owner, the late Paul Oliver, a legend in the Tanzanian safari industry.

In Randilen WMA, Tarangire Treetops lodge has 20 large rooms with views over the tops of surrounding marula and baobab trees. It's part of the **Elewana Collection**, known for its extensive range of stylish safari lodges in Tanzania and Kenya. As well as the usual game drives, guided walks are offered at Treetops, available all year, with the best conditions just after the green season, which is usually April to May. Setting off at dawn, the walk duration is about two hours, ending with a breakfast in the bush. It's an option to go out on foot during the afternoon 'golden hour' and end with sundowner drinks back at the vehicle. Tarangire is often combined with the Serengeti National Park, where Elewana's Serengeti Migration Camp and Serengeti Pioneer Camp also run guided walks. Treetops takes three hours to reach by road from Arusha, and it's possible to drive through the national park on the way.

Nimali Africa has three camps in Tanzania, one of which is in its own private concession in Randilen WMA not far from the Entara and Elewana camps. From here, morning and afternoon walks are available by advance arrangement and at an additional fee. A short walk to a sundowner spot is a popular choice.

Between Tarangire and Lake Manyara National Parks, Lake Burunge is one of the smaller lakes of the rift valley; it's a soda lake that's an important waterbird habitat. The picturesque Burunge WMA surrounds the lake and has open boundaries with both Tarangire and Lake Manyara parks. The Kwakuchinja Corridor is a vital wildlife migratory route linking the two national parks, and there are a number of lodges guiding walks within this area. The pick of them is **Chem Chem**, which has a choice of three properties – Chem Chem Lodge and two camps, Forest Chem Chem and Little Chem Chem. Guests at the lodge can go on Maasai-led nature walks to Lake Manyara; guests at Forest Chem Chem and Little Chem Chem can take a walking safari along the shores of Lake Burunge with their private guide and a vehicle in close proximity. If preferred, walks can be taken in complete silence or in 'power walk' style as a 6–10 km workout. Walks are available throughout the season, which runs from June to March.

Lake Manyara National Park and the Eyasi basin

Lake Manyara National Park is a popular first stop on the northern safari circuit, as it can be combined with a road trip from Arusha to the Ngorongoro and Serengeti. The lake can vary in size depending on the season, but it covers an area of approximately 230 sq. km. In recent years, water levels have been high, which does not suit the flamingos, who have relocated to other alkaline rift valley lakes. The park has elephant, giraffe, buffalo, zebra and numerous primates, and its tree-climbing lions are a famous highlight for those lucky enough to see them. Visitors find a range of ecosystems, from the lake itself to grassy floodplains, acacia woodlands, and lush groundwater forests. The reason that tours often start with Manyara is that its relatively dense woodlands make wildlife spotting tricky, so it can be disappointing if visiting after the Serengeti. Walks are allowed in the park, guided by TANAPA staff or from the Wayo Manyara Green Camp.

Lake Manyara **TANAPA** parks staff have been trained to guide walks in the park on set routes, and they should be booked in advance. There are three defined trails in the park, each with its own flavour. Nearest the gate is the Msasa Trail, about 11 km into the park. This tracks the Msasa River up onto the escarpment to a look-out point. Another trail, the Lake Shore Trail, is the best in terms of looking for waterbirds and big game. The third, Iyambi River Trail, is 50 km deep in the park, and explores a forest that's another good area for bird-spotting.

Wayo Manyara Green Camp is a permanent camp with eight tents on the edge of a seasonal river beneath the Endabash Waterfalls, a splendid location away from the game drive tracks, with views of wooded peaks. The river and waterfalls run between late December and late August, and pools in the falls are usually at their deepest between February and May. The tents are set on decks and have en suites with warm water suspended bucket showers and low-flush toilets. Guests can see herds of elephants every evening in front of the camp between the months of July and October. It's an ideal base to mix safari activities; apart from game drives, guests can visit the treetop walkway, go on canoe safaris or take a guided walk. These walks range from a leisurely birding stroll along the lake shore to energetic climbs to the top of the waterfalls and day-long demanding hikes up the Rift Valley.

Mobile camping with the Hadzabe

Tanzania's four main operators of mobile walking camps bring visitors to stay near a Hadzabe camp and take part in walks and cultural activities. The format of each is similar: guests spend the days getting to know community members and participating in whatever daily activities are happening. During a stay, visitors are given the opportunity to go on a hunting trip, to learn of the traditional ways and the skills developed over thousands of years. It's an authentic experience that can last for anything from one to four hours depending on what game is found and on the skill of the hunters. It's not a requirement to go hunting, and many guests enjoy other daily routines such as foraging for tubers and edible berries, and learning about the medicinal uses for plants, including the ones that are used to make the poison to bring down bigger game. The distinctive call of a honey guide bird could be the signal to follow and try to collect honey from a wild hive. There are opportunities to learn traditional skills, from starting a fire without matches to making an arrow and learning to shoot it.

African Environments operates a four-day Hadzabe Cultural Walking Safari, which can include not just walking but running and hunting with the Hadzabe for those up for it. African Environments have worked with a particular clan of Hadzabe for more than 30 years – supporting members of the community and helping them to gain title to some of their own land. It's a valuable partnership that gives guests wonderful access to this unique and disappearing lifestyle.

Dorobo Safaris brings its low-impact fly-camping set-up for each bespoke group, and uses it as a base for stays alongside the Hadzabe in the Yaeda valley. This is normally paired with visits to Tarangire or Serengeti national parks; see page 239 for more about the Dorobo fly-camp experience. For a contrast to the savannah and cultural experience of the Yaeda valley, Dorobo can bring walkers to the Nou Forest, a few hours' drive south of Lake Manyara. There, in partnership with a local Iraqw community, the company guides guests in the heavily forested

Walking with Hadzabe

Lake Eyasi is a soda lake located in an offshoot of the Great African Rift to the west of Lake Manyara and south of the Serengeti. It's a shallow lake that covers an area of over 1,000 sq. km and is fed by several small rivers, including the Sibiti and the Baray. The lake is surrounded by a diverse landscape of savannah, woodland and rocky outcroppings, and is habitat for a wide variety of plant and animal species. It can be visited as a side trip when moving between Lake Manyara and Ngorongoro Crater.

The area at the northern end of Lake Eyasi is fascinating for being the homeland of several indigenous tribes, including the Hadzabe, who have preserved a long tradition of hunting and foraging that's similar to that of the Khoisan of the Kalahari. The valley is in a rain shadow that precludes intensive agriculture, and it's an area where livestock naturally shares land with wildlife in a dry savannah dotted with baobab and acacia trees. Cultural visits in Africa can get a bad press, often because of their fleeting and commercial nature, and poor visitor behaviour that has been labelled 'human safaris'. Visits to the Hadzabe are carefully managed by a few long-standing safari companies that have built relationships over decades and conduct the visits on the terms of the Hadzabe themselves. Don't expect a day visit – to get to know the people, plan on spending at least three nights.

Specialist walking companies bring their mobile camp experiences to the valley, while Entara's Kisima Ngeda lodge has a walking and fly-camping option. A visit here is about much more than walking safaris; it's a chance to appreciate traditional skills through time spent hunting, foraging and interacting with one of Africa's last remaining hunter-gatherer tribes. On a trajectory similar to that of the Khoisan of Southern Africa, these skills are at risk of being lost, but well-managed tourist visits are a means to channel funds directly to the Hadzabe and help them to make self-determined decisions about preserving their way of life.

ROSHNI LODHIA

Traditional arrow making is a skill preserved by the Hadzabe people.

slopes on foot. It's unlikely to find the few elephant that live in this habitat, but it's a place to enjoy the flora, birdlife and reptiles, and all the forest lifeforms. It's a pleasant and cool escape from the heat of the valley floor, and a longer walk can be rewarded with a swim under a remote waterfall.

Mark Thornton Safaris runs three- to four-night camping trips, always combined with Tarangire or the Serengeti. The visits are conducted in ways that are authentic and educational, and the camps are set with the permission of the Hadzabe who join guests to tell stories, demonstrate arrow-making and engage in lively bow and arrow shooting contests. The mobile camp set-up is the same as that used by MTS for its journeys in the Serengeti and Tarangire. Visits include a range of supports to the local communities, so guests can be sure to be practising responsible tourism on these safaris.

Wayo Africa operates trips either as a stand-alone visit or as part of an itinerary that takes in Lake Eyasi while moving between Lake Manyara and Ngorongoro. To fully appreciate and engage with the Hadzabe, it's recommended that three nights are spent sleeping in a small mobile camp close to a Hadzabe village. This gives time to devote a day with the men to hunting and honey gathering trips, and another with the women of the village, joining them as they forage for roots, tubers and berries. Apart from sharing time with the Hadzabe people, it's a trip that includes walking in a beautiful area amid baobabs and wildlife. Some camps are set at the foot of a rocky outcrop that's sacred to the Hadzabe, and from the top there are stunning views of the valley and beyond to the reaches of Lake Eyasi. Most afternoons are spent in and around camp, relaxing and taking bush walks in the area. The sunsets from the escarpment are always memorable.

Kisima Ngeda

An alternative to the mobile camps operated by the companies previously mentioned is to stay at a lodge in the area, several of which can organise time with the Hadzabe. A good choice is the **Entara Lodges & Camps** venue, Kisima Ngeda, as it can arrange a night of fly-camping. Kisima Ngeda is in a lovely location on the eastern shore of Lake Eyasi with palm-thatch shaded tents amid fever trees, all rebuilt in 2024 following a fire. From here, guests can pick from a range of guided activities, and the most popular are guided walks and fly-camping with the Hadzabe. These trips, which are on offer all year, venture into the wilderness areas in which the Hadzabe live, hunt and gather, along with their neighbours, the intriguing Datoga people, fiercely traditional pastoralists who roam the region with cattle herds.

The private fly-camp can have up to four tents, which are extremely light touch, made of netting that allows the starlight through while keeping any insects out. There are cosy bedrolls and bedding, a short-drop toilet and a warm water suspended bucket shower (when two nights out are booked). The walking is not difficult, with an emphasis on appreciation of the Hadzabe's fascinating knowledge of their natural world. In addition, a 5 km gorge hike and similar distanced Yasaneda ridge hike can be arranged, accompanied by Hadzabe for a more subtle cultural experience, as well as visiting ancient rock painting sites. Kisima Ngeda Camp can be conveniently combined with Entara's Olkeri Camp in Tarangire, and during the June–October dry season it's possible to transfer by small plane to the Serengeti to add walking from the Esirai Migration Camp and fly-camping from Olmara Camp.

Ngorongoro Conservation Area

The Ngorongoro Conservation Area (NCA) protects a huge conservation zone east of the Serengeti and it contains some of Tanzania's most stunning volcanic landscapes. It's best known for the Ngorongoro Crater and Olduvai Gorge, and its mix of wildlife, forest and views makes for magical walking, especially in the green season from December to May when the migration is passing through and calving on the short grass plains.

While there's no walking in the actual Ngorongoro caldera, walks on the rim and surrounding slopes are highly recommended. The NCA can be an excellent destination in itself, but it's more usual to visit it as part of an itinerary to the Serengeti. African Environments, Nomad and Asilia have lodges and camps with walks, while Wayo and Dorobo bring their mobile camps in for bespoke trips. From Empakaai crater north to the border with Kenya, there's less wildlife to see, and multi-day hikes pass through a splendid 'crater highlands' landscape of grasslands and towering volcanoes.

African Environments

African Environments run walks with the Maasai from its tented Mysigio Camp in the NCA west of the crater. This semi-permanent camp has ten large tents and a mess/lounge tent warmed by a woodburning stove. It's located away from the busy crater rim in a grove of venerable acacia trees, and there are no permanent platforms or plumbing for the tents – which would be damaging to the environment within the conservation zone. The company has a long presence in this area, which makes it a good location for authentic engagement with the local Maasai community, rather than the highly commercial flying visits typical of many tours in the area.

From Mysigio Camp, a two-night walking itinerary starts with a climb towards the ridge that leads into the highlands. It's not too steep, and the open grasslands make it possible to enjoy fantastic views westwards to the Serengeti plains. As well as a Maasai guide, walkers are accompanied by a nature guide and armed park ranger, and along the way, the group meets other Maasai herders grazing their cows and goats. By late morning, walkers reach the high point of the ridge, exposing further vistas towards Oldonyo Lengai to the north. The route then drops steeply to the plains far below, following footpaths and animal tracks on grassy slopes, before entering the woodland where it levels out into the cooler shade. The lightweight camp is ready in a sheltered glade in the woods for the overnight.

On the second day, the walking is through woodland with a chance of occasional glimpses of wildlife amidst the trees. The woods gradually thin out and there's better wildlife viewing in the open grassy plain. Depending on the conditions and guests, there are several route options: to follow the treelines on the dry river courses or to stay within the shaded woodland before reaching camp for the night. On the third day, the walking party leaves the camp crew and sets off across the plains, perhaps following one of the dry watercourses or heading for a small kopje to explore. By late morning there's a rendezvous with the safari vehicle for lunch, before travel onwards by vehicle.

Nomad Tanzania

Set in a unique location, with views of both the Ngorongoro Crater and the

Serengeti plains, Entamanu Camp is part of the **Nomad Tanzania** collection. In keeping with their enthusiasm for walking, it has a range of options to keep you on your feet for days and walks are guided by a Nomad guide along with a Maasai walking guide and an NCA Authority armed ranger. The ideal choice is to walk from here westwards down towards Nomad's Serengeti Safari Camp. Depending on the time of year, this is about 10–14 km and takes four to six hours, so you need to be prepared. When the bush is thick in the green season, the longer route is taken to avoid any thickets where wildlife might be hiding. The day begins with a 30-minute game drive to the walk start point. From there, it meanders through Maasai grazing land and acacia woodlands, with great views of Lemakarot Mountain to the south. The route descends and the habitat gradually changes as it reaches the plains. Along the way, a bush brunch is magicked up, and from there guests can either drive back to Entamanu or onwards to Serengeti Safari Camp when it's set in the Lake Ndutu area. In the green season, it's possible to extend this walk by another few kilometres in the direction of Olduvai Gorge for an extra dose of scenery and plains game.

Another demanding walk is to allocate a day to target Lemakarot. This is similar in duration to the above walk but involves more uphill hiking. It's a 90-minute game drive to the walk starting point, and from there guests follow ancient cattle trails and pass pretty Maasai settlements on the approach to Lemakarot's incline. The climb takes about three and a half hours, ascending grassy slopes before entering a belt of dense highland vegetation: mystical trees are cloaked in old man's beard, and leafy shrubs and giant ferns brush the path. This gives way to open highveld grassland wreathed with wildflowers, and a view of Lemakarot's peak through patches of montane evergreen forest. Looking back reveals part of Ngorongoro crater, the peaks of Mount Satiman and Mount Oldeani, and endless undulating highland hills. At the summit, walkers are rewarded with a 360-degree view from Lake Eyasi to the Serengeti plains, Ngorongoro highlands and all the way to the Gol mountains, with Oldonyo Lengai in the distance toward the northern side of the mountain.

Other easier walk options are available from Entamanu, such as the 3–4 km excursion to a fine crater viewpoint. This walk is avoided when the bush is thick between April and June, in case of unexpected close encounters with an elephant or buffalo. A longer version takes up to half a day and explores a section of the crater rim for 6–8 km over three to five hours.

Ngorongoro mobile walking camps

Dorobo Safaris has some of the most interesting walk options, as they explore parts of the NCA remote from the caldera that others don't. The walks show the range of habitats to be found in the area from the Upper Kitete corridor and Selela forest east of Ngorongoro crater to the classic short grass plains of Kakesyo west of the crater. Some areas work better at certain times of the year.

Upper Kitete lies along a timeless elephant route between the Ngorongoro Highlands and the Manyara rift valley floor. Walks follow this 'elephant corridor', which is around 3 km wide and extends 8 km to the valley floor; elephant still use the trail, primarily at night. Walking here is best in the drier months from June to November. Time is spent in Selela forest, which is a mature groundwater forest at the base of the Great Rift wall, a habitat that's both a sanctuary for wildlife and the Maasai community who own and manage

The Dorobo mobile camp set in the lush bushlands of Kakesyo in February.

it. Some of the income from walks in this area supports the village via bed night fees and payment to local guides elected by the community. With one of these local guides and an armed Dorobo Safaris guide, the forest walks focus on birding and spotting primates such as blue monkeys and olive baboons. It's possible to hike into the Ngorongoro highland forest, which is a great option in the morning as you ascend the escarpment and get views of the Selela forest along with Losimingur and Lopurko volcanoes.

The walking camp is set amid a grove of highland red thorn acacia that provides welcome shade. In camp, guests are hosted by Maasai selected by the village. These Maasai help when interacting with other Maasai herd boys who attend their cattle close to the camp. While in the area guests can meet the 'Forest Guardians', a group of rangers who are there to help keep the elephant from moving out of the corridor area into the neighbouring villages. One of the ways they do this is to put up 'chilli fences', which the elephant can't abide.

Another interesting locus for Dorobo walks in the NCA is the Nasera Rock area, some 40 km north of the Ngorongoro crater rim. This makes for a good expedition in the December to May green season. The rock itself is an inselberg and an important archaeological site. The trees below it make for a lovely shady campsite, a spot to just sit and look out on the short grass plains. At this time of year, it's a key calving area for wildebeest and zebra, and if rains have been good the grasslands attract prolific numbers of game, including eland, giraffe, gazelle, hyena and – if lucky – lion. The camp is the base for walks that can venture onto the plains or ascend some of the smaller ridges and use drainage lines as cover. The wildlife shares the area with Maasai cattle herds, so the animals are habituated to humans and one can approach closer than in the parks.

As well as these two remote areas, Dorobo runs multi-day walks in the Kakesyo area, west of the crater and south of the Serengeti. Logistically these can be done as part of an itinerary that takes in the Serengeti or as a stand-alone trip out of Arusha. This is splendid walking territory, an area called Loirujruj by the local Maasai, and affords the choice of walking on the endless southern plains or moving farther in towards the escarpment with stunning vistas over the Eyasi rift and basin. On all of Dorobo's NCA walks there's the option to enjoy the company of the local Maasai and witness their way of life. It's interesting to visit a boma in the early morning or evenings while the livestock are around and getting milked. These interactions are not staged and provide a genuine insight into the daily life of Maasai.

Wayo Africa itineraries almost always include overnights in the NCA, both for its attractions and the logistical sense. While the company does not camp on Ngorongoro crater rim (owing to the large number of visitors), it runs a Wayo Walking Camp remote from the caldera. This is designed for guests who want to experience the crater in a different way; the wildlife viewing is less than when walking in the Serengeti, and walks are more focused on the landscape and Maasai interaction.

The Walking Camp combines well with a stay at a crater rim lodge or camp, with the option of game drives onto the crater floor, before doing a couple of nights at the Walking Camp and then proceeding to the Serengeti. Such an itinerary provides time for a full day of walking, followed by another morning's walk. It starts early from the Lemala gate on the eastern side of the crater and follows a track through thick forest along the contour line, looking down into the caldera. A picnic lunch is taken along the way, and the Wayo Walking Camp is reached in the early afternoon. The next morning's walk is through more open terrain just inside the crater rim, with incredible views: take binoculars to spot the game. The walk ends at around midday at the Leneto Crater descent road, to rendezvous with the vehicle for onward travel. This trek is 15–20 km a day, and can be muddy during the rainy season.

The Highlands

The Highlands is an **Asilia Africa** lodge that presents something different in terms of walks. It's more remote than most Ngorongoro lodges, deliberately located away from the busy Ngorongoro Crater, with eight unusual domed suites overlooking the Olmoti Crater. It's an area of forests and vistas begging for walks rather than drives, and there are a couple of options. One is to start with a short drive to the ranger post at the base of Olmoti and ascend to a viewpoint at the top, looking over the interior of the crater. This walk can be extended into the interior to an impressive waterfall. Alternatively, drive a little north to Empakaai Crater for a walk down the inside of the crater, where a flamingo-lined lake awaits. It's about 45 minutes down to the floor, and about an hour and a half back up the steep inner wall. It's unlikely that you'll see big game in this area, but the walks have plenty of interest, including birdlife and smaller bush game, and the chance to meet the occasional Maasai herdsman with his cattle along the way.

Crater highlands

So far, this chapter has focused on big-game walks in Tanzania's national parks and surrounding conservancies, but the north of the country is a superb destination for other sorts of hikes. These, while highly recommended and hugely enjoyable, would not fit the usual description of a walking safari, as they lack the slow nature interpretation aspect.

The best known hike is the ascent of Africa's highest peak, Kilimanjaro. While no doubt rewarding, it's superseded by a lesser known neighbour in terms of wildlife viewing and interesting terrain: the volcanic peak of Mount Meru that fills the sky north of Arusha town and is protected in Arusha National Park. During an ascent of Meru, which usually requires three nights in mountain huts, walkers can expect to spot elephant, giraffe, zebra and perhaps buffalo and blue monkeys. There are shorter walks in the park that don't involve the ascent, such as just doing the first day of the climb to Njeku Viewpoint. **Wayo Africa** offer a choice of two-hour and four-hour walks through the Napuru forest with the chance to spot monkeys, and the guides are good at birding and knowledgeable about the forest flora. The longer walk is more demanding, with steep inclines.

Between the Ngorongoro caldera and Kenya, the area of the NCA known as the crater highlands has some of Africa's best grassland walking. The wildlife thins out and Maasai herds are common, making it more of a hiking and cultural experience than a walking safari. The altitude makes conditions very pleasant compared with the valley floors, and walkers avail themselves of donkey portage, spending a couple of nights camping along the way. The usual route passes Olmoti and Empakaai craters (with an option to descend into them), before skirting to the west of the volcanically active Oldonyo Lengai and ending at Lake Natron; Oldonyo Lengai is a demanding night-time ascent. It's not hard to find a company in Arusha to organise these crater highland treks.

An interesting alternative is the **Footsteps of Mankind** trek, which links Lake Natron and Olduvai gorge, the 'cradle of mankind'. This timeless journey begins appropriately at the site of ancient

Serengeti National Park

The Serengeti is part of an ecosystem of global importance that spans northern Tanzania and southern Kenya. Its natural beauty and abundant wildlife have made it one of the most desirable safari destinations in Africa, and it stands alongside the Kruger, Luangwa River valley and Laikipia as a major walking safari destination.

A UNESCO World Heritage Site, the terrain of the Serengeti National Park includes open grasslands, rocky outcrops, woodlands and riverine forests. The grasslands are particularly noteworthy and are the primary habitat for the wildebeest migration, which is one of the most magnificent events in the natural world calendar. It's a year-round destination as safari operators have devised mobile camps that move in sync with the seasonal migrations. Broadly speaking, they set camp in the north from May to October and in the south from November to April. While it's no doubt an attraction to see the vast herds of blue wildebeest and other plains animals associated with the

Walkers on the Footsteps of Mankind trek negotiate a scenic section of the Sanjan River.

footprints preserved on the edge of Lake Natron. Guided by local Maasai, the hike passes from lake shore, to volcano, up the Great Rift valley and through rocky gorges before easing into the edge of the Serengeti plains. Here, there's a chance to search for fossils and cave paintings and take time to reflect on the journey before visiting the 3.6 million-year-old *Australopithecus afarensis* casts at Olduvai gorge. The trek makes for a good prequel to further safari travel in the Serengeti, or alternatively can be walked in reverse.

migration, there can be a tendency for too many visitors to chase the best river crossing photographic locations – all the more reason to seek out walking safaris that run in remote areas of the park.

For a long walking safari – and an unforgettable experience – the best option is to go with one of the specialist multi-day companies: African Environments, Dorobo, Mark Thornton Safaris and Wayo. These operate small mobile walking expeditions in wilderness-zoned areas where no vehicles are allowed other than the one that moves the camp. Strictly controlled by the park authorities, the emphasis is on preserving the wilderness experience with walking only, no game drives. The camps are lightweight: they must pack up in a single pick-up truck per five people and can't spend longer than two nights at one spot. These walking safaris are up there with the best in Africa as journeys in real wilderness.

Apart from the wilderness zone walks, there are plenty of other opportunities to get on foot in the park. There are a number of safari operators that guide walks from their fixed and mobile camps as an alternative to a game drive. In this category, Nomad Tanzania is known for its

On foot on the endless plains near Kusini in the Serengeti.

strong walks focus, while Serian, Entara, Lemala, Elewana, Asilia and Laba Laba all cater for walkers. Their walks are generally confined to the 'low use zones' near their lodge or seasonal camp, and make a very satisfying alternative to confinement in the vehicle.

Note that the term 'mobile' is used a bit differently in the Serengeti; it describes a seasonal camp that follows the migration and changes location two or three times a year. Not all Serengeti mobile camps include walks in the experience. For the wilderness-zone walk operators, a mobile safari is one where the camp is moved for the walking group each day, or every other day.

TANAPA staff operate guided walks in the park, and these are generally short (less than an hour). While it would be a stretch to call them walking safaris, they facilitate welcome opportunities to get down from the vehicle and stroll in safety.

African Environments

African Environments operates a year-round camp at Pembezoni on the margin of Serengeti's eastern designated wilderness zone. The camp is set on the ledge of a small river gorge that attracts plenty of wildlife traffic; it has ten large en-suite tents and an airy mess tent for relaxation. Its location makes it possible to walk directly from camp into the wilderness zone, for anything from a half-day or full day to a couple of nights of fly-camping. There are no vehicle crossing points on the rivers around the camp, so walkers won't encounter vehicles. Even in the dry season, the river holds a series of deep pools, and there's always game attracted to it. Pembezoni guests can either fly into Seronera airstrip or drive in from Arusha – ideally with a night or two at Mysigio Camp along the way. A minimum three-night stay is recommended.

For longer walking safaris, guests overnight in the lightweight Wilderness Walking Camp. This is carefully designed to have as many comforts as possible while being easy to relocate each day as guests walk with just their day packs. It features dome tents with cot beds, thick mattresses, real sheets, and duvets and pillows. Outside the tent a washstand is topped up with warm water for hand and face washing, and a bath towel is provided for hot suspended bucket-style showers. There's an enclosed dining tent, in case of bad weather. As at Pembezoni, there's a focus on fine food and fresh ingredients – meals are waiter served either in the mess or, if the weather permits, tables are set up around the campfire. African Environments works hard to minimise the environmental impact of its activities. All the camps are solar powered and water for drinking and cooking is filtered. Sufficient water is brought in for cooking, washing and drinking needs, and nothing is wasted. The Wilderness Walking Camps leave no trace behind, not even the remnants of the campfire.

On a three-night itinerary, the first day starts with a drive of two to three hours deeper into the wilderness zone, the exact location dictated by the movement of the game, with a bush picnic lunch along the way. The walk to the first camp takes place as the sun starts to dip and the shadows lengthen, arriving in camp in time for a shower followed by a cold drink at the campfire. The next two days are full walking days, wandering amid towering rock kopjes that dot the landscape and unlocking the secrets of this magical area. The group moves slowly, taking time to rest under a cool overhang or the spreading branches of a fig tree. The whole camp is packed up and moved each day to a new site so that the walk has a true feeling of being a journey across the wilderness. On the fourth day, everyone is up before dawn, keen to make the most of the last morning walk and a 'surprise' bush breakfast. Back at camp, it's time to pack up camp and drive out, with time along the way to stop for whatever game appears, far from any other vehicles.

Alex Walker's Serian

Alex Walker's Serian is totally focused on the Serengeti/Mara ecosystem, with fixed and mobile camps in both Tanzania and Kenya. The camps are small, and while 'high end' in terms of comfort, tend to have an informal ambience and eschew anything that might distract from the simple enjoyment of wild places: no pools, spas or gyms, and definitely no Wi-Fi. The company operates a mix of fixed and seasonal camps that cater to both walks and game drives, and these combine with bespoke fly-camps designed for overnight walks.

In the Serengeti, Serian Lamai is a fine walking base for exploring the north and operates all year, with the peak for migratory wildlife from mid-June to October. Set among acacias less than a kilometre from the river opposite Crossing Point 4, Lamai sleeps 24 split into two zones with separate mess tents. There's a minimum three-night stay, and ideally more time can be spent in the area to really explore it on foot. Serian has a 'Soul Drifter' walking safari itinerary that affords five nights of fly-camping bookended by two-night stays at Lamai camp, for a total of nine nights. The fly-camp has four stand-up bell tents, sleeping a maximum of eight guests. Once the herds have moved on, Lamai enjoys having the run of the area, allowing guests to take in the beauty of the surroundings. The silver birds, bateleur eagles and the boisterous calls of the striking black-headed gonoleks add to the ambience.

In the green season from December to May, when the large herds have migrated to the south, there are Serian mobile camps in that area – Serian's Serengeti South (open from October to April) and Serian's Serengeti Kusini (open from December to March). Fly-camping is an option from Serengeti South, with the same format as the Lamai fly-camp. There's a five night minimum stay, but these nights can be a combination of both of the camps and some fly-camping. The experience can include as much walking as you want, and most guests do a mix of drives and walks. As in the north, Serian offers a walks-centric itinerary from Serengeti South; this is called 'Soul Searchers'. With a seven-night stay, three can be devoted to the fly-camping and longer walks, with two nights in camp at each end, these with more of a focus on game drives. Both this and the north's 'Soul Drifter' itinerary have a minimum booking of two guests but there's no single supplement, meaning each can have their own tent. Serian Lamai is accessed via Lamai airstrip, Serian Serengeti South via Mwiba airstrip, while Serian Kusini is nearest to Serengeti South airstrip.

Dorobo Safaris

Many years ago, **Dorobo Safaris** began multi-day walking safaris in the community owned areas to the east of the national park, but later shifted to the wilderness zones within the park. The walks operate from a mobile camp that's relocated by vehicle, and itineraries can be designed for anything from three to seven days or longer. Each trip is planned in consideration with current conditions and game movements, and the camp may move each day or stay put for a couple of nights.

Two wilderness zones are used, and walks are operated pretty much all year.

The north-west zone is walked during the June to November dry season. Here, the landscape has a pleasing diversity of rounded ridges and hills, rocky kopjes and open plains. The river valleys have year-round water that attracts an abundance of wildlife. In the 'green season', from December to May, the mobile walking shifts to the southern wilderness zone, a landscape of expansive open plains and woodlands with waterholes. At this time of year, the grasslands attract vast numbers of wildebeest and zebra and their young – and their predators.

The mobile walking safaris operate with a maximum of six guests in keeping with the low impact ethos of wilderness zone walking. Depending on its location, guests travel by road or air to rendezvous with their vehicle in the park and then to drive into the wilderness zone. There, they link up with the camp crew who will be their companions for the duration of the adventure, and find their first camp ready. The next day starts with an early breakfast and coffee by a low fire, and guests shoulder a day pack with water for the walking ahead. Accompanied by an armed Dorobo guide, the exploration begins as the crew break camp for transfer to the next location. The aim is to reach camp for lunch, and the pace allows plenty of time to take in the vistas and wildlife, and to rest and rehydrate along the way. Afternoon at camp is spent relaxing and spotting whatever passes close. The golden hour is the time for a short walk to a vantage point. The pattern of the days is repeated as the group traverse the pristine wilderness; it's easy to see why repeat guests opt for longer stays.

Entara Lodges & Camps

Entara guides walks from its Serengeti camps, with the permanent Olmara Camp the best pick as walks there can be combined with fly-camping. Located in the Soit Le Motonyi region of eastern Serengeti, its tented suites merge seamlessly into a gnarled grove of acacias and furnish vistas of grassy plains and the Ngare Nanyuki valley, dotted with time-weathered rocky outcrops. Walks explore a remote river valley, and ideally should be booked with a night or two of wild fly-camping in a wilderness-zoned walking area. The fly-camp features mesh tents that combine comfort with the 'under the stars' experience, and meals are taken at the campfire.

Apart from Olmara, Esirai Migration Camp is a seasonal camp that does as it sounds: moves to follow the migration. It has the low footprint of such mobile camps, with eight tents. Both Esirai and Olmara are good bases to look for cheetah. Apart from the Serengeti, Entara has guided walks from its properties in Tarangire and Lake Eyasi, making walks-centric northern circuit itineraries easy to arrange.

Mark Thornton Safaris

Mark Thornton Safaris (MTS) was among the first to guide walking safaris inside Serengeti National Park, building on Mark's years of walking experience in other parts of Tanzania. Here, MTS walking safaris are multi-day mobile trips, ranging from three nights to the signature **Great Serengeti Traverse**, a ten day, 100 km expedition across the entire western wilderness zone of the park. These longer walks provide a chance for guests to really disconnect and have an immersive experience, without seeing a road, camp, vehicle or other person for the duration of the safari, a rare privilege. Most trips involve a walking safari of three to ten days, and then time at private camps or lodges in the wildebeest migration areas. For those who want a real in-depth experience, MTS combines its Tarangire and Serengeti walking safaris for a 10–14-day trip, flying between the two to maximise time in the bush. MTS walking safaris are almost all private trips for specific groups of friends or families, but each year it runs three open, set-departure trips for individual travellers with a seven-day traverse on foot, followed by two days in a private tented camp by the Mara River.

During the multi-day Serengeti walking safaris, guests explore three river systems and a diverse terrain of kopjes, acacia savannah and rolling hills dotted with buffalo, gazelle, eland and other resident wildlife. There's a very good likelihood to spot lion from afoot on these treks, and a chance to explore a series of cave paintings hidden in the rocks. Mobile camps are comfortable set-ups with sit-down loos, hot showers and tents with cots, mattresses and fresh bedding. Meals are usually taken with a cold drink around the campfire and under the stars. Each day, guests set off on foot with their walking guide to a new location as the camp is moved by vehicle to the next spot. In addition to the guide, trips are often accompanied by a local tracker, who provides unique insight into the environment, human history and wildlife.

Nomad Tanzania

Nomad Tanzania has the best park coverage of any Tanzanian safari company, and walks are always in the activity mix. The Nomad mobile camp, Serengeti Safari Camp, was one of the first to operate in the park, and as with others it moves to follow the wildlife movements including the 'great migration'. Nomad takes pride in setting the camp in remote and secluded locations, allowing guests to enjoy a more private and authentic encounter with nature. The camps are

Encounters on the Great Serengeti Traverse

Mark Thornton

It is usually about the third day when it really kicks in. The feeling that you have truly escaped. I could see it in everyone's movements: slower gaits, calmer demeanours, relaxed postures. The phones we saw on arrival at the airstrip in Serengeti had disappeared, only retrieved now and then for the odd photo. People seemed to be reading more, either from our field guide books or from that novel that one has wanted to dig into for so long, but just never had the time, between work or kids or commutes. There was no Wi-Fi or cell signal to distract us with news or social media.

Earlier in the morning, we had stood over the top of a bull elephant. Up until then, we had spotted a few family groups and enjoyed approaches to a certain distance before the wind circled and trunks went up like periscopes and we retreated. Here, on foot in the enormous, roadless wilderness zones of Serengeti National Park, elephants do not normally encounter humans, and remain wary.

This time, however, it was a bull, broad-headed and heavy-trunked, alone in the riverbed. We checked the wind – steady from the east – and edged our way to the security of an enormous fallen tree on the edge of the bank. Safe from our vantage, we stared down upon this venerable beast, as it suctioned water into its trunk from small pools in the sand. Remaining silent, we listened to him drink and fill his cavernous belly. At some point he moved on down the river, rose up the other side and into the shade of a Kigelia tree. And we moved on too.

As we lazed in the shade that afternoon, we each reflected on the day in our own personal ways. For some of the guests, it was a second or third safari with me. For others, this was their first trip: a full-on ten-day trek across the little-explored parts of the Serengeti, a journey I first walked many years ago that we call the Great Serengeti Traverse. It's a chance to explore this landscape entirely on foot, to savour meaningful encounters with wildlife, and, perhaps more than anything, to escape the speed and stress of modern life.

For me, this was another 'Day Three', a time to appreciate just where we were and to be thankful that there is still such big, open and truly wild country across which to meander. There is no other place where one can be in such a rich landscape with such densities of African wildlife, from lion and leopard to elephant and the great herds of buffalo, and for ten days to never set foot in a vehicle. Instead, this is walking country – whether trekking the ridges or clambering up kopjes to take in the view over a vast and pristine habitat, unmarred by humanity, all the way to the distant hills of the park and the far stretches of Maasailand beyond.

About 15 years ago, this area was off limits to all entry, and it still is, with the exception of low-impact, lightweight, multi-day walking safaris. Vehicles are only permitted to move gear and a couple camp crew members. Since that time, we have poked and meandered through this landscape, finding those perfect little spots to put up camp, each with its own flavour. Sometimes there is the sweeping view; other times, it's a quiet spot on the river, tucked away and serene.

The next morning, we got an early start. Our terrain for most of the morning was a magnificent landscape of granitic kopjes along the edge of a seasonal river. Still holding water throughout the dry season, the river is a lifeblood attracting wildlife from all around: zebra, buffalo, eland and countless others, the kopjes little ecosystems themselves. Hyrax, baboons and klipspringers eyed us from the ledges; a multitude of species rely on their tangles of vegetation as secure shelter.

We walked game trails up into the rocks, slowly and in silence. Checking our wind direction, we continued, always aware of the many old bull buffalo that retire to the quiet of these areas. Beside me was good friend and fellow guide Chagamba, who has walked these landscapes with me for over a decade, and Toroye, a hunter-gatherer, whom I've known for over two decades.

On our way up through the rocks, we paused to notice the small things: lion scratch marks on the soft bark of a Ficus tree, bones collected by a porcupine at the entrance to a small cave, and in the cave itself a series of paintings by those who had sheltered here long before it was a national park. In fact, while we may have escaped modern humanity with its cell phones, luxury safari camps and crowds, we see ancient humanity all around us in the Serengeti. It is there in the rock art, on the smoke-stained rockface of an overhang or in the shards of chert and obsidian, and the stone tools we find on the land – which we hold to the sky searching for chips and clues before letting them fall back to the earth to remain there for another millennium.

As we reached the top, we spotted that distinct shape – an outline of a

We walked game trails up into the rocks, slowly and in silence.

body and feline ears silhouetted in the shadow of a tree. She was facing the other way, scanning the valley below. We moved closer to another set of rocks, then another. We had good terrain in front of us, providing enough of a safe barrier, and we remained at a distance both safe and exciting. We took our time in silence. There would be plenty of time for chatting later at the campfire. I watched the guests, looking through their binoculars or just with wide open eyes, amazed to be standing and watching a lion in the wild, on common ground.

We enjoyed our sighting and began to move away from the lion, hoping to leave her in peace and enjoy one of those special sightings where the animal never even knew you were there. But alas, catlike as always, she busted us – perhaps it was from a flash of movement by one of us or a snap of a twig – and she gave us her guttural growl before turning on her heels and disappearing over the ledge and down the other side to safety. We too retreated some distance, to breathe and recap the event. There were smiles, laughter and, from some, just a silent appreciation.

The mid-morning sun was now strong, and we still had several kilometres to go. On our way, we divided herds of gazelles, Thomsons and Grants, like a boat parts waves upon the ocean. We spooked a striped hyena, which burst out of a bush in flight, and we navigated around a few other lone buffalo bulls. Finally, there it was: down in the valley in a shaded grove of Tortilis trees, our tents set up and a fresh lunch waiting for us. So much had happened, so much had been learned, and we still had more days to go.

MARK THORNTON has guided walking safaris for 25 years, has a master's degree in environmental management and has consulted on conservation projects for UNDP, European Union, the governments of Zanzibar and South Africa, Conservation International and UNESCO. His second novel, *Nothing is Wrong*, was published in 2024.

designed thoughtfully, and the guiding is tuned to ensure guests go home with memories of diverse experiences, and not just spotting the headline animals. Wildlife photography, ornithology, cultural visits and of course walks are all part of that.

About 10 km south of the Mara River, Nomad Lamai is a fixed venue with an eight-room main lodge and four private suites. It operates from June to mid-March. As with all Nomad venues, walks are high on the recommended activities list and available when the grass is short and safe to move through. Departing from the lodge, walkers explore an attractive landscape where small valleys, river lines and rocky kopjes make for frequent changes of scenery – and provide perfect cover for approaching wild animals.

The Expeditionary Walking Camp is a relatively new venture for Nomad. It works as it sounds, a light footprint mobile camp with a focus on walking. At the start of the season in November it's set in the Ngare Nanyuki area of the eastern Serengeti, then around March shifts to the Gol Mountains and Salei Plains. From May to June it's relocated to the Mbalageti Western Corridor in western Serengeti. See page 241 for more about this camp.

Wayo Africa

There are three styles of **Wayo Africa** seasonal camp in the Serengeti: the Green Camp, which has ten tents and is

The Nomad Expeditionary Walking Camp on a misty Serengeti morning.

semi-fixed, moving with the migration, and has both game drives and walks; The Little Green Camp, which is smaller and likewise moves seasonally; and Wayo Walking Camp, which is the same scale but designed for mobility and delves into the park's wilderness-zoned areas for more intensive walks. For walking, the two smaller camps are recommended. The Wayo Little Green Camp is set in different locations in the Serengeti depending on wildlife movements: in the south from December to March; central Serengeti from April to July; and in the north from August to November. These are camps with a strong focus on walking. Six tents are of the mesh 'stargazing' design, and the camp has a large stretch-tent mess area. Each tent has an attached bathroom with suspended bucket shower and composting toilet.

From camp, game viewing is run in a flexible way on foot or by vehicle depending on guest wishes, conditions and animal movements. It's not all action, but equally about being in nature and resting in camp during the heat of the day, sitting under a tree with a packed breakfast, or enjoying sundowners at the bewitching hour on the top of a remote kopje. You do not have to be ultra-fit or active to enjoy the Little Green Camp experience, and some days you don't need to walk anywhere if you don't feel like it. Wayo Little Green Camp can be combined with the Wayo Serengeti Green Camp, which is a larger seasonal camp that's more focused on game drives. It's set in the north from July to October and south from December to March.

The Wayo Walking Camp is for more demanding walks, and participants will enjoy it more if they are regular walkers. It takes participants deep into wilderness-zoned areas of the park away from the vehicle tracks. These areas are strictly controlled and only a few companies have permission to access them, and then only for walking safaris. While vehicles can be used to move the camp, there are no game drives allowed in these zones. The actual location walked is decided a couple of weeks before departure, to take advantage of the best wildlife sighting opportunities. Normally, guests fly from Arusha into the nominated airstrip, and from there straight to the first camp, arriving for an afternoon walk to a sundowner spot. Guided by a Wayo Africa guide and escorted by a park ranger, the walking is done in the morning, taking a packed breakfast. The aim is to arrive at camp for lunch, and then afternoons are devoted to resting there, with a short walk in early evening when conditions are cooler. The camps normally move every second day for an opportunity to explore different areas, but it's possible to plan walks whereby the camp moves every day. The Walking Camp has a maximum of seven tents, which are of a gauze construction that maximises the sleeping under the stars feeling. Fly-sheets are available in case of rain.

Serengeti lodge walks

A signature feature of the Serengeti is the mobile camp that relocates two or three times each year to follow the migration. These tented camps tend to be smaller than fixed lodges, at a scale suited to walking groups, and for walks in the Serengeti such camps are an alternative to the longer walks in the wilderness-zoned areas. As the main reason for the existence of these camps is to get visitors close to the biggest numbers of plains game and their predators, there's the chance to get on foot with vistas of grasslands full of wildlife. On the other hand, the vehicle safaris have the same idea, so it detracts from the walking experience when it's shared with vehicles, even distant ones. Ideally, a walking tour of Serengeti would combine some days on a walking trail in the wilderness zones with some days doing walks and drives from a mobile camp. Of the mobile camp operators, some have a stronger focus than others. As described in preceding sections, Nomad Tanzania, Wayo Africa and Serian all operate mobile camps that offer side escapes to small fly-camps for walks. There are a myriad of other mobile and fixed camps that can run excellent guided walks as an alternative to a drive.

Wilderness is best known for its extensive network of camps and lodges in Southern Africa and is a recent arrival in the Serengeti. Wilderness Usawa is a well-appointed tented camp that moves with the migration. It's at the typical scale of a mobile camp – six tents for 12 guests – and walking safaris in remote areas are part of the experience. Although it has all the expected comforts, the camp is designed to leave no trace behind when it moves on to track the movement of the plains game. With a variety of locations throughout the park, the timing of the relocation is determined by what's happening on the savannah rather than the calendar. The aim is to give guests a real wilderness experience – avoiding other vehicles – while being in the right place to witness the vast wildlife migration. The camp locations make it possible to walk out directly into wilderness zoned areas of the park, where no vehicles roam. The usual routine is to get out early for a few hours before returning to camp for brunch, and then do a game drive in the afternoon.

Close to Nomad Lemai, **Lemala** Kuria Hills Lodge is a year-round property that's often combined with the company's classic-style mobile tented camps, Mara and Ndutu. It makes for a good walking destination outside the migration crossing season, as there are very few permanent properties in the north and there's still plenty of game but few visitors. This is East Africa as she should be – remote, wild and exciting. Alternatively, Lemala Nanyukie Lodge is more central in the park and located in superb walking territory. It sits on a grassy savannah that's dotted with rocky kopjes and shaded by ancient acacia trees, and the combination of Serengeti grasslands, elevated lookouts and secret wooded valleys makes for interesting walking conditions all year. There's plentiful wildlife that includes all the endemic game species and rich birdlife, and the area is known for its population of big cats – in fact, it was previously set aside for scientific research into large feline predators. Meeting these can add to the excitement if encountered on foot, and there's a rare and elusive melanistic genet that has been spotted by lucky guests. Lemala Nanyukie is the home base for the company's walking guide trainer, Andrea Pompele, and one of Tanzania's few female walking guides, Namsikia Joysack.

Elewana Collection's Serengeti Pioneer Camp and Serengeti Migration Camp are both fine bases for camp-based guided walks. The 12-tent Pioneer Camp is sited on a rocky outcrop in the central Southern Serengeti overlooking the Moru Kopjes, and these distinctive hills make for interesting walking terrain. Migration Camp is a larger camp overlooking the Grumeti River in an area where the migration begins in late November or December. The latest addition to the company's Serengeti portfolio is Serengeti Explorer, which is a large property – 74 rooms – designed with the 'active safari' market in mind: more activities at a lower cost. It's a fixed lodge set high in the Nyaboro Hills in the

Sunset at Nanyuki Lodge.

Evening light at Little Okavango Camp, set in wetlands on Lake Victoria's shore.

south-central area of the park. Another Explorer camp has recently opened at a desirable location on the Ngorongoro crater rim. Walks from all camps can be requested for two or four hours and they can take place early in the morning or late afternoon, when conditions are at their best, and usually end with a bush breakfast or sundowners in the wild. For guests who are interested, the walks can include cultural elements, such as discussions about the local Maasai culture or visits to nearby communities.

Asilia Africa has three camps in the Serengeti that are good walking bases, with two in the north. Sayari Camp is close to the Mara River, and Ubuntu Migration Camp operates from the remote 'Lamai wedge' in the season from mid-June to mid-November. Namiri Plains Camp is in eastern Serengeti, where there are wide open short grass plains presenting beautiful walking territory. The dry season months from July to October are best for walking, while April and May are the most likely to be wet and muddy, and are to be avoided.

Laba Migration Camp is a ten-tent seasonal camp, and three times a year it's completely taken down and moves to follow the 'great migration' of plains game. It's in the southern Ndutu region from November to March, before shifting to Masabi in the west of the park from April until the end of July. From there it moves north until November, when the cycle restarts. The primary activity at the camp is private game driving, but walks are on the menu too. The camp is part of the **Laba Laba** collection, which operates Laba Jongomero in Ruaha National Park, where seasonal walks are guided.

Apart from the above venues, which have walks from both their mobile and fixed camps, there are numerous other Serengeti lodges that offer splendid accommodation and walks as part of their activities.

In the west, **&Beyond** Grumeti Serengeti River Lodge guides walks in a contrasting terrain in a remote and exclusive area. It's located in the wildlife-rich 'western corridor' between the Serengeti plains and Lake Victoria. The central feature of this area is the Grumeti River, which in season flows westwards to the lake. It's a fine location for walks with a small number of expensive lodges. Note that &Beyond's mobile camp in the Serengeti National Park, &Beyond Serengeti Under Canvas, does not do walks.

South African conservation and ecotourism group, **Singita**, is another excellent walking choice in the Grumeti area. There's a choice of five sumptuous lodges, including Singita Sabora Tented Camp on the grassy plains and Faru Faru overlooking the river. Singita Explore is an exclusive-use mobile camp that can have up to six single bed tents. Guided walks are available from all of the lodges, and are of the high standards associated with Singita.

West again of Grumeti, not far from Serengeti's Ndabaka Gate, **A Tent With a View** has a lodge on the shore of Lake Victoria. Little Okavango Camp has raised walkways that make it a water camp for much of the year, and walks from here are focused on the outstanding birdlife, which includes shoebills close to camp. Walking can be combined with canoeing to get close to the waterbirds, and these outings can be extended to up to four hours to take in local *shambas* and village life in the area.

On the other extreme of the Serengeti, 100 km to the east, **Taasa Lodge** is perched on a ridge on community land just outside the park's eastern boundary, and is well located close to the junction of the Ngorongoro Conservation Area, Maasai Mara National Reserve and Serengeti National Park. It takes advantage of its location in having a wide range of activities that include walks, ballooning, Maasai cultural visits and night drives. The walks are inclusive in rates and available all year.

In the same general area as Taasa Lodge and at a higher price bracket, **&Beyond** Klein's Camp is set on the edge of the rugged Kuka Hills in a large private concession leased from the Maasai community. It feels remote, and walks explore the wooded hillsides, rolling grasslands and forested riverbanks. Both Taasa Lodge and Klein's Camp are accessed via Lobo airstrip, around 20 km away.

North of Klein's Camp, 15 km as the goshawk flies, across a savannah broken by kopjes and clusters of fig trees, a series of concrete zebra scratching posts delineate the frontier with Kenya, a celebrated land that's the subject of the final chapter in this guide.

12 Kenya

Kenya is the idealised romantic Africa destination, the one perhaps most often twinned with the word 'safari'. With good connections to Nairobi and a sophisticated network of air transfer services, the country's parks and conservancies are very accessible. It's feasible to arrive on an overnight flight, transfer to Wilson Airport for a domestic connection and have brunch in a lodge in Laikipia or the Mara.

Although Kenya straddles the equator, the main safari zones are at an altitude that affords pleasant conditions for most of the year. The Greater Mara conservancies are at around 1,500–2,000 m, and the Laikipia plateau is even higher. In fact, Laikipia is a year-round destination, as even in the wetter months, from March to May, it's usually possible to avoid a soaking. Low-lying areas of the country can be oppressively hot in certain months. The only significant walk destination where heat is a factor is Tsavo, which tends to be hot and dry all year, peaking in January and February.

The impact of climate change on conservation areas is becoming more evident in Kenya. The northern half of the country is arid and sensitive to drought, and a prolonged lack of rainfall and grazing sometimes forces Maasai to herd cattle into the unfenced conservancies of Laikipia and the Mara. Climate change, combined with the huge growth in population of people and cattle, puts Kenya on the front line of habitat loss. The tradition of semi-nomadic pastoralism is integral to Kenya's walking safaris, which are typically guided by Samburu or Maasai tribesmen in colourful attire and carrying their preferred selection of implements – the *rundu*, a short fighting stick; the *fimbo*, a long stick for poking cattle and leaning on; the *embere*, a spear for hunting and defence; and the *Samsung* with optional solar charger.

Walking safaris in Kenya

The Kenya Wildlife Service (KWS) administers the country's national parks, and the policy on walking varies by park. Unlike with the government agencies in Tanzania or Zambia, the KWS does not provide rifle escorts for walks, a role left to walk operators.

Kenya's pre-eminent walking destination is the central Laikipia Plateau, an area with an altitude and climate well suited to the activity. There, and in remote northern wilderness areas, camel-supported mobile safaris are a speciality. It's not necessary to embark on overnight walks, as many lodges in the Laikipia and Samburu areas have trained walking guides for shorter outings. Elsewhere in Kenya, multi-day walking safaris are limited. Maasai Trails runs donkey-supported walks in the Loita Hills, east of the Maasai Mara, and Tropical Ice operates Africa's longest scheduled walking safari in Tsavo National Park. The Maasai Mara National Reserve is not run by the KWS and does not allow walks, but there are a number of excellent lodges with walks in the adjacent northern conservancies and some do walking/fly-camping combinations. In the east, the Chyulu Hills have attractive walking terrain, and there

Northern Kenya is known for its camel-ported walking safaris.

are lodge walks in reserves adjacent to the national parks of Amboseli and Tsavo.

Kenya has some excellent safari companies with a focus on multi-day walks, including Bobong Camels, Karisia Walking Safaris, Lewa's Walking Wild, Maasai Trails, Remote'n'Wild and Tropical Ice. It's possible to organise itineraries directly with lodges and walk operators, and they are generally happy to stitch together multiple venues and activities; for example, to enjoy walks from a comfortable lodge in the Laikipia area, followed by some days out on a multi-day camel-supported walking safari; or walking the Loita Hills with Maasai Trails and then flying north for a completely different experience with Kitich Forest Camp in the Mathews mountain range.

A number of lodge operators with walks have collections that span both Kenya and northern Tanzania, facilitating cross-border itineraries. These include Alex Walker's Serian, Asilia Africa and the Elewana Collection. As in South Africa and Zimbabwe, there are companies owned by walking guides who know everything there is to know about the best walking options in the country, and a selection is covered here.

Africa Off Track

Africa Off Track is operated by Dan Peel who is a professional Zimbabwean, Kenyan and South African walking guide, as well as a published wildlife photographer. He has worked in some of the most pristine wilderness Africa has to offer. Based at Laikipia Wilderness, Dan's focus over the last two years has been the famous black leopard named Giza, and following and photographing her has been one of the highlights of his career. However, Dan's main interest is walking safaris, and he has led walks over the last 15 years through South Africa, Zimbabwe and Kenya. His love for the peace and tranquillity that walking in the bush provides is matched by his sense of adventure, and encounters with Africa's megafauna on foot are always a goal on his walks. Dan tailors trips to create unique wildlife encounters, and the special emphasis on capturing photographic opportunities requires that every corner of Africa needs to be explored and considered, depending on the time of year, the seasons and the animal movements.

Dan says: 'My passion for everything wild has led to a lifelong obsession with sharing Africa's wilderness with the world. Engaging and teaching guests the art of tracking and the subtle reading of animal behaviour helps unlock secrets of the bush that have transcended history.'

Andreas Fox Safaris

Andreas Fox specialises in wilderness walking trails, field guide instruction and custom safaris across sub-Saharan Africa. With an unwavering curiosity and desire to keep discovering and learning, he has become one of East Africa's most qualified guides. With years of experience in Kenya, South Africa and Botswana, and forays into Zimbabwe, Zambia and Tanzania, he is in a position to create and lead truly custom itineraries – be they walking trails, specialist naturalist courses, adventurous 4x4 expeditions or bespoke private safaris.

As a director of **The Original Ker & Downey Safaris**, Andreas conducts walks based at his mobile camps on a variety of conservancies and national reserves, wherever the local regulations allow. Working with trained rangers, Andreas also leads walks into Tsavo East's seasonal riverbeds, as well as along the Ewaso Nyiro in Shaba National Reserve and various conservancies in the Northern Rangelands. In partnership with a number of preferred lodges and private houses, he conducts walking on Laikipia conservancies such

Andreas Fox on a walk in Laikipia.

as Borana, Lewa and Lolldaiga Hills. Here he is able to lead walks into areas where no vehicle is able to go, regularly encountering elephants, rhinos and northern Kenya's special mammal and bird species. All of these walks can either be short excursions from a vehicle to full days out or multi-night expeditions. Beyond Kenya, Andreas regularly includes favourite walking safari products, such as Kweene Trails in Botswana or the Makuleke region in Kruger National Park, in his client proposals.

Andreas was born and raised in Kenya and has been organising and guiding safaris since he was a teenager. Despite qualifying with a law degree in the United Kingdom, it was wilderness and the desire to get into formal conservation work that lured him back to Africa. His career began in South Africa on a research project in the Greater Kruger conservation area, studying big cats. It was there and in eastern Botswana that he cut his teeth as a walking guide, with a special affinity for tracking and safely approaching elephants. From there he moved into teaching full time, specifically the Field Guides Association of Southern Africa curriculum for training walking guides.

As Andreas says: 'I always try to get people out of a safari vehicle, be it to safely track and approach game on foot, explore nuances of an ecosystem or engage with local cultures, conservationists and personalities.'

Mark Ross Safaris

Mark Ross Safaris runs safaris throughout East and Southern Africa. In Kenya, reserves include Samburu and Meru National Reserves, the Greater Mara conservancies and Lewa Wilderness Conservancy. Founder Mark Ross has decades of experience of organising safaris in remote corners of Africa, and a special fondness for exploring on foot wherever possible. He is as much at home on horseback, even running annual trips to the western borderlands of Mongolia.

Mark is a wildlife biologist by profession, attaining his advanced degrees in the Maasai Mara in 1977. He has been guiding for 40 years, and takes pride in bringing his deep experience to bear to ensure that his guests are treated to a personalised experience. He is a commercial pilot and transfers guests in his own aircraft. Impromptu stops and side-trips and interacting with local people enrich the journey. Mark's favourite walking destination is Lewa, thanks to its combination of open grasslands, rich wildlife, and the freedom to drive and walk as he wishes.

To quote Mark: 'I believe it is important to go slowly, spend time with the wildlife and spend some time on foot with the wildlife as well. That simple change in perspective is hugely valuable and educational; and fun.'

New African Territories

Based in Nairobi, **New African Territories** handles marketing and reservations for some of Kenya's best walking safari venues, including Speke's Camp, Maasai Trails, Alex Walker's Serian and Kitich Forest Camp. As such, they are very well positioned to put together interesting walks-centred itineraries and handle the pre-trip planning advice and trip logistics for both tour operators and individual travellers.

Zarek Cockar Safaris

Born and raised in Kenya, and having taken every opportunity to go camping, hiking or on safari from a young age, **Zarek Cockar** has developed a deep connection to East Africa's wilderness areas. A privately guided safari with Zarek is defined by his wide-eyed wonder at the natural world, from hopping through muddy puddles catching frogs to slowly roving a riverbank searching for an elusive leopard. When he's not guiding international clients, Zarek occupies most of his low season with training guides at some of East Africa's finest safari camps and lodges. Emphasis is put on spending time on foot, looking at flowers, amphibians, spiders, birds, ecological relationships and the stories that bind them.

Zarek takes great joy in exploring some of the lesser known areas of East and Central Africa to get away from the well-worn safari trail for new adventures and unique wildlife. He is happiest on foot, whether in the thick forests of Gabon looking for lowland gorillas or the dry acacia woodlands of Laikipia in high central Kenya, the domain of leopards and elephants. As a Gold Level guide with the Kenya Professional Safari Guides Association, he's familiar with local wildlife, cultures and conditions. He holds a Field Guide (NQF4) qualification with the Field Guides Association of Southern Africa and a Level 3 Track & Sign qualification with Cybertracker, a non-profit network for wildlife trackers. These widely recognised qualifications, along with over 15 years of experience, have provided him with useful tools to interpret the natural world encountered on safari.

Greater Mara conservancies

The Maasai Mara National Reserve (MMNR) does not allow walking safaris – nor night drives nor horseback safaris – and the reason, as stated in the MMNR Management Plan, is that it allows 'the surrounding community areas of the Greater Mara Ecosystem to capitalise on these niche markets, giving the community areas a potential tourism boost'. Given that the eastern sector of the MMNR, managed by Narok County, has a reputation for poor visitor management, it's just as well that walks are prohibited, as participants would be at risk of getting mown down by a fleet of vehicles chasing a cheetah. It remains to be seen if the ratcheting up of park fees will have a positive impact on management of this overburdened park.

This is all the more reason to seek out locations with walking safaris where better wildlife viewing experiences can be found. The lands north of the national reserve are managed under conservancy agreements in partnership with local communities, and there are some fine lodge-based walking options in these 'Greater Mara conservancies'. Fly-camping and walking combinations are rare, but Kicheche has a five-night itinerary that includes a night of wild camping between two of its camps; and similar fly-camping and walking combinations are offered in Naboisho by Asilia and Saruni Basecamp. East of the Mara ecosystem in the Loita Hills, Maasai Trails runs donkey-supported hiking safaris through the hills and down into the Gregory Rift.

Asilia Naboisho

Guests at **Asilia Africa** Naboisho Camp not only enjoy sweeping views of a wildlife-filled savannah, but also can set off to explore it on foot. The camp was rebuilt in 2023 and is classed by Asilia as a Reserve Camp – their top tier. The gentle terrain is good for walks, and the mix of open grasslands and thickets close to camp gives cover for spying on big game,

A giraffe browsing a desert date tree: a signature image of the Mara savannah.

including elephant and giraffe. Beyond, low hills provide look-out points, and perhaps the chance to spot a leopard at rest in a favourite tree.

Guests can choose between staying at the camp and swapping a morning game drive for a walk or setting out on foot in the rich afternoon light to spend a night or two at a pop-up fly-camp. The usual routine is to leave camp after afternoon tea carrying just binoculars and a water bottle in a sling, in the company of a rifle-carrying guide and a Maasai tracker. It takes a couple of hours to meander to the fly-camp, which will be reached before sunset to a welcome by the camp crew and a cold drink. The dome tents will already be set up with guests' overnight bags, and a warm bucket shower, hidden behind a canvas screen, is usually first item on the agenda. The tents have thick and comfortable mattresses made up with duvet, pillows and blankets, and there's even a hot water bottle to keep things cosy. Dinner is cooked on the campfire, and then it's time to swap stories and do some star gazing.

In the morning there's a pre-dawn wake-up and light breakfast so guests and guides can be back on foot as the sun breaks the horizon, leaving the team to break camp. The return route to Naboisho Camp differs from the previous day's walk, and there's a chance to see some interesting wildlife on the move at this time of the day. The area has a very active

Sharing common ground

The backpacks were first to be discarded. Next to go were our hats, which snagged on the branches as we pushed through thicker bush. Doubled over, I followed Roelof, trying to place my feet softly in his tracks. We'd spotted the leopard relaxing in a tree from over a kilometre away, her rump glowing in a ray of light from the rising sun. If she had looked our way, she would have seen us too as we zig-zagged from scraggly spike-thorn to bushy camphor, seeking cover. Now, we crouched to stay low on the final approach. The leopard had not moved and had her back to us.

On a walk, we always aim to observe animals without disturbing their normal behaviour, and we had this in mind as we closed the distance. So it was gratifying that the cat never saw us, her attention focused in the other direction. Peering through the branches, I could see her legs dangling from the side of the branch and tail flicking at flies. Abruptly, in one fluid movement, she stood and dropped without a sound to the dust and vanished. Roelof paced to the tree. 'Thirty-three metres. That's as close as I've ever been to a leopard on foot.'

Pleased with the first action of the day, we retraced our steps, picking up the discarded belongings, and found tracker Mpatinga who had stayed back. He has seen plenty of leopards here in his homeland in the north of the Maasai Mara/Serengeti ecosystem. It was the second day of our overnight walk in Naboisho Conservancy, and on the first day we had animal encounters of a different kind. We'd set out from Asilia Naboisho camp on foot, our ankles brushing the thick climax grasslands, led by Mpatinga and Head Guide Roelof Schutte, and accompanied by a real sense of anticipation. A loud pride of lion had sounded all night from the riverbed beyond the trees. And the number of elephant on the conservancy was evident; as we walked, we could see some moving along the treeline to our left and gave them a wide berth. They were busy feeding, one tree each. We reached a point where we had no option but to pass through the woodlands, but the elephants were evenly ranged, one every 20 m – no safe gaps for us. With impenetrable scrub to the right and the main herd to the left, we decided to wait it out.

Waiting in this habitat was no hardship. It gave us time to scan with binoculars. A lone lion ambled through the drainage line a few hundred metres away, spooking the elephants; there are two prides on Naboisho, the Nkisiausiau pride with over 20 lions, and the smaller Enesikiria pride. A steppe eagle circled overhead. In the scrub, a chatter of yellow-fronted canary and Rüppell's long-tailed starling. The elephant feeding continued, and the main herd moved, now closing off our retreat to the lodge. We were surrounded.

Bush walking is not an adventure sport, and safety always comes first; Roelof and Mpatinga consulted quietly, taking into account how low the sun was in the sky. There was no shame in using the radio to call for a vehicle extraction from this predicament, and soon we were transferred around the elephant blockade, and, in twilight, descended on foot to the fly-camp.

Reflecting by the campfire, we talked about the situation. It was not dangerous, but the wrong decision could have put us at risk – it's never wise to be surrounded by elephant in the half-light.

For Roelof and Mpatinga it was all in a day's work, nothing unusual. They both have huge experience, coming from different directions: Roelof's via training in Zambia and many years of guiding safaris, and then as a guide trainer; Mpatinga's from a lifetime on the land, interacting with wildlife since he was a boy. Traditionally his subgroup of the Maasai were semi-nomadic hunter-gatherers, and in his youth, it was not unusual for him and his friends to steal part of a lion kill for a meal – not something he needs to do these days, except for the benefit of the occasional documentary film maker.

On the fire, potjes steamed. Pea soup, then beef stew. I thought about how these two men interacted while walking, a relationship built over years of common purpose. A motion of the hand from one and both would stop and gaze in the same direction, hands cupping their ears – catching the barely perceptible sound of an elephant chewing 100 m away. And then that leopard. Mpatinga spotted it first, and there was no question but that they would both relish the challenge of sneaking up to it. This was fun – it was easy to imagine the ten-year-old version of either man doing exactly that. And countless generations before too – for a couple of days, we all shared an experience common to humanity for tens of thousands of years, before most of us became urbanised, 'modern', detached from the natural world. Chocolate mousse was the final course. As the fire embers dimmed, we could hear the 'churr' of a square-tailed nightjar. Time for bed and its hot water bottle.

Our collective impact on nature was something to ponder as we left the leopard's tree and walked through yellow-barked acacia, into the basalt hills and back towards Naboisho Camp. We stopped at a look-out point and remarked how perfect the area would

We took advantage of an outcrop to scan for wildlife.

be for black rhino, and how the view was diminished by their absence. A gabar goshawk sounded from a tree, but otherwise the bush was still.

As we walked, Roelof took time to tell tales. He pointed at Mpatinga's beautifully crafted rungu stick, and then the tree it came from – *Acacia gerrardii*. Nearby, wild olive and wild date trees also provide good wood for crafting into tools and weapon shafts. He spotted a clump of knitted hair caught in an orange-leaf croton branch – wildebeest tail and beard hair, a favoured nesting material. Roelof said the leaves of this tree are insect repellent and can be rubbed on the skin, and its branches are used as brooms in villages. 'And lions like to sleep inside these croton thickets, probably as the flies are kept at bay.' Along with the crotons, the most common tree in that area was magic gwarri. Roelof fondled a branch. 'It's evergreen and stays soft and smooth after it's plucked, so martial eagles use it as the last lining of their nest before laying eggs.'

We emerged from the hills onto a high open plain. In the distance, three southern ground hornbills strutted in a line. It was getting hot, and we paused in the shade of a small-leaved shepherd's tree for a final scan. Up – pallid harrier, lappet-faced vulture. Down – dik-dik, second dik-dik, a lone hyena. Up again – grey kestrel, black-chested snake eagle.

From this high plain, Naboisho's riverways were evident as rich green ribbons straggling across the landscape. With binoculars, it was possible to see zebra and wildebeest herds scattered to graze. Dozens of elephant, no doubt the ones we'd seen the previous day, heading for their morning drink. Somewhere in the shade, a cheetah mother called Entito and her three cubs were out there – we'd seen them on a game drive on the first day. We stood a long time there, absorbed in the calmness that immersion in nature brings. Then a glance between Mpatinga and Roelof was the subtle signal it was time to move. There would be more days like this to come.

lion pride. The fly-camping is booked exclusively for groups of two to six guests at a supplementary nightly fee in addition to the camp rate, and the activity should be prebooked so the logistics can be organised. June to October are the best months.

Asilia Africa has a network of camps in Kenya and Tanzania, making it easy to stitch together multi-park trips. For stays of two guests over seven consecutive nights, the road or air transfers are included, subject to terms. Naboisho is the only camp in the portfolio that has the fly-camping option, and in Tanzania there are Asilia camps with walks in the Serengeti, Ngorongoro, Tarangire, Nyerere and Ruaha.

Saruni Basecamp

Formed through the merger of two well-established safari companies in 2021, **Saruni Basecamp** has 12 camps and lodges in the Maasai Mara and Samburu regions, and is now among Kenya's largest safari companies. It's proud of its record of community engagement and employment, and is a partner in six conservancies owned by the Maasai and the Samburu people. Safari walks are guided from most of the camps and lodges in the Mara and Samburu regions, led by experienced local guides. These can range from leisurely two-hour explorations to multi-day walks. For the longer adventures, fly-camps are deployed, and this experience is available in two Mara conservancies.

In Naboisho, Basecamp Wilderness is a fixed camp; it has five tents set in Saddle Valley in the middle of the conservancy. Each tent has a king-size or twin beds and a separate bathroom unit with bio-flush toilets and a traditional bucket shower, which is heated on request. Basecamp Dorobo Mobile is an overnight fly-camping experience and can be used for both vehicle and walking safaris. It's a classic-style mobile camp that is relocated by vehicle while guests walk, 'slackpacking' style. The fly-camp has five tents with twin beds, and walks are restricted to a maximum of ten people inclusive of guests, Maasai guides and rangers. Basecamp Hill Top has the same camp set-up as Basecamp Dorobo Mobile in a different location. It runs a little to the north in a neighbouring conservancy, Pardamat Conservation Area. This is a new 'triple use' area, meaning that wildlife protection, human development and livestock share the land as core activities. Guests here spend time with the local Maasai and witness how this tourism model works.

Kicheche Camps

Kicheche Camps guides walks from three camps in the Mara, plus one in Laikipia. Kicheche Valley Naboisho has six tents tucked discreetly below a wooded ridge in the heart of Naboisho Conservancy. Kicheche Bush Olare is about 20 km to the west in Olare Motorogi Conservancy and is the same scale but with a more rustic bush camp aspect. Kicheche Mara is further west again, set in a valley of acacias in Mara North Conservancy. All camps offer their guests walks as an alternative to game drives, which can be short nature walks close to camp or longer walks if desired. The walks are guided by Maasai Kenya Professional Safari Guides Association (KPSGA) silver-rated guides, and the group is accompanied by an armed ranger. For a more intensive walking safari, Kicheche has walks with fly-camping on a bespoke basis. These involve around four to five hours per day on foot, but as the walks are run on an exclusive basis, there's flexibility to reduce the distance walked, and there's a backup tent reserved in a fixed camp in the case of bad weather requiring the wild camp to be cancelled. The fly-camping can be arranged from all three Mara camps.

The Kicheche five-night Walking Wilderness package takes guests on foot between Kicheche Valley Naboisho and Kicheche Bush Olare, camps that are separated by a distance that's ideal for a meandering exploration at a gentle pace, with a night spent wild camping along the way. This can be done in either direction. Starting from Naboisho, the distance covered is around 10 km on the first day and 13 km on the second day. The fly-camp is transferred by vehicle, along with the guests' overnight bags. It's staffed by a cook and a camp hand, and has small dome tents for two people equipped with camp beds, bedrolls and a washstand. Simple bathroom facilities are available, comprising a long-drop toilet and bush-style bucket shower. A lightweight mess shelter is used in the event of rain. The fly-camp caters for a maximum of six people and operates all year apart from a break from mid-April to the end of May, when rain is most likely.

The first day of the itinerary sees guests fly into Naboisho on a scheduled morning flight from Nairobi. After meeting their guide, there's a slow drive to camp, stopping to spot the first wildlife. Following lunch, there's time to rest before the afternoon drive. Two nights are spent at Kicheche Valley, with at least two game drives a day – a night drive is recommended. On the third day, there's a final dawn game drive, along with a picnic breakfast. Back at camp, after lunch and a

Kicheche Valley Naboisho is set below a well-wooded ridge.

trail briefing, the walking starts. The route heads west from Kicheche Valley, crossing a number of beautiful valleys with frequent stops to examine spoor, flora and whatever wildlife pops up en route. It takes three to four hours to reach the fly-camp on the western side of Naboisho Conservancy with enough daylight remaining to wind down, shower and sit back with a drink as the sun slips below the horizon. The Maasai guide is host for the evening and dinner is cooked on an open fire.

The fourth morning is spent on foot continuing westwards along the escarpment and Seketa Valley in Olare Motorogi Conservancy. It takes four to five hours to reach Kicheche Bush Olare, with arrival in time for a refresh and lunch. After a siesta, it's time for a game drive in the conservancy.

Greater Mara lodge walks

Away from Naboisho, a good number of lodges and camps in the Greater Mara conservancies have lodge-based walks. In Olerai Conservancy and Ol Kinyei Conservancy there's Lerai Safari Camp and the set of Porini camps; then in Mara North Conservancy options are Offbeat Mara and Tangulia Mara Camp east of the Mara River. Angama Mara and Mara Elatia are both high-end and high on the Oloololo Escarpment west of the Mara River, while Alex Walker's Serian's pair of camps are directly on the river. Some lodges inside the MMNR offer walks, especially those along the Talek River not far from the northern boundary and on the Mara River inside Oloololo Gate in the west. As walking is not permitted inside the park, they must drive guests outside the park into a private conservancy, which is not ideal in terms of getting on foot at dawn.

Lerai Safari Camp is on a private conservancy west of Naboisho, a short distance north of the MMNR's Talek Gate, and has six tents shaded in a dense acacia forest next to a stream. Walks are available all year at an extra fee. Led by local Maasai guides, these usually go direct from camp as the wooded valley and its stream make for nice walking habitat. There's a likelihood to spot Maasai giraffe, impala, warthog, Thompson's gazelle and other plains game, and possibly encounter elephant. Alongside the stream there are some magnificent fig trees, amazing stand-alone ecosystems packed with life that provide roosting and brooding sites for critically endangered vulture species, including the lappet-faced vulture and Rüppell's griffon vulture. A popular short sundowner walk is to Leopard Hill to witness the sunset over the Oloololo Escarpment.

The **Porini Safari Camps** company operates four camps and safari cottages in the Greater Mara conservancies and all run Maasai-guided walks. These are available all year and range from short outings to several hours in duration; the maximum group size is generally six. Porini Mara and Porini Cheetah are in Ol Kinyei Conservancy. This game-rich 7,500 ha reserve has a diverse terrain of plains, forests and rivers, and is habitat for a broad range of species including the big cats. For game drives, guests additionally have access to the Mara National Reserve and the adjacent 20,000 ha Naboisho Conservancy. Porini Ol Kinyei Safari Cottages are another option here. Porini Lion is to the west in the Olare Motorogi Conservancy. It's a low-footprint ten-tent camp, and walks are guided by Maasai from the local area. Night drives are possible in the 13,300 ha wilderness.

Finally, Porini Giraffe Camp is an eight-tent camp in a forested area of camphor bush and yellow-bark acacia along the Ripole River in the Mara Ripoi Conservancy. This exclusive 8,000 ha wildlife reserve comprises beautiful hills, forests and open plains, and has an abundance of mammals, including lion and leopard. The conservancy connects onto Siana Conservancy and then directly to the Mara National Reserve, and so allows free movement of wildlife from the reserve as well as through a wildlife corridor along the Ripole River to Ol Kinyei Conservancy. Porini operates a full safari booking agency, Gamewatchers Safaris, which can organise travel throughout Africa.

There's a cluster of lodges just outside the MMNR Oloololo Gate that can offer walks in their local area between the Mara River and the escarpment. One such is **Tangulia Mara Camp**, which overlooks the Olotulo-Murt salt lick; although it is primarily a game drive venue, walks are included as an activity, guests being accompanied by a trained guide and armed ranger. Tangulia is 25 minutes' drive to Musiara airstrip and a similar distance to Kichwa Tembo airstrip.

A small number of lodges occupy a prime position on the top of the Oloololo Escarpment, with views over the Mara River and the Mara Triangle to the horizon. The Mara Triangle is the area of the MMNR west of the Mara River bordered by the Oloololo Escarpment to the west and the Tanzanian border to the south. It's managed by the not-for-profit Mara Conservancy and in contrast to the eastern side of the reserve, the game viewing is well controlled; it does not have excessive day visitors owing to its remoteness. It's well known for its Musiara Marsh and the associated TV-star lion pride. Lodges on the escarpment have a private road into the reserve, which means quicker access than driving to the Oloololo Gate.

As with the rest of the MMNR, walks don't take place inside the Mara Triangle, but the unfenced conserved lands outside are accessible. **Angama** Mara's guided walks take place high on the escarpment near the lodge. There are a number of routes depending on guests' preferences and mostly the walks go into the forested areas that have lovely streams running through them and abundant birdlife. Guests are able to choose their own pace and distance, guided by a Maasai naturalist who has grown up in the area. As well as the human history and ethnobotanical aspects, the naturalists are highly knowledgeable about the animals and birdlife. An *askari* accompanies the group, and may be armed depending on recent activity in the area and the length of the walk. It's possible to arrange to have a picnic at the lodge's favourite spot or to end the walk with lunch at the *shamba* to see where the fresh kitchen produce is grown.

Angama runs the mobile sole-use Angama Safari Camp at various locations deep in the Mara Triangle. If camp guests are keen for a walk, they can drive to one of the ranger outposts on the border of the Triangle. What follows is more of a hiking safari than a walking safari, as the escarpment is ascended. There are plenty of opportunities to stop and spot birds or simply enjoy the unfolding vista behind. Some light refreshment is the reward for making it to the top, while a vehicle with cold drinks and more substantial food awaits at the bottom. Angama has a sister lodge, Angama Amboseli, which runs guided walks as an alternative to game drives.

Next door to Angama Mara is Mara Elatia, a lodge of the **Heritage Group**. The name means 'the good neighbour' in Maa and the lodge's neighbours are in the Partakilat Wildlife Conservancy, an area that mixes community led conservation and cattle farming. Revenue from tourism activities supports the Partakilat rhino sanctuary and community healthcare and education initiatives. Mara Elatia has 12 tents set in hilly terrain, and from their private decks guests have views of the

Walkers on the Oloololo Escarpment enjoy Maasi Mara vistas to the horizon.

Serian's camps are connected by an elegant footbridge over the Mara River.

Mara below. Apart from game drives in the MMNR, guided walks are conducted on the escarpment rim in the vicinity of the lodge. The Heritage Group also has walks from Voyager Ziwani, which is a small tented camp sited just outside Tsavo National Park, and from Samburu Intrepids camp in the north of Kenya.

Mara North Conservancy has over 28,000 ha spanning the Mara and Olare Orok Rivers as they flow southwards into the national reserve, and is a perfect place to mix vehicle and foot safaris while staying at a full service camp. **Offbeat** Mara and Offbeat Ndoto camps are neighbours on a meandering section of the Olare Orok in the east of the conservancy. This area is rich in wildlife and well known for spotting leopard and the local 'Offbeat pride' of lion. Typically, guests stay for four nights, and on at least one day swap their morning or afternoon game drive for a walk. These tend to last two to three hours, and guests are led by both their Maasai guide and a professional walking guide who carries a firearm. Both camps are small and designed in the classic Mara tented style. Offbeat shares its ownership with Sosian in Laikipia, where adventurous walking and horseback safaris can be found.

On the western boundary of Mara North Conservancy, **Alex Walker's Serian** has a pair of camps directly by the Mara River. On the left bank, Serian 'The Original' is an elevated camp with five spacious tents, of which one is a family unit. All tents are set on sustainable hardwood decking and overlook the river and across to the Oloololo Escarpment, less than a kilometre away. Each tent has an en-suite bathroom with hot and cold running water, flush toilet, and a shower and custom-made bathtub with a view. The camp is a home for the Allen family and has a pleasant informal ambience, with guests usually dining at a communal table; Adrian Allen often guides walks himself.

Through the Rift Safari Trail

Maasai Trails is unique, offering the only genuine mobile walking safari in western Kenya. Guided by local Loita Maasai, this is a zero-trace expedition best spread over three nights. More than a hike, it's ecotourism in action, a means to engage with one of East Africa's most traditional communities and to support rural livelihoods. The route traces long-trodden elephant paths through the forested Loita Hills; it's punctuated by splendid lookout points and threaded by rivers. Each lunch and camping site seems more wonderful than the last, and along the way the guides explain what local plants they use for ceremonial purposes, sharing their extensive knowledge of the trees and their medicinal uses.

Maasai Trails is operated by Adrian Hughes, the owner of **Speke's Camp**, and often walkers spend a few nights at the camp prior to doing the trail. The Through the Rift Safari Trail package includes three nights at the camp and three nights on trail. Located on a private conservancy between Olare Orok and Mara North Conservancies, Speke's is a classic tented safari camp with all the comforts. Guests each have their own game viewing vehicle, and walks can be swapped in when requested, with the guests accompanied by their guide and a spotter. Guests normally fly into Musiara airstrip to access the camp.

For guests who first visit Speke's Camp, the trail starts with a beautiful morning drive east from camp to meet the walking guides and pack donkeys at Entersekera. Alternatively, trail walkers can rendezvous with the guides at the trailhead, a six-hour drive from Nairobi. The multi-day trail is always hiked from west to east, from altitude to the rift valley floor. The walking group can number anything up to 14 guests, and at least eight Maasai manage the guiding and the pack donkey caravan that carries the camp kit and luggage. The roomy bell or dome tents have camp cots and cotton bedding, and there are environmentally friendly short-drop toilets.

With the overnight bags sorted, the walking begins with around three hours through hilly terrain to the Ol Lasur Valley where River Camp is set for the first night. Cold drinks and hot bucket showers await, and after sunset the evening is devoted to dinner and chats around the campfire under the stars. Departing at a leisurely 10:00, the second day of walking ascends the Loita Hills, reaching their highest point at Oltyiani, with the chance to visit the Ol Lasur waterfall and perhaps a cooling swim. Lunch is taken along the way, accompanied by endless hazy Rift Valley views. In total, there are five to six hours of walking on this day, with arrival at

Ngare Serian is a separate camp at river level on the right bank. It's accessed by a lovely footbridge, and there's always some wildlife to spot in the water or nearby trees.

The primary activity from the camps is game driving, with a very good chance to find lion, while cheetah and leopard are in the area too. Walks take place both in Mara North and in 800 ha of exclusive walking area on the western side of the river. A picnic breakfast is carried and enjoyed at a shady spot overlooking the river or under a rock fig on the escarpment slope. The Serian camps are solar powered and open all year, best accessed via Mara North airstrip, with scheduled daily flights from Nairobi.

Hot water basins create mist at River Camp in Ol Lasur Valley, the first stop on the Through the Rift Safari Trail.

the second camp, Oltyiani Camp, in late afternoon; time to have a wash before a sunset drink. The third day begins as usual with an early cooked breakfast before camp is broken. It takes another five to six hours to reach the final camp, Ngurumans. The undulating terrain has first a mix of forest and open glades and then descends an old cattle and game track. On the final day, guests say farewell to the camp crew, who turn for the return journey. After an early breakfast, the walking starts, and it's a three-hour 1,000 m drop into the Gregory Rift to rendezvous with a vehicle at a place called Enkomongo, north of Lake Natron.

As well as the Through the Rift Safari Trail, Speke's Camp has an arrangement with Kitich Forest Camp (see page 321), whereby three nights can be spent at Speke's absorbing the Mara, before flying to the northern rangelands for a multi-day expedition with camels and donkeys in the Mathews Range.

South African nature training company **EcoTraining** (see page 51) runs courses at the Mara Training Centre camp overlooking the Mara River in Enonkishu, a private conservancy that's part of the Maasai Mara ecosystem, with additional access to Ol Chorro and Lemek conservancies. The camp is comfortable and functional, with two-bed tents and shared ablutions. It's not unusual to see hippos grazing in camp after dark. Courses are based on both FGASA and KPSGA curriculums; trails guide courses are not an option here, but other courses involve plenty of time stepping down from the vehicle to get close to all the little wonders typically encountered on a walking safari.

Amboseli National Park

Amboseli is a renowned national park located in southern Kenya, near the border with Tanzania. The park is notable for its views of Mount Kilimanjaro, the highest peak in Africa, which dominates the horizon and provides a distinctive backdrop for wildlife photography. It's known for its large elephant herds and extensive wetlands, and is the second most popular wildlife destination in Kenya after the Mara area. The park does not allow walks, but there are good lodges with guided walks on the park boundary, while, to the east, the Chyulu Hills make for an attractive alternative walking area – fewer animals, but a more interesting landscape.

Tortilis Camp, part of the **Elewana Collection**, is in the private Kitirua Conservancy adjacent to the south-west corner of Amboseli National Park. It's named for the flat-topped *Acacia Tortilis*, an iconic tree of East Africa. The camp is 100% solar powered and has large tents on a wooded hillside, and accommodation options include a family tent and private house. Game drives are conducted in both the conservancy and Amboseli National Park, while walks are led in the 12,000 ha conservancy. These can be taken in the early morning or late afternoon for a couple of hours. They are guided by Maasai from the local community who have been walking over these plains since childhood; the aim is not to track big game, but to observe and learn about the smaller things that make up a healthy ecosystem. The guides share their knowledge of the habitat, traditional uses of wild herbs and barks, and the Maasai way of life. It's nice to end the walk with a

Mount Kilimanjaro is the backdrop to a Maasai-guided afternoon walk from Tortilis Camp.

bush breakfast or sundowners with a view of Mount Kilimanjaro. Walks are available all year; pack a light rain jacket in April, May and November.

A recent arrival to the area, Mnara Amboseli is a sister lodge to Angama Mara. It's set in the Kimana Sanctuary, which lies in a wildlife corridor linking Amboseli National Park with the Chyulu Hills and Tsavo protected areas. The lodge has sole use of the 2,300 ha concession, and walks are recommended as part of the experience, especially birding walks; with a wonderful variety of ecosystems, the birdlife is diverse and abundant throughout the year. Walkers will see warthog, impala, giraffe and more often than not, breeding herds of elephant and the famous super tuskers of the area. These walks are led by Angama's guides and an *askari* to share stories and information on the animals, plants and habitats, and to keep guests safe. Usually walks conclude at Mnara, which is an observation deck overlooking a marshland with sweeping views of the sanctuary backed by Mount Kilimanjaro, before the group returns by vehicle to the lodge for breakfast.

Porini Safari Camps' Amboseli camp is in a remote wilderness area in the Selenkay Conservancy north of Amboseli, which is an important wildlife dispersal area for wildlife moving out of the national park. It has ten classic safari tents with en-suite bathrooms and solar lighting. As with most of the Porini camps, Maasai-guided walks are available, and the duration is customised to guests' wishes. The company has a lower cost alternative to the north of the lodge, Selenkay Adventure Camp, where accommodation is in dome tents, each with its own ablutions.

Another low cost option, **Maasai Simba Camp** is a Maasai-community-owned venture set on a bend of the seasonal Kiboko River about one hour from the park. It runs morning and afternoon bush walks in the local area, which has plenty of plains game and runs vehicle safaris to Amboseli National Park, meeting Maasai village elders, and beading with a local Maasai women's cooperative.

Chyulu Hills

Chyulu Hills National Park, and the private lands adjacent, are a green oasis in a part of Kenya that's usually found in shades of brown. It was a stand-in for the Ngong Hills in the film *Out of Africa*, and it's still sparsely populated by tourists. It's part of the gigantic Tsavo Conservancy Area, which comprises almost half of all of Kenya's national parks extent. As such, it makes a decent jumping off point for visits to both Tsavo to the south and east and Amboseli National Park to the west. It has sufficient wildlife to keep walks interesting, but the real stars are the scenery and mist belt woodlands. The hills have a reputation as a bit of an activity hub, as in addition to walks there are game drives by day and night, horse riding, cave visits, rock climbing, mountain biking and Maasai cultural visits.

At the northern end of the Chyulu Hills, ol Donyo is a **Great Plains Conservation** Réserve Collection property in a large conservancy, Mbirikani Group Ranch, owned by local Maasai. Set on a hillside with endless classic savannah views that stretch to Mount Kilimanjaro on the southern horizon, the lodge is a base for game drives, walks and other activities. The guided walks explore the varied terrain surrounding the lodge, from rolling grassland hills to the open plains, and venture into the nearby mist forest that can really only be appreciated on foot. All walks are accompanied by qualified and knowledgeable guides.

At the southern end of Chyulu Game Conservation area, **Campi ya Kanzi** is owned by a community trust. The camp takes pride in its commitment to regenerative tourism and is 100% solar, including powering of its electric game viewing vehicles. It's convenient to combine with its sister camp next to Tsavo National Park, Chyulu Club, and an Amboseli side trip can be arranged. Given the splendid location in the hills, guests are encouraged to get out on foot or horseback, and a moderate level of fitness is desirable to cope with the terrain. Led by Maasai guides, guests explore the open grassland slopes, hike the magnificent cloud forest of the Chyulu or drop into a well-wooded valley to follow the Ol Turesh River, looking out for silvery-cheeked hornbill, Hartlaub's turaco and the elusive Narina trogon. A cathedral-like strangler fig is a highlight of this walk. Morning walks can be concluded with breakfast in the bush, while afternoon excursions last about one and a half hours, and culminate at a good sundowner spot before guests return to camp by vehicle in the twilight.

Tsavo National Park

Tsavo is a vast conservation area in southeastern Kenya, known for its expansive landscapes and abundant wildlife. The park is divided into two sections, Tsavo East and Tsavo West, which together cover an area of over 22,000 sq. km. The western part is more accessible and therefore more visited, especially the northern end, which has an attractive terrain of rolling, well-wooded hills and the Mzima Springs. The larger eastern park is drier bushland, but also features fine baobabs and riverine woodlands along the Galana and Voi Rivers. One of its most notable geographic features is the Yatta Plateau, a lava flow of planetary scale.

Expect to find the full range of East African wildlife, including maneless lion and exceptionally large elephant, characteristically sporting a red hue from dust baths in the iron-rich sands. Tsavo is a place redolent with history, and being on foot with these legendary elephant herds is an intense experience. One of East Africa's stand-out walking safaris, The Great Walk of Africa, is operated here by Tropical Ice.

The Great Walk of Africa

The Great Walk of Africa is a ten-day walking safari in one of the highest density elephant regions left in Africa. Participants hike a total distance of 160 km, which makes it the longest scheduled walking safari on the continent. The genesis of this expedition was in 1980, when Iain Allan, the founder of **Tropical Ice**, expanded his business away from East Africa's mountains, into the dry, wild country of Tsavo. For many years Iain guided walking safaris down the remote Tsavo River, and then moved eastwards to incorporate the beautiful Galana River into his itineraries. Following on the heels of a heroic 25-day expedition in which Iain and a group of friends hiked from the summit of Kilimanjaro to the Indian Ocean, the idea of the Great Walk of Africa began to take root in his mind.

The most interesting section of his hike to the Indian Ocean was the ten-day crossing of Tsavo West and East National Parks, walking eastwards along the banks of the Tsavo and Galana Rivers. Using seven private campsites along the route, Tropical

Ice fine-tuned its camping style into a remarkable mobile deluxe unit, with an emphasis on comfort and fine cuisine. The concept of the Great Walk is 'hunting with cameras'. Using Samburu warrior trackers and protected by several armed guides, including Iain or his partner, Alex Fiksman, walking groups are able to be in surprisingly close proximity to elephants.

The walk is on generally flat terrain, but it's long: those who embark upon it should think of it as expeditionary in concept and should have a good level of fitness. Along the route, visitors receive thorough interpretations of the environment and history of the region; 15–20-minute rests take place every hour. Many species of wildlife are seen along the way, including lions and common game such as giraffe, zebra, Cape buffalo, hippo and gazelle. The hiking is all done in the morning. As soon as camp is reached, clients sit down to a lunch spread, followed by a welcome siesta period. In the late afternoon, game drives provide an opportunity to get even closer to big game.

The Great Walk of Africa is a journey into an Africa that existed over a century ago, and those who do it are very much aware of the fact that they are participating in, rather than merely observing, the African natural world. The experience is open to both group and individual bookings, the maximum group size is eight and the minimum age is 18. Walks depart on scheduled dates from February to October each year, and usually sell out quickly. June to October are the best months in terms of temperature. The itinerary includes hotel accommodation in Nairobi on the first night and dayrooms at an airport hotel prior to departure. Taking the Great Walk as their model, Tropical Ice has brought its style of walking safaris to the wilds of India and Japan.

Tsavo lodge walks

Kipalo Hills lodge is part of the **Secluded Africa** portfolio. It's located atop an escarpment in the Mbulia Conservancy surrounded by Tsavo West National Park and with distant views of Mount Kilimanjaro. It has six classic safari tents, plus a suite and a villa, and overlooks a

Guests on the Great Walk of Africa pause to observe hippos in Tsavo River.

waterhole popular with elephants. Game drives are operated to both Tsavo East and Tsavo West National Parks. Short guided walks are included, and are about much more than spotting fauna, with fun to be had tracking spoor, learning about traditional and medicinal usage of plants found and a chance to witness conservation projects and community activities.

Voyager Ziwani is a big camp set on a dam on the Sante River in a private farm between the western edge of Tsavo West National Park and the border with Tanzania. It's part of the **Heritage Hotels** group. There's a full range of activities, and as well as guided walks on its own property, there are night drives, agritourism farm visits, trips to the volcanic lakes of Chala and Jipe and tours of First and Second World War battlefields. Walks are conducted against the photogenic backdrop of Mount Kilimanjaro.

Laikipia Plateau

In central Kenya, the Laikipia Plateau has all the ingredients needed for a top-class walking destination. Its elevation of 1,500–2,000 m contributes to pleasant conditions for expeditions on foot for most of the year. Shaped by volcanic forces, the terrain is varied, with plentiful rocky hills and wooded valleys; reliable water sources, fed from the moorland slopes of Mount Kenya and the Aberdare Range, give the area a high density of wildlife. That animal life can be surprising because the area is a transitional zone between the vast grasslands found in the Mara/Serengeti ecosystem to the south and the arid lands to the north. Walkers spot local specials such as the reticulated giraffe, Somali ostrich, Günther's dik-dik, Grévy's zebra and squadrons of gorgeous vulturine guinea fowl. About half of Kenya's black rhino population inhabit the plateau's conservancies. And the area is malaria free.

While much of the plateau is acacia-dotted savannahs, olive forests and scrubby bush, there are dense forested areas, including Ngare Ndare, best accessed via the lodges of Lewa Wildlife Conservancy, and Mukogodo forest north of the plateau, which is walked by Tassia and Il Ngwesi lodges. The plains stretch from the Great Rift Valley to magnificent escarpments, which then drop to what used to be known as the Northern Frontier District.

There are multiple ethnic communities here, with the Kikuyus and Maasai communities forming the largest portion of its residents, as well as Borana, Pokot, Samburu, Kalenjin, Meru and Europeans forming its minorities. The land is owned by private and community conservancies, and 43 of these cooperate under the umbrella of the Northern Rangelands Trust (NRT), an organisation set up to ensure that conservation involves and benefits the pastoralist communities of the plateau and surrounding areas. While the plateau itself is around 10,000 sq. km, the NRT reserves span an area of 62,000 sq. km – the size of Portugal.

Laikipia is the gateway to Kenya's northern expanses, and no other place in Africa has the type of extended camel-ported walking safaris on offer on the plateau and in the rangelands to its north. These are authentic journeys, sharing a style with the age-old migrations of the semi-nomadic people of East Africa, the Maasai, Turkana, Samburu and Meru. By evening, the sounds of owls, jackals and hyenas are mixed with the grumbles of the

LAIKIPIA PLATEAU

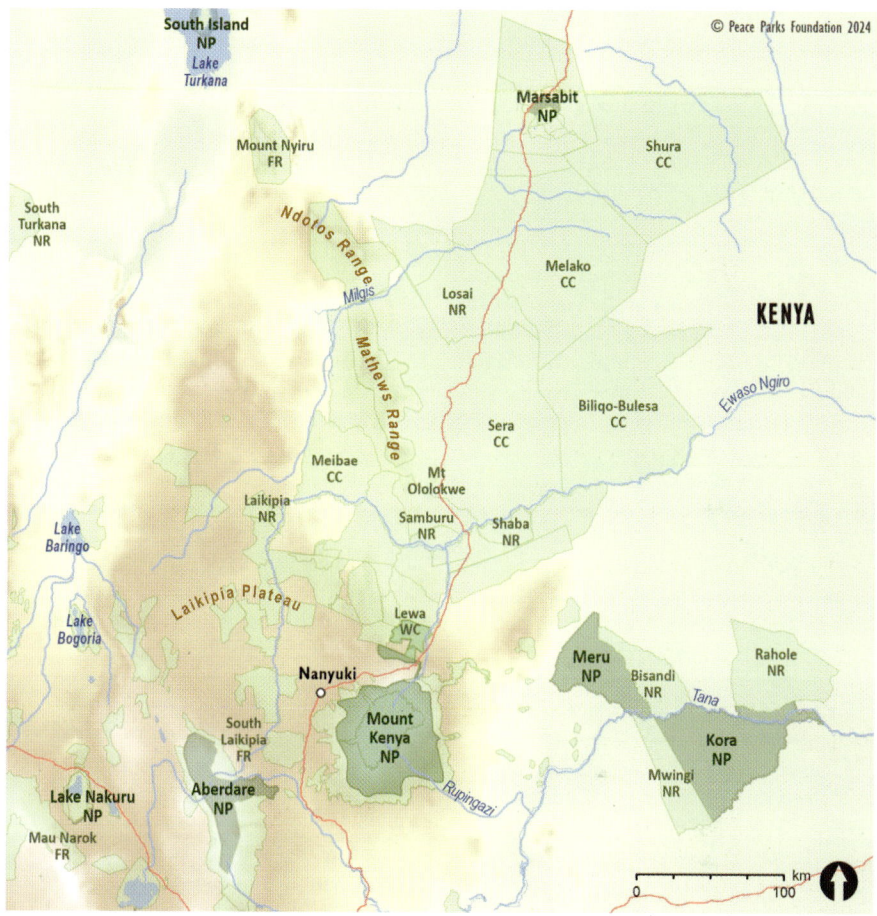

Map 10: Northern Kenya

camels at camp, a timeless and romantic experience.

Laikipia is a major walking safari destination thanks to its collection of safari companies that run such adventurous walking safaris. Bobong Camels, Karisia Walking Safaris, Laikipia Wilderness, Northern Frontier Ventures and Ol Malo can all arrange camel or vehicle-ported multi-day walks, and some have their own permanent camps to use as walking bases. Borana Lodge, Kicheche Laikipia, Ol Malo, Safari Series and Sosian have fly-camp/walk combinations, and at least a dozen other lodges serve as bases for safaris by vehicle, foot and horseback. Starting in the east of the plateau, there's a well-known conservancy that affords both lodge-based and mobile walking: Lewa Wilderness.

Lewa Wilderness and Walking Wild

The 26,000 ha Lewa Wildlife Conservancy (LWC) is often referred to as Lewa Downs, which was the name of one of the original farms in the area and reflects the nature of the landscape: it reminded British settlers of the grassy chalk hills of the Downs in southern England. It's at the eastern end of the plateau – actually in Meru county rather than Laikipia county – with views of Mount Kenya to the south. Today, farming has been supplanted by tourism as the main income source and it's a renowned conservation area known for its thriving population of both black and white rhino. Its importance was confirmed in 2013, when the conservancy and adjacent Ngare Ndare Forest Reserve were added to the UNESCO World Heritage site of Mount Kenya National Park/Natural Forest.

There's a handful of lodges on the conservancy and all guide walks. Lewa Wilderness runs walks from its lodge, as a fly-camping experience on Lewa and as Walking Wild – multi-day camel supported walking safaris. A little to the west, Lewa House and two Elewana Camps make for lovely walking bases.

Lewa has one of the highest populations of rhino in Kenya, and they are restricted to the Lewa and Borana conservancies by some clever boundary controls that allow pretty much any animal other than rhino to pass through. It's easy to find lion and elephant, and leopard too. Herds of Grévy's zebra, gazelle, eland, waterbuck, impala and reticulated giraffe are sprinkled across the hills and plains. Apart from the wildlife, what attracted the settlers in the past is what attracts walkers today: splendid rolling hills of grassland, divided by wooded, well-watered valleys; plenty of water sources and springs; a temperate climate; and its acacias and cedars. Many of the valleys intentionally don't have roads in them, and the only way to explore them is on foot.

Driving north from Lewa airfield, a small sign points to 'Wilderness Trails'. This is the former name for what is now called **Lewa Wilderness**, and gives a clue to the long history of walking and horseback safaris here. Lewa's hilltop camp of thatched cottages has the feel of a family home that has organically grown to add guest cottages. And that's exactly what it is, with guests hosted by long-standing manager Karmushu Kiama and the Craig family, who over several generations have overseen the successful shift from farming to conservation tourism. The farm is still a small part of the operation, including growing feed for the elephants at the Sheldrick Trust sanctuary.

Led by experienced and well-trained Maasai guides, walks here are distinguished by the splendid variety of landscapes, from woodland valleys to more open ridgelines and grasslands. On clear mornings, the distinctive shape of Mount Kenya punctuates the southern horizon. From the lodge, the Eastern Marania River valley below is an enticing walking destination, accessed directly via the steps from the dining area. For variation, drive east towards the plain or west into the hills, and walk in very different habitats. The whole Lewa area is remarkable for its wildlife viewing on foot: the open terrain is ideal for spotting wildlife from afar, and it's possible to pause during a walk and have a dozen species of animal in sight including rhino, giraffe, elephant, gazelle – and perhaps lion too. The steep slopes and gullies make it feasible to approach wildlife safely on foot in the care of the guides.

For a little extra adventure, it's possible to blend walking with a night or two of fly-camping on the conservancy. The usual routine is to take afternoon tea and then set off on foot with the walking guides, reaching the camp in time for sunset, drinks and hot bucket showers. Dinner is cooked on the campfire before guests settle either into canvas tents or sleep under the stars with just a mesh dome tent.

For an alternative multi-day experience, Walking Wild takes guests on camel-supported explorations of the full

LWC and the conserved lands beyond in Leparua and Il Ngwesi Community Ranch. The venture is owned by the community, and the walks are staffed and guided by people with a lifetime of experience of coexistence with the wildlife and know how to keep guests safe. Walking Wild offers anything from two to four nights fly-camping out in the bush. Depending on the arrival time, these trips set off from the airstrip or lodge, with guests just carrying water. The daily rhythm is redolent of timeless journeys in the Horn of Africa: breaking camp, loading camels, moving in a caravan and resetting camp. Walkers and their Maasai guides take a more circuitous route than the camel train, pausing to investigate natural treasures, climbing to look-outs, stopping to examine tracks or spot birds.

Walks are undertaken during the cooler early hours of the day and late in the afternoon, but can still be demanding for those not used to the heat and altitude, are best enjoyed by those who walk regularly. At camp, dome tents have bedrolls, feather pillows, sheets and blankets. They are netted to catch the night breeze and sky view, with a flysheet rig available in case of rain. Each tent has its own bucket shower and long-drop loo in a separate tent nearby. The longer Walking Wild itineraries that go into Leparua Community Conservancy and Il Ngwesi Conservancy provide a real sense of expedition, moving from the green hills of Lewa to the drier area where the plateau drops off to the north. At the conclusion, guests transfer by vehicle to Lewa or the airstrip for onward travel.

Northern Frontier Ventures

Charlie Wheeler is a third-generation Kenyan brought up in the bush, where he absorbed knowledge of the wilds from the local tribesmen and women. As a conservationist he has played a leading role in the protection of indigenous forest, and today his company, **Northern Frontier Ventures**, operates walking safaris assisted by camels and a crew of knowledgeable local people from the Samburu, Rendille and local Maa-speaking people. He has been guiding walking safaris for 25 years, beginning by doing solo trips into the wilds of Northern Kenya in the 1980s. His stories of adventures spread organically to friends and friends of friends, and his safaris are now sustained by their reputation among those who share a similar sensibility and quest for adventure.

Charlie mainly operates along elephant migration routes between their favourite habitats in Northern Kenya, ranging from Lewa Wildlife Conservancy northwards through community-owned conservancies towards Samburu National Reserve. For the more adventurous with time on their hands, expeditions explore the Mathews Range and further north, walking from one mountainous island to the next through semi-arid country. The walks vary from a minimum of three days to two weeks, and can start and end at one of the many fine lodges that are situated on the community owned conservation areas in Northern Kenya. During the camel-ported journey, overnighting is in a comfortable fly-camp with tented showers, long-drop toilets and netted sleeping tents. Food is fresh and sourced from local producers, and is cooked over an open fire. Huge parts of Charlie's walks are the sense of adventure, the wonder of a wild and natural environment, the interesting conversations around the campfire and the feeling of achievement at the end of each day's walk. Charlie also runs fly-fishing trips on the mountain rivers, fishing outings to Lake Turkana and sea fishing trips out of Kiwayu Island.

Borana Lodge

Immediately west of Lewa Wildlife Conservancy lies Borana Wildlife Conservancy, where **Borana Lodge** has six cottages set on a hill. Each one is different, beautifully crafted and decorated in local materials. Walks are guided either before breakfast for a few hours or in the late afternoon, in the company of a guide and an armed member of the anti-poaching team. The terrain is hilly, but the route and duration can be varied depending on guests' fitness levels and preferences. A favourite destination is a walk to Pride Rock, a location that provided inspiration for Disney's *Lion King* films. There, guests can sip sundowners with a view across Borana Conservancy, Lewa Wildlife Conservancy and deep into the arid landscapes of northern Kenya.

There's a fly-camping option for guests who stay three nights or more, and this is set up at a nice distance to reach on an afternoon walk. It's a comfortable camping style and the tents are furnished with real beds and linen. A separate mess tent is used for meals and relaxation; it has a fully stocked bar. The fly-camp sleeps a maximum of 12 and a minimum of two guests on an exclusive basis at a fee additional to the room booking at the lodge. Apart from walking, horse and e-bike riding are popular activities at Borana, and full day trips to the Ngare Ndare forest can be arranged. The forest can be reached by horse or via a game drive, and the day is passed with shady walks (including the canopy walk), swimming and a picnic lunch.

The Safari Series

The rolling Lolldaiga Hills are west of Borana in the eastern part of Laikipia plateau, and are accessible by road from the town of Nanyuki. It's a scenic landscape for walking with a mix of open plains, woodlands and rocky lookouts. The best option in this area for overnight walks is **The Safari Series**, which is a small, owner-managed tented camp on the southern slopes of the hills. It has five en-suite tents overlooking a waterhole. The conservancy has the full range of Laikipia wildlife, and on walks it's fun to find and track the big cats with the Maasai guides. A fly-camp is available for overnight walks; this can be set in an attractive location at a suitable walking distance from the main camp. The mesh tents give the feeling of being really in the wilds, while keeping any bugs at bay, and a watchman stands guard in case of any wandering elephants or other wildlife during the night.

Kicheche Laikipia

With 36,000 ha of southern plateau land conserved, Ol Pejeta Conservancy has a high profile thanks to its healthy population of black rhino. While they are the star attraction, there's plenty of other Laikipia game to be spotted here, including elephant and plains game such as Grévy's zebra, Jackson's hartebeest and East African (or beisa) oryx. There's a chance to spot all the big cats and African wild dog. Some visitors like to visit the chimpanzee sanctuary.

The conservancy has a number of accommodation options. **Kicheche Camps** Laikipia is set at the foot of an indigenous forest overlooking a waterhole with views to Mount Kenya. It's the best option in the conservancy for walking and fly-camping combinations. Walkers are escorted by an armed ranger from Ol Pejeta, along with a Kicheche KPSGA silver-level guide to overnight at a pop-up camp with views over the Aberdares. As the walk is run on an exclusive basis it's very flexible, and guests can walk for as little or as long as desired. The low-footprint fly-camp is similar in style to that offered by Kicheche Camps in the Greater Mara: there are cosy dome tents equipped with camp beds, bedrolls and a washstand. The usual fly-camp style ablutions are provided with a long-drop toilet and hot bucket showers. Also on Ol Pejeta, **Porini** Rhino Camp is an eight-tent all-inclusive camp that has guided walks included in rates.

Karisia Walking Safaris

Karisia Walking Safaris is a genuine walks specialist with a wide choice of trails options, which range from camp-based experiences to mobile walking safaris of a few days, a week or longer. The main base is Tumaren camp in the north of Laikipia plateau in a land of whistling thorn and other acacias and weathered granite whalebacks. The camp is not your standard tented safari camp; the tents are open to the long side, providing an airy North African ambience, with views of wildlife at a salt lick nearby and the granite monolith, Loseramuru, in the distance. Tumaren has seven spacious tents and following a recent upgrade they all have en-suite bathrooms. Using the camp as a base affords a high level of comfort, and makes it possible to include game drives in the daily mix. Note that while Tumaren has seven tents, four of which can accommodate families, walks are generally arranged so that there are no more than eight guests in a walking group, allowing a better chance for walkers to see and approach wildlife.

Walks from Tumaren are morning or evening affairs, and are generally shorter than the mileage covered on a multi-day mobile safari. The day starts early with hot water basins to wash followed by a light breakfast. As the sun breaks on the horizon, guests set out with a guide and tracker. Each morning, the ground shows evidence of fresh tracks as the area has a rich diversity of game animals: these can include Grévy's zebra, gerenuk, African wild dog, reticulated giraffe and Kenya Highland hartebeest, among many others. Big cats and elephant are around, and the guide and tracker are skilled in making sure that unplanned close encounters are avoided. There's no urgency on the walking pace, so there's plenty of time to pause to appreciate the small finds that make walking so interesting: the remains of the meal of an eagle owl, some unusual seedpods or archaeological artefacts such as flints and pottery sherds that litter the area. Normally a spot with a view is selected for a snack and rehydration, and then the walk returns to camp via a different route.

As the day heats up, the camp provides shade and a chance to cool off in the pool, to alternate siesta time with wildlife and bird-spotting. Then, as the sun gets lower, guests gather again for a shorter walk or drive. Sundowners with a view of a Laikipia sunset provide some of the best moments of the day, and crepuscular animals might be spotted on the way back to camp.

While some guests decide to stay just in Tumaren, multi-day camel-supported walks are the Karisia speciality. The attraction is that timeless lure of wildlife, mountain and forest topped up with fascinating nomadic culture. These expeditions can go out for three nights to a week or more, and are led by Maasai, Turkana and Samburu guides who know every tree and track. The fly-camp and guest kit are moved separately by camels, allowing guests to arrive to a cool drink and warm bucket shower. The walking is on gentle terrain and suitable for all ages, and five nights is a good option for a real wilderness adventure. For bespoke trips, the pricing is dependent on the group size, and there are different options in terms of camp facilities. The entry level is the cutely

A Laikipia murder mystery

On the second morning, we came upon a murder scene. We were an hour out of camp, a time of long shadows and bird song, and as we walked our eyes scanned the ground, in search of fresh tracks. We'd already found a leopard's print sharply outlined in the firm sand, but we were hoping for more. Perhaps the splatter of prints from a pack of African wild dogs that roam over a big territory in this remote western end of the Laikipia Plateau. Or an aardwolf – I'd had my first ever sighting just a day before. A flash of movement caught my eye to the side – gerenuk, dancing away and lost to sight in a flash. We walked on, gravitating towards an acacia festooned with weaver nests.

That's where we found the mysterious evidence. What looked like a little huddle of hedgehogs turned out to be a neatly discarded pile of hedgehog skins. Joseph Ekai, my Turkana guide, beckoned to where he stood alongside Laikipiak Maasai tracker Ntogore Kosika. More discarded hedgehog. Heads down, we slowly circumnavigated the tree. A dozen, then 20, maybe 25, all picked clean. I'd never even seen a hedgehog in Africa, and was surprised to see that this area was evidently well stocked and providing good hunting for some predator.

Let's return to the beginning. We'd met at Tumaren camp, the home of Karisia Walking Safaris. The access road weaves through the bushland, twisting as if designed to protect a secret place. In November, before the 'short rains' come, the ground is dust dry, and a squad of vulturine guineafowl created a vivid flurry of colour against the shades of sand and bark. Tumaren came suddenly, a little oasis of canvas and timbers. Named for dragonfly in the Maa language, the word also refers to light morning rain. For us, it was a place of welcome with cold drinks and a leafy lunch.

It was the middle of the day, and with the waterhole deserted, the whole world stood still. Then, Joseph took a handful of seed and scattered it near one of the bird baths. As if waiting – and they probably were – a half dozen feathery ruby bundles landed: chestnut sparrows. They were instantly followed by an even larger flock of black-capped social weavers, and in a few minutes it was weaver bedlam, including species I'd never seen before. Joseph kept me up to date on the names of the arrivals: speckle-fronted weaver; Kenya rufous sparrow; parrot-billed sparrow; vitelline masked-weaver; a pair of greater blue-eared starlings, bullying the smaller birds away.

I could have passed the day happily there, but Joseph had other ideas. He and Kosika stood, and he asked if I was ready to go. I'd expected to see at least a little camel train to carry our camp, but he explained that they had already gone ahead, and would be moving a lot faster than we would. And how right he was – we had many reasons to pause. Within 100 m we stopped to examine a very sorry umbrella thorn tree and a pile of stripped bark. Joseph explained how the elephants lever the bark with a favoured tusk and chew each strip, extracting the nutritious underlayers and leaving the tougher material; and how it's still used to create traditional African fabric dyes.

We pushed on, aware of the need to get to camp before nightfall. The larger animals did not detain us. A couple of giraffe stared over the top of a tree, then turned and loped off. A brown blur danced away. 'Günther's dik-dik,' said Joseph, marrying his knowledge of what animals live on his patch with the briefest of glimpses of its movement. We stopped for baboon spider holes, and to admire acacia thorns – useful as sewing needles or as toothpicks. We frowned at the succulents that thrive here, that no browser wants to eat – invasive prickly pear and sansevieria. 'Mother-in-law's tongue,' said Joseph, for its sharp edges. Kosika's face had the expression of a man who had heard that joke more than once.

It was heartening to see gerenuk, surely the most comical of the antelopes, like a cross between an impala and alpaca. We spent an hour wandering towards one of the granitic whalebacks that are distinctive of the Laikipia landscape. It looked high, but we approached it by a route that left only a short scramble to the top. The sun was low now, bathing the woodlands in a warm light. In the distance, a band of forest-green indicated the course of the Ewaso Nyiro, and the location of our first camp. Somewhere in the woodlands below, a white-bellied go-away-bird called. The world turned, a cloud on the horizon obscured the sun and the sky transformed into a deep indigo. It was time to go to camp and wash off the dust.

The woodlands got thicker as the ground dropped gradually to the river – Salvia mellifera, more umbrella acacias and desert dates. The first sign of the camp was an unmistakable mess of camel tracks. Then the camels themselves, tethered behind the kitchen tent. A whiff of wood smoke and a chorus of welcomes from the camp crew, each busy with a different task. Joseph and I sank into our camp chairs overlooking the river – Ewaso Nyiro translates to 'river of brown', but it seemed no more or less muddy than the other rivers of Laikipia. It flowed silently, and the only sounds were the murmurs from the cooking fire area and the

A cluster of hedgehog skins was evidence of a good hunter.

go-away bird duetting with an emerald-spotted wood dove. With darkness, they too fell quiet, and we settled into the fly-camp routine, starting with a bucket shower and ending with the last drink of the evening and a retreat to the tent.

The next sounds I heard were of the spotted hyena. Then a throaty growl – leopard – and the alarm response calls of vervet monkeys upriver; they'd heard it too. There was no question of going back to sleep, and I listened to the bush sounds until the 'wake up' call came, along with a bowlful of warm water. Outside, the pre-dawn morning light filtered through the smoke rising over a cauldron of porridge. I ate quickly, keen to get out and track the leopard.

We followed the river for a while, jumping on the grippy boulders. A martial eagle quartered overhead. The air was thick with birdsong – rattling cisticola, spotted morning thrush, African hoopoe. Joseph stopped and bent double over a track. Hyena? 'Yes,' he replied, 'but look at how small the back prints are – it's a striped hyena.' Not the bigger cousin, which had woken me an hour before. This animal had passed close to camp in the night.

We moved on, scanning the tracks. And that's when we found the feeding tree of a successful predator. But which one? We ruminated awhile. The fact that the skins were all discarded under the tree indicated it was the work of a hunting bird, and a creature of habit, a local suspect. 'A night hunter,' said Joseph. 'That's when hedgehogs are active and vulnerable.' He had an animal in mind but was waiting to see if I could guess. 'Owl?' I ventured. 'For sure,' said Joseph. It was most likely a Verreaux's eagle owl; they're skilled hunters and fairly common on the plateau.

An almost imperceptible plume of dust hung in the air in the middle distance: the camel caravan was on the move. We left the owl's dining tree and made for the shade near a hill, and a rendezvous with a bush brunch. This journey would have more to come – mystery sounds, tracks and trees, campfire stories, unexpected encounters. All of the elements that make Laikipia walking so special.

name 'AirBnC' that features stand-up dome tents with a thick mattress and bedding and shared ablutions. The second level, the Classic Walking Safari, has larger safari tents of canvas and net mesh. The Luxury Walking Safari has the same tents, but each has its own ablution tent. All options include meals, and there's no single supplement on these mobile safaris.

Karisia's mobile safaris are a proper journey, and the camp generally moves each day. Sometimes it can stay in the same spot for a couple of nights to explore a particular area, have brunch, maybe go rock climbing or visit a local market. A typical four-night expedition in Laikipia would cover between 8 and 16 km each morning, depending on the group. Walkers are accompanied by an armed guide, a Laikipia Maasai tracker and riding camels that carry the refreshments and daypacks. Walkers can stay with the caravan and witness the entire process of breaking camp, loading the camels and setting off on a more direct routing to the next camp. However, most prefer to get out of camp as soon as there's enough light, to enjoy the cool conditions. If the terrain is suitable, guests can choose to ride on the camels.

Along the way, there are occasional stops for water and snacks. Depending on the route walked, the camel train

Karisia guide Joseph Ekai and assistant Ntogore Kosika with Andreas Fox on the Ewaso Nyiro.

might catch up or may pass unnoticed – walkers arrive to find the camp magically set again, together with welcome cold drinks. Over the three days of walking, the terrain varies from open savannahs to lush bushlands along winding *luggas* – dry riverbeds. Afternoons at camp are spent resting, perhaps enjoying a stream or river, or doing some birdwatching. In late afternoon, activities could include another short walk, rock climbing, visiting a *manyatta* (Maasai homestead) or just finding the perfect spot for sundowners. Hot showers are provided in the evenings before drinks and a three-course meal at the campfire.

Apart from doing a mobile walk or staying at Tumaren, there's an intermediate option of requesting a fixed fly-camp. It's the same camping set-up as used for the Luxury Walking Safari, and each tent has its own bucket shower and toilet facility. There's a minimum booking requirement of two nights, the same as for the main camp, and nights spread across the two work well together. As well as the game viewing vehicle, camels are on stand-by for those who want a taste of safari on camelback.

Karisia Walking Safaris is accessed by air via scheduled flights to Nanyuki or Loisaba or by charter flight to the local airstrip. Airport transfers – and transfers to and from other Laikipia camps – can be arranged. Most of the mobile safaris begin from Tumaren, but remoter areas are used too, including the Lower Ewaso Wilderness, Karisia Hills and the Mathews Range.

Laikipia Wilderness Camp

In Ol Donyo Lemboro Conservancy, **Laikipia Wilderness Camp** is set on a breeze-catching ridge above the Ewaso Narok with views of alternating shades of green and brown to the horizon haze. The atmosphere at camp is relaxed and informal, and the walking has a unique flavour, reflecting the personality of host and Zimbabwe native Steve Carey. A trail with Steve means sharing his love for Laikipia – tracking leopard and African wild dog, getting close to a herd of elephant on foot without disturbing them or simply admiring an ancient shepherd's tree. It's not all walk action, and there's time to sit on a clifftop for an hour, take a cooling swim in the chocolate waters of the Ewaso Narok or enjoy a leisurely al fresco brunch.

The main camp has six tents set on palm-wood decking each with an open-air bathroom, veranda and day bed. In addition, there are two satellite camps, River Camp and Palm Camp. River Camp has four thatched cottages on the riverbank, ideal for groups. Palm Camp is the latest addition: it has four en-suite tents on raised platforms and a common mess area that overlooks an animal-cropped lawn and the Ewaso Narok. Laikipia Wilderness Camp is a five-hour drive from Nairobi or can be accessed via Nanyuki or Loisaba airstrips, both two hours from camp with pick-ups available. For a mini-adventure, it's possible to spend a night on a camp-out, as part of a minimum four night stay. From all camps, walks are available as an alternative to (or during) a game drive and are good most of the year, with the 'long rains' around April and May best avoided.

There's a huge expanse of 70,000 ha of the central plateau available for multi-day walking. Mobile Walking Safari guests normally spend their first and last night at base camp and trail nights at a fly-camp which is relocated each day by vehicle. The standard format has a minimum of three nights in the wilds, although with the huge and diverse area available, this can easily be extended. The walks mostly follow the rivers, with ascents to onion skin weathered granite whalebacks over expanses of semi-arid grasslands and groves of woolly caper bushes.

On the first day, the walking party is dropped at the northern end of Ngorare ranch. The habitat here is not dissimilar to the Mara: flat open plains: yellow fever tree forests snaking along a small river, and plenty of Thompson's gazelles and spotted hyenas. The walking is unhurried, with time to investigate any interesting finds along the way, and take a leisurely picnic lunch and rest in the middle of the day. In the afternoon, the trail continues through riparian woodlands to the first night's camp, located in a grove of fever trees. The camp facilities are just the essentials – tented bucket showers and a long-drop toilet. Meals are cooked on the campfire and accommodation is on stretcher beds in mosquito-proof dome tents, which have privacy but mesh roofs, allowing for stargazing. As the vehicle remains at camp, night drives are a possibility, and apart from the ubiquitous dik-diks it's an opportunity to look for hyena, leopard and smaller cats.

On the next day, the walking starts early and continues on Ngorare across the stunted whistling thorn forest, typical of black cotton soils. From there, it crosses over into the Mutara River valley on Ol Donyo Lemboro ranch. The valley drops down from the Laikipia plateau providing stunning views. Rocky outcrops and woolly caper bush forests dot the landscape, and there's the chance to spy a leopard at rest in one of the ancient *Boscia* trees. On the third day of walking, the Mutara River valley widens, and there are rocky kopjes to be scaled to do some wildlife spotting. Those game for it can enjoy cooling swims in the brown river waters, as long as no hippos are present (the rivers are free of crocodiles). On the final day, the walking party returns to Laikipia Wilderness Camp along the Ewaso Narok in a much drier habitat. The landscape flattens and opens up as the bigger river snakes through the landscape. By mid-morning the camp can be seen on the top of its rocky hill, and the full comforts can be appreciated for the final night.

The mobile camp is not restricted to Laikipia, and Steve and his team are always keen to bring guests on 'Laikipia expeditions' to remote parts of northern Kenya. While primarily vehicle trips, these always have plenty of walking in the mix, especially if there has been a long drive. Horse riding and fishing are popular inclusions. Guests on these ventures sleep in large dome tents with separate short-drop toilets and hot shower tents. Allow eight to ten days for such expeditions, which can start either in Laikipia or Samburu. On a northern circuit journey, a night is spent camped at Mount Ololokwe, to climb this famous rocky peak. Then there are two nights in the Ndoto Hills, hiking, visiting Samburu tribespeople and swimming in waterfalls (if they are flowing). The next two nights are at Porr village, camping on the edge of the lake, visiting the Turkana tribes and fishing villages, swimming in the lake and cooking dinner on a fire – often freshly caught that day. From there, the expedition moves up the eastern side of Lake Turkana to spend three nights in Sibiloi, exploring and looking for fossils, fishing for Nile Perch, camping near the lake in tents – or sleeping out on stretchers under the stars. On a south-western circuit trip, Lakes Baringo and Bogoria are visited, using Samatian Island in Baringo as a base, with the option to camp at Bogoria. There are plenty of walking opportunities, including on Mount Elgon and in the Kakamega forest.

Laikipia Wilderness Camp has an alternative larger camping set-up that can be used for bespoke 'luxury mobile camping' in the Aberdare National Park

Steve Carey of Laikipia Wilderness Camp enjoys approaching elephants without disturbing their natural behaviour.

or Meru National Park – both primarily vehicle-based trips. An Aberdare's Wilderness Mobile trip would typically run for a minimum of three nights, exploring this little-visited highland park and its wildlife that includes forest hog, leopard, elephant, buffalo, black serval and the very rare bongo, a forest antelope. With the mobile camp set in the Aberdare Salient in the east of the range, it becomes the base for game drives, fly-fishing in the waterfalls and short walks. For Meru expeditions, the Wilderness Mobile Camp is set in a private glade overlooking the Rojerwero River, which is an excellent spot for tilapia fishing. Walking is not allowed in Meru National park, but guests can enjoy game drives seeking out black and white rhino.

Bobong Camels

Bobong Camels operates multi-day camel-supported walking safaris in the west of Laikipia and in the lands to the north – the Mathews and Ndoto mountains and even as far afield as Lake Turkana. These can be short two- or three-night affairs or multi-week bespoke expeditions. Camp is moved by a team of Turkana cameleers with an impressive caravan of a dozen camels or more. Guests can ride camels at the front of the train if they want, but most prefer to walk separately.

These walks give a real sense of a journey and they are not so focused on nature interpretation, but of course stop for interesting wildlife, specimen trees and other features. The guides are good company, speak English and are knowledgeable about their natural world. The camp has the ambience of age-old travel, with cooking over the fire as the tethered camels chew the cud nearby. It's designed to be easy to set and take down, based on a long history of this style of travel, in the original meaning of 'safari'. Spacious tents have comfortable cots, mattresses, sheets and blankets, and solar lamps. A hot suspended bucket shower and short-drop toilet make up the bathroom facilities.

When not walking, the camels are based in Rumuruti, on the southern edge of Laikipia plateau, and from there are walked to the rendezvous point for the expedition. One favoured walking area explores the Soysambu Conservancy near Nakuru and journeys through a dramatic Rift Valley landscape of high valley walls, skirting the alkaline Lake Elmenteita, a haven for waterbirds. Another longer option travels south to north from Ol Maisor Ranch to Mugie Conservancy, which takes three days and covers around 50 km. And why stop there? The forested Rift Valley ranges that extend from Laikipia plateau northwards to Lake Turkana, the Mathews and Ndotos, become progressively wilder, an alluring invitation for those with an explorer's heart.

Thanks to the adventurous spirit of its Kenyan owners John and Amanda Perrett, Bobong is a company that takes on really long expeditions. Once, they walked a circuit of Lake Turkana, crossing the Omo River in Ethiopia. A more recent walk was an epic three-month, 750 km journey from Laikipia to the Indian Ocean. Passing through Tsavo, it recreated what was once the standard mode of commerce between the coast of East Africa and the interior. On such longer expeditions, walkers do not need to commit to the entire route but can join and leave for sections.

Sosian Lodge

The genesis of Offbeat Safaris was as a horseback safari company, and that's still a big element of activities at its **Sosian Lodge** in Laikipia as well as at its properties in Amboseli and Mara North

Conservancy. Walking is also popular on the Sosian Conservancy, which spans the Ewaso Narok upstream from Laikipia Wilderness. The area was formerly devoted to rangelands, and cattle ranching continues to be part of the operations, but it is now better known for wildlife conservation and its variety of tourism activities. As well as horse riding and walking safaris, camel treks, cultural visits to neighbouring villages and fly-camping are available all year, apart from in May when the lodge closes.

Walks are especially enjoyable in the riverine woodlands along the Ewaso Narok, which has several waterfalls and safe pools for swimming. Away from the river, the walking is on open plains that provide distant views of Mount Kenya, and, as well as encountering plains game, elephant and buffalo, birding enthusiasts have plenty to enjoy. An afternoon walk can be ended in the wilds with a night of fly-camping. After dinner by the campfire, guests retire to dome tents with cot beds, immersed in the nocturnal sounds of Africa. Hot water suspended bucket showers and long-drop toilets are provided.

Ol Malo

In the north of Lakipia, **Ol Malo** is perched at 1,600 m in a dramatic setting on the edge of the Laikipia plateau. It overlooks a land that falls away via a network of valleys that stretch down to the Ewaso Nyiro and the arid expanses of the Samburu, with the misty slopes of Mount Kenya in the distance. The lodge dates from 1991 and is operated by the Francombe family, who have lived in Kenya for five generations; there are aviators, philanthropists, conservationists and pioneers in the family tree. This is a wild and remote area that calls for adventure, and Ol Malo offers just that for those seeking a blend of comfort and exploration – and an opportunity to connect with a land and its people. There is a good selection of walking options, from excursions on foot on the savannah to learn about the medicinal plants of the Samburu, to a walk-out alongside camels for a bush breakfast or picnic lunch, or to investigate some markets or livestock wells. At night there's the option to swap a cottage for a night in the Ol Malo Treehouse or Leopard Hide, or, at an additional fee, a fly-camp.

Guests are able to combine their lodge stay with Ol Malo Nomad mobile camps. These are tailor-made trips that blend fly-camping with walking safaris, with the camp ported by camel. Trips are small and privately guided per group, and can be for as many nights as desired. The camp is lightweight expedition style under canvas, with walk-in tents, a bucket shower and short-drop toilet. Trees are used for shade during the day and a lightweight fly is used for a mess area if a rainstorm moves through. The walking terrain is steep and rocky through semi-arid acacia scrub, exploring outcrops and dry *luggas* along the Ewaso Nyiro valley. Walks are more focused on plants, landscape, culture and birding than big game. Camp might be stationary or moving, depending on the length of the trip, water availability and physical ability of guests. There are no vehicles for game drives: for a transfer into or out of campsites, guests walk to an area that a vehicle can access or alternatively book a transfer with an Ol Malo helicopter.

Laikipia lodge walks

Scattered across the Laikipia plateau from Lewa in the east to Mugie in the north-west are dozens of lodges and camps, and pretty much all have activities other than game drives on offer. Walking is more common than not, and a selection is covered here.

In the LWC, apart from Lewa Wilderness, there's a small number of other attractive high-end lodges with excellent walking guides, where walks – including rhino tracking – can be arranged. **Lewa House** is the most notable, a small owner-run lodge where a long family history of ranching predates its use as a tourism venue. The house and cottages are to the west of Lewa Wilderness on higher ground, with splendid views of Mount Kenya to the south and the rugged Mathews Range and the sacred mountain of Ololokwe to the north.

The accommodation is in the form of cottage-style rooms that are spread out along the hillside, all looking to the expanse of wilderness to the north. The heart of the property is a substantial, elegant building with an open fireplace and a large family dining table where the evening meals are served. Beautiful, shaded gardens surround the house, and breakfast or lunch is often served on the lawn, while the swimming pool overlooks a waterhole.

Guests have complete flexibility in how they spend their days, and walks are encouraged: with such a landscape, walking is the way to really appreciate Lewa. These can be in the mornings or evenings – short ambles near the lodge that are suited to children or excursions of up to four hours. Walks are usually led by Calum Macfarlane, a zoologist and one of the few FGASA-qualified guides in Kenya. His wife Sophie is from the family that previously worked Lewa as a cattle ranch. When Calum is not around, Wilfred Legei leads, and he too is an accomplished guide. He grew up in a small Maasai community in the Mokogodo Forest not

Ngare Ndare forest is an enjoyable walking destination from lodges in Lewa Wildlife Conservancy.

far from Lewa, and has deep knowledge of the area and its history, including that of the bygone hunter-gatherer Ndorobo life. It's rare for a walk to go by without seeing rhino, elephant and buffalo, and if guests are keen it's an option to join the LWC rhino monitors as they head out in the morning to try and find, identify and report on the rhino in their assigned areas. This demands a level of fitness, as the monitors move quickly.

Lewa House can arrange for walks in the Ngare Ndare Forest as a half-day trip with a picnic breakfast or lunch. This is one of the last remaining patches of indigenous forest that used to stretch all the way around the base of Mount Kenya. While not owned by Lewa, the forest is fenced into the LWC, and its rangers assist the Ngare Ndare Forest Trust in protecting the wildlife there. This is quite a contrast to the classic bush walk associated with Laikipia, with challenging hilly trails through thick forest. There's a 400 m canopy walkway to experience and a chance to swim below the waterfalls in the Ngare Ndare 'blue pools'. Lewa House can be a base for acclimatisation before Mount Kenya ascents or combined with multi-day walks with nearby Walking Wild (see page 303) or Karisia Walking Safaris to the west (see page 307). Horse and camel riding are further options, both adding a unique perspective to traditional game viewing.

The **Elewana Collection** has lodges in Loisaba in the west of the Laikipia plateau and in the LWC in the east; and further east again, Elewana Elsa's Kopje Meru in Meru National Park is notable for its history and has short walks. With lodges in several other parks in Kenya and Tanzania, Elewana is a company that can conveniently put together some interesting itineraries. In all of the venues, walks can be requested for anything from two to four hours.

Elewana's Loisaba Tented Camp is in a 23,000 ha conservancy owned by the Loisaba Community Trust. Walks are just one of a range of activities that include horse-riding, camel-trekking, fishing, mountain biking, cultural visits to Samburu villages and visits to the anti-poaching tracker dogs. For something special, the camp can arrange a night on 'star beds' – four-posters rolled out from under thatch at dusk onto to a platform overlooking a waterhole. Walks from the camp, and the exclusive Elewana Loisaba Lodo Springs close by, are led by Samburu guides who share not just their knowledge of natural history, but also stories of their culture and that of the Maasai. There's an opportunity to seek out some of the black rhino reintroduced in 2014. Loisaba is accessed via its own airstrip, close to the two properties. Similar walks are guided from Elewana's Lewa Safari Camp and Kifaru House, both in the LWC. Both camps use the conservancy's Samburu rangers to guide walks, and apart from their knowledge of rhino conservation, they are experts on the tracks and ethnobotany of the area. Generally, walks leave directly from camps.

Laragai House is a family-owned exclusive-use property on Borana Conservancy, west of Lewa. Borana is known for its population of both black and white rhino, which have a sizeable ranger team keeping care of them. Guests at Laragai can avail themselves of early morning walks all year (subject to the weather), and these can track the rhino on foot with a guide and armed ranger from the conservancy. The walks are on the gentle side, and a nice way to end them is with breakfast in the bush.

Il Ngwesi Eco-lodge is on a conservancy on the northern edge of the Laikipia Plateau that's owned and run by the Maasai community, designed to protect wildlife and habitats while simultaneously improving the livelihoods of that community. The lodge operates activities including game drives, sundowners, bush breakfasts by the Ngare Ndare and visits to the Mukogodo Forest, with an option to camp out overnight for visitors who have their own gear. The forest is the largest in Laikipia and makes for more challenging walks. The lodge itself is a pleasant place to pass the day, with a swimming pool, waterhole and hide. Visitors can walk accompanied to the rhino sanctuary, either directly or circuitously, with the rangers tracking and following the rhinos as they are on the move. Also an option is a visit to a local Maasai cultural boma to learn about traditional hunting techniques and honey collecting, and to enjoy traditional music and dancing.

Where the Laikipia Plateau drops off to the north towards Samburu, the Lekurruki Community Ranch conserves 26,600 ha of land. Set on a rocky outcrop of the Mukogodo escarpment overlooking a wooded valley, **Tassia Lodge** is the sole tourism venue in the conservancy; it's as remote as you can get. This genuine off-grid escape has artfully constructed rooms of local materials that are open to the wilderness view. It's not the sort of place to be confined to the vehicle, and the lodge's manager Martin Wheeler is only too happy to lead guests into the bush alongside Simintai, a local Mukogodo Maasai naturalist and expert tracker, and a rifle escort. There are short walks to explore caves, once used as dwellings, or to examine the botany and its traditional uses; or longer walks that seek birds and game, showing off traditional tracking skills and bushcraft. The walk variety is seemingly endless. On a hot day, it's good to explore under the Mukogodo forest canopy, and on a cool morning or late afternoon to choose a hill or mountain for a more challenging walk. Night drives afford the chance to spot leopard and hyena, and perhaps an African wild cat or porcupine. Walks are inclusive in the rates, and revenue from the lodge goes to support community projects and 80% of staff are from the local area. Martin's father Charlie Wheeler (see page 305) is a frequent visitor; he leads multi-day camel supported walks that either start or end at Tassia Lodge. The lodge can arrange a fascinating Nomadic Trail itinerary that combines a lodge stay with days on trail with Charlie followed by nights at the Elephant Watch camp on the Ewaso Nyiro.

A little to the north of The Safari Series in the Lolldaiga Hills, there are two further lodges that run walks alongside game drives. Set on a ridge, **Lolldaiga House** is sprawling old settler-style house, with six stylish double en-suite bedrooms. The diversity of the surrounding landscape makes for great walking, with everything from cedar forests to sweeping plains and hundreds of craggy outcrops and rockfaces to scramble up. There's a big cave with significant archaeological heritage, featuring paintings from nomadic tribes that mark it as an ancient meeting place. Lolldaiga has many dams, a wealth of birdlife and the full range of Laikipiak fauna. Although elephants and buffalo have become more used to meeting humans on foot here in recent years, the walking guides are careful not to approach beyond their comfort zone.

Nearby, **Enasoit Camp** is in a valley that acts as a natural wildlife corridor. Short walks are guided by manager Peter Glover with a tracker, and these stay on the easy flat terrain of the valley floor. The vegetation is a mix of whistling thorns and shepherd's trees, and there are some attractive kopjes. As well as encountering the wildlife on foot, it's a good place to see from the mess tent what visits the waterhole. The camp has six tents and a

Joseph Kaluu and his team birdwatching by a dam on El Karama.

spacious family tent plus the pool house, a five-minute drive from the camp, with two double bedrooms.

El Karama Lodge is embraced in acacia bushland on a remote section of the Ewaso Nyiro in the centre of Laikipia plateau. It's attractive to those seeking exclusivity as the lodge and Nilotica Private House are the only properties on the 6,000 ha of El Karama Wildlife Conservancy, and guests leave a positive impact by contributing directly to the conservation costs there. El Karama is a place that believes in sustainable tourism practices and offers much more than game drives. It's a family-friendly venue – there's a swimming pool and a bush school where kids can be entertained while parents head out for a morning drive or a hike on foot. It has a small new tented gym, running track and a little bush spa for those who like to keep fit on safari, and other activities include horse riding and fishing, fly-camping and enjoying the organic *shamba* and food experiences.

The lodge is the home of owners Sophie and Murray Grant, and features art and books from Lavinia Grant, the matriarch of the family. Murray is an accomplished wildlife sculptor and Sophie is a writer who runs the lodge with her crew from behind the scenes. Head guide and main host Joseph Kaluu is a Meru with three decades of experience guiding on El Karama, and he and his team of four guides are experts in showing why going on foot is such a rewarding activity. The walking terrain has good variety, a mix of rolling hills and acacia scrub plains with plenty of water sources – ideal for 'sit and wait'-style wildlife viewing. El Karama Wild is a private pop-up bush camp that's available during the dry season on a bespoke basis. It can have up to four elegant tents sleeping a minimum of four and maximum of eight guests, and can be used for exploring on foot, horseback and by game viewing vehicle.

New to the plateau, **&Beyond** Suyian Lodge is cleverly integrated into an escarpment with views to the Rock Sanctuary, a formation of ancient stone pillars on the opposite side of the valley. Its curved appearance, topped with plant growth, is designed to organically blend with its environment. It's the only lodge on Suyian Conservancy, an area with an interesting variety of walking habitats that includes grassland, savannah, rocky outcrops, dense acacia woodland and more than 16 km of the Ewaso Narok. Suyian refers to the African wild dog in the Maa language. Walks are an option all year alongside a full suite of adventurous activities from horseback and camel safaris to night drives, local community village visits, conservation and research experiences, and catch-and-release fishing trips.

For a genuinely remote Laikipia experience, the Mugie Conservancy in the far north-west of the plateau is the place to visit. Guests at **Governor's Mugie House** are hosted by George and Theresa van Wyk and stay in lovely hilltop cottages thatched with *makuti* (coconut palm tree leaves). It has the same high standards as its sister property, Governor's Il Moran Camp, a long-time fixture in the west of the Maasai Mara; both are at Governor's 'premier' level. George is a Zimbabwean professional guide and – not surprisingly – is a strong advocate for getting out on foot. Walkers in his company can expect to see an expert display of tracking skills, as there are often leopard or lion around, along with all of the game usual to Laikipia. Regardless of what is spotted, the walks are absorbing, and generally end with a treat – a bush breakfast or sundowners, depending on the time of day – followed by a leisurely game drive back to the lodge. Fly-camping should be available in 2025. Guests will be able to walk (or e-bike) to the camp for a night or two.

The other option on Mugie Conservancy is **Ekorian's** Mugie Camp. It has six roomy tents on sustainable hardwood decks, tastefully decorated with local craftwork. It's a place to go beyond game drives and there are kayaking, fishing and walking to enjoy. Walks are led on the open plains amid herds of plains game typical of the plateau, including Grévy's zebra, Grant's gazelle and Thomson's gazelle. There are Laikipiak archaeological sites to see during a walk near Mugie Camp. Little is known about these sacred Galla graves, but some are believed to be from the nineteenth century. A pleasant afternoon stroll is from camp to the reservoir for a sundowner.

Samburu and the Mathews Range

North of the Ewaso Nyiro, Kenya's northern districts are known for their rugged and remote landscapes, with vast deserts, rocky hills and dry riverbeds providing a stunning backdrop for walking safaris and wildlife viewing. Ancient Rift Valley mountain ranges extend longitudinally towards Lake Turkana; first the Mathews (or Ol Donyo Lenkiyio) and then the Ndotos further north. Although the arid landscape supports smaller densities of wildlife, there are elephant, rhino and the same 'specials' as in Laikipia – Grévy's zebra, reticulated giraffe and Somali ostrich. Visitors to the region learn about the fascinating history and culture of the local communities, including the Samburu and Turkana peoples. A popular walking activity is to take in some of the traditional 'singing wells' that are distinctive to the area, and perhaps witness one in use: Samburu herders form a human chain and chant traditional songs as they pass water up by hand for the cattle.

Northern Kenya lends itself to learning and to escaping the mainstream safari trips in favour of more active styles of adventure. The lodges and camps here tend to offer much more than just game drives, and short walks are usually in the mix. It's a land traditionally traversed by camel caravan, and this style of walking safari is popular here. Bobong Camels (see page 314), Northern Frontier Ventures (see page 305), Laikipia Wilderness Camp (see page 311), Kitich Forest Trails and Remote'n'Wild are the prime operators of overnight walks in the northern districts. In the Samburu area, Samburu Intrepids, Elephant Watch and Sasaab Samburu guide walks, as do a handful of camps further north – the Saruni camps, Sarara Camp and Kalepo Camp.

Kitich Forest Trails

Kitich Forest Camp is hidden in a remote and well-watered valley favoured by elephant, forest buffalo and waterbuck in the north of the Mathews Range. It's a classic old-world safari camp with six tents set under a cooling canopy on the Ngeng River, and is a place for those who want to go off the beaten track and get out by foot on an island of green amid an arid sea. The forest around camp is buzzing with life, from birdlife – over 350 bird species

'Singing wells' are encountered on walks in northern Kenya.

recorded – and more than 150 species of butterfly, to a number of wild forest orchids, a rare and endemic giant cycad and behemoth trees. Wildlife includes forest elephant, leopard, buffalo, wild dog, greater kudu, waterbuck and the giant forest hog. This is idyllic trekking country, with the constant promise of a surprise wildlife encounter – perhaps a De Brazza's monkey, a flamboyantly handsome water-loving primate. Walking in the forest is a daily activity from the camp, always with a Samburu guide and an armed ranger escort. There's the chance to swim in rock pools, try some fishing, and enjoy picnics and sundowners in the wilds. Visits to the 'singing wells' or – on market day – the nearby Ngilai village are possible too.

Kitich Forest Trails are multi-day pack animal-supported walking safaris that explore from the Samburu lowlands to the heights of the Mathews Range, taking in a stay at Kitich Forest Camp. A typical three-night walking safari begins with a scheduled morning flight into Kalama airstrip and a drive of around one and a half hours to link up with the guides and cameleers. It's possible to ride the camels but most guests find it more comfortable to walk. The journey starts in the low country, following the wide sandy riverbeds known as *luggas*. The wildlife shares the land with livestock and its Samburu herders, and some encounters with both are likely. Lunch is taken in a shady spot, perhaps under a venerable giant fig; a post-prandial siesta on a bedroll usually follows. As the heat of the sun abates, tea and biscuits are served before setting off again for a shorter walk, arriving at the fly-camp before sunset.

The fly-camp is simple and comfortable; it has dome tents, tall enough to stand up in, with mosquito net ceilings that allow stargazing from bed. There are comfy bedrolls or camp beds, kerosene lanterns for lighting and bucket showers. After a warm wash and cold drink, there's time to reflect on the day by the campfire before dinner is taken at an outdoor

Nightfall at the Kitich fly-camp set on the bank of Ngenge Lugga.

dining table. On the second day, there's a pre-dawn wake up and a light snack before setting off again, leaving the camp crew to pack up the camels. It's a good time of day for wildlife spotting, and the walking terrain gets greener as the route ascends slowly into the Mathews. It's 18 km to Kitich Forest Camp and, along the way, there's a stop for a full breakfast and perhaps a picnic lunch too. If the distance is too far for guests, a vehicle pick up can be arranged. At camp, there's time to wash, lunch and rest. The altitude gives a relief in temperatures compared with previous days, and an afternoon walk to springs for a swim is an option.

The next morning, the journey continues, this time with donkey portage in place of camels. There are giant cycads to be seen as the route threads the Kojos Valley, pausing for lunch before reaching the precipitous edge of the escarpment of the Murit Pass. Again, there's about five hours of walking this day, and the fly-camp is set in a glade of shady trees. In the cool air of morning, the final walk descends the Murit for 9 km through a landscape of more cycads and boulders. Breakfast is served under a grand *Newtonia* tree. Once the donkey train arrives with the luggage, the group transfers by vehicle back to the airstrip for onward travel.

Kitich Forest Camp is reachable by road in five hours from Nanyuki; a high ground clearance vehicle is required. It's an enjoyable drive taking in mountains, crossing dry riverbeds and passing through traditional Samburu villages and markets along the way. Kitich Forest Trails operate all year and have no single supplement. Bookings for Kitich are handled by **New African Territories**, who facilitate a walk-focused itinerary that combines Kitich and the Through the Rift Safari Trail in the Loita Hills, as well as some vehicle based game viewing at Speke's Camp in the Mara.

Remote'n'Wild

It's a long way from where this book started, amid the vineyards and fynbos of the Cape, to the semi-arid lands of Kenya's northern districts. The two landscapes could not be more contrasting, and although hot and dry, the 'northern rangelands' have some of the most interesting, varied and beautiful walking safari territory in Africa. Graced by ancient metamorphic mountains, arid plains and lakes, and both old and more recent volcanic activity, this land feels very isolated, and the people still mainly live nomadic lives, moving to where the best rains have fallen along with their livestock and the wildlife.

Walking safaris in this landscape take on an expeditionary air. There's no better way to organise such a journey than with **Remote'n'Wild**, based on the Milgis Lugga at the point where it flows east to divide the Ndoto and Lenkiyio ranges. From here, camel-supported walks can be organised throughout these incredibly scenic mountains and it's an option, weather and security permitting, to venture further afield towards Lake Turkana. Mounts Nyiru and Kulal, the Suguta Valley and the deserts to the east all make for remote and adventurous expeditions. The journeys operate on a bespoke basis, with each exclusive to the booking party. There are no set dates for departures nor starting points, and no defined routes. The climate is hot and dry, and walks operate all year; in ideal circumstances, rains are expected in April or May and again in October or November.

The safari can be as long as desired, but a minimum of six days. The distance covered each day is flexible to suit the guests, and walkers do not need to be athletes, just in good fitness to cover 8–20 km a day on foot. Depending on the length of trip, walks can cover a variety of

A scene old as time, the Remote'n'Wild caravan departing into the Lenkiyio hills.

terrain from desert to afro-montane cloud forests. If exploring any of these 'islands in the desert' takes your fancy, a trip with local porters, and taking lighter gear, can be organised, and the camels can meet you on the other side. Owner Helen Douglas-Dufresne, who has huge knowledge of the region, escorts every safari, along with husband Pete, who is in charge of all the background support, and their exceptional traditional crew. Despite traversing rugged and remote terrain, guests are well looked after in comfortable fly-camps. The cuisine is simple and healthy, with 'en route' full breakfasts, a full spread for lunches and a moon- or candle-lit dinner around the fire, surrounded by the hobbled camels.

Access to the region is usually by air charter, with the airstrip dependent on the location of the walk. Remote'n'Wild does not operate a fixed lodge or camp – when guests arrive, they transfer directly to the first location of the mobile camp.

Northern Kenya lodge walks

Part of the Kenyan **Heritage Group**, Samburu Intrepids is a large camp set amid the trees on the banks of the Ewaso Nyiro in Samburu National Reserve. The tent decks overlook the brown river waters and the wildlife it attracts, and the primary activity is game driving in Samburu National Reserve. The lodge's naturalist leads walks, which can be birding strolls inside the camp perimeter or longer walks in the park, escorted by a park ranger. The camp is best accessed via the Buffalo Springs airstrip and transfers are possible from Sasaab and Kalama airstrips. Other hotels in the group with walks are Voyager Ziwani in Tsavo and Mara Elatia.

A short distance upriver, **Elephant Watch Camp** was established by zoologist and elephant conservation pioneer Iain Douglas-Hamilton and his wife Oria, and has a strong connection to their foundation, Save the Elephants: the nearby research camp is well worth a visit. The camp's six airy tents and their bathrooms make good use of the sculptural wood of fallen trees. Guided by local Samburu, walks close to camp are fun, searching out hornbill nests along the riverbank or looking for the resident pair of Verreaux's eagle owls. For those who are more adventurous, a day can be spent on a guided ascent of the sacred flat-topped mountain, Ololokwe (also known as Ol Donyo Sapache), which is visible from the camp on the northern horizon. Longer camel-supported walking journeys into the Mathews Range can be arranged, as can walks from Laikipia through a partnership with Northern Frontier Ventures (see page 305). Normally these run over three nights, ending with a crossing of the Ewaso Nyiro to reach Elephant Watch Camp and its comforts. Elephant Watch can be reached via daily flights to Oryx airstrip, or via a six-hour road trip from Nairobi. Walks are available whenever the camp is open – it closes for six weeks at the start of April and start of November for the long and short rains.

Sasaab Samburu is in West Gate Community Conservancy within easy reach of both Samburu National Reserve and Buffalo Springs National Reserve. Large Moroccan-style rooms are designed to maximise natural cooling, each having a spacious open-air bathroom and private plunge pool. The lodge is part of The Safari Collection group, best known for the Giraffe Manor in Nairobi. It operates Solio Lodge in Laikipia and Sala's Camp in the Maasai Mara National Reserve, but Sasaab is the best geared for guided walks. These can range from a 45-minute leg-stretch to the summit of a nearby kopje, to longer half-day walks. The walks are recommended for the expansive views as far as the Aberdare Mountains. Closer by the river below, there's a chance to spot northern Kenya endemic species such as the Beisa oryx, reticulated giraffe, Grévy's zebra, gerenuk antelope and Somali ostrich. The lodge is proud of its '4C centre', which highlights Conservation, Community, Commerce and Culture, and showcases geology, Samburu culture and community partnerships alongside its wellness centre, the 'Spasaab'.

Saruni Basecamp has a portfolio of twelve camps in the Maasai Mara and Samburu areas. The two in the north are Saruni Samburu in Kalama Conservancy and Saruni Rhino 50 km further north in Sera Conservancy. The six villas at Saruni Samburu are nestled into a rocky hillside with superb views, and walks are guided by skilled Samburu guides from the area who share their knowledge of the natural world and stories of traditional life in a harsh landscape. Saruni Rhino is one of the remotest camps in northern Kenya and even smaller, with four stone cottages overlooking an arid terrain. It's significant for its local population of black and white rhinos, which are GPS-collared for their protection and monitoring. Tracking walks are a recommended experience: it's a privilege to be able to approach this endangered species on foot in their natural habitat. The normal routine is to drive to pick up a signal and then start walking – the distance depends on the animal's location. In addition to tracking rhinos, walks here can focus on the birdlife or on visiting the 'singing wells' in the company of Samburu guides.

Meaning 'meeting place' in Samburu, **Sarara** refers to the place where the indigenous Samburu and wildlife have harmoniously coexisted for generations. Located within the 3,440 sq. km Namunyak Community Conservancy, Sarara has four lodges, each in a remote natural setting, perfect for those who enjoy the stark and dramatic landscapes of Kenya's north. The conservancy hosts Kenya's second-largest herd of elephant and has the full range of northern Kenya wildlife, including the endangered African wild dog. Namunyak is habitat for an astounding number of endemic, migratory and predatory birds. The accommodation options are Sarara Camp and Sarara Treehouses, both with eight tented suites; the exclusive-use six-tent mobile camp, Sarara Wilderness; and the five-tent Reteti House, all of which are run by the Samburu community.

Guided walks and hikes are highlights, with various options available at each camp. Guests at Sarara Treehouses can set off in the early morning to explore the Mathews mountains and discover ancient cycad trees on foot, while from Sarara Camp traditional 'singing wells' make for an interesting outing: with water being such a precious resource in the region, warriors dig deep wells to access drinking water for their livestock. Guests at Sarara Camp can hike up Millennium Hill, which is located right in front of the lodge. It's a relatively easy walk that rewards you with incredible views – and it's recommended on your first day. At Reteti House, options include sunrise and sunset hikes up Reteti Rock – a favourite for photographers – as well as the short walk to the community-owned Reteti Elephant Sanctuary. This route is favoured by elephants, and you'll often see their footprints in the sand. For an energetic full-day outing, hiking up Mount Ololokwe is an option for fit walkers. While ascending this sacred mountain – which rises 1,000 m above the surrounding plains – guests stop halfway for a packed breakfast before hiking to the top, where endless views await.

In the neighbourhood of Meru National Park, a couple of venues can guide short walks. In the park, Elsa's Kopje is an **Elewana Collection** lodge named for a lion made famous in *Born Free*. It's beautifully set on Mughwango Hill, above the site of George Adamson's original camp where he raised and released orphan lions before the advent of conservation tourism. Each cottage is crafted around the rocks, with a large bedroom, open sitting room, veranda and spacious bathroom, and all have breathtaking views. Guests here can enjoy a climb to the summit of Mughwango, enjoying a 360-degree view from snow-capped Mount Kenya in the west to the vast Meru plains to the east. Just outside the park, **Porini Safari's** Rhino River Camp has guided walks in the indigenous forest around camp.

Kalepo Camp is *Endstation*, the most northerly walking safari venue in this guidebook. It's a small exclusive-use camp designed for families in the north of the Mathews, even more remote than Kitich Forest Camp. Guests come here to enjoy the isolation, the views of mountains and Kikwar Lugga, and the pleasure of having 1,570 sq. km of wilderness, spanning the range, to themselves. Kalepo is a place that likes to give guests something different from the usual game drives, and guided walks are part of that. These explore the network of *luggas* and woodland trails in the Mathews and, guided by local Samburu, cultural walks are encouraged too, with visits to 'singing wells' and the nearby villages.

Beyond here, walks in the north are expeditionary in nature, with Bobong Camels, Northern Frontier Ventures and Remote'n'Wild being the go-to options.

Afterword

This journey through Africa has taken us from the thickets of the Eastern Cape to the forests of the Northern Rift Valley, but it does not have to end there. We've stayed in areas where at least some of the African charismatic megafauna are present, but a wider definition of 'walking safari' can encompass primate treks, birding walks or simply exploration of areas with fascinating wildlife that do not include the 'stars'.

Beyond northern Kenya's arid expanses, the Bale and Simien mountains of Ethiopia have some of Africa's best trekking terrain and fabulous fauna from the naked mole-rat to the lammergeier. Nkuringo Walking Safaris are a notable walks operator in Uganda, and Bwindi is the prime destination for walks to encounter mountain gorilla, while in the north-western Kibale National Park, Kibale Lodge is part of a network of lodges operated by Volcanoes Safaris and a base for walking to find wild chimpanzees. In Murchison Falls, Bush Wonderers have recently started operating multi-night walking safaris using a mobile camp. Rwanda is famous for primate-viewing walks in Volcans National Park, but visitors can consider exploring Akagera National Park in the east. In recent years, Akagera has been restored and has reintroduced several key species, including lion and eastern black rhino, making it an exciting destination for wildlife enthusiasts. In the Volcans area, there's no shortage of attractive lodges to arrange walks, including Wilderness Bisate Reserve.

There are other marvellous safari destinations that are off the beaten track, some of them expensive and difficult to reach. Attracting wildlife visitors is part of the strategy to rehabilitate such special places. In Chad, Zakouma National Park is in the stewardship of African Parks and is a beacon of hope in a challenging part of the world. The wildlife – and especially birdlife – is magnificent, and some parts can only be reached on foot; the best time for this is in December or January, when the heat is least intense. The other area of Chad that's made for adventure is Ennedi Natural and Cultural Reserve in the north: Sahara landscapes, rock art and nocturnal wildlife all feature. Like Zakouma, the reserve is co-managed by African Parks, and here multi-day camel supported trips are the way to go.

South of Chad, the rainforest parks of the Central African Republic and Congo attract a steady flow of intrepid wildlife tourists, and walking is often the best (or only) way to seek out the wealth of birdlife and primates. In West Africa, Gabon's coastal Loango National Park protects chimpanzees, lowland gorillas and forest elephants. Walking is the default means of exploring Madagascar's stunning landscapes and fascinating endemic flora and fauna.

Every couple of months I hear a report of a new walking safari opportunity somewhere in Africa. Safari industry insiders testify that there's a genuine trend for travellers to seek active safaris on foot, horseback and water. There's no doubt that every time we experience the profound immersion of wilderness walking, our love for the natural world is enhanced. And we will become even more determined to protect it.

Safari operator contacts

South Africa

Africa on Foot	africaonfoot.com
Africa on Foot Wilderness Trails	wilderness-trails.co.za
African-Born Safaris	africanbornsafaris.com
African Bush Company	africanbushco.com
Amakhosi Private Game Reserve	amakhosi.com
&Beyond	andbeyond.com
Babanango Game Reserve	babanango.com
Bateleur Safari Camp	bateleursafaricamp.com
Bayala Private Safari Lodge	bayalagamelodge.co.za
Bhejane Nature Training	bhejanenaturetraining.com
BHS Safari Company	bhs-safari.co
Big Game Parks (Kingdom of Eswatini)	biggameparks.org
Bruce Lawson Trails	bruce.e.lawson@gmail.com
Bush Explorations Africa	jd@bushexplorationsafrica.co.za
Bushwise Field Guides	bushwise.co.za
Cheetah Ridge Lodge	cheetahridge.com
Clearly Africa	clearlyafrica.com
EcoTraining	ecotraining.co.za
Entabeni Safari Conservancy	entabeni.co.za
Ezemvelo KZN Wildlife	kznwildlife.com
Fraser Gear	andersonexpeditions.com
Gondwana Game Reserve	gondwanagr.co.za
iLala Safaris	ilalasafaris.com
Ingwenya Field Guide Training & Consulting	ingwenyatraining@gmail.com
Inyati Game Lodge	inyati.co.za
Jock Safari Lodge	jocksafarilodge.com
Kruger Trail, The	thekrugertrail.com
Kruger Untamed	krugeruntamed.com
Kwandwe Private Game Reserve	kwandwe.com
Lalibela Wildlife Reserve	lalibela.net
Lapalala Wilderness	lepogolodges.com
Legacy Hotels	legacyhotels.co.za
Leopard Hills Private Game Reserve	leopardhills.com
Lion Sands Game Reserve	more.co.za
Londolozi Private Game Reserve	londolozi.com
Lowveld Trails Co.	lowveldtrails.co.za
Makumu Private Game Lodge	makumu.com
Mala Mala Game Reserve	malamala.com
Manukuza Wilderness Safaris	manukuza.co.za
Mapesu Game Reserve	mapesu.com
Marataba	marataba.co.za

SAFARI OPERATOR CONTACTS

mFulaWozi Wilderness	mfulawozi.com
Molori Safari	roraprivatecollection.com
MORE Family Collection	more.co.za
Motsumi Bush Courses	motsumibush.co.za
Motswari Game Lodge	newmarkhotels.com
Nambiti Private Game Reserve	nambiti.com
Nare Walking Safaris	nare.walks@gmail.com
Nightjar Training	nightjar.co.za
Notten's Bush Camp	nottens.com
Pafuri Walking Safaris	returnafrica.com
Phinda Private Game Reserve	andbeyond.com
Primal Pathways	primalpathways.org
Pungwe Safari Camp	pungwe.co.za
Quatermain's 1920s Safari Camp	quatermainscamp.co.za
Rare Earth	rareearth.co.za
RETURNAfrica	returnafrica.com
Rhino Ridge Safari Lodge	rhinoridge.co.za
Rhino Walking Safaris	rws.co.za
Royal Malewane	theroyalportfolio.com
Samara Karoo Reserve	samara.co.za
Sanbona Wildlife Reserve	sanbona.com
SANParks	sanparks.org
Shambala Private Game Reserve	shambalaprivategamereserve.co.za
Shamwari Private Game Reserve	shamwari.com
Simbavati	simbavati.com
Singita	singita.com
Siyafunda Wildlife & Conservation	siyafundaconservation.com
Stones Safaris	stonessafaris.co.za
Tchagra Trails	tchagratrails.com
Thanda Safari	thanda.com
The Kruger Trail	thekrugertrail.com
Thornybush Game Lodge	thornybush.com
Tsala Trails	tsalatrails.com
Tswalu Kalahari Reserve	tswalu.com
Umkhiwane Sacred Pathways	umkhiwanesacredpathways.com
Untravelled Trails	untravelled.co.za
Welgevonden Game Reserve	welgevonden.org
Wild Wanderer Safaris	wildwanderersafaris.com
Wilderness Leadership School	wildernesstrails.org.za
Wildside Trails	wildsidetrails.com
World Trackers	worldtrackers.co.za
!Xaus Lodge	xauslodge.co.za
Zuka Private Game Reserve	zuka.earth
Zululand Explorers	zululandexplorers.com

Namibia

Etendeka Mountain Camp	etendeka-namibia.com
Etendeka Walking Trails	etendeka-hikes.com
Nambwa Tented Lodge	africanmonarchlodges.com
Natural Selection	naturalselection.travel
Onguma Private Nature Reserve	onguma.com
Ultimate Safaris	ultimatesafaris.na
Wilderness	wildernessdestinations.com

Botswana

African Bush Camps	africanbushcamps.com
African Guide Academy	guidetrainingcourses.com
&Beyond	andbeyond.com
Beagle Expeditions	beagle-expeditions.com
David Foot Safaris	davidfootsafaris.com
Deception Valley Lodge	deceptionvalleyprivatereserve.com
EcoTraining	ecotraining.co.za
Endeavour Safaris	endeavour-safaris.com
Footsteps in Africa	footsteps-in-africa.com
Great Plains Conservation	greatplainsconservation.com
Ker & Downey Botswana	kerdowneybotswana.com
Kwando Safaris	kwando.co.bw
Kweene Trails	beagle-expeditions.com
Machaba Safaris	machabasafaris.com
Mashatu Game Reserve	mashatu.com
Muchenje Safari Lodge	muchenje.com
Natural Selection	naturalselection.travel
Okavango Walking Safaris	okavangowalkingsafaris.com
Tswehe Wildlife Reserve	tswehewildlifereserve.com
Tuli Wilderness	tulitrails.com
Walk Botswana Safaris	walkbotswanasafaris.com
Wild Expeditions Africa	wild-expeditions.africa

Zimbabwe

African Bush Camps	africanbushcamps.com
Amalinda Safari Collection	amalindacollection.com
Big Cave Camp	bigcavematopos.com
Bumbusi Wilderness Camp	bumbusi.com
Bushlife Safaris	bushlifesafaris.com
Camp Mana	campmana.com
Changa Safari Camp	changasafaricamp.com
Chilo Gorge Safari Lodge	chilogorge.com
Daka Plains	dakaplains.org
Discover Safaris	discovervictoriafalls.com
Doug McDonald's Safaris to Africa	dougmacsafaris.com

SAFARI OPERATOR CONTACTS

Fothergill Island	fothergill-matusadona.com
Great Plains Conservation	greatplainsconservation.com
Hide, The	thehide.com
Hwange Bush Camp	hwangebushcamp.com
Imvelo Safari Lodges	imvelosafarilodges.com
Inzila Mobile Safaris	inzilasafaris.com
John Stevens Guided Safaris Africa	johnstevenssafaris.com
Kavinga Safari Camp	kavingasafaris.com
Khangela Safaris	khangelasafaris.com
Machaba Safaris	machabasafaris.com
Matetsi Victoria Falls	matetsivictoriafalls.com
Matobo Hills lodge	matobohillslodge.co.zw
Matusadona Conservation Trust	visitmatusadona.org
Mutondo Safaris	mutondosafaris.com
Natureways Safaris	natureways.com
Off the Track	offthetrack.co.zw
Rhino Safari Camp	rhinosafaricamp.com
Robin Pope Safaris	robinpopesafaris.net
Robins Camp	robinscamp.com
Seola Africa	seoloafrica.co.za
Singita	singita.com
16° South	16degreessouth.com
Stretch Ferreira Safaris	stretchsafaris.com
Tented Expeditions	tentedexpeditions.co.za
The Hide	thehide.com
Tsowa Safari Island	tsowasafariisland.co.za
Umdingi Safaris	umdingisafaris.com
Wild Expeditions Africa	wild-expeditions.africa
Wilderness	wildernessdestinations.com

Zambia

African Bush Camps	africanbushcamps.com
Amanzi	amanzizambezi.com
Anabezi	anabezi.com
Chiawa Safaris	chiawa.com
Chikunto Safaris	chikunto.com
Classic Zambia Safaris	classiczambiasafaris.com
Flatdogs Camp	flatdogscamp.com
Green Safaris	greensafaris.com
Kafunta Safaris	kafuntasafaris.com
Ker & Downey Zambia	kerdowneyzambia.com
Lion Camp	lioncamp.com
Liuwa Camp	visitliuwa.org
Luangwa Valley Safaris	luangwavalleysafaris.com
Lumbe Pools	lumbepoolscamp.com
Malala Wilderness Trail	visitkafue.org

McBrides Camp	mcbridescamp.com
Msandile River Lodge	msandileriverlodge.com
Mukambi Safaris	mukambi.com
Mwambashi River Lodge	mwambashiriverlodge.com
Nanzhila	nanzhila.com
Nkonzi Camp	gavinopiesafaris.com
Northern Kafue Safaris	northernkafuesafaris.com
Remote Africa Safaris	remoteafrica.com
Robin Pope Safaris	robinpopesafaris.net
Shenton Safaris	shentonsafaris.com
Sungani Lodge	sungani.com
The Bushcamp Company	bushcampcompany.com
Thornicroft Lodge	thornicroft-lodge.com
Time + Tide	timeandtideafrica.com
Track and Trail River Camp	trackandtrailrivercamp.com
Wilderness	wildernessdestinations.com
Wildlife Camp	wildlifezambia.com

Malawi

Bua River Lodge	buariverlodge.com
Central African Wilderness Safaris	cawsmw.com
Robin Pope Safaris	robinpopesafaris.net
Tongole Wilderness Retreat	tongole.com

Mozambique

Gorongosa Safaris	gorongosasafaris.com
Khangela Safaris	khangelasafaris.com
Niassa Expeditions	niassaexpeditions.com

Tanzania

A Tent With a View	tentwithaview.com
African Environments	africanenvironments.com
Alex Walker's Serian	serian.com
&Beyond	andbeyond.com
Asilia Africa	asiliaafrica.com
Babu's Camp	babuscamp.co.tz
Beho Beho	behobeho.co.tz
Chem Chem	chemchemsafari.com
Dorobo Safaris	dorobosafaris.com
Elewana Collection	elewanacollection.com
Entara Lodges & Camps	entara.co.tz
Essential Destinations	ed.co.tz
Ethan Kinsey Safaris	ethan-kinsey.com
Footsteps of Mankind	footstepsofmantrek.com

SAFARI OPERATOR CONTACTS

Great Serengeti Traverse	greatserengetitraverse.com
Hodi Hodi Bush Camp	hodihodizanzibar.com
Ikuka Safari Camp	ikukasafaricamp.com
Isyankisu	isyankisu.com
Katavi Wildlife Camp	kataviwildlifecamp.com
Kichaka Expeditions	kichakaexpeditions.com
Laba Laba	labalaba.com
Lemala	lemalacamp.com
Mark Thornton Safaris	thorntonsafaris.com
Mikumi Safari Lodge	mikumisafarilodge.com
Mkomazi Wilderness Retreat	mkomaziwilderness.com
Nimali Africa	nimaliafrica.com
Nomad Tanzania	nomad-tanzania.com
Ruaha River Lodge	ruahariverlodge.com
Rufiji River Camp	rufijirivercamp.com
Selous Impala Tented Camp	selousimpala.net
Singita	singita.com
Taasa Lodge	taasalodge.com
Tanzania National Parks Authority	tanzaniaparks.go.tz
Tarangire Safari Lodge	tarangiresafarilodge.com
Vuma Hills	vumahills.com
Wayo Africa	wayoafrica.com
Wilderness	wildernessdestinations.com

Kenya

Africa Off Track	africaofftrack.com
Alex Walker's Serian	serian.com
&Beyond	andbeyond.com
Andreas Fox Safaris	andreasfoxsafaris.com
Angama	angama.com
Asilia Africa	asiliaafrica.com
Bobong Camels	bobongcamels.com
Borana Lodge	borana.co.ke
Campi ya Kanzi	maasai.com
EcoTraining	ecotraining.co.za
Ekorian	ekorian.com
El Karama Lodge	elkaramalodge.com
Elephant Watch Camp	elephantwatchportfolio.com
Elewana Collection	elewanacollection.com
Enasoit Camp	enasoitcollection.com
Govenors' Mugie House	governorscamp.com
Great Plains Conservation	greatplainsconservation.com
Heritage Group	heritage-eastafrica.com
Il Ngwesi Eco-lodge	ilngwesi.com
Kalepo Camp	kalepocamp.com
Karisia Walking Safaris	karisia.com

Kicheche Camps	kicheche.com
Kitich Forest Camp	kitichforestcamp.com
Laikipia Wilderness Camp	laikipia-wilderness.com
Laragai House	laragaihouse.com
Lerai Safari Camp	leraisafaricamp.com
Lewa House	lewahouse.com
Lewa Wilderness	lewawilderness.com
Lolldaiga House	lolldaigahouse.com
Maasai Simba Camp	maasaicamp.com
Maasai Trails	spekescamp.com
Mark Ross Safaris	markrosssafaris.com
New African Territories	africanterritories.co.ke
Northern Frontier Ventures	4wheeler@northernfrontiers.com
Offbeat Safaris	offbeatsafaris.com
Ol Malo	olmalo.com
Porini Safari Camps	porinisafaricamps.com
Remote'n'Wild	remotenwild.com
Sarara	sarara.co
Saruni Basecamp	sarunibasecamp.com
Sasaab Samburu	thesafaricollection.com
Secluded Africa	secludedafrica.com
Sosian Lodge	sosian.com
Speke's Camp	spekescamp.com
Tangulia Mara Camp	tanguliamara.com
Tassia Lodge	tassiasafaris.com
The Original Ker & Downey	kerdowneysafaris.com
The Safari Series	safari-series.com
Tropical Ice	tropical-ice.com
Zarek Cockar	zarekcockarsafaris.com

Useful websites

africanparks.org	African Parks; NGO that manages parks in partnership with national government agencies.
africawild-forum.com	A forum for information about and discussion of conservation issues.
fgaea.org	Field Guides Association of East Africa, a new regional body for professional guides.
fgasa.co.za	Field Guides Association of Southern Africa, the largest African industry body for professional guides.
ifga.pro	International Field Guide Association, a global wildlife guide standards and certification group.
inaturalist.org	A citizen science site where amateur and professional naturalists can post images and other details of their encounters with flora and fauna.
peaceparks.org	Peace Parks Foundation; South Africa-based NGO developing Transfrontier Conservation Areas throughout Africa.
trackeracademy.co.za	An accredited training institute, Tracker Academy was founded in 2010 to train disadvantaged rural people in traditional skills of wildlife tracking.
tracks4africa.co.za	Publisher of self-drive guides and mapping for Africa.
walkingsafaris.africa	Author's listing of walking safaris.

Bibliography

Allan, Iain. *Outsider: A Life with the Elephants and Mountains of Africa*. Cambridge: Vanguard Press, 2024.

Bryden, Bruce. *A Game Ranger Remembers*. Johannesburg: Jonathan Ball, 2009.

Bulpin, T.V. *Lost Trails on the Lowveld*. Johannesburg: Protea Boekhuis, 2013.

Carnaby, Trevor. *Beat about the Bush: Mammals and Birds*. Johannesburg: Jacana Media, 2014.

Carr, Norman. *Kakuli: a Story About Wild Animals*. Harare: CBC Publishing, 1976.

Carr, Norman. *Return to the Wild*. London: Dutton, 1962.

Carr, Norman. *Valley of the Elephants*. London: Collins, 1979.

Carr, Norman. *White Impala – The Story of a Game Ranger*. London: Collins, 1969.

Carruthers, Vincent. *The Wildlife of Southern Africa – A Field Guide to the Animals and Plants of the Region*. Cape Town: Struik Nature, 2018.

Cazenove, Susie. *Licensed to Guide*. Johannesburg: Jacana Media, 2006.

Cesare, Mario; Noble, Peter; et al. *Heart of a Game Ranger: Stories from a Wild Life*. Johannesburg: Jonathan Ball, 2017.

Cooke, Graham. *My Life With Leopards – Graham Cooke's Story*. Penguin Global, 2013.

Coppinger, Mike. *Luangwa: Zambia's Treasure*. Lusaka: Inyathi Pub, 1998.

Coppinger, Mike; William Jumbo. *Zambezi: River of Africa*. Harare: Baobab Books, 1991.

Costello, Denis; Magagula, Hlengiwe. *Walking Safaris of South Africa: Guided Walks and Trails in National Parks and Game Reserves*. Cape Town: Struik Nature, 2021.

Douglas-Hamilton, Iain. *Among the Elephants*. New York: Doubleday, 1975.

Douglas-Hamilton, Iain. *Battle for the Elephants*. New York: Viking, 1992.

Emmett, Megan; Pattrick, Sean. *Game Ranger in Your Backpack: All-in-One Interpretative Guide to the Lowveld*. Pretoria: Briza, 2012.

Estes, Richard D. *The Behaviour Guide to African Mammals*. Berkeley: University of California Press, 2012.

Estes, Richard D. *The Safari Companion: A Guide to Watching African Mammals Including Hoofed Mammals, Carnivores, and Primates*. White River Junction: Chelsea Green Publishing Co, 2nd Revised edition, 1999.

Gordon, Jeff. *101 Kruger Tales: Extraordinary Stories from Ordinary Visitors to the Kruger National Park*. Cape Town: Struik Nature, 2015.

Gutteridge, Lee; Liebenberg, Louis. *Mammals of Southern Africa and their Tracks and Signs*. Johannesburg: Jacana Media, 2013.

Heever, Alex van den; Mhlongo, Renias; Benadie, Karel; Thomas, Ian. *Tracker Manual: A Practical Guide to Animal Tracking in Southern Africa*. Cape Town: Struik Nature, 2024.

Kingdon, Jonathan. *Origin Africa: Safaris in Deep Time*. London: William Collins, 2023.

Linscott, Graham. *Into the River of Life: A Biography of Ian Player*. Johannesburg: Jonathan Ball, 2013.

Mbatha, Sicelo. *Black Lion – Alive in the Wilderness*. Johannesburg: Jonathan Ball, 2021.

Orford, Bryan. *Kamchacha: Rhodesian Game Ranger*. Independently published, 2018.

Owens, Mark James. *The Eye of the Elephant: An Epic Adventure in the African Wilderness.* Boston: Mariner Books, 1993.
Player, Ian. *The White Rhino Saga.* New York: Stein and Day, 1973.
Player, Ian. *Zululand Wilderness: Shadow and Soul.* Cape Town: David Philip, 1998.
Ryan, Peter. *Sasol Birds of Southern Africa* (5th Revised Edition). Cape Town: Struik Nature, 2020.
Steele, Nick. *Game Ranger on Horseback.* Cape Town: Books of Africa, 1968.
Stuart, Chris; Stuart, Mathilde. *Stuarts' Field Guide to the Tracks and Signs of Southern, Central and East African Wildlife.* Cape Town: Struik Nature, 2019.
Thompson, Garth. *Guides Guide to Guiding.* Johannesburg: Jacana Media, 2007.
Van Wyk, Braam; Van Wyk, Piet. *Field Guide to Trees of Southern Africa.* Cape Town: Struik Nature, 2018.
Varty, Boyd. *The Lion Tracker's Guide to Life.* New York: HarperOne, 2019.